A RABBLE OF DEAD MONEY

A RABBLE

—— OF ——

DEAD MONEY

THE GREAT CRASH AND THE GLOBAL
DEPRESSION: 1929–1939

CHARLES R. MORRIS

PUBLICAFFAIRS
NEW YORK

PublicAffairs books are available at special discounts for bulk purchases in
the U.S. by corporations, institutions, and other organizations. For more
information, please contact the Special Markets Department at the Perseus
Books Group, 2300 Chestnut Street, Suite 200, Philadelphia, PA 19103, call
(800) 810-4145, ext. 5000, or e-mail special.markets@perseusbooks.com.

Book Design by Jack Lenzo

Library of Congress Control Number: 2016962748
ISBN 978-1-61039-534-2 (HC)
ISBN 978-1-61039-535-9 (EB)

First Edition
10 9 8 7 6 5 4 3 2 1

With love, to Beverly

—CONTENTS———————

List of Figures   *xii*
Foreword   *xv*

Prelude   1

PART ONE: **AMERICA DISCOVERS THE MODERN**   **17**
   I. The Jazz Age   19
  II. Edison, Tesla, Westinghouse, and Insull   24
 III. And Then Came Ford   30
 IV. Transformations: New York City   40
  V. The View from Below: Muncie, Indiana   50
 VI. Dislocations   58

PART TWO: **"ONE HECKUVA BOOM"**   **67**
    I. Trickle-down Economics   69
   II. From War to Prosperity   72
  III. Electrifying Chicago   78
  IV. David Buick, Billy Durant, Alfred Sloan,
     and the Modern Car Industry   84
    V. What Happened to Ford?   92
  VI. A Productivity Bonanza   97
 VII. Spinoffs   100
VIII. Laggards: Agriculture   103

IX. Laggards: Real Estate   106
X. On the Eve of the Crash   110

PART THREE: **THE CRASH IN THE UNITED STATES**   **117**
I. New York Stock Exchange   119
II. The Rise of Herbert Hoover   124
III. Charting the Fall   130
IV. The Worm's Eye View   137
V. The Banking Crises of the Great Depression   149
VI. The Twilight of the Gods I: Insull   155
VII. The Twilight of the Gods II: Kreuger   167

PART FOUR: **BLOOD, GOLD, AND UNPAID DEBTS**   **179**
I. Entanglements   181
II. The Gold Standard   182
III. Germany, 1919–1925: Vengeance,
Reparations, and War Debts   189
IV. The Dawes and Young Plans   196
V. England, 1919–1925: Churchill (Sort of)
Chooses Resumption   206
VI. The French Rollercoaster   217
VII. The End of Cooperation   221
VIII. Germany Unravels   225
IX. The Golden Jihad   231
X. Getting What You Wish For   234

PART FIVE: **ROOSEVELT, REFLATION, AND RECOVERY**   **241**
I. World Monetary & Economic Conference   243
II. Devaluing the Dollar   246
III. Creating the "New Deal"   257
IV. The New Deal in Overview   262
V. The New Deal in Detail   266
VI. The Rest of the New Deal: A Roundup   271
VII. Econometric Analyses   274
VIII. Catastrophe   279
IX. The Unemployment Conundrum   287
X. The Great Leap Forward   298

PART SIX: **THE GEOLOGY OF THE COLLAPSE**   **301**

  I. The Legacy of War   303
  II. The Big Picture   306
  III. The Details   313
  IV. A Postscript to the Reader   319

  Acknowledgments   *323*
  Photo Credits   *325*
  Appendix: Milking the Insull Structure   *327*
  Notes   *335*
  Index   *365*

I was lucky enough to see with my own eyes the recent stock-market crash, where they lost several million dollars, a rabble of dead money that went sliding off into the sea.

—Federico Garcia Lorca

——LIST OF FIGURES——

FIGURE P.1— European Defense Spending

FIGURE 2.1— Real ($1929) and Nominal US GNP, 1900–1929

FIGURE 2.2— Buick Sales, 1905–1910

FIGURE 2.3— Relative Sales Performance of Ford and GM, 1919–1929

FIGURE 2.4— Manufacturing Productivity in the United States, 1899–1937

FIGURE 2.5— US Crop and Meat Prices plus Output per Farm Worker, 1910–1930

FIGURE 2.6— US Monthly Industrial Production: 1920–1929

FIGURE 3.1— Dow Jones Industrial Average Monthly Close

FIGURE 3.2— US Real and Nominal GDP, 1929–1937

FIGURE 3.3— Percent Unemployed in United States: Civilian Labor Force, Civilian Private Nonfarm Labor Force, 1926–1941

FIGURE 3.4— Annual US Corporate Capital Flotations, 1926–1936

FIGURE 3.5— Ivar Kreuger : Closing Financial Position, at Book Value, 1932

FIGURE 4.1— Monetary Gold Holdings, Selected Countries

FIGURE 4.2— Newspaper Posting of Apartment Rental Rates, German Hyperinflation, 1923

FIGURE 4.3— Great Britain's Current Account Woes

FIGURE 4.4— German Fiscal Follies, 1924–1929

FIGURE 5.1— US All-Farm Price Index

FIGURE 5.2— Ratio Hourly Manufacturing Pay per Unit of Output in the United States, 1919–1941

FIGURE 5.3—Changes in Federal Liabilities (Percent GDP), 1930–1939

FIGURE 5.4—Apples-to-Apples Comparison, Roosevelt and Hoover Social Spending (Per Year, Per Capita, 1930 dollars)

FIGURE 5.5—US Industrial Production, March 1933–January 1940

FIGURE 5.6—US Unemployment and Wages, 1929–1940

FIGURE 5.7—Combined US Manufacturing Payrolls and Gross Revenues, 1929–1934

FIGURE 5.8—Changes in Hours, Real and Nominal Wages, and Employment in Manufacturing, 1929–1933

FIGURE 5.9—US Durable Manufacturers' Production, Prices, and Gross Revenues, 1929–1934

FIGURE 5.10—Comparison of US Durable/Nondurable Depression Production and Pricing Strategies

FIGURE 5.11—US Productivity Growth, 1929–1941

FIGURE 6.1—Collapse of Farm Prices

FIGURE A.1—AZ Power with Standard Rates

FIGURE A.2—A Five-Tier Holding Company Pyramid atop a Standard Utility Operating Capital Structure

FIGURE A.3—Same Pyramid with 5 Percent on Equity

FIGURE A.4—How Accountants Manufacture Earnings

── FOREWORD ───────────

T he Great Depression is an evergreen topic, and it's gotten a particular boost from the events of the Great Recession. If nothing else, the disdain that practitioners of modern economic management often exhibit for the officialdom of the 1930s may now be leavened with some empathy. Noting all exceptions, and there weren't many, the best people in the world of finance and economics were blindsided by the Recession, and the recovery has been long and frustrating. The lessons of the Depression did serve modern policy makers well, however, in designing remediations. Flooding the world with new liquidity would have been anathema to the managers of the 1930s.

I understand the Great Depression as a world phenomenon, with roots in World War I and its sequelae. The United States enjoyed the most successful economy, but signs of overheating were rife. By the time of the stock market crash, it was due for a major, possibly a nasty, correction. But it was the global Crash that turned an American correction into a Great Depression.

My perspective throughout the book is an American one, filtering the international events through American eyes, while keeping the important European events always in sight.

Part One is devoted to a description of American daily living in the 1920s. Radical changes were afoot in every aspect of life, many of them driven by new technology, especially the automobile and AC electricity. It was both a heady and a frightening time, with population migrations from south to north and from rural areas to cities. There were deep changes in the workplace and in relations between men and women. Electricity-enabled mass communications created "flash-crowd" mass events long before the internet.

Part Two lays out the industrial structure of America and details its underlying economic performance. The 1920s was a time when employers first grappled with the implications of mass production and their relations with employees, and there were the first fumbling attempts by big business to sort out its relations with government. The remarkable boom in financial markets unbalanced ethical compasses and set the sector up for a fall.

Part Three concentrates on the Crash in America. It happened in the first year of the presidency of the supremely gifted Herbert Hoover, a man who had never failed at anything. I examine the astonishing speed of the downturn, the impact on common people, the minimal attempts at remediation, and the consequences of the collapse. Two concluding sections chart the ruin of Samuel Insull and Ivar Kreuger.

Part Four takes a global perspective. It sketches a history of the gold standard, and the monetary *pax Britannica* that kept it on keel for so long. The central issue was how to reconstruct the international trading system, amid the poisonous atmosphere of mistrust and dishonesty that was the heritage of the war and the Treaty of Versailles. The major powers—the United States, Great Britain, France, and Germany—each had quite different views on issues of war debts and reparations, on reconstructing the gold standard, and on the desirability of inflation or deflation.

Part Five returns to America and analyzes the initial recovery under Roosevelt, the 1937 downturn, and the subsequent recovery. I review a large swath of the current scholarship on the New Deal to appraise where it helped and where it got in the way. I also show that it wasn't World War II that ended the Depression, for it was already over before the war started.

The book ends with Part Six, a compact analysis of the underlying forces that brought on the world Depression, and the important micro-developments that gave the American experience its own exceptional flavor.

──PRELUDE────────────────────

K aiser Wilhelm II, king of Prussia and emperor of Germany, was jubilant. It was the thirty-fifth day after the mobilization, and the German army was approaching Paris in three great arrays, with salients already as close as thirty miles from the city. The kaiser's troops had traveled hundreds of miles, mostly on foot, moving the lines forward by almost six miles a day against the flower of the French army. Within a week, they were expected to have overwhelmed Paris and forced its surrender, bringing the war to a glorious close.*[1]

The kaiser was especially delighted because his armies' positioning was almost precisely in accord with the "Schlieffen Plan," the brainchild of Alfred von Schlieffen, the head of the German Imperial General Staff from 1890 to 1906. Schlieffen had calculated that on or about the fortieth day after the invasion of Belgium, France's ally Russia would have completed its mobilization and begun to attack in the east. With Paris fallen, Russia would likely withdraw rather than fight alone against the full power of the German war machine, which could be rapidly deployed to the east by railroad. In 1914, war planning was the prerogative of General Helmuth von Moltke "the Younger," the nephew of the great Helmuth von Moltke "the Elder," who had masterminded the lightning six-week

---

* The brief account of the war here is restricted only to the western front and to the major industrial powers engaged in the war.

| 1

victory in the Franco-Prussian War of 1870–1871, and preceded Schlieffen as chief of the general staff.

The elder Moltke believed that his stunning 1871 victory was not repeatable, in great part because the French had built such a strong system of fortresses from Verdun, just below the border with Belgium south to Belfort just above the northern border of Switzerland, effectively covering the approaches to France from German territory. Moltke was also one of the very few European commanders who had studied the American Civil War, and understood how easily two armies with vast numbers of well-equipped troops might fall into a prolonged stalemate.

Schlieffen was a brilliant tactician, but had a highly abstract conception of strategy, disdain for naval operations, and little feel for politics or the tug of nationalisms. He agreed with Moltke on the difficulties of attacking the formidable networks of French forts, and without apologies or compunction, developed a plan that depended on invading neutral Holland and Belgium to skirt the French defenses. German statesmen and generals, from the kaiser on down, seem to have readily adopted the plan, while piously swearing that they never would invade a neutral country unless their enemy had already invaded it. But their behavior betrayed their intentions, for the national railroad, which was essentially an arm of the military, was steadily reconfigured to support a massive movement of men and matériel to the Belgian and Dutch borders. As Winston Churchill pointed out in 1911: "The great military camps in close proximity to the frontier, the enormous depots, the reticulation of railways, the endless sidings, revealed with the utmost clearness and beyond all doubt [the German] design."[2]

The "Schlieffen Plan" went through many iterations. The final version, the famous "1905 memorandum" assumed that practically all the German striking power would be in the right wing: it would comprise thirty-five corps—about a million men—who would strike France from the north through Amiens to Paris. The plan was for an essentially one-front war, save for a covering force of five corps to protect the coal-rich Alsace-Lorraine region that the Germans had taken from France in 1871. Schlieffen paid no attention to the possibility that Great Britain might be compelled to join France in the face of brutal attacks on neutral countries, perhaps a symptom of his tin ear for politics. He also paid no attention to the eastern front, which was reasonable enough in 1905, given the string of Russian fiascos in the 1904–1905 Russo-Japanese War. Ignoring Russia was not possible in 1914, however, since the tsar, with the help of France, had been diligently strengthening his military and had achieved several years of respectable industrial growth, although from a very low base.[3]

The military historian John Keegan has criticized the Schlieffen Plan for its rigidity and for its impracticality. Even in 1914, the German military did not dispose of the manpower that the plan required. (Schlieffen himself had expressed his doubts on the adequacy of the attacking force.) The marching times required for the extreme German right wing may have been impossible, and the timing of the attack took no account of the likely destruction of French bridges and rail lines. Schlieffen had insisted on an additional eight corps for the right wing—about 200,000 men— but while they could be accommodated by the railroads to the German borders, transportation would probably fail once they crossed into the neutral countries. Schlieffen and his successor as chief, the younger Moltke, ignored those constraints—as Keegan put it, the extra 200,000 troops "simply appear" outside Paris, an example of the "wishful thinking" that he finds throughout the plan.[4]

The younger Moltke was not of the same fiber as his uncle. He was a fine staff officer, but openly admitted that he might not be up to the job of chief of staff. "I lack the power of rapid decision," he said. "I am too reflective, too scrupulous, or if you like too conscientious for such a post. I lack the capacity for risking all on a single throw." He has been savagely criticized for his departures from the master plan, and the fairness of such criticisms is still debated today. One distinguished scholar, for example, heaps blame on Moltke, claiming that his changes in the Schlieffen Plan "had disastrous effects on the German prospects of victory in 1914 . . . [and] effectively nullified his chances of victory," while the military expert Liddell Hart commented that "Schlieffen's formula for a quick victory amounted to little more than a gambler's belief in the virtuosity of sheer audacity."[5]

The spark that set off the war was the June 28 assassination of the Grand Duke Franz Ferdinand, the heir to the throne of the Austrian-Hungarian empire and his wife, in Sarajevo.

The Balkans were seething with independence and pro-Slavic movements, often with the covert assistance of Russia, seeking to advance its vision of a great Slavic empire at the expense of Austria-Hungary's Haps-burgs. In response to the assassination, Austria sent an ultimatum to Ser-bia, backed by a German note to other great powers. Serbia promptly mobilized, but much of this was posturing. In previous Balkan flare-ups, hostilities had been deflected by the intervention of the big powers. On cue, the British proposed an international conference. The French and Italian governments eagerly accepted the invitation, setting the stage for the time-honored face-saving adjustments that could usually keep an inherently unstable situation tottering along for another few years.

Austria, almost inadvertently it seems, refused to play by the script and mobilized against Serbia. Russia's Tsar Nicholas, after hesitating a day, responded with a general mobilization, implicitly including Ger-many. The German government requested that Great Britain declare its neutrality, which they refused on July 30. On August 1, Germany mobi-lized, declared war on Russia, and demanded right of passage through Belgium. Over the next few days, Germany declared war on France and Belgium, and Great Britain declared war on Germany, cementing the alliance of France, Russia, and Great Britain against the "Central Pow-ers," led by Germany. The first elements of the German army crossed the Belgian border on August 4. All of these events transpired in an atmo-sphere of distrust, prevarication, hysteria, indecision, misunderstanding, and intentional misdirection.

———

John Maynard Keynes famously wrote:

> What an extraordinary episode in the economic progress of man that age was which came to an end in August, 1914! . . . The inhabitant of London could order by telephone, sipping his morning tea in bed, the various products of the whole earth, in such quantity as he might see fit, and reasonably expect their early delivery upon his doorstep. . . . He could secure forthwith, if he wished it, cheap and comfortable means of transit to any country or climate without passport or other formality, . . . and could then proceed abroad to foreign quarters, with-out knowledge of their religion, language, or customs, bearing coined

wealth upon his person, and would consider himself greatly aggrieved and much surprised at the least interference. But, most important of all, he regarded this state of affairs as normal, certain, and permanent. . . . The projects and politics of militarism and imperialism, of racial and cultural rivalries, of monopolies, restrictions, and exclusion, which were to play the serpent to this paradise, were little more than the amusements of his daily newspaper, and appeared to exercise almost no influence at all on the ordinary course of social and economic life.[6]

Keynes was eulogizing the high culture of Europe, its common heritage of Greek philosophy and Roman jurisprudence, the shared literature of Shakespeare, Molière, Schiller and Lessing, Tolstoy and Pushkin, the music of Mozart, Beethoven, and Verdi. Reminders of the ancientness of the common culture were everywhere, in the great cathedrals and castles and in the universities. Although most countries still had kings and queens, they usually ruled in accommodation with somewhat representative parliaments, amid slow but steady expansion of the franchise. There was an inchoate, but growing, attention to social insurance, the legacy of Germany's great chancellor, Otto von Bismarck. A glittering international café society dazzled with its wit, its taste, its curiosity.

But those splendid vistas were constantly shadowed by the black specter of war. It was not an alien presence, but part of the same cultural inheritance. States maintained armies, polished battle plans, and declared wars. Wars were an essential element in maintaining a polity's health and ensuring its progress. In his famous 1910 antiwar book, *The Great Illusion*, Norman Angell collected a sample of journalistic arguments for the obvious necessity for wars.

From the *National Review*: [Without] a powerful fleet, a perfect organization behind the fleet, and an army of defence . . . all security will disappear, and British commerce and industry . . . must rapidly decline, thus accentuating British national degeneracy and decadence.

From the *Fortnightly Review*: Does any man who understands the subject think there is . . . any power in the world that can prevent Germany . . . from now closing with Great Britain for her ultimate share of . . . overseas trade? . . . [This is] behind all the colossal armaments that indicate the present preparations for a new struggle for sea-power.

From the London *World*: Great Britain . . . exists by virtue of her foreign trade and her control of the carrying trade of the world; defeat in war would mean the transference of both to other hands and consequent starvation for a large percent of wage-earners.

And from *Blackwood's Magazine*: We appear to have forgotten the fundamental truth . . . that the warlike races inherit the earth, and that Nature decrees the survival of the fittest. . . . Our . . . parrot-like repetition . . . that the "greatest of all British interests is peace" . . . must inevitably give to any people who covet our wealth and our possessions . . . the ambition to strike a swift and deadly blow at the heart of the Empire—undefended London.[7]

Germany had its own fears. The banker Max Warburg reported on an unsettling conversation with the kaiser in June 1914:

He was worried about the Russian armaments [programme and] about the planned railway construction and detected [in these] the preparations for war against us in 1916. He complained about the inadequacy of the railway-links that we had at the Western Front against France; and hinted [. . .] whether it would not be better to strike now, rather than wait.

Warburg "decidedly advised against this," citing British domestic politics, French military and financial problems, and the backwardness of the Russian military. He advised the kaiser "to wait patiently, keeping our heads down for a few more years. 'We are growing stronger every year; our enemies are getting weaker internally.'"[8]

The general staff, however, fed the kaiser's paranoia, and they had reasons for their discomfort. Germany was far from the most militarized nation in Europe. France took those honors, for a full 83 percent of its military-aged males had undergone serious military training, compared to 53 percent in Germany. Germany's peacetime army was maintained at 761,000 men compared to 827,000 in France and 1,445,000 in Russia. In wartime the French-Russian/German-Austrian ratio became 5,200,000 to 3,485,000. Besides its huge population advantage, Russia was engaged in a surprisingly fast modernization program, much of it driven by the private sector and focused on railroads, electricity, and heavy industry. Germany also recently had been forced into a humiliating climb-down in a contest of *Dreadnought* battleship building with Great Britain.[9]

Much to the German generals' chagrin, they had little success in pressing their views on the government. When they pleaded for expanded capabilities, the civilian war minister scoffed that "the entire structure of the army, instructors, barracks, etc., could not digest more recruits," and blamed the constant badgering for more forces on the "agitation of the Army League and the Pan-Germans." There was even subtle opposition to military expansion within the senior officers. The top echelons of the military were dominated by Prussian aristocrats, who were concerned about the dilution of quality that would follow upon an increasingly "technocratic" rather than aristocratic officer corps.[10]

The pattern of European military spending supported the German generals' case. Of the most likely combatants in a European war, the Germans, with their Austrian allies, were spending just over 60 percent of the total of Great Britain, France, and Russia (see Figure P. 1).

But much of that can be discounted. A war in Europe was likely to be primarily a ground war, with naval power largely used to blockade supplies. The British held a clear dominance of sea power, but were still debating whether and how much to build up their infantry when the war broke out. Russia had been arming prodigiously, but the quality of its military officers, its impoverished and torpid peasantry, and the deficiencies of its infrastructure greatly limited its effectiveness. The historian

FIGURE P.1: EUROPEAN DEFENSE SPENDING

DEFENSE APPROPRIATIONS 1890–1914 ($ MILLIONS)

	Britain	France	Russia	Germany	Austria
1890	157	142	145	121	64
1900	253	139	204	168	68
1910	340	188	312	204	87
1914	384	197	441	442	182

Source: Kennedy, "The First World War."

Paul Kennedy points out that, of all the European countries, Germany had much the best balance of economic and military power. Due to its rapid industrial growth it could bear its growing military burdens with *"less strain* than virtually every other combatant . . . and had enormous staying power." Its populace may have been the best educated in Europe, its industrial production was greater than Britain's, its steel production was greater than the British, French, and Russian combined, and it was a world leader in advanced industries like chemicals, machine tools, communications, and optics.[11]

German military capabilities reflected all those advantages. It was the only major power to have adjusted its military strategies to comport with the leaps in weapon technologies. Traditional land warfare was mostly a matter of men with rifles standing in a line and shooting at each other. The German military had evolved a strategy of "defense in depth," with a zone of continuous defense with scattered small group outposts and machine gun nests firing at the attackers' flanks. The same concepts, or "storm-troop tactics" applied to the offense, emphasizing rapid movement and rapid fire by small detachments with considerable independence. Other advances included trenching technology and synchronization of infantry and artillery practice, like the "creeping bombardment"—all of it backed up by careful analysis and institutionalization of proven innovations.

The German tactical edge was evident in their remarkable success in killing their opponents. Over the course of the war, 5.4 million combatants on the Allied side lost their lives, with the great majority killed by the enemy, while the Central Powers (Germany and Austria) lost 4 million, for a 35 percent net body count advantage. British statisticians had even higher figures, showing a 50 percent advantage for the Germans, although some of that difference doubtless stemmed from the allies' penchant for mass attacks. One day's battle at the Somme River—a British assault under Field Marshal Douglas Haig—cost the British 60,000 casualties against 8,000 for the Germans.[12]

———

When the German armies came pouring across the Belgian border, they met a populace ready to fight. The system of forts at Liège and Namur guarding the Meuse River crossings were formidable obstacles. The Liège system was twenty-five miles in circumference, with most of the buildings underground, disposing of twelve equally spaced forts with four hundred heavy guns, with the whole protected by a thirty-foot-deep moat. It took about a week for the Germans to destroy the Liège forts, and another two weeks to level Namur. The decisive weapons were four massive new artillery pieces, two from Krupp, and two from the Austrian Skoda, each more powerful than those on *Dreadnought*-class battleships. Once they had secured their passage, the Germans descended on the civilian population with vindictive fury. More than a thousand Belgian civilians were systematically massacred. The nadir of their revenge came on August 25, when the Germans torched the leafy university town of Louvain, the "Oxford of Belgium," and its priceless trove of ancient manuscripts.[13]

The French had a war strategy of their own. General Joseph Joffre positioned the bulk of his armies in northeast France with access to Belgium and to Alsace-Lorraine, the "sacred" territory transferred to Germany after the 1870–1871 Franco-Prussian War. In effect, Joffre hoped to exploit the German focus on Belgium by unleashing a major attack to push them out of Alsace. It was badly misconceived. Alsace was well defended, and the Germans had by far the greater grasp of field tactics. At the first French attacks, the Germans retreated, sucking the French farther away from their support, and then fell on them. The French held several towns, then lost them, then held and lost them again.

By the last week in August 1914, the French were essentially fighting desperate holding actions all along their lines in a wide outward-facing semicircle that was centered on Paris. Its perimeter originally stretched from the channel ports along the Belgian and Luxembourg borders down to the western edges of the French Ardennes, but the whole space was rapidly imploding in the direction of Paris. By this time, a modest British Expeditionary Force (BEF), comprising one cavalry and four army divisions, had been landed on the channel ports to bolster the beleaguered French and Belgians. The BEF was immediately confronted by a powerful German army near the Belgian town of Mons. Although they gave a good account of themselves as steady fighters and marksmen, they were greatly outnumbered by the Germans, and they escaped only with heavy casualties. In the first two months of the war, the French suffered 329,000 killed in battle, a toll that rose to a half million by the end of 1914.

In the crisis, Joffre proved his mettle. He forthrightly recognized his own mistakes, fired dozens of nonperforming generals, and promoted younger high-fliers, including Ferdinand Foch, an aggressive and creative battle manager. Strategically, Joffre went into full retreat mode, with marching men carrying sixty-pound packs and covering as much as sixteen to twenty miles a day. Impressively, Joffre reconstituted the remnants of two nearly decimated armies into a new force, and organized the defense of Paris around the rivers of the Seine, the Marne, and the Ourcq on the north and eastern side.

Almost in parallel, Moltke's weaknesses as a field commander began to be exposed. The pursuing German soldiers were energized by the prospect of a stunning victory, but they were as physically exhausted as their opponents. As their supply lines lengthened, their fighting ranks dwindled as they were redeployed in securing their rear, pacifying the civilian populations and managing prisoners. It was at that point, in the midst of the drive toward Paris, that Moltke, feeling victory was assured, detached two corps—at full strength about 70,000 men—for service in the east against Russia. This was not necessarily a violation of the Schlieffen Plan as many commentators have had it, for Russia had mobilized with surprising speed. Two separate massive armies entered East Prussia on August 15 and August 22, well ahead even of the French concentration of forces in the west. Worse, the Germans got badly pounded in an early artillery battle, and the commander in the east was showing signs of panicking. But a more confident commander than Moltke might have recognized the folly of endangering the essential goal of a quick victory in France for the sake of a minor reverse in a fringe area.

Moltke had also never been known for his skill in large-scale force management, and he clearly muffed the management of his forces closing on Paris around the Marne River. He failed to intervene in a dispute between two commanders, Karl von Bülow and Alexander von Kluck, that resulted in a glaring thirty-mile gap between their forces. Even worse, Moltke and his staff seem to have been unaware of Joffre's repositioning of his forces. When Kluck was finally ordered to take his proper position, which would have closed the gap, he unwittingly exposed his flank on the Paris side to a large French army, which attacked vigorously. Kluck escaped, but it was a near thing. Bülow then maneuvered to help Kluck, and came under attack by another repositioned French force, which widened the German "gap" to forty miles. German aerial surveillance showed more French troops and an augmented BEF marching rapidly to exploit the opening. Moltke, probably correctly, decided that the position was irretrievable and ordered a pullback to higher country beyond the Aisne River east of Paris, about forty miles in his rear, where the Germans dug in.

The Battle of the Marne, as it was called, was a major strategic defeat for the Germans and a turning point in the war. It was succeeded by the so-called Race to the Sea. The German trenches on the Aisne anchored the southern end of the battle line. Both sides almost immediately tried to outflank each other at the battle line's northern point. There was a series of sharp actions, the most famous of which may have been at the Belgian town of Ypres, "First Ypres" as it came to be called. It was bloodily contested, and on the Allied side, demonstrated exemplary cooperation between Foch and the BEF, which now included a division from India. Each action ended in stalemate locked in by trenching. By November,

British soldiers and medics in Northern France, struggling in knee-deep mud transporting a wounded man. Soldiers' stories of the war often reflected the demoralization that came from months or years of slogging through mud.

the line of trenches extended from below Paris all the way to the channel ports. The last few miles in soggy, dreary, Flanders was finally secured when the exhausted Belgians opened the sluices of the Yser River and flooded the area.

In retrospect, the successful defense of Paris was the climactic event of the war, in the sense that all those immense forces were frozen—it appeared permanently—in deadly embrace with the other. And they stayed frozen in those positions for four more horrible years. Towns like Ypres, Passchendaele, Amiens, Messines, and the Somme River all wrote their doleful, sadly repetitive, histories in blood and mud. Essentially the same battles were fought over and over, but with more lethal tools. Gas, tanks, armor-piercing shells, and aerial bombing were used freely by both sides. As time went on, the skills of both forces converged. The "peace-trained" German army—the elite professional core of the German forces—had been badly depleted, and their replacements were no better or worse than the green soldiers in the opposing trenches. The fortified lines on both sides thickened and became more invulnerable to attack.

As the war dragged on, the body counts steadily mounted— literally millions on both sides. Casualty counts are far from reliable, but near-consensus figures capture the horror: 500,000 casualties at the Battle of the Marne in 1914, 850,000 at Passchendaele in 1917, 1,000,000 at Verdun in 1916, 1,200,000 at the Somme in 1916, 1,500,000 during the German "Spring Offensive" in 1918, and 1,900,000 during the "Hundred Days" offensive that finally broke the German resistance and led to the armistice.

The breakthrough was made possible only by the sudden flood of millions of men and mountains of matériel from the United States. The influx more than countered the transfer of German forces from the Russian front in consequence of the 1918 Treaty of Brest-Litovsk. Under the pressure of a broad Allied summer offensive, the German army simply disintegrated; in a matter of days, sixteen divisions were lost, amid widespread reports of German soldiers refusing to fight. In mid-August 1918, General Ludendorf, the effective chief of staff, suggested that the kaiser might think about an armistice; just weeks later, he was pleading for peace at any price. And within another few weeks, both Ludendorf and the kaiser had fled the country.[14]

Total casualties were 32.8 million, including wounded, killed, and in prison at the war's end, about 7.2 million of whom were killed in battle. Surplus civilian deaths from illness, starvation, and other causes have been crudely estimated at about 6.5 million. Total war spending was about $220 billion in current dollars, or about $5 trillion in 2016 prices.[15]

THE COST OF PEACE

Ordinary Germans could hardly believe that they had lost the war. Unlike in World War II, when Germans saw their homeland reduced to rubble, the fighting in World War I took place almost entirely on French and Belgian soil. At the time of the armistice, except in a few fringe areas, there were no Allied troops in Germany. Thomas Lamont, a senior Morgan banker, who was then acting as an unofficial adviser to President Wilson, described a visit to Germany passing through Verdun during the armistice negotiations. He was appalled by the "vast wasteland of gray stumps . . . and muddy shellholes and craters" and equally stunned by the contrast when they drove into Germany: it was Easter, and everyone was dressed in their best; the store windows were full, the children were rosy cheeked."[*16]

Germans had eyes to see as well. It was the German military that marched into Berlin after the armistice was signed, to be hailed by the chancellor, Friedrich Ebert, as troops returning "unconquered from the field of battle." Allied troops, mostly American, took months to arrive and establish control. That set the stage for the "stab in the back" legend that Germany had been sold out by "pacifists, Jews, and socialists." The officially cultivated sense of injustice fostered pervasive violations of the German peace treaty obligations. Matthias Erzberger, the German armistice commissioner who signed the documents, was assassinated in 1921.[17]

France had suffered dreadfully in the war. It had lost a quarter of its military-age youth, its northern industrial areas had been almost utterly wasted, and the Germans had taken particular care to destroy key industrial assets—flooding mines, smashing machine tools, shipping home

---

* This is what Lamont said, but the contrast was likely exaggerated—although understandably so. German stores were not "full" when Lamont made his trip, and German housewives were up in arms at the lack of food supplies. Still, the contrast with the devastation in Belgium and northern France was as one of different worlds.

agricultural equipment—meticulously documenting the economic havoc they were inflicting. The stripping of Belgium by German troops was, if anything, even worse than in France, and both countries were desperate for reasonable reparations to restart their economies. Great Britain, on the other hand, was not nearly as bloody-minded. Their casualties had been dreadful, but the death rate was only about half that of France. (The toll on sons of the upper classes, however, was devastating—20 percent of former Eton pupils in the armed forces were killed.) But the war had not come to the home country, there were no daily reminders of physical devastation, and British statesmen were far more anxious to resume their lucrative trading relationship with Germany than to exact punishment.[18]

The Versailles Peace Conference officially convened in Paris on January 18, 1919. There were twenty-nine nations* represented—any country with a plausible claim to have been on the winning side was invited. The Germans and Austrians were pointedly excluded, signaling that this would be an imposed, rather than a negotiated treaty. The key parties were Georges Clémenceau, the French prime minister, David Lloyd George, the British prime minister, and Woodrow Wilson, the American president. When Wilson's ship arrived in France, he was treated like a conquering hero. His right-hand man Colonel Edward House had been circulating Wilson's "Fourteen Points" as the large-minded and "Christian" path to reasonable settlements. Clémenceau and George viewed them as lovely sentiments, but about as relevant to a war settlement as, say, Jesus's Sermon on the Mount. The Germans were particularly enamored of Wilson because he had made statements that his points implied "no annexations, no contributions, no punitive damages." But the Fourteen Points expressly allowed monetary restitution: Point VII and Point VIII specified that the damage done to Belgium and France must be "restored." (Wilson insisted that those clauses covered only restitution for damage done by unlawful acts of war, and not for the parties' own war costs, but that just shifted the issue of allocating the charges.)[19]

---

* This account of the proceedings at Versailles is focused only on the decisions involving the western front, major industrial countries. The twenty-nine countries at the conference had a long list of war-fed grievances, especially on boundaries, including, for example, ratifying the famous 1916 Sykes-Picot boundaries for the major countries of the Middle East.

Much of the work of the Versailles conference was accomplished by the chief ministers of the Western powers. From left to right: Prime Ministers David Lloyd George (Britain), Vittorio Orlando (Italy), Georges Clémenceau (France), and US President Woodrow Wilson

The Germans were deeply offended at being shut out of the treaty discussions, and were distraught and angry when they got the final terms. They objected strongly to the famous Article 231, the "war guilt" clause for holding Germany accountable for starting the war, arguing that all the great powers were complicit. They strongly objected to losing territory and German-speaking populations. They were deeply aggrieved by the necessity of paying reparations, the more so since the treaty did not specify a limit, leaving that to a later conference of experts. And they were disdainful of Wilson, who they felt had betrayed his principles, and had simply caved to the French. The British tended to agree with the Germans, and John Maynard Keynes made a best seller out of his savagely sarcastic *The Economic Consequences of the Peace*.[20]

A vast literature has sprung up on the post-Versailles attempts at final war settlements. The French, by bitter experience, had learned to fear German expansionism, its growing population, its military and industrial prowess. Reparations were hardly unfair given the diligence with which the Germans destroyed French and Belgian industrial infrastructure. The final number, in fact, after being massaged by various international expert panels, was about what Keynes had said would be reasonable. In proportion to Germany's wealth, it was certainly no more than the 5 billion gold French franc indemnity that Germany imposed on France at the end of the 1870–1871 war—in addition to the annexation of the rich coal district of Alsace-Lorraine. Germany finally paid about half of the reparations, the great part of it with borrowed money that was never repaid.

A fitting symbol of Versailles may have been the pathetic figure of Woodrow Wilson, incapacitated by a stroke, grimly refusing compromise with the American Senate, at the cost of scotching American membership in his cherished League of Nations. It was a sour ending to a dreadful decade. Europe was awash with fear and mistrust. Its markets were broken, its treasuries impoverished, its populations restive, and radicals of the left and the right were sowing violence and disorder. In most countries, governments were dysfunctional, alternating between inflationary binges and harsh monetary repression. The forces that caused the Great Depression originated in the disordered aftermath of World War I. Absent the war, it is almost impossible to imagine a Great Depression.

PART ONE

America Discovers the Modern

——— I. THE JAZZ AGE ———

A fter they were married, Anthony Patch and Gloria Gilbert moved into his New York City apartment, and from there,

> they sallied triumphantly to Yale-Harvard and Harvard-Princeton football games, to the St. Nicholas ice-skating rink, to a thorough round of the theatres and to a miscellany of entertainments—from small, staid dances to the great affairs that Gloria loved, held in those few houses where lackeys with powdered wigs scurried around in magnificent Anglomania under the direction of gigantic majordomos. . . . [Then] through a golden enervating spring, they had loitered, restive and lazily extravagant, along the California coast, joining other parties intermittently and drifting from Pasadena to Coronado, from Coronado to Santa Barbara, with no purpose more apparent than Gloria's desire to dance by different music or catch some infinitesimal variant among the changing colors of the sea.

Anthony and Gloria, of course, were the fictional alter egos of Scott and Zelda Fitzgerald in Scott's *The Beautiful and the Damned* (1922) chronicling the antics of the "lost generation." To be sure that readers understood the reference, the book's jacket cover was a drawing of a handsome but discontented young couple in evening clothes, who were unmistakably Scott and Zelda.[1]

When Scott's first book, *This Side of Paradise*, burst on the literary scene in 1920, he and Zelda became instant celebrities. It is a beautifully written tale of the existential and amorous quests of Amory Blaine, a Princeton man very much like Scott, and captures the confusions of the Jazz Age—the gross excesses of a war-fueled new hyper-rich, the modernist assaults on traditional literary and artistic canons, the waverings of established religion, the visible corruptions of the political order.

Scott and Zelda were mostly amused by their sudden status as cultural icons. They scoffed at the notion that he had invented the "Jazz Age" label, and that she had been dubbed "first flapper" on her first trip to New York. But they were young—Scott was just twenty-four, Zelda twenty—and they *were* beautiful. Women rhapsodized over the perfections of Scott's face, his charm and wit, the way he looked in a dinner jacket. Zelda was the daughter of an Alabama Supreme Court justice, and she was a beauty of sufficient note that her presence at a Georgia Tech football game had been reported in both the Alabama and Georgia press.

They plunged into their new roles with gusto. Dorothy Parker first saw them arriving at the Ritz in a taxi, Zelda riding on the hood, Scott on the roof, both looking "as though they had just stepped out of the sun."[2] Zelda was a true original, with a quicksilver mind and a knack for making surprising but insightful connections between disparate topics. And she was utterly uninhibited—jumping into fountains, diving off high cliffs, flirting with everybody, dancing by herself in the middle of a crowded floor, lost in the music. A talented writer, she published a novel and a number of magazine pieces—although her stories often listed Scott as co-author in order to command higher fees. Scott lacked Zelda's physical grace, but he spoke as elegantly and as fluently as he wrote, and he readily commanded a room. The two showed up anywhere likely to be in a gossip column, enthralling the press with their splashy spending, high-wattage charm, and calculated boorishness. Lillian Gish said, "They didn't make the twenties, they *were* the twenties."[3]

Their lives fed seamlessly into Scott's novels. Large chunks of *The Beautiful and the Damned* were drawn from Zelda's diary, often word for word. His last completed novel, *Tender Is the Night*, which took him nine years to write, was drawn mostly from their experiences in Europe, as part of a brilliant salon of American and French literary and artistic figures assembled on the French Riviera by a rich American couple, Gerald and Sara Murphy. Gerald was an accomplished modernist painter in his own right, who had exhibited in Paris alongside Picasso and Léger. Both painters were regulars at chez Murphy, along with a shifting cast that might at any time include Ernest Hemingway, Archibald MacLeish, John Dos Passos, Gertrude Stein, Monty Woolley, Gilbert Seldes, Piet Mondrian, Jean Cocteau, Igor Stravinsky, and George Antheil. *Tender* opens with a lovely portrait of the Murphys (dubbed Dick and Nicole Diver) smoothly welding a set of contentious guests into a contented and harmonious group. Over the course of the novel, however, the Divers morph into Scott and Zelda—the one an obnoxious falling-down drunk, and the other mirroring Zelda's mental breakdowns.

Scott's masterpiece, *The Great Gatsby* (1924), was his least autobiographical novel. The main female character, Daisy Buchanan, had some affinities with Zelda, and the narrator, Nick Carraway, was also a Princeton man, but he is more a cynical observer than an independent character. Gatsby is a composite. A friend of Scott's, Robert Kerr, once rowed out in a Great Lakes storm to warn a yachtsman of a dangerous tide; Gatsby does the same thing, and the yachtsman, a fabulously wealthy copper tycoon, becomes Gatsby's tutor in the ways of high society. The seamy side of Gatsby is usually traced to one or the other of several Long Island bootleggers, and his wild parties may be modeled after George Gordon Moore's, a Canadian who parlayed World War I munitions profits into a street railway and utilities fortune. He entered international society by staging Gatsby-style bacchanals both on his Long Island estate and in London where he was avidly pursuing Lady Diana Cooper, heiress to one of England's top families. Lady Diana was a free spirit, an icon of female rebellion in London well before Zelda's emergence in New York. She had naturally befriended the Fitzgeralds on their European jaunts, and visited them in America.[4]

By the mid-1920s the Fitzgeralds' star was waning. *Gatsby* was warmly praised by serious critics but was a commercial disappointment. Scott commenced his long struggle to produce *Tender Is the Night* and failed as a Hollywood script writer, but still collected top rates for slick, catchy stories in mass circulation magazines like *Colliers* and the *Saturday Evening Post*. But he was nearly always drunk, and his antics had alienated even long-standing friends. Zelda meanwhile had been eclipsed by new celebrities like Clara Bow and Mary Pickford. Her relations with Scott had turned toxic, and her behavior was increasingly bizarre. She was first institutionalized in Switzerland in 1930, with symptoms that suggest bipolar disorder. During one hospitalization, Zelda wrote her novel, *Save Me the Waltz*, which was, in effect, her side of the story. Scott intervened at a late stage to insist that she excise her diary materials, since he needed them for his own work. Zelda eventually returned to Montgomery and lived quietly with her mother. She and Scott stayed in close touch, although they rarely saw each other. In shaky health from his years of binge drinking, Scott died of a heart attack in 1944. After her mother died, Zelda moved to a Montgomery nursing home and was killed in a fire in 1948.

———

E xtraordinary cultural changes were afoot in the United States. The elites, of course, were the first to take advantage of electricity; automobiles; radios and telephones; modern plumbing; air travel; a flood of smart journalism, novels, and new criticism; and remarkable developments in mass entertainment. But for them, none of it was life-changing. Servants had always coddled their travel. They had the finest foods and wines on their tables and discreet venues for their debauches. Theater, the arts, and deep information networks were all taken for granted. But for working people, the automobile's casual mobility and privacy were entirely new. The radio presented a feast of music, news, comedy, sports, drama, and political conventions—right in your living room. Movies, tabloids, and salacious fan magazines made the private lives of celebrities the stuff of back-fence gossip. Working-class teenage girls did not become flappers, but the new media showed them that females could break rules—and so they did, timidly at first, with cigarettes, makeup, and less constricting clothing, and then with regard to more important things, like the canons of sex and marriage and the protocols of finance and careers.

There was a tectonic shift in the perspectives of ordinary people. Before the war, the United States was still predominately an agrarian nation, not all that far away from Jefferson's dream of a polity of yeomen. For working farmers, the highlight of a week was likely a wagon ride into a nearby small town to get supplies and to meet and gossip with other farmers. The new media of the 1920s, especially the movies, opened strange worlds—of fabulous riches, exotic travel, casual sex, and fiery romance. Elites were not always shown to best advantage. Daddy Warbucks was obviously a war profiteer. Sinclair Lewis won the 1930 Nobel Prize in literature for his scathing portraits of small-city corruption and the hypocrisies of official religion.

The revolution was greased with rising incomes even for common people, amplified by new access to credit. From 1921 through 1929, the economy grew by 5 percent per year in real (inflation-adjusted) terms—one of the best performances on record. The underlying dynamism was fueled, above all, by two revolutionary industries—AC power transmission and the gasoline-powered internal combustion engine, with its flagship product, the personal automobile, and its corollary technology of mass manufacturing, spitting out identical, highly complex, precisely engineered products at prices almost anyone could afford. Each had been evolving over the previous couple of decades, and both reached transformational scales in the 1920s. We will briefly sketch the technologies and the visionaries who piloted the new industries to their revolutionary promise.

The most consequential transformation, however, may have been the creation of the world's first consumer society. Many of the leading brands, especially in food, cigarettes, and fashions, reached back as far as the 1880s, but it was not until the 1920s that the consumer culture took hold up and down the income ladder. New York City became the national metropolis, where fashions and fads were born, nurtured, and cast aside. We will examine its emergence, not just in finance, but as a prime mover in mass communications, publishing, and standards of dress and behavior. And then we'll reverse the glass and take a look from the bottom up, examining the same phenomena through the eyes of the working people of Muncie, Indiana.

—— II. EDISON, TESLA, WESTINGHOUSE, AND INSULL ——

Ⓣhe Niagara River, only thirty miles long, connects Lake Erie with Lake Ontario. The rate of turnover in Lake Erie water is very high, and average flow rates through the Niagara and over the falls into Lake Ontario approach 100,000 cubic feet per second, making it the single greatest source of potential hydroelectric power in North America. Over several years in the mid-1890s, a massive power-producing development took shape around the falls, with the explicit intention of being, as a later commentator put it, the "pioneer hydro-electric system, forerunner of modern utility power service . . . the great step in the transition from the century of mechanical power to the century of electrical power."[5]

The ancient Greeks were fascinated by electricity and magnetism, but European interest languished until the heroic age of sail spurred interest in the magnetic compass. A burst of development in the early nineteenth century—Volta, Ampère, Ohm, Faraday, and others—unveiled electricity's potential as an energy source. By the 1830s, weak electrical pulses were sending telegraphs, and by the 1870s, European cities had begun to install electric outdoor arc-lighting.

Arc-light was produced when a high-voltage spark leaped between two filaments. The light was harsh, very hot, and often uncomfortably bright. Thomas Edison, the first time he saw an arc-light demonstration in 1878, decided it was a dead end. But he saw a huge opportunity if electrical power could be "subdivided" to power softer, cooler, lower-voltage lighting solutions for the home. When Edison was seized with an idea, he became a bulldozer. Within a week he had invented a working prototype of an incandescent light bulb. He immediately announced it in the press, organized public tours of his laboratory in Menlo Park, New Jersey, and in due course roped in J. P. Morgan to raise the development capital.

When his publicist's hat was on, Edison could be reckless, and he announced that he would have a domestic electric lighting system in operation "within months." Back in the lab, however, he set out methodically to create not just a long-lasting incandescent bulb but a whole congeries of improved generators, circuits, wiring systems, meters, and countless accessories—resistors, conductors, insulators, and so on. His system for generating remote electrical power and conducting it safely to the home was specified down to the last screw. He made two complete working models of the generating plant and the transmission system, and personally supervised every detail of its installation—manufacturing his own wire and insisting that it be encased in pipes and buried underground. To keep Morgan happy, he built a private lighting system for his new house, powered by a basement coal-fueled steam engine. The neighbors hated it, but Morgan was delighted, and the press duly swooned when the interior of the mansion sprang marvelously to life with bright, steady, easy-on-the-eyes lamps and ceiling fixtures.

Finally, in August of 1882, after six months of careful testing, the first Edison generating plant, at Pearl Street in lower Manhattan, went on line, with eighty-five customers using four hundred 110-volt DC lamps. Within two years Edison had more than five hundred customers with more than 10,000 lamps, and was making a small profit. As soon as Pearl Street stabilized, he began multiplying central power stations in Manhattan and opening Edison power companies in other states. The industry exploded. By 1890, there were a thousand central power stations in America, plus thousands more dedicated generators in office buildings and factories. Street railways were also electrifying rapidly. By then, Edison had serious competition, especially Westinghouse Electric and Thomson-Houston.

The Niagara project, however, completely changed the profile of the industry. Rather unexpectedly, it turned into a shoot-out between Edison-style DC (direct current) technology—dominated by General Electric—and AC (alternating current) technology owned by Westinghouse. George Westinghouse, one of America's greatest entrepreneurs, and one of the few with a good grasp of science, had bought up most of the important AC patents, especially those of the eccentric Serbian genius, Nikola Tesla. AC was still a relatively untested technology, but its theoretical advantages over DC for a national system were hard to overlook. At the currents required for residential service, DC power could be transmitted only about a half mile, so electrifying a major city required honeycombing it with unsightly coal-fed steam generator plants. Westinghouse had lit the 1893 Chicago World's Fair with AC, but since it was only a local system, it did not settle the critical question of long-distance transmission. The assurances that it would work came almost entirely from the mathematicians.*

The Niagara chief executive, Edward Dean Adams, and his chief engineer, Coleman Sellers Jr., made the decision to go with AC, and carried a majority of the directors, despite dissents from some of the experts. Adams, a small man with a large drooping mustache, was a banker and a lawyer who had gotten the job on Morgan's insistence—Morgan had been impressed by his performance in several complex railroad restructurings. Sellers, in his sixties, semi-retired, with an elegant white Van Dyke beard, was one of the country's premier engineers. Westinghouse's willingness to bet his company on AC was also a big factor in the final decision.

But the three must have endured night sweats at the sheer daredeviltry of their undertaking. The major elements of the system were all constructed in parallel and were almost all started before major design decisions had been settled. The tailrace tunnel, the huge underground pipe that carried the discharged plant water back to the river, was started well before the power technology was sorted out. As excavation proceeded, the tunnel's specifications were changed several times, and it finally emerged as a mile-and-a-quarter-long, 24-foot-diameter monster, bigger than any high-pressure tunnel in the world. The beating heart of the complex was housed in a 200-foot long Stanford White limestone building about a mile from the falls. It comprised ten 5,000 horsepower (hp) alternators, or AC generators, 50,000 hp in all, each connected by a shaft to a water turbine 140 feet below. Beneath the powerhouse, at the top of each shaft, a seven-foot-six-inch-diameter pipe delivered free-falling

---

* The equations of electricity show that the rate of power loss in transmission increases as the *square* of the current. Long-distance transmission, therefore, is feasible only with very low current. But power (work output) equals voltage x current, so a specific power value could be transmitted at a range of different voltage/current ratios (100V x 1C = 10V x 10C = 1V x 100C). With AC technology, a vendor could transmit power at a very high V/C ratio, then "transform" it to the ratio required for the target application. By the use of multiple transformers, the same power supply could service both heavy machinery and residential lighting. With only a slight loss in efficiency, it could also be converted to DC, so the installed base of DC equipment could remain in place.

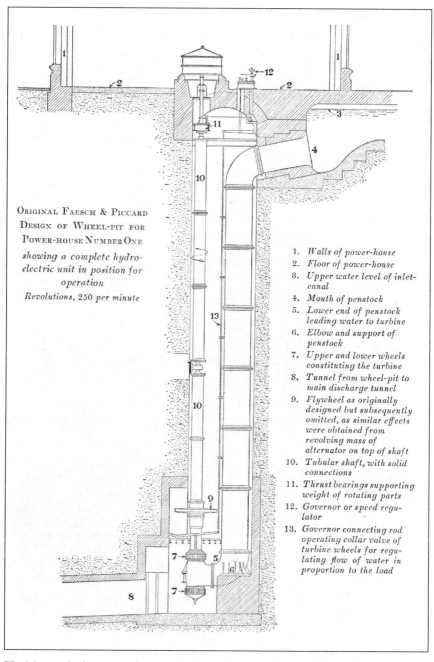

ORIGINAL FAESCH & PICCARD
DESIGN OF WHEEL-PIT FOR
POWER-HOUSE NUMBER ONE
showing a complete hydro-
electric unit in position for
operation
Revolutions, 250 per minute

1. *Walls of power-house*
2. *Floor of power-house*
3. *Upper water level of inlet-canal*
4. *Mouth of penstock*
5. *Lower end of penstock leading water to turbine*
6. *Elbow and support of penstock*
7. *Upper and lower wheels constituting the turbine*
8. *Tunnel from wheel-pit to main discharge tunnel*
9. *Flywheel as originally designed but subsequently omitted, as similar effects were obtained from revolving mass of alternator on top of shaft*
10. *Tubular shaft, with solid connections*
11. *Thrust bearings supporting weight of rotating parts*
12. *Governor or speed regulator*
13. *Governor connecting rod operating collar valve of turbine wheels for regulating flow of water in proportion to the load*

The Niagara hydropower plant was by far the largest in the world. The schematic shows one of the alternator/turbine mechanisms that drove the plant. Niagara water entered at the top right (4), fell 140 feet to a massive turbine below (7) turning it at 250 rpm, driving the shaft (10) to the alternator on the surface, which produced the electricity.

river water to drive the turbine. The arrangement "far exceeded in power and speed and head of water any then in existence."[6]

Each combined alternator/turbine system weighed seventy-six tons, so the operational stresses would be extreme, requiring all system elements, like shafting and gearing, to be balanced with great accuracy. By itself, the complex turbine shape was a world-class machining challenge. After the first two alternator/turbine systems were constructed, there was a nine-month testing and adjustment process. The first power was delivered to customers in August, 1895, about a year later than originally projected. Successfully completing the project would have been a splendid accomplishment by any measure; given the lack of technical consensus at the outset, it bordered on the miraculous.

The first customers were heavy manufacturers close to the power plant. The acid test, however, was transmitting power to Buffalo, some twenty-six miles away. Excruciating street-franchise details first had to be worked through with the city fathers, but finally, at 12:01 on a Monday morning, on November 16, 1896, a switch was pulled in the powerhouse of the Buffalo street railway company, the lights came on, the dynamos hummed, and the nearly unlimited power of the Niagara River had been placed at the disposal of the citizens of Buffalo.

Over the next twenty years or so, AC became the utility power standard. The economics of large generating complexes serving extensive geographic regions were too compelling. That meant tricky conversions of existing power stations, and the gradual replacement of DC equipment by AC. The construction of ever-larger generating complexes and the retooling of industry away from steam and water power to electricity were major boosts to the engineering disciplines. Electricity may also have been the first American industry to be dominated by qualified engineers and scientists, rather than by ingenious tinkerers, like Edison. Tesla, who did calculus in his head, always maintained that "a little theory and calculation would have saved [Edison] 90 percent of his labor."[7]

The stunning growth of electrical utility companies, at the outset of the Progressive Era, naturally created an anti-monopoly backlash. Samuel Insull, a native Briton who emigrated to the United States to take a job as Edison's secretary and rose to become one of the greatest of utility moguls, took the issue head on, lecturing around the country. Using his flagship company in Chicago as his example—it had the country's highest customer penetration—he showed how the economics naturally drove to local monopolies: utilities had to build to meet peak demand, which varied greatly within a day. The greater the customer base, the greater variety of demand profiles, and the greater the opportunity to balance loads throughout the day, thus lowering costs and driving down rates. Insull's charts showed that as per capita revenue in the Chicago region had increased, prices to customers had fallen sharply. He argued forthrightly that electrical utilities should be exempted from the anti-monopoly laws, but in return they should accept state regulation of their rates and service standards. That message was skeptically received by many of his fellow power executives, but by getting out in front of the issue, he helped assure that regulatory schemes would be more to the industry's liking. We will come back to Insull, for he was a major figure in accelerating the growth of America's unique consumer-oriented economy before he became the poster boy for the consequences of excess leverage in an economic crash.

When all ten of the Niagara alternators were in service in 1900, they produced about a fifth of all electrical energy in the United States. By 1920, American electric power consumption had increased tenfold, and it more than doubled during the twenties. By then it was an independent force in driving social and economic changes throughout the country.

H enry Ford once described the mission of his Model T as follows:

> I will build a motor car for the great multitude. It will be large
> enough for the family but small enough for the individual to run and
> care for. It will be constructed of the best material, by the best men
> to be hired, after the simplest designs that modern engineering can
> devise. But it will be so low in price that no man making a good salary
> will be unable to own one—and to enjoy with his family the blessing of
> hours of pleasure in God's great open spaces.[8]

The automobile was not an American invention, and Henry Ford was
not the first in the industry. While he was a fine intuitive engineer in the
American tinkerer tradition, his genius lay both in perceiving that the
automobile could be a mass-market consumer product and then in creating the production and marketing systems to make his vision a reality.

Henry Ford was born in 1863, the oldest of six children on a prosperous farm in Dearborn, Michigan. He had little interest in farming but
had a pronounced mechanical bent—as a young boy he made his own
tools for repairing watches. By the time he was sixteen, a confident youth,
lean and athletic, he left the farm for Detroit, had a string of mechanical employments, and became a qualified machinist. His next few years
were spent moving between mechanical jobs in Detroit and working in
Dearborn, both lumbering and repairing farm machinery. Along the way
he became obsessed with the idea of building a practical car. Recently
married, he finally moved permanently back to Detroit and took a job as a
machinist at the Detroit Edison generating plant.

Ford's ability to fix almost any machine became a legend in Detroit
machining circles. Within a few years, he was made Detroit Edison's chief
engineer, essentially the primary troubleshooter, on call 24/7. His managers knew of his inventive interests, and they were anxious to keep him, so

they allowed him to set up a workshop at the company and more or less come and go as he pleased.

Ford finished a prototype working car, the Quadricycle, in 1896. Another local inventor had his own horseless carriage out on the roads three months earlier, but Ford's was by far the more advanced machine, with a rear-mounted, two-cylinder, four-stroke engine* and a sophisticated transmission with a neutral, low, and high gear, but no reverse, and a top speed of twenty miles per hour.

At the time, the leadership in automotive technology clearly rested in Germany. Nikolaus Otto had patented a one-cylinder, four-stroke engine in 1867, although he manufactured them for stationery uses. (Ford had repaired one in a Dearborn neighbor's threshing machine.) Gottlieb Daimler, who managed Otto's engine factory, and Karl Benz had both used them in prototype automobiles in the 1880s and had joined to form what is now Daimler AG in 1890.

The excitement over automobiles at the turn of the twentieth century was something like the dotcom boom at the turn of the twenty-first. More than five hundred automotive startups were founded within a decade, most of which quickly failed. The Duryea brothers, Frank and Charles of Springfield, Massachusetts, opened the first commercial plant in 1895, and were the first to actually sell a car. Elwood Haynes, an Indiana metallurgist, opened his factory in 1896, and may have been the first American car maker to make a profit. Ransom E. Olds's company opened in 1897, then relocated to Detroit and sold six hundred cars in 1901. Olds is also credited with the first automotive assembly line.

Ford's resolve had been greatly reinforced by a conversation with Thomas Edison at a 1896 New York technical conference for Edison engineers. Learning that Ford had built a "gas car," Edison pressed him for details, then, according to Ford:

banged his fist on the table and said: "Young man, that's the thing: you have it. Electric cars must keep to power stations. The storage battery

---

* The four strokes are air intake, compression, ignition, and discharge. Compared to the one-cylinder Otto engines, Ford's was more efficient because the two piston cycles reinforced each other, which allowed a lighter flywheel and made crank-starting easier. Reducing vehicle weight was a constant with Ford.

is too heavy. Steam cars won't do it either, for they have to carry a boiler and fire. Your car is self-contained—it carries its own power plant—no fire, no boiler, no smoke, no steam. You have the thing. Keep at it."⁹

Ford joined the ranks of manufacturing hopefuls the next year. After building a much improved Quadricycle, with a more passenger-friendly design, he raised $2,500 from a small circle of businessmen to finance a demonstration model. The new car sufficiently impressed Thomas Murphy, a Detroit banker, businessman, and car aficionado, that he led a local syndicate that raised $150,000 in 1899. Ford severed his ties with Detroit Edison to manage his first car company.

The venture was a failure, possibly because the investors insisted on a heavier, more upscale car than Ford wanted to build. But a second venture financed by Murphy failed as well. This time Murphy gave Ford his head on the design, but, almost fecklessly, Ford spent most of his time on a racing car. Frustrated, Murphy asked a local engineer, Henry Leland—a charter member of America's machinist hall of fame—to review the company's operations. Ford left in a huff—which might have been Murphy's intention. Leland took over, and he and Murphy created the Cadillac Motor Company.* Ford finished his racing car and actually won two races against the then-national champion racer.

Ford's racing success prompted new interest from investors. Alexander Malcomson, a local coal magnate and a serial investor, agreed to finance a demonstration model that Ford called the Model A (not to be confused with the 1927 Model A that succeeded the famous Model T). The car was finished in early 1903, and a financing was closed in June—a very tight $49,000.

Ford quickly set up a factory and contracted out all the parts manufacture, enough to make 650 cars. By later standards, the cars were dogs,

---

* Murphy and Leland had a big payday when they sold Cadillac to General Motors in 1909. After the war, Leland, his son, and Murphy formed the Lincoln Motor Company to compete with Cadillac, but they ran into liquidity problems during the very sharp 1921 economic downturn, and sold it to Ford. A standard tale is that, as the only bidder, he bought at a big discount and savored firing the Lelands. In fact, Leland and his son remained in charge of Lincoln until 1924, and appear to have been treated respectfully. The split finally came over the degree to which the Lincoln designs could be consistent with Ford technology while remaining an up-market brand.

but as Allan Nevins points out, "Nobody in 1903–04 expected a car to run dependably."[10] Events confirm Nevins' point. The first sale came on July 15, 1903, for $850 to a Chicago dentist. By the end of the summer, the company was already in the black; in November they paid their first dividend. Within two years, the company had built a new factory ten times bigger than the first plant and employed three hundred men making twenty-five cars a day. Sales the first three years averaged 1,681 cars at an average annual net of $217,000.[11]

Yet again, internal conflicts threatened to derail the enterprise. At the founding, Malcomson had been designated as the business administrator. Instead, he appointed a young subordinate, James Couzens, to act in his stead. Couzens turned out to be a brilliant manager, the perfect man for a high-growth startup. He installed accounting, cost-tracking, and inventory-control systems, and built a formidable sales and dealership network. Ford was impressed, and the two slowly bonded; by about 1905, they thought alike on almost every critical issue.

Then Malcomson decided to reclaim his place as business manager. In particular, he wanted to shift the emphasis to a high-end, more luxurious, and heavier car. Sensing a coming clash, Ford took it to the board, and over the next year, he and the board majority rather brutally squeezed out Malcomson. Ford was made president, with Couzens as number two.[†]

The new Model N, introduced in 1906, was a turning point. The first version sold for $500, cheaper than the Model A, although it was a far better car. With a vertical four-cylinder, fifteen hp engine, positioned in the front, it was even lighter, but far more powerful than its predecessors, with a top speed of forty-five miles per hour. It also had better brakes,

---

† The squeeze tactic was to form a new company to manufacture parts, owned by all the shareholders except Malcomson. It is not likely that the arrangement would have survived a court test, since it was blatantly discriminatory. More flagrantly, parts pricing was adjusted to ensure that most of the profits would accrue to the new company. Instead of suing, an outraged Malcomson formed a competing company, which allowed the directors to vote him off the board because of the conflict of interest. He was paid $175,900 for his shares, or about $4 million in today's money. That was probably fair, given the risks ahead, but was far less than they would have been worth a few years later. Malcomson's supporters also sold back most of their stock, which allowed Ford to obtain a majority position.

better springs, and a smoother two-speed planetary transmission. Ford announced that they would produce 10,000 of them in 1906, more than five times their previous single-year production record. No other automobile manufacturer had ever come close to such numbers.

The car drew raves from the trade journals—"distinctly the most important mechanical traction event of 1906," said an editorialist.[12] One dealer sent Couzens a check for $30,000 to secure his hoped-for three hundred cars. By May, Couzens was sending money back to avid customers to keep the order backlog within reason. In the event, they produced 8,250 cars, all of them sold before they rolled out of the factory. Ford was disappointed by the shortfall, but the ramp-up was still a signal accomplishment, for it was the same year that they internalized the manufacture of their engines, axles, and transmissions, which required opening a new factory and hiring a new workforce.

Ford was determined to write a new chapter in the history of mass production. Americans, at least outside of the slave-based South, had long embraced mass manufacturing. Well before the Civil War, the average farmer could buy factory-made stoves, and mass-produced shoes and clothing, soap, candles, and clocks. By the 1880s, packaged fresh meat and varieties of canned goods diversified diets. Branded goods like Heinz foods, Campbell's soups, Ivory soap, and Lucky Strike cigarettes were all well-established before the turn of the century. Henry Ford's Model T took it to a new level. It was a superb car, one of the best made up to that time, and Ford insisted on driving the price down to the point where almost any working family could afford it.

Achieving mass production of cars entailed first making all parts to such a fine degree of precision that they would be truly interchangeable—any part would fit accurately to any chassis. Rather than apply skills to machining individual parts, Ford lavished his ingenuity on designing and prototyping the high-precision machine tools to produce parts that needed no fitting. Ford didn't do it by himself; as usual he surrounded himself with a superb crew. But the vision was his, as in the main were the strategy, the mechanical designs, and the factory. He dreamed of a great car, sold at low costs, and in such volumes that costs would always fall, driving ever greater volume and cost reductions. And at a deep practical level, he understood how to make that happen.

The design of the Model T stretched over 1907; it was accomplished by an elite team in a cramped room in the production factory. For much of that year, Ford spent a great part of his day with the designers—the usual routine was that he would roughly sketch what he wanted, and they would take it from there, iterating through multiple sketches and blueprints until they finally got it right. The car that emerged made maximum use of the newest, lightest steel alloys, and incorporated greatly improved transmission gearing, and a much better carburetor. It was also very rugged. Ford intentionally targeted a rural market, so the Model T was something of an all-terrain vehicle, with a suspension system that allowed considerable independent adjustment for each wheel, perfect for deeply rutted rural roads. Ford also insisted on making it easy to repair. Some farmers reconfigured their Model Ts to work as tractors.

The production system evolved over a number of years. First, the machinery lines were reconfigured to match the sequence of manufacturing instead of being grouped by machine type. Attention was lavished on redesigning parts to facilitate automated manufacturing. The engine block became a single casting, instead of two separate casts that had to be welded together; that was difficult, but once achieved, it paid dividends forever. The use of vanadium steel, the best and most expensive new alloy, allowed a shift from machining small parts to much faster and cheaper precision stamping; taking full advantage of that required redesigning hundreds of parts. Cylinder blocks had to be machined to close tolerances and drilled, tapped, and milled to accommodate hundreds of connections and insertions. There were no skilled machinists involved, only operators to load the parts, start the machines, and send the finished work on its way.

Creating the final Ford factory took about seven years. After automating the machining of individual parts, the team shifted attention to the subassembly. The magneto-flywheel (the starter) had always been assembled by one man working from an ordered array of all of its parts. Breaking up the job among several men, each concentrating on a specific task, improved productivity by about a third. The next step was to design the part's moving assembly line. The line for each big subassembly took a while to get right—the work specification for each station, the speed of the line, its height and placement of the work pieces to minimize bending and stretching. When it went into production, magneto-flywheel assembly

Early Ford Assembly Line: "Fordism" dramatically increased manufacturing productivity. The men hated the mind-numbing tedium of performing the same small task over and over every day. Ford secured their loyalty by paying about twice the prevailing manufacturing wage.

time was reduced by factor of four. The chassis was the most spectacular success: assembly time was reduced eightfold, from 12.5 hours to only 1.5 hours. The last, and quite extraordinary, step was to choreograph the entire plant, from the foundry through three major subassembly lines to the final assembly, assuring that end to end, everything cohered to produce a stream of identical automobiles in ever-growing numbers.[13]

The beauty of the Ford system was that, even with such enormous productivity gains, he was driving output so hard that his workforce exploded—between 1910 and 1913, factory employees almost quintupled, from 3,000 to 14,000. The men did not like the line, but Ford secured their loyalty with his March 1, 1914, announcement of the $5 per day, eight-hour day, about double the previous wage. A famous lament from a worker's wife in a letter to Ford was: "The chain system you have is a *slave driver! My God!*, Mr. Ford. . . . That $5 a day is a blessing—a bigger one than you know but *oh* they earn it."[14]

Nevins has described the $5 per day wage as an act of magnanimity on the part of Ford. Doubling the wage was clearly generous, for it took years for other companies to catch up to the Ford pay scale. But Ford got more than spiritual solace from it. His factories suffered from extreme absenteeism, a consequence of the long hours of absolutely unremitting work at the preset pace of the mechanical line. Men could "automatize" the job—work purely on reflex—but as one worker said, "If I keep putting on Nut No. 86 for about 86 more days, I will be Nut No. 86 in the . . . bughouse." Like most other factories of the time, Ford tolerated arbitrary foremen and disciplinary practices, inconsistent pay scales, and vile conditions on factory floors. A measure of the Ford workers' hatred of the line was an appalling turnover rate of 370 percent in 1913, almost twice as much as the still-high average of 200 percent at the other big Detroit manufacturers. To maintain an average force of 13,600 men, the company had to hire 50,500 men annually. A 10 percent daily absentee rate also required bringing on 1,300–1,400 replacement workers each day—while most men could be trained for an assembly line job in less than an hour, the delay in filling a slot was disruptive of schedules.

The company's personnel department, after conducting a study in 1913, made a number of changes, including granting a 15 percent overall pay raise, reining in abusive foremen, and improving plant conditions. For a short time, the absenteeism dropped, but then it spiked up again at the end of the year, and in January Ford and Couzens made the decision to adopt the $5 per day wage. That contradicts the Nevins assertion that, while there had been serious management issues when the line first became effective, the personnel department had effectively solved them.

Classical economics assumes that, within skill bands, workers are interchangeable, and that markets clear, assuring that like companies will pay like amounts to similar workers. Difficulty in recruiting workers is a sure sign of below-market wages; while long lines at the hiring gate suggests that the proprietors are paying too much. The solution in both cases is to ensure that wages are adjusted to the market-clearing level. More recently, economists have identified the "efficiency wage"—an above-market wage designed to improve employee morale and productivity. The position of the Ford company is something of an anomaly. It had no trouble finding men—the application queue at the front gate each morning was almost a tourist attraction. And despite the worker churn, the Ford system produced staggering profits. Its 1912 earnings were 132 percent of tangible assets, and its bottom-line return on sales was an eye-popping 31 percent. So was the famous $5 per day pay package an efficiency wage, adopted to improve productivity and profits over the long run? Or was it an enlightened act of corporate statesmanship to elevate the status and earning power of the ordinary worker, as Ford, and Nevins, portrayed it?*

The answer is likely a mix of the two. Ford and Couzens were complicated people. Ford was never much motivated by money, and Couzens, although he was a demanding boss and a hard negotiator, took pride in his business ethics. The two of them made the decision to double the company's wage bill pretty much by themselves, with only minimum consultation with their directors. (Ford held 58.5 percent of the voting shares.) If their only objective had been to sweeten labor relations, a much smaller increase, perhaps to $3.50 would have sufficed. The Ford personnel department also began to sponsor citizenship training (for their many immigrant workers) and literacy training, and hired social workers to assist in disruptive family problems. Turnover dropped like a rock after the new wage policy was installed, but it still cost them about half of their gaudy profits. In short, it is reasonable to take Ford and Couzens at their word when they said that directors, managers, and shareholders had been making extraordinary financial gains, and the time had come to share the bounty with their workers; but at the same time, they must have been aware that a smoothly running plant and attentive workers would make it much easier to achieve their volume objectives.[15]

For the next decade and a half, Ford dominated the automobile industry. When the Model T was first introduced in 1908, it sold a then-spectacular 11,000 cars its first year. As Ford phased in his production system, the company roughly doubled sales each year, hitting the 500,000 mark in 1915–1916, which would have been inconceivable with traditional

---

* In this period, all of the other car factories required more skilled men than Ford and more men per unit of output. So it's likely that, by the standards of unskilled men, Ford was already paying a wage premium, which would explain the long hiring queues, but it was not enough to quell the turnover. The inherent productivity of his factories still generated the boffo profits. When General Motors caught, and surpassed, Ford in the ingenuity of its factory methods, it paid its workers more than Ford.

manufacturing methods. The economies of scale were demonstrated in 1913, when Ford Motors accounted for nearly half of all automobile sales: Ford sold 261,000 cars against the rest of the industry's 287,000. But Ford did it with 13,000 employees, while the 299 other companies required 66,000 employees, or five times as many.[16]

For New York City, the 1920s was the most splendid of decades. For one thing, it was swimming in money. In consequence of the devastation in Europe and Churchill's mismanagement of the pound, global monetary rivers had rechanneled to run through New York. The deepening sediments of gold dust provided the loose change to pay for great advances in broadcasting and publishing, in advertising and popular entertainment, in couture, in culture and the arts, and finally for the decade's great building boom that established skyscraper art deco as the characteristic New York City design standard.[17]

New York was the country's communications hub. David Sarnoff, born on a Russian *shtetl*, and running his own shoeshine and newsstand businesses in the New York ghetto at thirteen, became an office boy at Marconi's Wireless, made himself a top wireless operator for ship-to-shore communications, and was part of the team that mediated the rescue of *Titanic* passengers. Sarnoff was also among the first to realize the potential entertainment value of radio. After the war, Marconi's Wireless was purchased by General Electric and renamed the Radio Corporation of America (RCA), headed by Sarnoff. His official job was to expand the market for General Electric radios, and his great insight was that the best way to sell radios was to create material people wanted to listen to. Sarnoff formed the National Broadcasting Company (NBC) by a merger that brought him AT&T's broadcasting infrastructure. (It was part of a broad communications patent-sharing agreement that left the radio market to General Electric and telephones to AT&T.) Sarnoff bought out a struggling Victor phonograph company for its music library, and fought off competitive challenges from Westinghouse and other companies. He recruited Arturo Toscanini to conduct the NBC Symphony Orchestra, and paid lavishly for the rights to broadcast Jack Dempsey's fights. *Amos 'n Andy*, played by two white men speaking in minstrel show accents, was on for fifteen minutes six nights a week, with probably the greatest percentage radio audience market share ever. Grantland Rice broadcast the 1923 World Series.

Sarnoff's flaw was that he was an aspiring highbrow, and much of his programming was dull. William Paley, a rich man's kid, saw his opening and took over a struggling Columbia Broadcasting System (CBS). Unlike Sarnoff, he did not try to soft-pedal the advertising, and pitched all of his programming to a mass audience. He targeted Toscanini with the much more popular Paul Whiteman, and countered Sarnoff's dramas with soaps and comics like Bob Hope and Jack Benny. But Sarnoff was a competitor, and quickly changed his programming and advertising policies to keep pace. His owners were content, as sales of radios soared from $60 million in 1922 to $843 million in 1929 (despite much cheaper small radios), while NBC's advertising revenues jumped proportionally.[18] Along the way, Sarnoff and Paley created the programming and revenue models that are still the basis of today's television industry.

The national print media was also concentrated in New York. The *New York World*, featuring Walter Lippmann on the editorial page, was the highest of the highbrow dailies, while other New York-based columnists—Walter Winchell, Damon Runyon, Ring Lardner, Westbrook Pegler—all achieved national syndication. The *Daily News* adopted the down-market tabloid format in 1919, and in 1924, Bernarr Macfadden, the former bodybuilder, launched the decidedly downscale *New York Evening Graphic*, sometimes referred to as the "Evening Porno-graphic." Macfadden also pioneered the "True" tag in confession and pulp adventure magazines—which spawned *True Story, True Romances, True Experiences*, and other progeny, often referred to as "sex magazines." At the other end of the economic scale, Harold Ross, from Salt Lake City, founded *The New Yorker*, and made it a success by focusing on the narrow class of Manhattan glitterati—emphasizing that it was specifically for "sophisticated" and "enlightened" readers who enjoyed the "metropolitan life," and decidedly "not edited for the old lady in Dubuque." Scott and Zelda, Dorothy Parker, Robert Benchley, and Edna St. Vincent Millay were regulars at *New Yorker* parties and helped recruit other writers. But the most creative departure in the magazine business was undoubtedly Henry Luce's and Brit Hadden's launch of *Time* in 1923, which Luce rapidly turned into a national media empire.

The 1920s were also one of the great ages of book publishing, almost all of it centered in New York. Maxwell Perkins of Scribner's launched the careers of Scott Fitzgerald, Ernest Hemingway, and Thomas Wolfe; Horace Liveright of Boni & Liveright published William Faulkner, Sherwood Anderson, Theodore Dreiser, Eugene O'Neill, Robinson Jeffers, and Hart Crane; Alfred A. Knopf was home to Willa Cather, H. L. Mencken, Langston Hughes, and Wallace Stevens. It was also an era of publishing projects—like The Harvard Classics and Will and Ariel Durant's multivolume bestseller, The Story of Civilization, which targeted a middlebrow audience aspiring to expand its tastes and erudition. Bennett Cerf acquired the splendid Modern Library from Liveright, and founded the very successful The Book of the Month Club.

Charles Lindbergh's solo flight from New York to Paris in 1927 was a watershed event in the history of mass communications—the first 1920s viral, social-media-like, flash-crowd event. Lindbergh was an appealing young man—a former army and mail-service pilot, a superb natural flier and stunt man, devoid of pretension, resourceful, and brave. The event itself, however, had a whiff of the artificial. A number of teams had already flown across the Atlantic—they just hadn't flown from New York to Paris nonstop, and a wealthy hotel owner had offered a $25,000 prize to the first team that made it. Lindbergh decided he would try, scraped up some $13,500 and, with the help of a start-up airplane company, designed a completely stripped down plane, and filed for the event.

But there was nothing artificial about Lindbergh's accomplishment, and it placed him in the ranks of the world's greatest aviators. At a full load of gas, his plane was dangerous to fly, so he had never tested it fully loaded. Taking off for the real event, he nearly consumed the entire runway before finally getting airborne and barely cleared a ribbon of telephone wires that would have destroyed the plane. Several of the most experienced competitors came to watch his takeoff, and all were deeply impressed. Richard Byrd, who led a forty-person team, and who had previously flown over the North Pole, told the press, "his takeoff was the most skillful thing I have ever seen from any aviator."

The flight itself was just as extraordinary. Lindbergh said he flew through "sleet and snow for a thousand miles; sometimes he flew as low as ten feet, sometimes as high as ten thousand." Although a number of other transoceanic attempts had gone far off course, Lindbergh not only hit Paris on the nose, but hit all of his intermediate points as well. Without a radio (to save weight) or a crew, he did it by dead reckoning with maps, compass, and slide rule in the cruelly cramped cockpit, often by flashlight, at times working the math even when he had been without sleep for more than two days. Charmingly, his main worries as he approached Paris were, in rough order, whether anyone knew he was coming, whether he needed a French visa, and how he would find the airport in the dark.

But the real event was the event itself. The press had not discovered Lindbergh until a few weeks before his flight, but were naturally drawn to him, for he made great copy. Weeks of bad weather delayed the start of the contest. Characteristically, Lindbergh was the first to decide that it was good to go, although he made no announcement. The night before the flight, he got almost no sleep, was at the airport by 3 a.m. with a small crew to ready his plane, and got off the ground at 8 a.m. During the flight, he had no idea that he was front page news throughout the country, or that ship-to-shore radio buzzed with possible "Lindy" sightings all that day, or that on that same evening, twenty-three thousand people at a heavyweight boxing match in Madison Square Garden stood with heads bowed to offer a silent prayer for his safety. And when he arrived in Paris late that night, he couldn't imagine why the area that he had calculated as Le Bourget airport appeared to be occupied by tens of thousands of torch-waving people, or why roads were clogged with traffic as far as he could see. When he finally decided to land, he was almost consumed by the jubilant mob, and his plane was damaged before he was whisked away along with the American ambassador and a panoply of French officials. Literally overnight Lindbergh became the most famous man in the world.

The power of the movies was that they could bring a constant stream of Lindbergh-like events to anyone for the modest price of a ticket. Filmmaking was also the most successful American media business, the fourth largest industry in the United States, producing 80 percent of the world's films, including some eight hundred features and 20,000 shorts each year. Its stars were world famous. Ironically, it was also in desperate financial straits. To attract audiences, movie theaters were piling on the extras— lavish décors, giant orchestras, live comedy acts. The Roxy theater in midtown Manhattan had 6,200 seats, dressing rooms for 300 performers, space for a 118-piece orchestra, and an organ so big it took three men to play it. After paying the hefty film rental fees, theater owners couldn't cover their overheads.

The savior was sound, beginning with Al Jolson's few minutes of speaking aloud exactly 354 words in the 1928 *The Jazz Singer*. It took time to work out the kinks in the technology, and even longer to complete the practical accommodations. The grandiose 1,000+-seat theaters were too big for the day's best sound equipment. Silent movie audiences were accustomed to talking freely during performances, and had to be retrained. Many actors who had built solid careers didn't have the voice or the diction, or even the command of English, to make it in the talkies, although figures like Peter Lorre, Greta Garbo, and Marlene Dietrich made a virtue of their accents. Scriptwriting was suddenly much more demanding, creating a new market for writers like Fitzgerald and Faulkner, while soundtracks were a boon for composers and conductors. The lure of vast profits accelerated the transition, and by the early 1930s, millions of new fans streamed to the talkies, and movies became the decade's quintessential recreation.

Movies, like much contemporary fiction, were frequently culturally transgressive, portraying a sexual ethic at odds with the prim official canons retailed by America's middle-class parents and pulpits. Actors like Clara Bow, Louise Brooks, Mae West, and Joan Crawford exemplified the recreational, the manipulative, and the comic sides of sex. From the very start producers had understood that nothing else sold quite as well as sex. The advertisements for movies, and frequently the content, were quite salacious, well after the "Code" had been ostensibly adopted by Hollywood. It was not until the mid-1930s, deep into the Depression, when the entire country was pulling away from the exuberances of the pre-Crash days, that Hollywood adopted a Code that, with the assistance of organizations like the Legion of Decency, actually worked.*

---

* Contrary to legend, studio moguls, as opposed to directors and producers, welcomed a strong Code. Middle American revulsion with highly sexual movies threatened to bring federal regulation on the industry. (It was actually part of Roosevelt's first National Industrial Recovery Act.) The era of Code dominance, ironically, was also the golden age of American movies. *Casablanca, Double Indemnity, Rope of Sand, The Postman Always Rings Twice, On the Waterfront, A Streetcar Named Desire, The*

Mass population movements created more upheavals. The American entrance into World War I triggered the first crumblings of the totalitarian regimes in the former Confederate states. Since Reconstruction, Southern whites had pinned their black citizens under a terror-enforced yoke of white rule. Lynch-law, the ultimate penalty for being "uppity," reigned throughout most of the South. The torture and mutilations that frequently accompanied it were object lessons to quell incipient restiveness. But both the draft and the war-time shutdown of immigration created severe labor shortages in northern factories, and the braver Southern black workers were delighted to seize the opportunity.

Isabel Wilkerson's splendid *The Warmth of Other Suns* is a close-to-the-ground story of the black hegira. During the decade of the war, 555,000 Southern blacks relocated to the North, more than in the entire half-century since Emancipation. Southern whites reacted with scorn at first: "As the North grows blacker, the South grows whiter," a New Orleans paper chuckled.[19]

As the labor shortage started to bite, the South swung to a posture of heavy-handed repression. Labor agents from the North were harassed and threatened. In Macon, agents had to pay a $25,000 fee and get forty-five recommendations from local luminaries. Police patrolled bus and train stations, stopped trains in mid-journey to search for escapees, and often enough arrested every black person in a station. If a black worker did not show up for work, it was not uncommon for a sheriff's officer to be dispatched to bring her in to be sure she wasn't absconding. Recalcitrant black workers could be imprisoned or taken into the woods and savagely beaten—but as a South Carolinian paper asked, "If you thought you might be lynched by mistake, would you stay in South Carolina?"[20]

The North was no picnic. A job in a modern "Ford-ized" factory was neither less back-breaking nor menial than picking cotton, but the pay was higher, and the boss didn't keep part of your paycheck. But even in the menial factory jobs, white workers often rebelled when blacks were hired. The plant owners exacerbated the animosities when they hired black strike-breakers.

Maltese Falcon, Mildred Pierce, and *The Naked City* were all made under the Code. Almost all movie critics would agree that the Lana Turner/John Garfield *Postman* was much sexier than the explicit, but lame, Jack Nicholson/Jessica Lange remake.

And there was anti-black violence in the North, although it wasn't state-sponsored, as in the South. When the war ended, and factory employment flagged in 1919, blacks became a target for struggling white workers. In Chicago, a black boy crossed an invisible line while swimming in Lake Michigan. A crowd of whites threw rocks at him, and he drowned. Blacks asked the police to arrest the whites, but they arrested a black man instead, apparently for protesting too forcefully. Unlike in the South, blacks often fought back in the North, but with the police generally backing the whites, the tolls were lopsided.[21]

Harlem became the de facto capital of the black North, with a half million people crammed into a 50-block long slice of Manhattan, just seven or eight blocks wide. Since realtors generally enforced informal, but strict, segregation rules, rents in the black zone rose to 40–60 percent higher than in comparable white areas. To meet the high rents, tenants often resorted to "rent parties" at the end of each month, when they "drank bathtub gin, ate pig knuckles and danced with the lights off," usually for twenty-five cents a head. It is likely that the profits were miniscule, but the parties at least were fun.[22]

The black northward migration left a profound stamp on American culture, especially in the arts, and in reinforcing the transgressiveness of the 1920s culture. In New York, the "Harlem Renaissance" was personified by writers and poets like Countee Cullen, Langston Hughes, Zora Neale Hurston, and James Weldon Johnson. Venues like the gangster-owned Cotton Club, featuring artists like Duke Ellington, Louis Armstrong, Billie Holiday, and Cab Calloway, exposed white audiences to the deeply sensual beats of blues and jazz. The Cotton Club and many of its competitors were still segregated—the entertainers and the waiters were black, but all the customers were white. Black audiences had their own clubs.

Critics like Carl Van Vechten, himself a man of fluid sexuality, explored the seamier sides of Harlem life, especially the small jazz clubs and polymorphic sex tourism industry, which had a mixed black and white clientele. Van Vechten threw lavish parties at his downtown apartment that mixed notable blacks and wealthy whites. Invitations were much sought-for, despite lingering suspicions of exploitation. Blacks were wary of being displayed like zoo animals, while whites were nervous about being hustled. Van Vechten himself illustrates the problem. He more or less single-handedly turned the spotlight on Langston Hughes's great talents, tirelessly boosted the careers of James Johnson and Paul Robeson, was very helpful to Ethel Waters, and played a major role in developing the production that introduced the nineteen-year-old Josephine Baker. His payback—aside from expanding his sexual menu—was to cement his position as the leading interpreter of black culture for the white world.

But perhaps nothing undermined respect for authority like Prohibition, one of history's signal demonstrations of unintended consequences. It was not imposed on an unwilling populace, for the temperance societies had clearly won the battle for public opinion. Forty-six of the forty-eight states ratified the constitutional amendment, which was quickly embodied in the Volstead Act. The law provided that no one could "manufacture, sell, barter, transport, import, export, deliver, or furnish any intoxicating liquor," except as specifically provided in the act, which generally exempted any beverage with less than 0.05 percent alcohol. It did not prohibit purchasing or drinking alcoholic beverages. So California vineyards made up some of their lost wine sales by selling concentrated grape pulp—add water and allow it to ferment and you had legal wine. The promise of Prohibition was that it would reduce crime and the prison population, keep families together, and lower spousal abuse.[23]

A fair review of the evidence suggests, first of all, that Prohibition did substantially reduce drinking. While data on the volume of drinking during Prohibition are necessarily speculative, the volume of drinking *after* Prohibition's repeal confirm its success. During the years 1900–1915, American adults consumed, on average, about 2.5 gallons of pure alcohol per year. In the first year after repeal, however, alcohol consumption was less than one gallon a year, and it increased only slowly thereafter—to 1.2 gallons in 1935, and 1.5 gallons in 1936–1941—and did not reach the 1900–1915 average until the 1960s. In addition, in the early years of Prohibition, admission to state hospitals for alcoholism dropped substantially, and a number of social service studies concluded that there had been a substantial decline in drinking, especially in smaller towns and among the working classes.[24]

But those gains came at a cost. For one thing, the actual workings of the law broke sharply along class lines. In big cities, and especially in New York and Chicago, the business, political, and social elites virtually ignored it. Scott, Zelda, and their friends never wanted for quality spirits, and flasks were freely displayed at Harvard-Yale games. Illegal supply networks quickly sprang up—like the bootlegger ships ringing New York harbor just outside Coast Guard jurisdiction and the Canadian border runners in Chicago and Detroit. Although Prohibition did not create the contending Jewish, Italian, and Irish gangster networks, it vastly expanded their revenues and facilitated their moves into casinos, prostitution, loan sharking, dope trafficking, and a number of legitimate businesses.

The repeal of Prohibition was driven in great part by the elite flaunting their noncompliance. In a representative sample of films that opened in 1930, more than three-quarters of them had references to liquor, and two-thirds showed people drinking.[25] Even the president of the United States drank—copiously during the Harding administration. Parental lectures on respect for law and social canons rang hollow when the parents had cocktails before dinner. The intermittent gangland slaughters, especially in Chicago, were frightening. The solid support for Prohibition was clearly waning by the 1930s. During his campaign, Franklin Roosevelt had been cautious of taking a position on repeal, but by the time he took office, repeal was almost as uncontroversial as its imposition had been in 1920.

Cultural transgression was also reflected in the couture industry. A business newspaper calculated in 1928 that, since the war, the material required for a woman's clothing had dropped from 19¼ yards to only 7. Even that would have been an intolerable weight for *The New Yorker's* fashion arbiter, Lois Long—who signed her restaurant and nightclub reviews "Lipstick." "I know nothing about men at all, being a modest and retiring type," she wrote. "I know only that they all love black lace over pink; they adore long, sheer black silk stockings, plain pumps without buckles or straps, and long eyelashes."[26]

Shoppers could have found all that and more on New York City's Fifth Avenue, the cynosure of American fashion. Earlier in the century, New York's fashionable ladies had their clothes hand-fitted by custom tailors, as often as not working from pirated Parisian designs. In the 1920s, however, Edwin Goodman, who had kept the trademark Bergdorf Goodman after his partner retired, achieved a smash-hit with high-quality, high-style off-the-rack clothing for upscale ladies. His secret was to pair standardized design with very personal service, and to complement his clothing with a full line of handbags, scarves, and other accessories.

The rest of the industry quickly followed suit, with most of the major stores creating their own lines, at first usually manufactured on-site. As the industry expanded, a new breed of Jewish real estate entrepreneurs, most of them with roots in the garment industry, concentrated the manufacture of clothing in the "garment district," the area bounded by Sixth and Ninth Avenues from 35th to 40th Streets. During the last half of the decade, they built 120 new high-rise garment district centers for clothing manufacture and showrooms. For many years the workers in a single garment-district building made half of all ladies' hats sold in the country.

The 1920s saw the United States rise to dominance in high-end service industries—not just finance, but insurance, law and accountancy, publishing and printing, advertising, radio and movies, air travel, and others. Broadway created new genres of staged musicals, while Tin Pan Alley churned out the nation's most popular songs. In all big cities, but especially in New York, there was a surge of demand for white-collar workers, and the age of the ultra-high skyscraper was born. In the last half of the 1920s, Manhattan office space roughly doubled, most of it in skyscrapers, mostly in Midtown, centered around Grand Central Station. By 1929, New York City had half of all the nation's buildings over twenty-one stories high. Not everyone approved. The critic Lewis Mumford wrote in 1926, "the less said about the aesthetic triumphs of the skyscraper the better. . . . The people who see our architectural salvation in the skyscraper know very little, I suspect, about either architecture or salvation." *Scientific American*, in a 1925 article "Panic!," calculated that if Manhattan subways and skyscrapers had to evacuate their occupants at the same time, the pile of people on the pavements would be eighteen feet high.

Yet the skyscraper has survived, and splendidly. Iconic 1920s buildings like the Chanin Building at Lexington and 42nd, and the French Building at Fifth and 45th are now national landmarks. The Chrysler Building eclipsed the downtown Woolworth Building (which opened in 1918) as the world's tallest, and was quickly dethroned by the 1930s Empire State Building. The Chrysler and Woolworth Buildings, however, still reign as consummate examples of the art deco style.[27]

Muncie, Indiana, in 1924 was an industrial city of about 36,000 people in the Midwestern corn belt. No one claimed it was lovely—its local newspaper, indeed, admitted that it was "unfortunate in not having many natural beauty spots." Its primary employers were mostly subsidiaries of the big automobile companies or suppliers to them, making glass, wire, and automobile parts. Its residents were more than 90 percent white, with scatterings of black and foreign-born populations. About half of its adult residents had been born on farms, and 70 percent of those in employment were working class—predominately factory workers, with an admixture of clerks in offices and retail stores and semi-skilled services, like waiters, barbers, and beauticians.

We know quite a lot about 1920s Muncie because a team of cultural anthropologists, led by Robert S. and Helen M. Lynd spent eighteen months there in 1924 and 1925. They called the city "Middletown" to ensure a measure of anonymity for their subjects. As anthropologists, they applied the methods they would have used if they were studying exotica like the Trobriand Islanders. They lived in the community, participated in many of its activities, conducted hundreds of interviews, and collected many more anonymous questionnaires. Their interviews ran the gamut from top officials down to a large sampling of high school students. The objective was to document how a middle American community made its living, the nature of people's home lives, how they worshipped, what they did for entertainment, the sources of their anxieties, the kinds of social pressures they were under, and their hopes and dreams for the future. The team returned in 1933, primarily to document how the townspeople had dealt with the Depression. [28]

Muncie had once been a strong union town. Around the turn of the century, half of all production workers were in unionized skilled or semi-skilled trades, and had completed apprenticeship programs. It was the unions that had insisted on workplace safety rules that sharply lowered accident rates, and the unions had also pushed through a state worker's compensation program. Much of the town's social life had been organized around the unions. Unions led the holiday parades, and the results of interunion baseball games—"the Sandmolders vs. the Machinists"— were grist for the sports pages. But the unions lost their base when Ford deskilled manufacturing. In a Ford plant, the machine embodied the required skills, while the human operator was its servant—turning it on, loading the work piece, keeping it lubricated, changing a cutting tool, all the time working to the machine's tempo. Some factory owners deliberately forced strikes so they could install new generations of machinery during the shutdowns.

By 1924, the median Muncie worker was a male factory machine operator. He had not finished high school, did not belong to a union, and had no formal apprenticeship training. He was paid by the hour for the time he actually worked. There were almost no benefits, although a handful of the bigger companies were experimenting with group life insurance. Despite the improvement in industrial accidents, the numbers were still atrocious. About 20 percent of the factory workforce lost time each year because of an industrial accident; 43 percent of them lost more than eight days of work, 5 percent lost an eye or some bodily appendage, and about half of 1 percent died. Few people had health insurance, but the day's medical capabilities were rudimentary and appropriately inexpensive. Several of the larger plants had a nurse or other medical professional either on site or on call in case of an accident.

In Muncie's new Ford-style plants, most jobs required only a few days of training. But even the work of the remaining skilled men had been substantially routinized. Gear-grinding was a skilled task in most plants, and when factories were smaller, a man qualified to grind gears was expected to work on a variety of other similarly demanding tasks. Not so in the new era of mass production. A Muncie plant manager pointed out a gear-grinder to one of the Lynd researchers and said, "There's a man who's ground diameters on gears here for fifteen years and done nothing else. It's a fairly highly skilled job . . . [but] it's so endlessly monotonous! That man is dead, just dead!"[29] The manager of a large metal-working plant told the researchers that 75 percent of their hires could be trained in a week or less, while in glassblowing, one of Muncie's premier industries, and formerly one of its most skilled, 84 percent of the workers needed a month or less training. Only about 6 percent of the tool-using jobs in 1925 Muncie's glass industries required journeyman glassblowers.

Blue-collar work was hard, and the hours were long. Most plants started work at 7 a.m.; the standard workweek was five ten-hour days, and a half day on Saturday. (Executives usually started their workday at 8:30 a.m.) And the pay was poor. The US Bureau of Labor calculated that a minimum standard of living for a Muncie family of five required annual earnings of $1,903, or about $36 a week. The Lynds' sample of Muncie working-class families with five or more members showed that only a quarter of them made that much, even counting the income of working wives and children. Jobs were also uncertain. The year 1923 was a good one for Muncie, so three-quarters of the male family heads had worked a full year without layoffs. The next year, the economy turned sour, and 43 percent of the sample lost a month or more of employment. One large plant that had ended 1923 with 802 men had cut back to 316 by midsummer 1924, with a third of them working on short hours. Except for the genuinely skilled men, and perhaps some favored long-term employees, employers generally did not commit to hire back their men when a layoff ended. Factory hands were factory hands: the laid-off men understood the game and lined up at other factory hiring offices as soon as they were let go.

Factory workers all faced the likelihood of dying in poverty, since the plants almost uniformly terminated men when they could no longer keep up. Plant managers told the Lynds: "The principal change . . . has been the speeding up of machines. . . . [We have] no definite policy of firing men when they reach a certain age . . . but in general we find that when a man reaches fifty he is slipping." "In production work forty to forty-five is the age limit because of the speed needed in the work. Men over forty are hired as sweepers and for similar jobs." "Fifty per cent of the men now employed by us are forty and over, but the company has decided to adopt a policy of firing every employee as he reaches sixty." "The age dead line is creeping down on those men—I'd say that by forty-five, they're through."[30]

Workers and their wives understood the bleakness ahead. "Whenever you get old they are done with you. The only thing a man can do is to stay as young as he can and save as much as he can." "The company is pretty apt [not to lay him off]. But when he gets older, I don't know."

"I worry about what we'll do when he gets older and isn't wanted at the factories and I am unable to go to work. We can't expect our children to support us and we can't seem to save any money for that time." "He is forty and in about ten years will be on the shelf. . . . What will we do? Well, that is just what I don't know. We are not saving a penny, but we are saving our boys [who were both in the local college]."[31] Many of these families had been raised on farms, at a time when the farm itself provided a modicum of security. If a farm couple managed their farm adequately and stayed healthy, they could pass the farm to their children and stay on in their dotage, contributing work as they were able. But in the 1920s, agriculture was industrializing as well, and forcing small farmers off the land. As the security of farming became ever more illusory, the chance to earn regular weekly cash packets in a booming urban industrial economy was tempting, safety net or no.

On top of the cruel financial pressures, working-class people were besieged with new ways to spend money. By 1924, Insull's company and other electrical conglomerates were steadily wiring up the towns and cities in the upper Midwest, and almost everyone in Muncie had electricity, with its spreading vistas of new things to buy. Electric irons and curling irons! Washing machines! Refrigerators! Toasters and waffle irons! Radios! For working-class women, who did not send the laundry out as their betters did, the washing machine was a miracle, much as the iron stove was for nineteenth-century farm women. No more boiling soiled clothes and scrubbing them on a washboard with raw-red hands. Working-class Muncie families frequently bought a washing machine before they had an indoor toilet.

It wasn't just about durables. The barrage of mass media—tabloids, radio shows, movies—turned advertising into an important industry. Muncie interviews confirm that children exerted considerable independent spending pressure. Fashion trends from New York were replicated in mass-produced knockoffs that sold throughout the country. Cosmetics became a major expense. In previous eras, women had used mostly powder and perfume, since "painting" one's face bordered on immorality. The heavy makeup used in Hollywood changed all that. Max Factor, who became famous as a movie cosmetologist, Helena Rubenstein, and Elizabeth Arden rolled out a flood of new products throughout the 1920s and

1930s—eyebrow pencils, mascara, lip gloss, liquid nail polish, rouges, and compacts to allow constant attention to the state of one's face. In Muncie, the push to conform escalated in high school for both boys and girls, although the pressures were greater on girls. One business-class mother said, "The dresses girls wear to school now used to be considered party dresses." Her daughter, she said, would feel "terribly abused" if she had to wear the same dress two days in a row. A fifteen-year-old boy admonished his mother that if his sister didn't have silk stockings when she started high school, "none of the boys will like her or have anything to do with her." There were many instances of the daughters of working-class mothers who could not afford the clothing standard simply dropping out of school.[32]

Measured by its economic impact, the evolution of consumer credit was nearly as portentous as the light bulb or the internal combustion engine. Credit was suddenly readily available for homes, for consumer durables like cars and washing machines, and even for routine purchases like clothing. At the turn of the century, people in Muncie rented their houses, but by the 1920s, they had clearly shifted to buying homes with borrowed money. There were four building and loan societies in Muncie in 1924. One of them, not the largest, had 7,090 members and $2.7 million in assets. Loan rates for members were $0.25 a week ($13 a year) for each $100 borrowed. Those were excellent terms: standard building society practice was to lend up to two-thirds of a property's value, with full amortization over an eleven to twelve year period, which implies an annual interest rate of 6–8 percent. People without building society accounts could get financing from other lenders, but the terms were harsher—the maximum loan was usually 50 percent of the purchase price, and amortization periods were five years or less. Even worse, if they missed a payment, they were subject to losing the home and all their accrued equity.

Point-of-sale credit radically changed working-class attitudes toward consumption. By 1925, consumer installment credit had soared to $11.5 billion, up from almost nothing in 1920. Big-ticket items like cars and furniture led the parade, but there were "easy" payment plans for pianos, radios, phonographs, vacuum cleaners, and even impulse items like jewelry and clothing, which by themselves accounted for half the total borrowing. Average maturity of the loans ranged between twelve and eighteen months for major durables, down to only five or six months for clothing and jewelry and smaller durables like radios.[33]

But the cultural artifact with the greatest impact on savings and social behavior was undoubtedly the affordable automobile. A new Model T, with a base price of $350, could be readily financed for $35 a month for a year, or about an average male's week's pay, and be owned free and clear—unless there was a layoff or a sickness. Some families, even in 1924, were financing new cars with mortgages on their homes. One advertisement had a gray-haired banker saying: "Before you can save money, you must make money. . . . I have often advised customers of mine to buy cars, as I felt that the increased stimulation and opportunity of observation would enable them to earn amounts equal to the cost of their cars." (Later during the Depression, advertisements pushed the value of a car in widening the job search.) One woman with nine children told the Muncie researchers, "We'd rather go without clothes than give up the car. We used to go to his sister's to visit, but by the time we'd get the children shoed and dressed, there wasn't any money for carfare. Now no matter how they look, we just poke 'em in the car and take 'em along." There was also evidence of people cutting down on food to keep the car.

At first, owning a car was a family-cohesive force. "Sunday drives" became a standard recreation. Working-class people, in particular, relished the opportunities to drive into the country for a picnic or just for sightseeing. But as cars became a standard piece of family equipment—by 1929, the ratio of cars to families in Muncie was about 1:1—they became a source of tension between parents and older children. One mother lamented that in the pre-automobile days, families would sit outside their houses on summer evenings chatting, maybe even playing music or singing. Now, a father reported, his daughter complained, "What on earth *do* you want me to do? Just sit around home all evening?"[34]

The combination of cars and pre-Code movies was especially potent. In 1925, Muncie had nine movie theaters, open daily from 1 p.m. to 11 p.m., showing twenty-two different films a week for a total of three hundred showings. Comedies, especially those of Harold Lloyd, were the most popular movies. Right behind, though, were so-called "sex" movies. In one week, *The Daring Years*, *Sinners in Silk*, *Woman Who Give*, and *The Price She Paid* were all running at the same time. The advertisement for

The movies were a peephole that allowed working-class, god-fearing Americans a glimpse into the lives of the upper classes. The poster for *Flaming Youth* promised the "Naked Truth" about a "spicy society" and its "gay life, its petting parties, its flapper dance, its jazz."

Flaming Youth proclaimed, "neckers, petters, white kisses, red kisses, pleasure-mad daughters, sensation craving mothers . . . the truth, bold, naked, sensational."

The famously straitlaced morality of American working classes had depended in some measure in not knowing how the elites really behaved.* Now the movies offered master classes in such deportment, even as the automobile supplied readily available privacy. One juvenile court judge noted that of thirty girls brought before him for "sex crimes"—how he defined them isn't clear—nineteen of them had occurred in cars, which

---

* There was, of course, a fair amount of hypocrisy involved in the earlier pose of strict morality. In 1890, there were twenty-five houses of prostitution operating in Muncie. Prostitution was outlawed in Indiana in 1915, and in the decade following, a number of Muncie officials were convicted of profiting from prostitution—shades of Sinclair Lewis's *Elmer Gantry*. At the time of the research, there were apparently only a handful of "fly-by-night" brothels catering to the working classes—or at least that was what the Lynd researchers were told.

had become "mobile houses of prostitution." The transition may have been particularly hard on working-class girls, who typically had much less access to sexual education than their better off peers. All of the "business-class" wives interviewed approved of and practiced contraception. But in the working class, fewer than half of the wives interviewed used any contraception at all, and 40 percent of those used primitive methods, like withdrawal. And of those using "scientific" methods, only half used the more up-to-date methods standard among the business-class wives. All the business-class wives had engaged in sex education with their daughters, while a large fraction of the working-class wives had not—or if they had, they might well have conveyed misinformation. The good news was that most mothers realized that sex education was important, although many working-class mothers felt incompetent to give it. There was no sex education in Muncie schools, churches, or social organizations like the YM/YWCAs.[35]

B y the end of the decade, ordinary Americans had seen their beliefs and values cruelly battered, not least by the arbiters of taste in New York and Hollywood. A signal episode that dramatized the gap between the gullible multitudes and the thinking elite was the 1925 John Scopes "Monkey Trial."

The short version is that the State of Tennessee outlawed the teaching of evolution as a scientific fact, under penalty of a fine or jail sentence. The American Civil Liberties Union (ACLU), hoping to head off a wave of such legislation, advertised in Tennessee newspapers that they would be willing to finance a test case. A transplanted New Yorker, George Rappleyea, who lived in the small town of Dayton, Tennessee, saw the ad, and convinced local school officials to make Dayton the site of a dramatic test case. Rappleyea was a Darwinist, while the two officials were not, but they all agreed that such a trial might be a "big sensation," and benefit the local economy. John Scopes, who taught biology at the local high school and was a committed Darwinist, volunteered to be the defendant. Rappleyea reached out to the ACLU, and the wheels were in motion.[36]

The established churches were delighted to join issue, and they assembled their own legal team, featuring William Jennings Bryan, who was a former secretary of state, a three-time progressive presidential candidate, and a senior figure in American Presbyterianism. Bryan, his biographer writes, was always "more interested in religion than in government." Darwinism had been a major focus of his energies since 1921. He was willing to lecture almost anywhere on the "gigantic conspiracy of atheists and agnostics" and had played a major role in mobilizing state educational authorities against Darwinism. Clarence Darrow, by then the nation's most famous criminal lawyer, offered his services free of charge to Scopes. He and Bryan had once been allies in Democratic politics, but the militance of Darrow's atheism and Bryan's fundamentalism* chilled

---

* "Fundamentalism" was a powerful evangelical movement within contemporary

their friendship to the point where Darrow referred to Bryan as the "the idol of all Morondom."[37]

Rappleyea's hope of creating a major spectacle was fully realized. Dayton, a town with a population of about five hundred, was inundated with sightseers, revivalists, carnival-style hawkers, more than one hundred working press representatives, and famous journalists like H. L. Mencken, who could not pass up the opportunity to ridicule the *booboiserie*. (Mencken was disappointed in Dayton: "I expected to find a squalid Southern village, with darkies snoozing on the houseblocks, pigs rooting under the houses and the inhabitants full of hookworm and malaria. What I found was a country town full of charm and even beauty.") An expanse of Dayton's main road was dedicated to the trial, with a speaker's platform and a tourist camp. The courtroom was equipped with telegraph and telephone wiring, movie-newsreel camera platforms, and radio microphones. The rental for just the telephone lines was $1,000 a day. It was the first-ever broadcast of a live trial over a national radio network, yet another 1920s flash-crowd media circus.[38]

The trial got underway on July 10, in blistering hot weather. Bryan made only occasional interjections during the early course of the trial, while Darrow was quite vocal from the outset. From the very start, the lawyers' exchanges grew nasty, with Darrow fulminating against a "narrow, ignorant, bigoted shrew of religion." The judge was a believing fundamentalist, but his rulings seem generally fair. The spectators were vocal and unruly throughout.

Once the preliminaries were over, Scopes entered a not-guilty plea and the defense presented its theory of the case, arguing that evolution was established science, and was not antireligious, since religion and science occupied different, but compatible, intellectual universes. The prosecution called two school officials and two boys to testify that Scopes had indeed taught the forbidden matter, which Scopes did not deny. Darrow then called a Johns Hopkins professor, who was both an eminent zoologist and a devout Protestant, to explain what was meant by

---

American Protestantism, inspired by a 1910 tract, *The Fundamentals*, prescribing a strictly literal interpretation of the Bible. It was especially strong in the South and Midwest, and Bryan, along with preachers like Billy Sunday, had adopted it in his religious work.

scientific evolution. At one point Darrow asked him whether evolution had commenced more than 6,000 years ago, and the witness replied, "Well, 600,000,000 years ago is a very modest guess," eliciting an audible gasp in the courtroom.[39] The next day, the attorneys debated the relevance of scientific evidence—in effect, was the trial a test of the science of evolution, or was it merely a question of whether Scopes had violated a very specific law? Bryan led off, and he was in top form—conversational, caustic, learned, and very funny. (The transcript records continual laughter throughout the talk.) The high point may have been his reading from Charles Darwin's *The Descent of Man*, doubtless savoring every syllable of the strange terminology—proceeding from the "ancient progenitors in the kingdom of the Vertebrata" through the Ascidians, the Ganoids, the Lepidosiren, and Monotremata to Simiadae, which "branched off into two great stems, the new world and the old world monkeys, and from the latter, at a remote period, man, the wonder and glory of the universe, proceeded."[40]

"Not even from American monkeys," Bryan lamented comically, "but from old world monkeys." Scopes said that he didn't listen to the argument but was thoroughly taken by the speech: "Every gesture and intonation of his voice blended so perfectly that it was almost like a symphony."[41]

The trial judge finally ruled that the scientific evidence was not probative on the main point—whether Scopes had taught material forbidden by the law. Since it appeared that little remained except the formality of Scopes's conviction and sentencing, a number of the press corps and celebrity visitors like Mencken traveled home over the weekend.

The defense, although they had expected the result, were unhappy with their performance. Despite his scornful harangues, Darrow had scored few points against Bryan. Bryan's parody of Darwin's book had gone over very well, and they knew he was planning a stemwinder of a closing speech. They came up with the idea of putting Bryan on the witness stand. It was highly irregular, but they thought Bryan would jump at the chance.

When Monday's court opened to oppressive heat, the judge adjourned the proceedings to the lawn, which had a podium and broadcasting equipment. As expected, Bryan readily agreed to be cross-examined, and Darrow then belabored him for two hours. Those two hours have gone down in history as exposing Bryan as a "bigoted, ill-informed, hopelessly outdated old man."[42] But that picture comes more from the 1960 Oscar-winning movie *Inherit the Wind*, which is avowedly fiction. In the movie, Spencer Tracy, playing the Darrow character (although the names were all changed), reduces Fredric March's Bryan to a gibbering, tearful fool, asking his wife why everybody is laughing at him.

In the real confrontation, a fair reading of the trial transcript shows Bryan rather holding his own, while Darrow comes across as hectoring and intemperate. Darrow's primary tactic was to raise a point of scientific consensus, like the age of the early Egyptian civilization, contrast it with the maximum age of the earth implied by the Bible, and then mock Bryan when he said that he accepted the biblical date. Darrow, presumably, was making a record for the big-city newspapers or future federal court judges. In Dayton, most of the audience, including the judge, the lead prosecutors, and the great majority of local spectators, would have given the same answers that Bryan did. Freethinkers and liberal Christians chuckled when Darrow badgered Bryan on whether fish survived the flood or where Cain found a wife, but Bryan's answer that anything was in the power of God would have sat well with his constituency.

As the back and forth became increasingly cantankerous, the judge finally called a halt and ruled that the examination had been irrelevant and would not be part of the record. Darrow then said that since they had already conceded that Scopes had taught the forbidden material and could not present their scientific evidence, the defense had no closing statement, foreclosing one from Bryan. The jury retired for nine minutes before returning a guilty verdict. The judge imposed a $100 fine on Scopes, which was paid by the *Baltimore Evening Sun*.

For Bryan, losing the opportunity for a comprehensive rebuttal was a disappointment, for he had assembled a great trove of apparently scientific cautions to Darwinism. So he went back on the road, using his Dayton closing statement as the basis for a new series of lectures and interviews. Rather than being broken and defeated, as some later accounts have it, he was marshalling his energies to see the fight through, and thousands of people turned out to see and hear him. The Sunday after the trial, he returned to Dayton for Sunday services, where he offered the opening prayers. After the service, he returned to his quarters, had a very large meal, lay down for a nap and was found dead some time later from "apoplexy," presumably a stroke of some kind. When Darrow was asked whether Bryan had died of a "broken heart" after the trial, he replied that he had died of "a busted belly."[43]

For Bryan, Biblical literalism was never the main objection to evolution. While he was no scientist, he was fairly well informed on intellectual trends, and more than once confided to friends that the hypothesis of gradual evolution of species was probably correct, but it could not explain the spiritual aspect of humans. He felt strongly that parents should determine what their children were taught on subjects that overlapped with their religious training. Even more strongly, he feared that if humans were taken to be naturally evolved organisms—just another primate—there would be no bar to immoralisms of all kinds. As his biographer put it, for Bryan, his "religion and the Bible [were] the foundation of an earthly kingdom of social justice and brotherhood among men and nations," the guiding light, as it were, of the progressive politics he had pursued throughout his life.[44]

The secular publishing industry determined the historiography of the trial. In the 1930s, Frederick Lewis Allen's immensely popular *Only Yesterday*, based mostly on press reports, presented the trial as a crushing blow against fundamentalism. Bryan, he wrote, was "covered with humiliation." And he went on: "Theoretically Fundamentalism had won, for the law stood. Yet really Fundamentalism had lost. . . . [C]ivilized opinion had regarded the Dayton trial with amazement and amusement, and the slow drift away from Fundamentalism certainly continued." In the 1950s, Richard Hofstadter and the playwrights of *Inherit the Wind* linked fundamentalism with the Ku Klux Klan and McCarthyism—one more of the sinister forces that education and intellectual progress had put to rout.[45] In fact, fundamentalists adopted a strategy much like the one American Catholics, another disfavored group, had chosen in the 1880s. They withdrew from American culture and created their own web of schools and social service institutions, all the time trumpeting their super-patriotism. Some sixty years later, Catholics were among the country's most powerful and influential religions. The high profile of fundamentalists in current politics suggests that they may be right on schedule.

B y the end of the decade, American intellectuals, especially those who had embraced scientific progressivism, were struggling with their own crumbling certainties. Confidence in scientific management of affairs reached a high point in the decades just before World War I. A touchstone was Karl Pearson's *The Grammar of Science* (1892), which claimed "the whole life, physical and mental, of the universe . . . [as] the material of science."[46] In his 1899 presidential address, John Dewey assured the American Psychological Association that science "will afford us insight into the conditions which control the formation and execution of aims, thus enable human effort to expend itself sanely, rationally, and with assurance."[47] The mission of the American Sociological Association, founded in 1905, was to identify "the social-equilibrating apparatus" to make possible a discipline of "social control."[48]

At the microlevel, progressivism displayed a tangle of motivations and ideologies, veering between quasi religiosity and *de haut en bàs* authoritarianism. The very idea of progress had a providential ring. When Darwin called man "the wonder and glory of the universe"—he was thinking, of course, of the contemporary English gentleman—it was the kind of Whig history that viewed the British constitution as the apex of human governance. But Darwin's own work exposed the fatuity of such speculations. The newest genetic research revealed that evolution really *was* random. Selection was about fitness for survival, not progress, and when it came to species' longevity and adaptability, cockroaches had it all over humans.

The whiff of the autocrat is apparent in Dewey's paean to education's ability "to control the formation and execution of aims." Progressives extolled democracy but often shrank from majoritarianism, as the Scopes trial demonstrated. Dewey seemed to believe that if his educational theories were adopted, the majority would necessarily become scientific progressives. But at a deeper level, Dewey's faith in rationality was mocked by the war. If an alien race had happened to survey the earth in the years after 1914, they might have concluded that humans were best at killing each other with monstrous instruments. Dewey broke the hearts of many of his followers when he supported the American entry into the war.

By the end of the decade, such worries were percolating from the cultural elite through the middlebrow press and journals like *The Nation*, *The New Republic*, and *The Saturday Review of Literature*. Just as Muncie parents were discovering that their teenage children were beginning to resist their pious platitudes, the golden rules of elite thought and behavior were turning into quicksilver. The literary and cultural critic Joseph Wood Krutch captured the sense of discontent in his *The Modern Temper* (1929), which lamented "the impasse to which the scientific spirit has conducted us." Nature "is ingenious in devising *means*," Krutch wrote, "But she has no *ends* which the human mind is able to discover."[49]

Walter Lippmann made his living sensing and analyzing elite cultural crosswinds, and like Krutch, he channeled his own anxieties of losing both God and scientific certainty. In his *A Preface to Morals* (1931), he tried to construct a secular creed to supply a moral compass for a random and impersonal world. William James, Lippmann acknowledged, had immense sympathy with popular religion and clearly envied its certainties: "He had the Will to Believe, he argued eloquently for the Right to Believe. But he did not wholly believe." Lippmann finally quotes Bertrand Russell on the harshness of the thinking human's spiritual environs:

> [Spent on] the dark ocean on whose rolling waves we toss for a brief hour; from the great night without, a chill blast breaks in upon our refuges; all the loneliness of humanity amid hostile forces is concentrated upon the individual soul . . .

Lippmann then proceeded to lay out the precepts of a "religion of the spirit," a doctrine of humanism, which he suggested could satisfy the spiritual yearnings of cultured people without the motley medieval trappings of traditional religions.[50]

James, Lippmann, and Russell could expatiate on their existential crises in the comfort of lovely homes, servants, and decent incomes. Such rarefied speculations were of little interest to the working classes because they really *were* at the mercy of malevolent impersonal forces, ones that were only too real and too imminent. Although the underlying technologies of the twenties had been percolating for a full generation, for ordinary people they didn't really take hold, in the sense of dominating their lives, until the postwar recovery of 1922. In effect, the whole phenomenon of the twenties was squeezed into just seven years. And it happened in a country with only the barest of governance, the most rudimentary of economic institutions, and little inkling of the cataclysm that was about to crash around it.

The next twenty years would bring, first, a decade of dark Depression, followed hard by a decade of raging war with hellish forces of Unreason.

PART TWO

"One Heckuva Boom"

── I. TRICKLE-DOWN ECONOMICS ──

N ate Shaw was the son of a slave, and sharecropped in Alabama, just as his daddy had done after the Civil War. Shaw was illiterate, but highly intelligent, strong and active, an aficionado of mules, able to manage their sulks and extract the full measure of their plodding diligence. His wife, Hannah, was literate, and he greatly admired her for it. He made a point of bringing her with him for any complex dealing with white men. He couldn't always avoid being cheated, but when Hannah was there, he at least knew when it happened, and how much it could cost him. Shaw was a careful, diligent farmer, who made sharecropping a profitable enterprise, putting away cash from his cotton crops—even though he was paid less for them than white sharecroppers were—and keeping his family in meat and fresh vegetables besides. He was also active in the Alabama Sharecroppers' Union, and was imprisoned for twelve years after being involved in a shootout with whites. That was in 1932. The important event for our story, however, happened in 1926. Shaw, a black sharecropper, in Alabama, a region with the tightest of barriers against trickle-down prosperity for the lower classes, bought a brand new Ford Model T, and he paid for it with cash. That's how far down the ladder the 1920s prosperity reached.

Here is Shaw's account:[*]

> I done reached out and got as high as four head of stock and a two-horse wagon and a rubber tire buggy. I was prosperin and when I married I didn't have decent clothes to wear, had nothin. But I never did have no

---

[*] Researchers on the sharecroppers' union tracked down Shaw in the 1960s, when he was in his eighties. Shaw turned out to be a consummate storyteller, who could go on for hours. The eventual transcripts were published as a 550 page book, a splendid ground-level documentary of the pre–Civil Rights deep South. The sharecroppers' union was organized by the American Communist Party, but was focused only on labor and civil rights issues; it was intended to be biracial, but the membership was all black.

view ahead to cause me to work as hard as I done. I did have it in view to support my family, keep em in shoes, clothes, groceries—and to accumulate what I could accordin to what I was makin at the time. Often, somethin to buy, I'd want it if I *could* buy it, but I wouldn't dote on it if I didn't have the money. I bought a brand new Ford car when I was haulin lumber. As colored people started to buyin cars, I started right along in there not very many months behind the first colored car buyer. . . .

We men would stand out and huddle or set out and talk. Here's the subject come up: we got to talkin about cars and I thought but little of that, in a way, because I knowed how the conversation would run.

I told em, "Yes, I'm thinkin of buyin me a car, get me a new Ford. Thinkin about it; I haven't done it yet but it's my thorough aim—my boys, anyway, they done got big enough to go and correspond with girls and I think I'll just buy me a new Ford to please them. I can make it all right with a car and the stock I got and my rubber tire buggy. So I think I'll get me a car."

And our colored race is a curious race of people. Don't want you to have nothin less'n he got it too—that's what I call a begrudgeful heart and a heap of em is that way, So, I said, "I think I'll get me a car, a new Ford."

Elijah looked at me and said in the presence of them other fellows, "Yeah, all of us will know when you get a car."

I wouldn't say nothin out of the way to him.

"All of us will know when you get a car."

He just thinkin I was talkin bout somethin that I was as far from, the way he expressed it to me, as the east from the west. Well, in a few days I bought a Ford car and drove it up there, drove it right across the yard . . . and my cousin Elijah Giddings was standin there lookin. He wouldn't turn his head hardly. . . . Elijah Giddings never did lose no time with me from that day until he died.[1]

Two years later the boys came to Shaw and asked if the Ford could be traded in for a 1928 Chevrolet, "a little faster and a little nicer car." It cost $650, and the difference Shaw got for the trade-in left him still paying more than he did for the Ford. Worse, it wouldn't fit in his garage. Shaw eventually bought another 1926 Ford, but still kept the Chevy. By then the boys wanted the new "closed" Model A Ford. Shaw's ever-sensible Hannah overheard that conversation:

"Darlin, what was Calvin nuzzlin you so close for this mornin?"

I looked around; it was her spoke, I knowed it was her. I said, "O, he just wants me to change that Ford off and get em a closed Ford with a glass department."

She said, "Are you goin to do it?"

I said, "Yeah, I'm goin to change it for em."

She said, "Uh-uh, you just pay attention to these boys and get em everything they want, if you can reach it. After a while we won't have nothin here but cars."

I said, "Them's my boys and they're your boys. I'm their daddy. They do whatever I tell them to do without a grumble. . . . Now, you got anything to do there in the house?"

She said, "Yeah, I got plenty to do in the house, and I got plenty to do out here too, watchin you and the boys full up our yard with cars."[2]

Nate Shaw bought his first Ford just four years after the country recovered from the 1920–1921 economic turndown, one of the nastiest in its history, but also one of the shortest. By the mid-twenties, the sense of prosperity was taking hold. Economists often cite the credit-driven consumer product boom as one of the contributors to the crash of 1929. But Nate and Hannah Shaw did not buy on credit. The two had once borrowed to purchase a lot, but after making all payments always on time, the white lender refused to return their note until they made a number of additional payments. Fair-minded whites liked Shaw: he was the first they hired for difficult jobs, and they respected his hard-working family and the quality of his farming. Several let him know that they were upset by the extortion, but in 1920s rural Alabama few whites would stop another white from cheating a colored man. Both Nate and Hannah understood the rules that applied to colored people in the pre-Civil Rights South, most especially in the deep South cotton regions like those of Alabama. But the good times of the 1920s were such that even people on the bottom rungs of the ladder—and few were lower than black sharecroppers—could claim a modest share of the booming consumer economy.

W orld War I was a rare opportunity for the United States to strut on the world stage, demonstrating both the raw power of its economy, and the capabilities of its new Federal Reserve system. In the year before President Wilson's 1917 war declaration, the federal budget was only $711 million, or about 1.5 percent of gross domestic product (GDP)—in keeping with the prevailing Jacksonian suspicion of federal power. The level of spending had been quite stable for some time, and since the turn of the century, the average inflation rate to 1914 was a modest 1.4 percent a year.[3]

Both major political parties had been officially opposed to entering the war, so there had been almost no military preparation for a war declaration. (Contemporary newsreels, however, show that the war announcement was greeted with ecstatic celebrations.) Considering that America was gearing up a war machine from scratch, its performance was impressive. There were only nineteen months between the war declaration and the November 1918 armistice. In that time the United States increased its military establishment from 174,000 men to 2.8 million, and despite some severe early equipment shortages, supplied them with bases, equipment, and transport. Two million Americans were sent overseas, and 1.4 million saw combat. Including civilian war workers, 6.5 million Americans were engaged in the war effort. Total military casualties exceeded 250,000, of whom 50,000 were killed, along with another 67,000 fatalities from disease, most frequently from pneumonia.[4]

US industries had waxed fat on military exports to the Allied powers from the start of the war, but war production ratcheted up dramatically once the United States joined the fighting and almost all big manufacturers converted a large share of their productive capacity to the war effort. The output of the well-regarded Liberty airplane engine, built by a half dozen automobile companies, hit an annual run rate of 46,000 in late 1918.[5] (Pundits scoffed at FDR's 1930s suggestion that the United States

could produce 50,000 planes a year. But if World War I had been prolonged a year or so, the country could easily have reached that number.)
For products in which Americans already held a leadership position, like
explosives, American companies provided the lion's share of the Allied
requirements from the outset.

Officially, the Wilson administration nationalized the railroads and
the telephone and telegraph companies, and set up bureaucracies to allocate industrial production and control prices. Although they served as
precedents for later New Deal initiatives, they were of little practical
importance. Most of the new agencies were still getting organized by the
armistice, so the nominally nationalized industries operated with minimum interference. Even the most vaunted of them, like Bernard Baruch's
War Industries Board—save for one dramatic confrontation that broke
the collusive pricing of the steel cartel—had done little but issue procla-
mations and press releases. Baruch paid his staff's travel expenses home
from Washington, because his agency had been shut down so fast that he
no longer had any spending authority.[6]

The fiscal consequences of the war were staggering. Total American
war expenditures were about $32 billion. In 1918, the war effort consumed
about a fifth of gross domestic product (GDP), expanding the federal
budget twentyfold. By the last months of the war, American war spending was nearly a third of GDP. About two-thirds of the new spending
was financed by borrowing, but taxes were also raised sharply—the top
bracket rate on the new income tax jumped from 6 to 66.3 percent.[7]

The lion's share of the borrowing, about $21 billion in all, was accom-
plished through the famous Liberty Bonds issued throughout the war,
followed up by Victory Bonds issued after the armistice. The bonds were
attractively priced and were snapped up by banks and professional investors. The Treasury also mounted a massive advertising campaign to place
bonds with ordinary people, with the avowed purpose to educate the populace on the benefits of saving.

The Fed was the fiscal agent for most of the bonds, taking care to supply the district banks with the reserves to finance their customers' bond
purchases. The Fed also facilitated the war spending by keeping rates at
ultra-low levels. In anticipation of wartime inflation, war bonds came with
specific protections against principal losses. It is no surprise, then, that in

BUY WAR BONDS

A print of a fearsome Uncle Sam, backed by vast military power, stirred Americans' militaristic impulses. Bonds paid for about two-thirds of the American costs of the war, and for many Americans, were the first encounter with financial savings instruments.

the three years from 1916 through 1919, the American inflation rate averaged 17.1 percent per year, pushing the overall price level up by 60 percent.[8]

The dotted line in Figure 2.1 tracks the actual spending by business and consumers in the dollar values prevailing at the time, while the solid line restates those same purchases, using the currency values that prevailed in 1929.* As the Figure shows, the dollar value of 1900 GNP was

---

* The year 1929 is the first one for which the government produced an official GNP statement, although it wasn't computed and published until 1942. Academic economists spent several decades replicating that reporting for the years prior to 1929. There are several versions, all of them converging around the same results, going as far back as the 1820s, although the data are much less reliable the further back they are carried. The pre-1929 twentieth century data shown in the Figure are considered to be quite good.

FIGURE 2.1: REAL ($1929) AND NOMINAL US GNP, 1900–1929

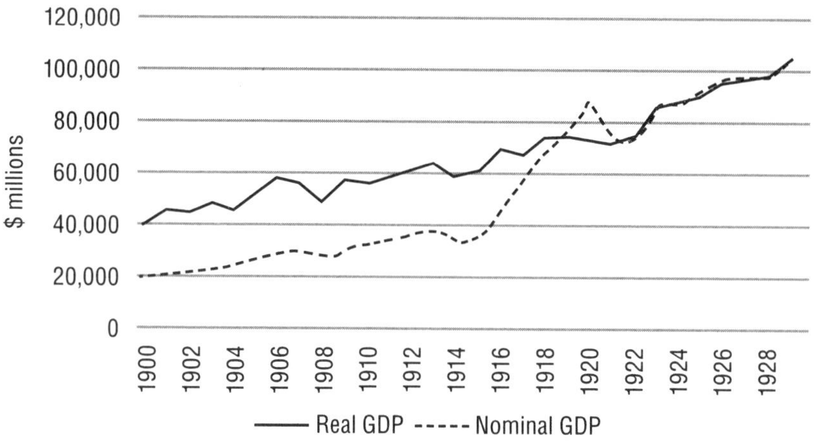

Source: *Historical Statistics of the United States*, Tables Ca213 and Ca214.

about $20 billion. But the solid line shows that a time traveler from 1929, with 1929 dollars, would have needed twice as many dollars for the same goods. In theory that would not would not be a hardship, because the time traveler's paycheck would have also doubled.

For many years, prevalent economic doctrine held that changes in money values were neutral, since efficient markets would quickly reestablish the appropriate relationships. But in the real world, prices never adjust so smoothly and seamlessly. For example, many contracts are not indexed to inflation. So bankers who have made fixed-price loans lose money as prices rise, while farmers with fixed-price mortgages may be in desperate circumstances if crop prices fall.

A prolonged, high rate of inflation, like that between 1915 and 1920, is always disruptive, producing boondoggles for some and disasters for others, merely because of the way they were positioned at the start. Normal gold standard rules, however, would have moderated the impact on international transactions. As soon as the US inflation kicked in, other countries would have dumped their dollar holdings and insisted that the United States make all payments in gold. But this was wartime, and all the major countries except the United States† had gone off the gold standard

---

† The US dollar price was linked to gold throughout the war, but its major trading partners had all suspended their gold linkages, so the United States did not export gold. The practical effect was that the dollar became a gold equivalent.

and were inflating even faster than America. When prices stopped rising, it created a sharp fall in nominal GNP—a year-on-year drop of 16 percent from 1920 to 1921 (made up of a 13 percent fall in prices and a 3 percent fall in real output). At that point, the solid and dotted lines in Figure 2.1 effectively merge. Prices had stabilized at near-zero inflation: for all practical purposes, nominal and real prices were the same.

But that left an awkward problem for the future. Since 1879, the dollar price of gold had been $20.67 per fine ounce. After the 1915–1920 inflation, even taking into account the 1921 fall in prices, the purchasing power of a dollar was only about half of what it had been in 1914. But an ounce of gold still bought you only $20.67 worth of goods. Gold, that is, was badly undervalued, and as we will see, that created no end of problems.

Victory in war breeds its own disasters. As a consequence of the military draft and the jump in factory output, the 1919 US labor market was unusually tight. Workers were restive, and unions feisty. With demobilization, the black workers who had moved North for wartime factory jobs were getting squeezed. There were bitter strikes throughout industry. A 1920 bombing attack on the Wall Street offices of the J.P. Morgan bank killed 38 people and injured 143. All of it fed into the J. Edgar Hoover-A. Mitchell Palmer "Red Scare." The victory itself was quickly soured by the bickering at Versailles, by the US insistence on repayment of war debts, by the explosion of Wilson's parliament-of-nations fantasies, and then by his incapacitation by a stroke. Warren Harding's "return to normalcy" 1920 campaign slogan made him a shoo-in.[9]

When the war ended, expectations were that the inflation would collapse in a recession; instead, it went on for almost another two years. The Fed was at fault here, but it was torn between its missions of controlling inflation and financing the government. Instead of immediately tightening rates, it held off until the last round of Victory Bonds were disposed of in the spring of 1920. Then it cracked down hard. Interest on short-term commercial transactions jumped to a viselike 8.13 percent. Long rates, however, were not much affected, suggesting that the markets believed, correctly, that the inflation genie would be quickly rebottled.[10]

Inflation broke in May 1920, and a very sharp recession set in as the Fed kept on the pressure. Although the real (inflation-adjusted) drop in GNP was modest, the violent price rejiggerings were disruptive for everyone, and crushingly hard on debtors, since debt principal doesn't change as nominal incomes shrink. Industries that had flourished in the wartime boom took it on the chin. From 1920 to 1921, annual revenues at Anaconda Copper, Bethlehem Steel, and US Steel, respectively, fell by 49, 46, and 44 percent. Consumer-oriented companies, like American Tobacco and Woolworth's fared much better.[11] The recession hit bottom in mid-1921, and by the end of the year coal, cotton, petroleum, and many agricultural products had recovered to at least their prewar levels.[12] Real GDP growth was a strong 7.2 percent in 1921, and a sparkling 14 percent in 1923. That was a year that the factory hands of Muncie, Indiana, recalled fondly as an exceptional one for laboring people. From the start of the recovery through the eight years from 1921 through 1929, the annual real growth rate in GDP was a very respectable 5 percent, although it came in a series of sharp spurts interspersed by mild downturns in 1924 and 1927.[13]

It is conceivable that real growth in the 1920s was even faster than the official data suggest. Muncie's working people, and even a Nate Shaw in rural Alabama, were rapidly changing their lifestyles. US history offers occasional examples of "productivity shocks," a period when rapid growth in output pushes down relative prices. Something like that may have been at work in the 1920s. Automobiles improved very rapidly over the decade, while competition kept prices down. The Ford Model T had a base price of $565 to start, and was down to only $300 by the mid-twenties. Chevrolets were better cars than the Model T, and carried a higher sticker price, but General Motors (GM) was careful to stay within a consistent dollar range of the Ford price. The same could be said for utility services—regional AC power distribution was far superior to any previous alternative for lighting or power, and its price fell consistently. Most electrical appliances, mass-produced clothing, and mass-produced food followed a similar pattern of rising quality and falling prices.*

The automobile industry and AC electric power remained the primary drivers of the 1920s boom. Automobiles were not only the dominant consumer purchase, but provided the critical demonstration of the productivity gains from electric factories. Overall manufacturing productivity in the 1920s was the best recorded within the era captured by modern statistics.

---

* Modern GDP accounting includes "hedonic" adjustments, introduced to reflect the fact that modern semiconductor technology has brought stunning improvements in capability at steeply falling prices.

S amuel Insull, the British immigrant who had become Thomas Edison's secretary and right-hand man, and who had also run the General Electric (GE) manufacturing businesses, assumed the presidency of what eventually became the Commonwealth Edison company of Chicago in 1892. He was thirty-two years old, small in stature, but compact and hardy, with boundless energy, a first-rate mind, and a direct, forceful, approach to every problem. While he was no glad-hander, he was still a superb salesman, taking pains to understand his customers' needs, and lucidly setting out the case for his products. He had some exposure to quality education in England, though not at a university level, and he worked hard to overcome his thick regional accent. His family was respectable, but of precarious means, and he related easily to union leaders and Chicago politicians. When it came to producing and selling electricity and electrical equipment, he was as knowledgeable as anyone in the country. Insull took a big pay cut to make the move to Chicago, but Marshall Field, the retail magnate and a Commonwealth Edison director, sweetened the package with a $250,000 loan so Sam could purchase a sizeable stock position in the company.[14]

Urban energy companies were in their Cenozoic era, a free-wheeling stew of new life-forms scrabbling for position and profits. Natural gas was displacing coal gas in municipal lighting and cooking. DC central power stations were proliferating—each one had a service radius of only a half mile or so. Building engineers were pushing "self-contained" commercial and factory buildings with their own steam-generated power supplies. Urban transport was shifting from horse carts to trolley systems, run from dedicated DC power plants. High-end developers offered pre-wired houses fed from a neighborhood generating station. But the penetration of new solutions was still thin. Ordinary folks' homes were still lit with kerosene lamps and heated with coal- or wood-burning stoves, domestic technologies on the level of the ubiquitous outdoor privy.

It took Insull almost twenty years to realize his vision—an integrated, metropolis-wide, all-purpose, highly affordable, almost infinitely expandable energy system, able to accommodate the deluge of labor- and money-saving products jostling to take advantage of the inexorable shift toward electrical power. His challenges were political, technical, strategic, and financial.

Chicago has always been famous for the rough-and-tumble of its politics and the blatant plundering of its politicians. For sheer rapacity, however, the Gilded Age politics of Insull's day may win the prize. The city council granted the gas, electric, and streetcar utilities franchises subject to a maximum term of twenty years. That was long enough to pay off the debt of a DC power station, but much too short to finance the behemoth generating complexes Insull had in mind. In 1897, the state legislature authorized fifty-year franchises, but repealed the law the next year. Before the repeal took effect, a meat-eating pack of Chicago aldermen known as the "Gray Wolves," took advantage of the window to create an unassigned fifty-year franchise, with the intention of selling it to Insull. When he peremptorily refused, they incorporated a new electrical utility under their own control and endowed it with the enviable fifty-year franchise. And then they discovered that every major electrical equipment maker had signed exclusive sales contracts with Insull. Good politicians are fatalists: the aldermen quickly negotiated a reasonable purchase price for the franchise. Insull reciprocated the respect. He never paid a bribe, but he gave generously to both political parties; his dealings with city and state officials were straightforward, and he always kept his word.[15]

Insull's common touch served him well in dealing with unions. When a militant union leader, Mike Boyle, called a strike action, Insull, with his five-year-old son, strolled over to Boyle's temporary quarters at the strike scene and suggested that they get together and settle things. Then he introduced his son to Boyle, stressing that Boyle was "a very important man." Insull had no objections to unions, and was happy to work with Boyle, on the sole condition, which Boyle readily agreed to, that he would not organize the administrative and management employees, since they would provide vital electrical services during a strike.

The same directness was evident in his dealings with coal and coal miners. Francis Peabody was a talented politician with a modest coal business on the side. Insull agreed to finance Peabody's expansion in return for first rights to all of his coal at a reasonable cost-plus price. Together with Peabody, Insull worked out a deal with the brilliant and tempestuous John L. Lewis, who was just then organizing the Midwest's coal mines. The union was recognized in all of Peabody's mines, and he and Insull agreed to encourage other mineowners in Illinois to do the same. They also agreed to support a progressive and enforceable mine safety law. In return, Insull asked only that all union contracts expire on April 30—so if coal was going to be short, it would not be during the winter months.[16]

The technical hurdle was serious but straightforward. The success at Niagara clinched the case for AC power. The missing piece of the puzzle was the power for the generating plant. The Niagara plant was powered by massive water turbines, which were well understood. But Chicago sat in prairieland, and its dynamos could be powered only by coal-generated steam. The biggest steam engines in the world were Corliss reciprocating engines—giant walking beams—a fifty-year-old design. One of them powered Insull's central business district generating station, but the strains from its whirling hundred-ton flywheels were worrying, and its coal consumption was fearsome. Europeans had been testing modestly-sized steam turbines, but none had approached the scales that Insull needed. So he reached out to his friends at GE and convinced them to undertake the joint, shared-risk development and installation of twin 5,000 kilowatt (kW) steam turbines. They were up and running in 1903, after just about a year of development, and were repeatedly enlarged. Since turbines were only a fraction of the weight of a Corliss, they brought huge fuel savings. With AC generators powered by steam turbines, Insull could build out high-voltage long-distance AC transmission lines, marble the city with substation transformers and DC converters, and supply reliable power at the correct current to all classes of users.[17]

A good franchise, peace with unions and politicians, and a state-of-the-art generating and distribution plant was still not enough to succeed. Insull understood from the start that without a well thought-out strategy, the enormous cost of the plant could sink him. Large-area AC electric power supply was a high-volume/low-unit-price business, with enormous startup costs. The good news was that once a plant was at breakeven, marginal profits rose almost without limit. So an obvious strategy was to go in big and ramp up sales very fast. But it couldn't be just *any* sales, as Insull quickly learned. In the early days, he had focused on the trolley companies, the city's biggest power consumers, and quickly won about 30 percent of the business. But that created a usage spike during the evening rush hour when trolley demand overlapped with lights being turned on all across the city. The kind of large-scale electricity provider that Insull envisioned could not survive with such skewed volume. In 1902, for example, he had to supply a peak demand of up to 4,500 kW, against a daily average usage of only 1,200 kW. So nearly three-quarters of his generating capacity was standing idle most of the time, even as his debt service meter ticked like a bass drum in the background.[18]

The challenge was to fill the empty hours, primarily in the daylight and late at night. Insull had a highly analytic mind, which he eventually embodied in a full-blown statistics department. Chicago was a pioneer in tall commercial buildings, which necessitated elevators. Steam elevators were noisy monsters, so electric elevators became the first choice of architects and builders. But they used a lot of power very intermittently, so both traditional DC central station vendors and building owners with on-site generators hated them. With Commonwealth Edison's wide AC service area, intermittent elevator usage in a large swath of buildings averaged out to a steady daytime load factor. Since Insull was selling idle capacity, it was almost pure profit.

Dozens of focused sales strategies followed that pattern. Apartment house hall lighting provided at very low rates to create income through the wee hours, with landlords paid commissions for signing up tenants for electrical service. Snapping up vacant stores in promising areas, and installing dazzling electrical displays to rope in the surrounding merchants. Deals with developers to include full wiring in all their new homes. Electrical appliances at near-wholesale prices paid off by small interest-free installments added to the electrical bill.

A critical technical fillip was a new meter, originally developed in England, that allowed Insull to measure usage volumes and split the charge between a connection fee and volume-based charges. Data from the metering also allowed the statistics department to conduct natural experiments on the effects of different charging plans. Industrial power took the longest to convert, because so many factories had only recently invested in their own DC power plants. But as Insull steadily pushed down prices and exploited his advantage in coal purchasing, the economics of switching to a regional power supplier became compelling.[19]

Between 1905 and 1912, Insull's power sales leaped from 100,000 kilowatt hours (kWh) to more than 700,000 kWh, but that was only the palest portent of the explosive growth to come. The middle-class residential market did not begin a broad adoption of electricity usage until after the war. Even in the early 1920s, middle-class customers still viewed electricity as just a lighting solution, although the electric iron was beginning to gain a decent market share. A typical Insull sales strategy was a political-campaign-style sound truck passing out electric irons for a free six-month trial. Later, he sponsored essay contests in schools in which the students wrote about the electrical products they would most like to have in their homes. Bruce Barton made advertising history with a heavy-handed full-page newspaper ad, "How Long Should a Wife Live?" extolling the benefits of labor-saving electrical appliances.[20]

The final challenge was a financing strategy to cover the crushing startup costs. The generation and transmission infrastructure was very expensive, as was the cost of connecting each individual customer. Residential customers needed time to grow their usage beyond lighting, while the electric appliance industry was still learning the nuances of developing and marketing new classes of appliance. Since Insull had unlimited faith that electricity markets would only expand, he built his generators with huge capacity margins, effectively ensuring a long period of underutilization. Financing with very long-term bonds, with maturities of forty-five years or so, was essential to keep his debt service affordable while utilization was building to profitable levels. The prewar US economy was very bumpy, and financiers told him that the London market had no appetite for American bonds. Characteristically, Insull went to London by himself, *sans* financiers, with only the most tenuous of connections in London finance, and quickly placed a $6 million equipment mortgage. Sam Insull, as Chicago already knew, was a salesman to the bone.

By the 1920s, Insull's silky-smooth financing machine was supplying hundreds of millions of highly attractive, very long-term, 8 percent mortgage bonds to an eager market. All of them were placed by a Chicago banker, Harold Stuart, of Halsey, Stuart. Midwestern investment banks were used to living off the slender financial pickings ignored by the great New York banking houses, and Stuart had specialized in placing the modest bond issues for Insull's acquisitions of rural and suburban utilities. During the money drought that followed the wartime inflation, Insull tried out Stuart on a $27 million issue; when he placed it in short order, he became Insull's banker, handling all of his issues from then on.[21]

As the 1920s drew to a close, Sam Insull sat on top of one of the nation's greatest business combines, providing about an eighth of all electric power in the country. He was a hero in Chicago, both for his business achievements and his philanthropy, the most powerful voice in nation's utility industries, and the darling of investors.

IV. DAVID BUICK, BILLY DURANT, ALFRED SLOAN, AND THE MODERN CAR INDUSTRY

D avid Buick was a Scotsman, a partner in a substantial Detroit plumbing supply business, and an owner of twenty-five patents, with a focus on gasoline engines. Around the turn of the century, after several years of selling stationary engines, he started experimenting with marine engines and automobiles. Soon after, Buick and his team came up with a more efficient engine design with a compact combustion chamber and faster fuel-burn rate. The design was known in Europe, but the Buick designers were the first to take full advantage of it, realizing high ratios of power to weight and fuel consumption for the time.[22]

Buick raised money from carriage makers in Flint to finance a small production run of "Buick Model Bs" in 1904, featuring the new, more powerful, engine. With the Buick order book filling up, Buick and his other backers turned to William Crapo "Billy" Durant for working capital. Durant was a self-made millionaire, whose carriage company was the biggest in the country, and probably the world. Although Durant claimed to dislike automobiles almost on principle, a road test of the Buick made him a convert. Convinced that the automobile was "the next big thing," Durant leaped headlong into the industry.

Headlong, in fact, was the only way Billy Durant knew how to jump. His family had long roots in Flint. His mother's father had been a successful lumberman, mayor of Flint, and governor of Michigan. His father, on the other hand, was a charmer but something of a wastrel. Billy was also a charmer, and a natural salesman, but with drive, a knack for business, boundless energy, and vision. Bored with high school, he had scored a string of modest successes in small local enterprises, when in 1886, still only twenty-four, he encountered a horse carriage with a spring seat that gave an unusually smooth ride. Interested, he took a train 120 miles to the small town where it was made, hoping to become an investor; instead he ended up buying the rights. Eighteen years later, Flint was "the carriage capital of the world," and Durant was rich, bored with carriages, fascinated with Wall Street, and spending most of his time in New York.

In November 1904, with Durant putting up the bulk of the money, the Buick Motor Company was recapitalized with subscriptions of $500,000, with Durant in effective control, a new factory, and a production group drawn mostly from the carriage industry. Durant understood talent and enticed people like Charles Stewart Mott, reputedly the country's best axle maker, to move his production to Flint and gradually integrate it into the Buick organization. David Buick fared less well. He was a director of the company for several years, but had "faded away" by 1908. He had a number of unsuccessful business ventures, apparently did not keep his auto stock, and before his death in 1929 was employed as a trades teacher in Detroit.[23]

Durant was a legendary salesman. Even before the new factory was ready, he took one of the model cars to the New York City auto show and came back with 1,108 orders. Walter Chrysler, a semi legendary figure himself, later wrote of Durant: "I cannot find words to express the charm of the man. He has the most winning personality I've ever known. He could coax a bird right down out of a tree."[24]

And the company was surely on a roll:

FIGURE 2.2: BUICK SALES, 1905–1910

1905	725
1906	1,400
1907	4,541
1908	8,820 *
1909	14,606
1910	30,525

* These are calendar year figures. Ford recorded his numbers from midyear to midyear. The Model T was introduced in June 1908, and sold 11,000 by the next midyear. Buick was the #1 seller for the calendar year 1908, but Ford rapidly outdistanced the field from that point.

Note that Buick's sales tripled in 1907, the year of a famous banking crash. All the car companies cut inventories once the crash hit, except Durant. Even when Buick agencies stopped taking cars, he kept producing them, storing them however he could. When the economy snapped back, Buick's inventory advantage allowed him to steal substantial new share.[25]

Durant enthusiastically supported Buick's entry into racing, and liked hand-picking daredevil drivers, one of whom, a stocky Belgian named Louis Chevrolet, eventually saw his name enshrined in the pantheon of industrial history. Durant also converted his carriage company's dealerships into Buick agencies, giving him the most "exposed" automobile in the country. Durant was not a production guy, but kept a finger on the pulse of the company, especially from talking to the agencies. Everyone loved the engines, but customers continued to complain about the quality of Buick parts, drawing hurricanes of Durant inquiries onto the engineers and production staff.[26]

Durant had only one gear—a charge-ahead focus on market share. He flirted with an attempt to roll up the entire industry with Morgan financing, but dropped the idea because of the Morgan group's ultracautious concern for profits. So Durant created a holding company of his own—General Motors, incorporated in September 1908, with William Eaton, a prominent Michigan businessman as president and himself as vice-president. (Durant almost always chose to be a vice-president of the companies he controlled, so he could focus on deal making and sales, free of administrivia.) Shortly thereafter, he inked the acquisition of the Olds Motor Vehicle Company, which had separated from its founder, Ransom Olds, and was struggling. Durant furnished it with a new product, essentially a bigger and more powerful Buick, at a higher price point. Before the year was out, he had also acquired Albert Champion's high-performance spark plugs and a car body-making company. The next year, Durant shifted into high gear, buying the Oakland Motor Car Company, later to become GM's Pontiac division, and Henry Leland's Cadillac Motor Company, plus *twenty* other companies, including five more struggling car companies, a wheel maker, and various parts and lamp makers.[27]

The economy was flat in 1910, not nearly a crisis, but enough to shake Durant's high-wire debt practices. GM entered 1910 with some $15 million in debt, by no means an egregious amount. Buick, by itself, earned

$10 million a year on $30 million in sales and Cadillac made 50 percent net margins on $4+ million in sales. But Durant, wary of the coils of powerful Wall Street bankers, had spread his borrowing among some two hundred small banks, GM suppliers, and dealerships, all of it short term and with his personal guarantee. The blip in the lending market terrified the small banks, forcing Durant to accept a humiliating deal with two bigger players, Boston's Lee, Higginson and New York's J. & W. Seligman. Although he stayed on the board, he lost control of the company—a new president was brought in, who recruited Walter Chrysler as production manager. The industry recovered strongly after the 1910 slump, just as Durant had predicted. But GM, now infused with banker sensibilities, was content to reap tidy profits, avoid risk, and pay off its debt—precisely the banker playbook that Durant, and Henry Ford, so abhorred. [28]

But Durant was irrepressible. In late 1910, without resigning his GM directorship, he financed three new automobile companies in Flint, including Chevrolet, with Louis Chevrolet as chief designer. Durant had decided to challenge Ford for control of the low-end market by creating a reliable car, at only a modest price premium to the Ford, but with style and sex appeal. All three of his companies produced prototypes before the end of 1911. None of them was what Durant was looking for, but by combining the best features of the three, he eventually came up with a good first-cut under the Chevrolet brand. (Louis Chevrolet left in a huff when Durant changed his designs, but he had a fine subsequent career in racing.)

Durant created another holding company in 1912, featuring his new Chevrolet design. He quickly raised $2.5 million in private subscriptions, and in late 1913, Chevrolet introduced two models and sold 5,000 of them. Durant feverishly added capacity, and opened Chevrolet assembly plants in New York and other major cities, so customers could see how they were made. According to Durant, Chevrolet had booked 46,611 cash-secured sales by June 19. Production was still catching up, however, and completed 1915 sales were just 13,292—good, but not a blowout. Lift-off came in 1916, with 70,701 sales.* Durant's Chevrolet was the new darling

---

* For perspective, Ford sold more than a half million cars in 1916. Still, Edsel and the other senior Ford executives, but not Henry, knew that Chevrolet was their first true, and very dangerous, challenger for control of the mass market.

of Wall Street, and Durant had created a plausible vehicle for making a triumphant return to GM.[29]

But there was now a new player in the GM game, the DuPont company, which had just completed a consolidation of the country's explosive manufacturers. Pierre Du Pont and his finance guru, John Raskob, had both made substantial investments in GM for their personal accounts and for a company investment trust. The following year, with GM's $15 million note soon to be discharged, and the bankers' operating authority about to end, GM's stock went on a surprising run, suggesting to Raskob that it was in play. The action, of course, was from Durant who was building a carefully concealed takeover position.

A New York banker, who happened to be close to both Durant and Pierre Du Pont, passed on an invitation to Du Pont to join the GM board. Du Pont tentatively accepted, but at his first meeting found himself in the middle of a proxy fight between Durant and the bankers. One of the bankers finally proposed that each of the proxy combatants have the same number of directors, and that Pierre take the chairmanship and name three more directors—he picked Raskob and two other DuPont veterans.[30]

Durant continued to increase his GM holdings, at one point offering five shares of Chevrolet for one of GM, a trade that even senior GM managers jumped at. Once he had a clear majority, Durant replaced the board with one comprising mostly GM executives. The headlines shouted, "Chevrolet Company Will Acquire Control of General Motors." Du Pont and Raskob tendered their resignations, but Durant asked them to stay, with Du Pont retaining the chairmanship and Raskob chairing the finance committee. Durant anointed Walter Chrysler as the president, locking him in with a high-pay package and a three-year contract.[31]

Durant's first moves were brilliant. He bought the Delco battery company, two roller bearing companies, a lighting company, a specialty steel company, and a wheel company, consolidating them all as the United Motors Company, headed by the redoubtable Alfred P. Sloan, who had founded one of the newly acquired ball bearing companies. Chevrolet, along with the existing GM car brands—Buick, Olds, Oakwood (Pontiac), Cadillac, and GM Trucks—made a formidable combination, and it got stronger when he closed an all-cash $26.7 million deal for the Fisher

Body company, which was well worth it. Raskob was closely involved, effectively managing the stock syndication for United Motors.

Raskob's assignment from Du Pont was to keep Durant from running wild. Durant basically ignored him: in 1916 all the GM businesses minted money, as did all of the in-house Durant supporters, which by that point included Raskob. But Durant was still flying without a risk barometer, eschewing budgets and financial controls, freely transferring money between companies, and keeping no one fully informed. He got away with it until the war declaration of April 1917 sent financial markets into a tailspin. Durant, who had once again built his control position with heavy margin debt, was dangerously exposed, as to a lesser extent was Raskob.

Pierre Du Pont and Raskob went back a long way, and if Du Pont criticized him, it was done very privately. Raskob fully informed the DuPont board of the troubles Durant was in, but also recommended a rescue plan. DuPont was earning rivers of money from its explosives business, especially now that the Americans were in the war, and had amassed a cash mountain nearing $100 million. Raskob proposed that DuPont—the company—make a $25 million investment in GM. GM's dividends would help support a diversification program, and the acquisition would lock up GM as a major customer for their paints, varnishes, and other new businesses. Durant's profligacies would be contained by putting Raskob in charge of finance. Even with Pierre Du Pont's strong support, the proposal just squeaked through a skeptical board.

Surprisingly, Raskob remained more of a Durant enabler than a curb. Pundits had expected that the year 1919 would see a typical postwar economic crash. Instead, there was a boom—a hollow one, to be sure, for it was driven primarily by price inflation. GM's 1919 sales were nearly half a billion dollars, with net profits of $60 million. Durant, without any objections from Raskob, was buying everything in sight. Some acquisitions, like the Fisher and the Frigidaire companies, turned out be long-term solid performers, but Raskob was once again standing idly by as Durant built another dangerous tower of debt. A measure of Raskob's cluelessness is that in early 1920, he marveled that in just a little more than three years, Durant had increased GM's assets eightfold—which should have been a source of alarm.

When the Fed cracked down hard on inflation in the spring of 1920, the automobile market crashed, and Raskob finally realized how exposed Durant and GM were. He brought in accounting help from DuPont, and discovered that the production divisions were losing millions of dollars a month. Durant's records were an utter tangle. After a difficult meeting, Raskob asked him whether he owed "six or twenty-six million dollars;" Durant said he would have to get back to him. Raskob and Du Pont turned to the Morgan bankers, who regarded Durant as a gambler and liar. They paid off the Durant debt by structuring a large loan secured by his stock. Durant complained that the valuation of his stock was unrealistically low, which was true, but such were the rewards of recklessness. The board was reorganized, with a strong Morgan presence, and Durant was unceremoniously separated from any management role. Pierre Du Pont replaced Durant as president, with Raskob in charge of budgets and finances. Alfred Sloan was drafted from United Motors to act as Du Pont's principal assistant, with a broad mission to impose order on the company.[32]

The 1920–1921 recession ran roughly from midyear to midyear. GM's 1920 full-year net profits, reflecting a strong first half, came in at $37 million, but collapsed to a loss of $39 million in 1921, a $76 million swing. Profits recovered strongly in 1922, to $51 million. In 1923, with the company stabilized, Du Pont retired from the presidency, with Sloan as his anointed successor. Sloan was cadaverously thin, hyper-intelligent, a tireless workaholic, and utterly methodical—just the solution for GM. He set about creating the famous GM organization, an adroit combination of centralization and decentralization. The company's "center" concentrated on broad policy making, like defining the markets for its product divisions, combined with tight budgeting and detailed statistical and financial controls. There were central research and engineering laboratories, but the division presidents had primary responsibility for product and design decisions. Much of it is astringently laid out, with generous samplings of his policy memoranda, in Sloan's *My Years with General Motors*, which is still holy scripture at American business schools.

My Years may underplay the enormous contribution made by good manufacturing practice, and particularly the use of common parts across several product lines. Sloan, for example, pushed hard to have Pontiacs manufactured in Chevrolet factories with mostly Chevrolet parts. As he said, the move would "give us everything for which we have been waiting, namely, the lowest-priced 6-cylinder car that is possible constructed with Chevrolet parts." Walter Chrysler later "hard-wired" the system by con-solidating engineering into one central staff to maximize parts-sharing. Production machines were also designed with cross-platform usage in mind, by simplifying jig and fixture changes rather than building a new machine.[33]

Under Sloan's steady hand, GM's sales hit the $1.5 billion mark in 1928, with $272 million in net profits, $1.2 billion in assets, a minuscule $2.2 million of debt, and a large cash trove. Its fortunate shareholders received dividends of $174 million, or 12 percent of sales, leaving plenty of cash to feed its investment requirements. It was one of just three indus-trial companies with that level of revenues—the others were US Steel and Standard Oil of New Jersey—but GM had more than double the profits of the other two.[34] The Ford revenue stream, in 1929, his best year to that point, was just over half of GM's, and GM's workers were better paid than Ford's.

In his memoir, Sloan analyzed the mid-twenties transformation of the automobile industry. Ford's initial success with the Model T proved that there was a huge market for inexpensive, reliable basic transportation. By the 1920s, however, the industry was maturing. Millions of cars were on the road, and as the first wave of car buyers traded up to more advanced automobiles, a growing used car market competed for the wallet of the basic transportation buyer. The price discount on a used Buick, with its powerful engine and elegant styling, made it a formidable competitor to a new Model T. Sloan writes that Ford somehow missed this, adding "Don't ask me why." And he skewers the legend that the Model T was a "great car expressive of the pure concept of basic, cheap transportation." It died, he says, because it was no longer "the best buy, even as raw, basic transportation" and was "noncompetitive as an engineering design."[35]

Ford's people, including Edsel Ford, his son and president of the company, had been telling him the same thing for years. They worried particularly about the Chevrolet, which was now openly targeted at the Model T market. Henry refused to consider any new model car, although he had long been working quietly on a "radical" new design without making much headway. Edsel did force a number of cosmetic improvements on the Model T in 1925—an option for a closed body (it was a kludge, because the basic Model T was too light to carry it), a slightly longer and lower chassis, a little more leg room, better cushions, some color choices for some models. But when the new Chevy came out, it sported a visible oil gauge, a speedometer, a modern sliding three-speed gear shift, a much better lubricating system, more reliable spark plugs, a foot accelerator (the Model T still used a hand accelerator), much better springs, and a water-pump cooling system (the Model T's siphon-based system boiled over at the slightest engine strain). As roads improved, people wanted faster cars, and the Chevy was a lot faster than the Model T. Henry Ford was still proud that the Model T was the workhorse of rural America. Sloan was content to allow him that honor.[36]

The year 1923 was the industry's first four million-unit sales year, and total sales of new cars and trucks plateaued at about that level for most of the rest of the decade. Ford's share of the postwar market peaked at 61 percent; by 1926, it slipped to only 36 percent, and its unit sales were 200,000 lower than its 1923 peak. Chevrolet hit 800,000 units by itself in 1926, while the rest of GM sold 450,000 units, for total unit sales of just under 70 percent of Ford's. Henry finally saw the light. While still insisting that the Model T would not be changed, in August 1926 he quietly convened his best engineers for a complete overhaul of the Ford product.[37]

The next two years may have been Henry's finest hour. Much as he had done during the design of the Model T, he spent almost all of his time directing the redesign. He made a few mistakes, like insisting on an in-house electric starter instead of the Bendix starter, which had become the industry standard. (After a burst of customer complaints, he adopted the Bendix.) But overall the Model A, as it was called, was a splendid car. The engine was powerful but unusually light—the product of a joint design between Ford's automobile engineers and designers from his aircraft division. The car was also very quick, with excellent acceleration, and a top speed of sixty-five miles per hour. There was unprecedented use of welding, rather than nuts and bolts, and generous use of high-quality steel forgings for durability and stability. The Model A was handsome enough, longer and lower than the Model T; some thought it looked like a "little Lincoln," which was a compliment. It had both a safety glass windshield and four hydraulic springs, so the ride was safer and smoother than the Chevy's. Standard features also included hydraulic brakes, a best-in-class slide gear shift and an excellent new transmission. Topping it off, there was a variety of colors, with high-fashion names like balsam green, rose beige, and andalusite blue.

Astonishingly, Ford made the switch cold turkey. In January 1927, he acknowledged that the company would produce fewer cars that year, with no "extraordinary changes in models." But the phrase that caught the press's attention was the throwaway, "although, of course, the whole industry is in a state of development and improvement." By spring, rumors were flying about a new Ford car. Finally, in May, Henry announced that the company would soon produce its fifteen millionth Model T, and then shut down the production line for good. The event was marked with a minimalist ceremony. Henry and Edsel drove the last Model T from the assembly line to the Dearborn Engineering Laboratory fourteen miles away. In the yard were Henry's first car, from 1896, and the first Model T. He drove each of them a lap around the plaza. That was it. Informed speculation was that the new car would be unveiled in July, or at least by early fall. But Ford made no announcements, for final designs weren't yet finished, and the engineers were still figuring out how to make it.

The death of the Model T brought a torrent of nostalgia. Dealer inventory rapidly cleared. Many Model Ts were sold at a premium over the list price, which helped to tide the Ford dealerships over the chasm between the Model T and the Model A. It was rough on the workers; the factories did not totally shut down—Ford still sold trucks, tractors, and airplanes—but the great majority of the rank and file were on layoff.

For the company's thousands of tool and die makers, the transition was a bonanza of overtime. A drawback of a Ford-style automated production line is that it assumes a stable product. But the Model A had 5,580 parts, all of them new, and many of them radically different from those of the Model T. Even for similar parts, the drive toward better stability and integrity required new manufacturing processes, like electric welding. Both the Model A and Model T production lines had about 45,000 machine tools, but only a quarter of them could be used in both lines. Another quarter were completely new, and often had to be designed from scratch, while the remainder required extensive rebuilding and refitting to be used on the new lines—adapting the machines for making two gears on an axle assembly, for example, cost $500,000. The production sequences for the two models were also quite different, so production and assembly lines had to revised and retimed, and the workforce retrained.[38]

Sightings of prototypes were breathlessly reported in the daily press. In November, two Chicago dealers, desperate for a glimpse, drove to Detroit. Fortuitously, they ran across Henry and Edsel test-driving one of the new Model As, and received an enthusiastic demonstration that got headlines in the trade press. The first press showing was on November 30, and it was a smash: "Through blinding eddies of snow and over rutty roads rim-deep in mud, the car was driven at sixty-two miles an hour, whirled about, brought to abrupt starts, and taken around curves at a breathtaking pace."[39] Models trickled into major dealerships and for exhibits in December auto shows.

Much like the Lindbergh flight, the Dempsey-Tunney battles, and Babe Ruth's home-run splurge, the actual release of the Model A became another 1920s media extravaganza. In the United States, ten million people were estimated to have seen it within the first thirty-six hours. In New York City, 50,000 people put down cash deposits. Special trains carried crowds to an exhibit in London; police had to control mobs in Berlin; 150,000 people showed up for a demonstration in Spain. Within two weeks, the company had 400,000 orders.[40]

Excruciatingly for Ford, year-end production was stuck at just a few hundred a day. Although the demonstration cars got raves, there were problems getting them out of the factory. A number of components needed to be redesigned and retooled. The production and assembly lines still weren't tuned. Almost all the Ford machine tools were highly specialized, single-purpose instruments ordered in small lots, and some were still not available. Hand workers could be substituted, but they slowed production. As deliveries to the agencies stayed at a trickle, the dealer network was in open-throated revolt. May 1928 marked a full year from the announcement that the Model T would be scrapped, and Model As still couldn't be had. A profitable black market was already developing; the lucky customer who had a Model A could resell it at a premium, and some dealers were rumored to be auctioning their inventories to the highest bidder. But by about midsummer the most annoying operating kinks were worked out, and production finally got untracked, soaring to more than 4,000 new cars a day—Model T-style volumes at last.

Allan Nevins called the Model T-to-Model A transition "one of the most striking achievements of twentieth century industrial history."[41] That's true enough, and a tribute to Henry Ford's vision and organizing capacities and the great skills of his team. From a broader perspective, however, the real story is one of colossal management failure, stark testimony to Henry's pigheadedness, his cultivated ignorance of market trends, and his cavalier dismissal of the rising panic among his senior team. Recovering from the disaster was a stunt-pilot's feat—almost willfully creating a crisis for the thrill of exercising his peculiar genius. Sloan was just then demonstrating how to manage a company bigger and more complex than Ford's with careful planning, focused market and technical research, regular and predictable product improvement, and a minimum of heroic rescue operations. Over the long term, the self-inflicted wound of the Model T not only cost Ford its industry leadership but opened the door to a powerful new third competitor in the person of Walter Chrysler.

Figure 2.3 shows the relative sales performance of Ford and GM. Note the 900,000 unit dip in national car and truck production in 1927 when Ford was in shutdown mode. Assuming a $500 price per unit, that would amount to about a half of a percent of lost GDP, although Ford's huge investment in new plants may have offset a fifth of that. Given the booming economy, few people beyond Ford shareholders and workers would have noticed.

FIGURE 2.3: RELATIVE SALES PERFORMANCE OF FORD AND GM, 1919–1929

	Total Cars and Trucks Thousands	Ford	% Share	GM	% Share
1919	1,900	941	49.5%	392	20.6%
1920 *	2,200	464	21.1%	393	17.9%
1921	1,600	972	60.8%	215	13.4%
1922	2,500	1,307	52.3%	457	18.3%
1923	4,000	2,019	50.5%	799	20.0%
1924	3,600	1,929	53.6%	587	16.3%
1925	4,300	1,919	44.6%	836	19.4%
1926	4,300	1,563	36.3%	1,245	29.0%
1927 **	3,400	424	12.5%	1,563	46.0%
1928	4,400	750	17.0%	1,811	41.2%
1929	5,300	1,870	35.3%	1,899	35.8%

* August 1–December 31, 1919 (Fiscal Year Change).
** Ford Model T replacement.
Source: Nevins and Hill, *Ford: Decline and Renewal*, Appendix 1; and Sloan, *My Years*, 151n, and Appendix 1: General Motors Corporation, Unit Sales.

The automobile industry was at the leading edge of the nation's astonishing increase in manufacturing productivity. Consider again Henry Ford's 1913 production: he produced nearly half of all automobiles produced that year, but with only a fifth the number of workers as his competitors. By 1929, all the automobile companies that mattered had adopted "Fordism" and had improved it. At GM, for example, Sloan and the central engineering staff had vowed they would never get caught in the kind of changeover hell that Ford had endured in 1927, and they had organized their plants around that objective, most especially by designing machinery with flexible tooling to adapt to different size parts.

The deeper productivity transition that underpinned Fordism was the marriage of electricity with mechanical production. In the mid-nineteenth century Samuel Colt's pistol factories were considered the apex of manufacturing technology. They were beautifully and thoughtfully laid out. They used a blend of special-purpose and flexible machinery, with a high degree of automation for the time. But productivity was drastically limited by their dependence on centralized coal-fired steam power connected to working machinery by belts and shafts. All the drive shafts turned all the time, although individual machines could be disconnected and reconnected. If the main drive shaft into a factory floor was interrupted for any reason, all the machines went down. Machines were necessarily grouped by their weight and torque to align them with the appropriate shafting and belting. Belting often drove shaft arrays on multiple floors, requiring elaborate belt towers. As belts loosened, precision was lost. Oil cylinders were located in factory ceilings to dribble oil on belt arrays to keep them flexible, ensuring slippery, greasy floors. The shaft and belt arrays blocked natural light and made it impossible to clean ceilings.

It took about twenty years after the advent of inexpensive AC power for manufacturers to realize its enormous efficiencies.* The first companies to embrace electrical power were textiles, print shops, and other businesses in which cleanliness was important. Typically, however, nothing changed but the power plant, which still drove the old system of shafts and belting. In the early 1900s, GE developed a "group" approach to power management. Recognizing the absurd inefficiency of driving all shafts all the time, they divided a large plant into units, each of which was powered electrically. The final step came mostly in the 1920s with the adoption of "unit-drive" layouts, in which each machine had its own electrical power source. It was also about this time that large electrical utilities began to market the advantages of unit-drive factory power, even providing free engineering consulting on the conversion process.

The obstacles to full unit-drive conversion were formidable. Virtually all the machinery had to be replaced. Variable-speed machinery needed DC power. (AC power could run DC machinery, but there was a loss of efficiency.) But the advantages were so patent as to be irresistible. The power savings were palpable, but the biggest opportunities were in the intangibles. Unit-drive machinery released the factory layout from the tyranny of the shafting design. Machinery layout could be freely changed to conform to the sequence of production flows. Without the massive shafts and shaft gearing, factories could be constructed of lighter and cheaper materials. One-floor factories were more suitable to straight-line flows, and cheaper than multiple-floored plants. Ditching the liana forests of ceiling shafting made for brighter, much cleaner plants with windows and skylights. Empty ceilings were ideal venues for overhead cranes. Factories could be readily expanded or contracted, without worrying about the distance from the central power source.

It was Ford, of course, that plowed the visible trail in all these areas. Big companies appeared generally on board with the new approaches

---

* That is not much different from the time it took the web and internet to be fully incorporated into business practice. The base internet technology developed slowly through most of the postwar period, before the advances in semiconductor design enabled a rapid expansion of applications starting officially in 1995 when the internet was privatized. That process is still underway, and is shifting from streamlining business processes to new paradigms like the "internet of things."

during the war, although this doesn't show up in the statistics. The Lynds' reports on Muncie, Indiana, in the mid-1920s, however, suggest that Fordism had penetrated nearly all their manufacturing establishments, since the majority of skilled workers had been supplanted by nonunion workers tending smart machines. That may be a biased sample, since Muncie was primarily a supplier to the automobile industry. But the national data show a stunning burst of manufacturing productivity (see Figure 2.4).[42]

FIGURE 2.4: MANUFACTURING PRODUCTIVITY IN THE UNITED STATES, 1899–1937

Decade (Annual %)	Labor Prod. %	Capital Prod. %
1899–1909	1.30	-1.62
1909–1919	1.14	-1.95
1919–1929	**5.44**	**4.21**
1929–1937	1.95	2.38

Source: Devine, "From Shafts to Wires," Table 2—percent change calculations by author.

The scale of the automobile and AC power industries sucked whole congeries of other industries in their wake, most notably, the oil, aluminum, and steel industries.

The advent of cheap electrical lighting had doomed the kerosene market, the mainstay of the old Rockefeller Standard Oil. The court-ordered breakup of Standard Oil in 1911 was a boon for the company since it had clearly lost its mojo after the elder Rockefeller's retirement.* The old Standard was late to the fuel oil market, and missed out on major new oil finds in Texas, California, Oklahoma, Kansas, and Illinois that were exploited by new companies like Union Oil, Gulf, and Texaco. Military requirements and the explosive growth of the American fleet of gasoline-powered cars, trucks, and farm equipment forced the pace of technological development—high-powered airplane engines and machine guns needed top-quality lubricants, while new refining techniques like molecular "cracking" were key to meeting the demand for high-octane gasoline. By the mid-1920s, of the 30 largest oil companies, 21 controlled some 52–53 percent of total production, and there was considerable rotation of the 30 companies through the top groups, suggesting a very competitive industry.[43]

The Aluminum Company of America, now Alcoa, was a monopoly, at first by virtue of its patented electrical method of smelting aluminum ore, and then by its extraordinary record in spotting and quickly dominating each next great market opportunity—moving quickly from cooking ware to automobiles and then to airplanes. It was also one of the first companies to take advantage of the vast new AC power complex that opened at

---

* The Standard breakup was simple: there were thirty-seven constituent companies, each with its own stock, which was held in trust for the shareholders by a New Jersey entity that effectively ran the conglomerate. The court simply abolished the trust, which it ruled was the real engine of monopoly, so the constituent firms all became competitors.

Niagara in 1903. Andrew Mellon was an early investor and stayed close to the company. Henry Ford, with his fetish for lightweight cars, was the first to make wide use of aluminum in his industry, and he also made the aluminum cylinders in the World War I Liberty airplane engine. Aluminum was still a modestly sized company when the twenties opened, but its balance sheet expanded more than tenfold during the decade, vaulting it into the ranks of major American industrial players.[†44]

The steel industry appeared in blooming health, benefiting not only from the automobile boom, but also from the rapid advances of steel-frame residential high-rises and office skyscrapers. Its economic performance, however, was dragged down by the near deadweight of the biggest company, US Steel. The great 1902 steel merger that created US Steel was essentially a defensive maneuver by J. P. Morgan to get Andrew Carnegie out of the steel business. J. P. Morgan had engineered roll-ups of a number of modestly sized end-product steel makers, most of whom bought their steel from Carnegie. Morgan went a step too far, however, when he organized an upstream steel maker to supplant Carnegie—fecklessly going head to head with the world's most efficient steel manufacturer. Carnegie detested Morgan, and gleefully announced expansions aimed at destroying the Morgan entities. Facing catastrophe, Morgan engineered the buyout.

Morgan and his hand-picked US Steel corporation chairman, Elbert H. Gary, a lawyer, shared the belief that the primary purpose of a corporation was to reliably pay its investors their expected streams of earnings. Jostling for market position by stealing customers or undercutting prices was "destructive competition," which would damage them all. US Steel controlled about 60 percent of the market, and Gary disciplined the industry by his famous "Gary dinners"—annual meetings of all the steel company executives at which they would reach a consensus on basic prices and individual shares. US Steel, under Gary, missed much of the boom in the automobile markets. It kept its plants in Pittsburgh instead

---

† Alcoa was subject to a long antitrust action by the Justice Department, finally losing only in 1938, on a finding by Learned Hand that the fact of monopoly is a violation of the antitrust law, even if the company did not intentionally create it. At the end of the war, in order to create effective competition, the government created two new aluminum companies, Reynolds and Kaiser, equipped with Alcoa technology.

of expanding to Michigan, and virtually all the breakthroughs in automobile steel—new alloys, continuous rolling, detailed chemical standards—
came from the automotive companies, or from innovative entrants like
American Rolling Mill Company (ARMCO). The Society of Automobile
Engineers (SAE) specifications for automotive steel reached five hundred
pages by 1920. US Steel played almost no role in the automotive industry, although dozens of other steel companies were involved, all of them
small and innovative, and not likely to be invited to the Gary dinners. The
steel historian Thomas Misa lists as one of the notable accomplishments
of Morgan's steel roll-up that it finally managed "to stamp out technical
innovation in steel structures."[45]

In 1928, US Steel and General Motors were virtually tied for the
leadership in sales among American companies—GM had revenues of
$1.46 billion, while US Steel had pulled in $1.37 billion. But the similari-
ties ended there. GM had a glittering 21.9 percent net profit on its assets,
while US Steel, with roughly twice the plant and equipment as GM,
much of it old and unproductive, returned a measly 4.7 percent on assets.
The two companies' returns on sales were similarly lopsided, 18.9 percent
for GM and 8.3 percent for US Steel.[46]

——— VIII. LAGGARDS: AGRICULTURE ————

M anufacturing was clearly the star industry of the 1920s. Its output doubled between 1921 and 1929, and it accounted for about 30 percent of all payrolls. Annual labor and capital productivity grew two to three times faster than ever before. Cars and electrically powered consumer and investment durables, especially communications-oriented products, changed the rhythms of daily living.

Some industries, however, did not keep pace. Agriculture had enjoyed halcyon years during the war, but struggled mightily with overproduction once the farm sectors in the warring countries came back on line. The 1920s marked the point when agriculture ceased to be the most important American industry. Muncie's factories were depopulating family farms, mechanization was forcing consolidation of smaller farms, and the farm labor force was steadily shrinking. So farmers as a group had a lot to be unhappy about, but the traditional meme that a rural collapse was a major cause of the Depression in America is an overstatement.

Giovanni Federico, an Italian historian of world agriculture, has reexamined the American data and taken issue with the standard story. Much of the rural perception of disaster, Federico suggests, was only by comparison with the golden years of the war. A longer view gives a different impression. In the 1900s, the American farmer's terms of trade (the ratio of farm prices to manufacturing prices) mostly languished in the 80s. It jumped to 100 in 1910, then took off in 1915, soaring to about 125 in 1917— the consequence of the "Western settlement" nations (United States, Canada, Australia, and New Zealand) enjoying a virtual monopoly on the international agricultural trade during the war years. The first blow was that the war ended, catching farmers with outsized debt incurred to expand their planting. The second was that European agriculture recovered faster than expected. And the third was the nasty 1920–1921 recession. Wholesale farm prices suffered a real drop of about 18 percent even as planned production declined. Deflation magnified the burden of farm mortgages, and many farmers defaulted.[47]

But Federico's data suggest that farmers coped. Based on a model that relates population growth and improving diets to food demand, he finds that American farm production had adjusted to demand by the end of the 1920–1921 downturn, and stayed that way for the rest of the decade. There was probably modest overproduction in 1928 and 1929, but not on a scale sufficient to cause a crisis. The 1929 *Survey of Current Business* shows that the index of farm labor output had increased by just over 14 percent over the 1923–1925 average. Farm prices had stayed flat, consistent with the slightly negative inflation for the entire economy. Nor did farm equipment manufacturers have a bad decade. The biggest of them, International Harvester, had gross profits of $11.4 million in 1922 and more than $59 million in both 1928 and 1929. That is far from GM territory, but it suggests a healthy, modernizing industry. Ford also continued to enjoy healthy sales of its tractors and trucks.

Figure 2.5 lends considerable support to Federico's thesis. Prices for meat animals and farm crops jumped enormously during the war,

FIGURE 2.5: US CROP AND MEAT PRICES PLUS OUTPUT PER FARM WORKER, 1910–1930[48]

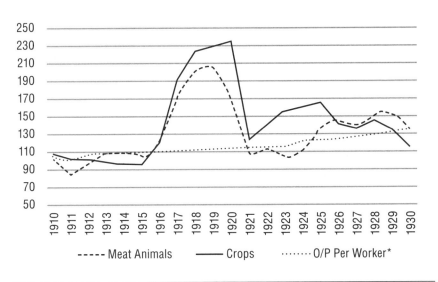

Source: FRED Indexes of Farm Prices for Meat Animals and for Crops; and Barger and Landsburg, "Agricultural Productivity," Table 38.

undoubtedly encouraging farmers' ambitions—although the real farmer price gains were no more than 10–30 percent depending on their product mix. The end of the war was brutal for all farmers, but by 1925, crop farmers had fully caught up: the combination of price increases and improved worker output put them ahead of the 80 percent postwar inflation in the overall economy, while meat farmers took until about 1928 to reach that blessed state. While that was no more than holding their own, it is a less dire picture than painted by farm advocates.

Having said that, however, a real collapse was just around the corner. The 1930s combination of deflation, bumper crops, and heavy debt loads prostrated farm belts throughout the world and was one of several major forces creating the Great Depression. Because of the diversity of the United States' economy, the debacle in global agriculture was less consequential in America than in most other countries with large agrarian sectors. In 1935, the Federal government effectively socialized the biggest cash crops—a bailout not unlike the one provided to the banking sector in 2007–2008.

Economics aside, the cultural loss from the disappearance of traditional agriculture was unsettling. The self-sufficient family farm, and its concomitant Jeffersonian vision of a nation of rural small producers was dying, the victim of the same mass production forces that had radically changed the manufacturing sector. Machinery was gradually replacing labor, and smaller farmers could not withstand the mechanized corporate competition. Family farmers were defaulting on their mortgages and losing their land, and with it, their sense of place and long-term security. For most, factory work in big, heartless cities was the only alternative, and it was a scary one, as documented in the Muncie interviews. In 1900, some 40 percent of the labor force worked in agriculture; by 1930 it was down to 22 percent, on its way to the almost invisible 2 percent that prevails today.

IX. LAGGARDS: REAL ESTATE

Henry Flagler, the very rich former number two man in John D. Rockefeller's Standard Oil, discovered Florida in 1877—indeed, many thought he had invented it. After sampling its legendary winter weather, he commenced a Florida development program of lavish beachfront hotels for plutocrats and, along with entrepreneurs who followed him to the state, built modern rail and seaboard transportation, docking, and storage facilities. Altogether, Flagler put between $40 and 50 million of his own money into Florida, or close to a $1 billion in today's dollars.

Flagler died in 1913, but other wealthy entrepreneurs had followed him into Florida. One of them, Carl Fisher, creator of the Fisher auto body company, may have been the first to concentrate on residential housing. Development flagged during the war and froze during the 1920–1921 downturn. But building activity in Florida picked up sharply in 1922–1923, and by 1924 the whole region was in the grip of a frenzied real estate gold rush.[49]

While the building boom took place along both the Atlantic and Gold coasts of the panhandle, the epicenter of the activity was Miami. Its population doubled to almost 7,000 between 1900 and 1910, and jumped to nearly 30,000 by 1920. Tourism was still the main industry, but real estate was growing apace to keep up with the population. Intensive investment in draining the Everglades opened up more interior land, for both agriculture and residential uses, and national land companies moved in to assemble parcels for residential subdivisions. More and more of Florida's casual vacationers fell in love with the state and put down permanent roots. By 1923, Miami's population had passed 47,000. The state legislature injected a cocaine hit into the frenzy by abolishing income and estate taxes. Land values went exponential, as local chambers of commerce howled gleefully from the sidelines.[50]

The "binder boys" capture the hallucinatory tinge to the whole episode. The binder was simply a purchase option to buy a property once title had been transferred and the first substantial payment made. Binders were typically priced at a small portion of the expected purchase price, they were "binding" on the seller, and could themselves be resold. The binder boys were the kind of gritty, street-smart, moving-up-fast lads so admired by Charles Dickens. They mostly worked the streets and arriving rail centers, with binder books in hand, hawking raw real estate options. Once a purchaser bought a binder, for cash usually, he and the seller would proceed to the records office and register the binder. The purchaser of course had never seen the lot, and often had no idea of its location, but had a small piece of the biggest lottery in America.[51]

Canny locals often made modest fortunes in the binder game. One longtime resident said of the boom: "everything kind of went crazy. . . . I'd leave in the morning and tell my wife, 'How much money do you want me to bring home?' . . . I'd come up town and it wasn't so long for I'd have a deposit on a piece of property. Maybe a few hundred dollars. In forty-eight hours you'd sell it and make several thousand dollars." Other proto-cities sprang up to take advantage of the boom. The most successful was Coral Gables, which had its own song, "Moon Shines in Coral Gables," contracted from Irving Berlin's songwriting team. William Jennings Bryan was one of their pitchmen.[52]

By 1925, the signs of an Everglades-sized bubble were unmistakable. The City of Miami had $60 million in new construction underway in 1925, and Greater Miami had $103 million worth, against $11 million in their 1923–1924 fiscal year. Sixteen giant luxury hotels were completed in Miami in 1925, and fourteen more started construction. Lots that were sold for $1,000 in the early 1900s were going for prices of up to $1 million. Parcels of land near a fashionable area sold for $7,000 in June and rose to $35,000 within six weeks. Total sales booked in Coral Gables in 1925 surpassed $100 million.

The seamy side of the boomtown was on full display, with mushrooming tent cities for construction workers, speculators renting sleeping spaces on residents' front porches, soaring crime rates, and impossible traffic. Miami had 105,000 automobiles, the highest per capita in the country. The boom cooled in 1926. A slow period in the stock market dampened the appetites of investors, and buyers from the late-stage boom began to default on their payments. The *coup de grâce* may have been a

125-mile per hour hurricane that nearly flattened Miami. By 1929, even Coral Gables was facing bankruptcy.[53]

The Florida real estate craze and collapse was an extreme example of 1920s mini housing booms and subsequent busts throughout the country. The economist Alexander Field suggests that they may have played a significant role in prolonging the Depression—but not for the usual reasons studied by economists, like damage to bank balance sheets, but for clogging the microeconomics of housing. Throughout the country, developers rushed into projects, often with poor site selection, poorly planned utilities, and awkward street layouts.*[54]

A 1947 study by the National Housing Administration commented on the legacy of the 1920s, noting that:

> In their eagerness to find tracts of land in single large ownership, unhampered by fixed arrangements of streets and utilities, developers . . . will pass by hundreds of thousands of plots already equipped with paved streets, curbs, sidewalks, water and other utility mains into which millions of dollars have already been sunk—enough, indeed, to have bankrupted many townships and villages.
>
> Many millions of lots still shown on assessors' books are entirely unimproved and never represented more than some stakes set out in a field. . . . [Others] are sterilized because the ownerships are dispersed in the hands of nonresidents who cannot be located and who have long since ceased to pay taxes.
>
> No sound estimates have been developed of the total amount of abandoned subdivisions, either in area or in cost. . . . [T]here may be from twenty to thirty million vacant subdivided lots of record in the whole country.[55]

Another 1947 report from the American Municipal Association noted that "foreclosure and forfeiture action since 1930 has in most places

---

* "Short blocks" were a particular problem. Studies by the Federal Housing Administration in the 1930s recommended block lengths of about 1,300 feet. Twenties developers often created blocks of no more than two hundred to six hundred feet, greatly increasing street area and thus reducing the space for housing, and requiring awkward utility arrangements.

reduced the problem of tax delinquent vacant land to minor proportions." That report, Field notes, marked the end of a twenty-year period of "lengthy, costly, and drawn out legal processes necessitated by the prior boom and deflation." The new Federal Housing Administration (FHA) played a leading role in working off the blockading detritus of ill-fated 1920s developments, both through education of municipal officials and the standards it insisted upon for approving FHA-insured financing.[56]

The collapse in residential construction, however, was another nail in the coffin of the 1920s business boom. Unfortunately it coincided with an overshoot in the late-decade boom in urban skyscrapers. Construction was the hardest-hit industry of all in the Depression looming ahead.

As the United States entered its seventh year of rapid growth in 1929, the country's businesses looked unstoppable. Car sales, which had become an economic bellwether, got off to a fast start, with a host of attractive new models. In 1922, the industry had sold 2.5 million new cars and trucks. That jumped to 4 million in the banner year of 1923 and, except for 1927, when Ford was out of the market, new car and truck sales averaged just above 4 million. But in 1929, they hit 5.3 million, a jump of about a quarter. Steel plants were running over capacity. Electricity sales were up by 12 percent, electrical machinery sales by 30 percent, machine tool orders by almost 20 percent. Radio audiences were growing apace, and the new talkies were packing them in at the theaters. Big cities were sprouting skyscrapers. There was stunning growth in both worker and capital productivity and no inflation to speak of.

Was there a bubble in stocks? The great contemporary economist, Irving Fisher, thought not, since the momentum of corporate earnings suggested that prices were fully justified. John Kenneth Galbraith's famous 1954 book, *The Great Crash, 1929*, makes the case for a "great speculative orgy," which for many years was the traditional view.[57]

The Galbraithian logic was supplanted in the 1960s and 1970s by "efficient market," theorists who begin from the premise that free market prices always best represent the current state of knowledge. Efficient market theorists believe that bubbles are impossible by definition, although the debacle of 2007–2008 may have dispelled the blind faith in efficient-market ideologies.

Barrie Wigmore, former head of research at Goldman Sachs, has produced the most complete microhistory of the 1929 stock market crash. He suggests that there is "room for debate" as to whether stock prices were excessively high in the first half of 1929. The Dow Jones Industrial Index had settled into a trading range of 300–320, or a price/earnings multiple about twenty-four times the anticipated 1929 profits. That was

A caricature of a "bullish" J. P. Morgan blowing stock market bubbles attests both to the prominence of the Morgan Bank (J. P. was long since dead) and the skepticism toward the market's sustained rise.

high by historic standards, but not crazy, given the apparent momentum of the economy.[58]

But the third quarter developments, Wigmore suggests, crossed the line into Galbraithian territory. Starting in late summer—when Wall Streeters were normally on the beach—the market turned decisively up, peaking at 381 on September 1. Signs of "irrational exuberance," in Alan Greenspan's famous phrase, had been building for some time. The number of brokerage offices—devoted pushers of stocks to retail customers— had jumped from 706 in 1925 to 1,685 by the fall of 1929, with almost all of the increase coming since 1928. Trading volume increased dramatically, from a daily average of 1.7 million in 1925, to 3.5 million in 1928, and 4.1 million to mid-October, 1929. New issuances of common stock in 1929 were two and a half times higher than in 1928, and more than six times higher than in any previous year. The great majority of 1929 issuances, moreover, were not for new shares but for highly leveraged investment companies aiming to invest in existing shares, in some cases their own shares. The price-earnings multiples for some high-flying stocks soared into the hundreds, some into the thousands. Columbia Graphophone sold at a 5,000+ multiple in September. Foreshadowings of the dotcom boom.[59]

Brokers jacked up sales with easy credit terms. The average retail customer could buy on 25 percent margin—that is, borrowing 75 percent of the purchase price. (Margin regulation came only with the New Deal securities legislation.) Regular customers routinely bought on 10 percent margin, and many had open credit lines with brokers and put up no cash at all. Securities lending to brokers and other investors grew from $3.3 billion in the spring of 1927 to $8.5 billion in October of 1929, or about 8 percent of GDP. After mid-1928, 90 percent of such lending were "call loans," that the lender could close out at any time—an important source of instability. To make it worse, almost 80 percent of the lending came from nonbanks. The Federal Reserve had clamped down on brokers' loans by banks, so corporate treasurers, investment funds, or anyone else with loose cash rushed in to scoop up loans paying annualized rates of up to 20 percent. The flood of new lending, of course, was purely opportunistic, so loans were called in at the first hint of trouble.[60]

The hucksterism was especially flagrant in the late stages of the 1929 stock run-up. There were more than a hundred new issuances that were organized by market professionals, usually comprising bundles of stocks, for the sole purpose of artificially pushing up prices. Tip sheets followed their every move and blared their virtues to naïve investors, who were left with the losses after the professionals made their exit. As Pecora's and other investigations showed, Wall Street's interlocking depositary and investment banking businesses were ripe fields for self-dealing, gross fiduciary violations, and rampant greed. When Clarence Dillon of Dillon, Read was asked how the insiders on a Dillon, Read flotation could justify their disproportionate share of the profits, he seemed mystified: "We could have taken 100 percent. We could have taken all that profit." A senator on the panel quoted Lord Clive of India's comment in his corruption trial: "When I consider my opportunities, I marvel at my moderation."[61]

Two 1990s papers by senior economists measured the degree of overpricing by comparing changes in the prices of shares to roughly comparable instruments. In the last stage of the closed-end fund craze in the late summer of 1929, the closed-end funds were 50 percent more expensive than the individual shares in their portfolios, which makes no sense at all. The second paper tracked the interest cost on broker loans to buy shares. When the Fed cracked down on brokers' loans in 1929, interest rates soared to 20 percent or even more. In normal times such a heavy cost of carry would cause a sharp market break, purely on the economics. Following the math through suggests a market bubble of about 30 percent. Still other research supports market plungers. A 1975 paper applies Burton Malkiel's well-known formula for forecasting price/earnings ratios of the stocks in the Dow Jones Industrial Average, and finds that, while there was "some over-indulgence . . . by the usual standards for such things, the conclusion would have to be: not much of an orgy."[62]

Allan H. Meltzer, in his history of the Federal Reserve, provides an arresting comparison of net corporate profits to the market capitalization of shares listed on the New York Stock Exchange. While real GDP rose strongly through most of the 1920s, corporate profits rose three times as fast. The ratio between stock capitalizations and net profits was 6.2 in 1925 and jumped to more than twice that by 1929. But almost all of the repricing had happened by 1927. The market cap/profits ratio dipped through much of 1928, but recovered in 1929, to slightly ahead of its 1927 high, based on the boffo first-half growth in revenues and profits. Even on Meltzer's comparison, stocks still could be considered high in the fall of 1929; that peak market cap/profits ratio has since been exceeded only twice.[63]

There were certainly conflicting signals. It is a commonplace among historians of the crash to say that industrial production had turned down after June 1929. Technically, that's true, as Figure 2.6 shows. But the question is whether anybody noticed it.

Industrial production peaked in June. The June data are dated July 1, but could not have been compiled and released until well into July,* when

---

* The US Department of Commerce warned in its *Survey of Current Business* reports: "As most data covering a particular month's business are not available until from 15 to 30 days after the close of the month, a complete picture of that month's operations can not be presented at an early date, but the weekly supplements give every week the latest data available." The reports were released in the third or fourth week of the publication month, and were revised as new data came in. Distribution of the reports was by mail to subscribers, who were most likely to be professional investors.

FIGURE 2.6: US MONTHLY INDUSTRIAL PRODUCTION: 1920–1929

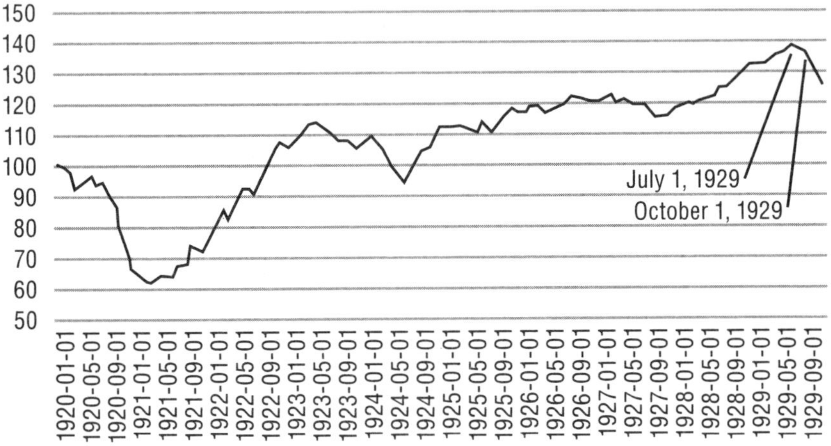

Source: St. Louis Federal Reserve, FRED, "Industrial Production Index." (INDPRO).

they were greeted with unalloyed cheering. Here is the commentary from the July *Survey of Current Business:*

> The general index of manufacturing production in June . . . was higher than any other month on record, showing a gain of more than 2 per cent over the preceding month and almost 15 per cent over June of last year. . . .
>
> Wholesale trade in June . . . showed a decline from May but was greater than a year ago. . . . Sales by department stores . . . were greater than in either the preceding month or June of last year.
>
> Sales by mail order houses in June were substantially greater than in the preceding month or the corresponding period of last year. . . . Sales by grocery chains in June . . . showed a considerable gain over a year ago. Ten-cent chain-store systems reported a gain of more than 13 per cent over June, 1928. . . .
>
> The total production of automobiles, both passenger cars and trucks, during the first half of 1929 was larger than in any other period on record. Exports of automobiles from the United States in June were greater than either the preceding month or June of last year, with the total for the first half showing the largest external trade than in any other

similar period. Imports of crude rubber in June showed a decline from the previous month, but were about 50 per cent higher than a year ago.[64]

July was a little less exuberant, but had the aspect of a modest slow-down from the torrid pace of the first half. Pig iron was up, but sheet steel (driven by autos) was down. Fabricated structural steel (skyscrapers) was up strongly, as were steel castings. Coal continued to slip, as it had been doing for a long time, but petroleum products were hitting new highs.[65] It is only in the September report, released in mid-October, that the slippage becomes visible, but it's far from dire. The *Survey* data is in the form of index numbers, using the averages for 1923–1925 as 100. Total manufacturing, which included textiles, packaged foods, cement, petroleum products, as well as iron and steel and machine tools and automobiles, had opened the year at 117, peaked at 128 in June, then slipped to 122 in September, with no obvious trend. Automobiles had been on a tear, opening the year at 121, before shooting up to 188 in April, then dropping back to 127 in September. Steel ingots had opened at 121, risen to 153 in May, and fallen to 130 in September. Electric power was at 159 in September, close to the average for the year. Factory employment was flat. While the summer cool-down in the enormous metals and metal products industries was evident, little else in those reports suggested a collapse. As Bethlehem's Schwab remarked with some puzzlement in the first days of the market break, steel factories were running at 110 percent of capacity, with healthy backlogs and no inventory buildups.[66]

The falloff in the industrial production reports, which was a broader index, doesn't really raise alarms, even with 20/20 hindsight. The blowout June number, 138, was the highest ever, and by the September report, which wasn't released until mid-October, had only dropped to 135. The collapse in October was clear, of course, but those reports weren't released until November and December. The National Bureau of Economic Research (NBER) later placed the 1929 business cycle peak in August.[67] A number of professional traders, however, had long since seen enough, particularly if they were following events in Europe, where economies had been turning down for some time. Bernard Baruch and Percy Rockefeller, a nephew of John D. and an active investor, were selling shares in early 1929. John Raskob had dumped almost all of his GM and DuPont shares starting in 1928. Certainly by September a number of broker newsletters were warning of a correction.[68]

A fair conclusion is that the market was too high in the late summer and early fall of 1929, and was due for a correction—which duly happened. But as Galbraith remarked, "it is easier to account for the boom and crash in the market than to explain their bearing on the depression which followed."[69]

PART THREE

The Crash in the United States

Richard Whitney, six foot two and powerfully built, had the cut and credentials of a charter member of the American nobility. His ancestors had arrived with John Winthrop on the ship *Arabella* in 1630 to lay down a Puritan plantation in the area of present day Cambridge, Massachusetts. He was a former Harvard crewman, a member of the exclusive Porcellian Club, a university overseer, and president of the New York Yacht Club. He lived in a mansion in New York City and took his leisure at an elegant horse and cattle farm in rural New Jersey. In his day job, he headed an important brokerage, and was also president of the New York Stock Exchange. A severe market crisis hit on Thursday, October 24, 1929, when as *Time* put it, "Stocks bought without reference to their earnings were being sold without reference to their dividends. At around noon there came the no-bid menace. . . . Sound stocks at shrunk prices— and nobody to buy them."

Then at 1:30 p.m., Whitney strode confidently onto the Exchange floor, heading straight for Post No. 2, where US Steel, a national bellwether, was traded. US Steel had broken through 200 down to 190. "Panic, with its most awful leer," *Time* purpled, "might surely take command." But Whitney, everybody knew, represented a "bankers' pool," reminiscent of Pierpont Morgan's famous pool that halted a dangerous financial unraveling in 1907. The new pool was also headed by the Morgan bank, represented by the suave and cultured Thomas Lamont, the Morgan operating partner. Whitney was Morgan's broker, and US Steel was a Morgan creation. In a commanding baritone, Whitney placed an order for 25,000 shares at 205—that was $5 million at a price 15 points above the previous sale. As he strode from trading post to trading post, booming out orders, traders were galvanized. Cheers broke out, and a flood of buy orders poured forth. "In an hour General Electric was up 21 points, Montgomery Ward up 23, Radio up 16, A.T.&T. up 22 [and] . . . the man who bid 205 for 25,000 shares of Steel had made himself a hero of a financially historic moment."[1]

The bankers' pool stayed in session on Friday and the half-day Saturday session, as the markets remained calm. On Friday morning, the pool was able to unload some of its shares at a small profit, and they moved quietly in and out of the market through the day—making an adroit purchase if an important stock faltered, and lightening up when a security seemed to find its own footing. Saturday was almost boring: the Dow Jones Industrial Average was steady, down 2, and the alarmists seemed to have been put to rout. Brokerage firms pumped out optimistic newsletters, while the Exchange worked throughout the weekend to complete the trading paperwork, and to clean up margin accounts.[2]

But the malevolent genies of the market unleashed full-blooded havoc on Monday, October 28, forever after known as "Black Monday." Margin calls generated from the weekend accounts cleanup caused a wave of forced sales, lien filings, and angry face-offs between brokers and their clients. The Fed added $25 million in liquidity to the New York banks to ease the shock, but it couldn't stop the pullback. Just before the Crash, brokers' loans outstanding from New York City banks were at $6.6 billion. A month later they were $3.6 billion, a level not seen since December 1927. The loss of $3 billion of market liquidity, equivalent to 3.5 percent of the New York Stock Exchange's total valuation, was enough by itself to sustain the market's dark downward momentum.[3]

On the next day, "Black Tuesday," foreign investors joined in the rout. Clarence Hatry was a London version of Billy Durant—a smart, flamboyant operator, with a taste for high leverage and lavish living, who had built a sprawling network of companies. He was about to close a giant iron and steel merger when a diligent brokerage clerk noticed that he had seen the same list of collateral securing a previous deal. Once the accountants looked closely, it took no time at all to confirm that Hatry was insolvent. The London market dropped like a stone, sucking yet more money out of New York. Hatry and his associates readily admitted to the charges, and after a short trial they went to prison—but with flair, treating themselves to a proper lunch at the Charing Cross Hotel before being remanded to custody. Hatry served fourteen years before beginning a new life as an antiquarian book dealer.[4]

The bankers participating in the New York pool were as overwhelmed by events as their clients. Charles E. Mitchell, head of the National City

Bank, had been on the verge of completing an all-stock merger with the Corn Exchange Bank, on the condition that National City stock was at least $400 a share. As the National City stock nosedived, Mitchell took out a personal loan of $12 million from the Morgans to bull the stock. It was hopeless: on Black Tuesday, National City was as low as $155. The merger blew up and Mitchell defaulted on his loan, although the Morgans, true to the rules of class solidarity, did not call it.[5]

Richard Whitney was not so lucky. Despite his Exchange floor bravado, the first days of the Crash had left him insolvent. His brother George, a senior Morgan partner, bailed him out, but Richard was consistently on the financial precipice, even when he made the cover of *Time* in 1934. He was finally convicted of embezzlement—from charitable funds he looked after, company trust funds, and the yacht club, among others—and was imprisoned from 1938 to 1943. He never expressed any public remorse, but was a model prisoner, played on the baseball team, and taught classes for the other prisoners, who always called him "Mr. Whitney." His last years were spent employed as the manager of a small New Jersey dairy.[6]

The Crash, in the sense of a cataclysm, ended on Thursday, November 14, not quite three weeks after Black Monday. The previous day, John D. Rockefeller had placed a bid for a million shares of Standard Oil at $50, 60 percent of its 1929 high. On Thursday, it opened up 8¼. General Motors announced a dividend increase, and Standard Oil of Kansas restored its dividend. The New York Fed cut its discount rate. Treasury secretary Andrew Mellon announced a 1 percent cut in income tax rates. The Federal Reserve Board said that credit conditions were returning to normalcy.[7]

Within a few days, market indexes were up about 25 percent. As investors calmed down, trading volumes fell back to about three million shares a day, or about where they were in 1927 and 1928. Utilities returned to their usual pace of raising money to deepen their regional networks. A $350 million leveraged merger created Republic Steel in late December. Billy Durant and Albert Wiggin, head of the Chase Bank, organized new stock pools. Peering out from their bunkers, stock and bond brokers discovered that they had survived the turmoil more or less intact. That was mostly because they had been ruthless in calling their security customers' margin loans, while the banks lending to the brokers had freely waived loan terms to keep them solvent.[8]

As 1930 opened, markets still bubbled with cautious optimism. Many companies had booked record-breaking profits in 1929, so the spring shareholders' meetings were pleasant affairs. Businessmen admired the new president, Herbert Hoover, and he fully returned their admiration. Mellon, himself a business Prometheus and one of the country's richest men, was the cautious manager of the national treasury. The dollar was strong, and Fort Knox was overflowing with gold. By April, the Dow Jones Industrial Average (DJIA) had bounced all the way back to 294, well under the 1929 high but only 20 points below the average close for the first six months of 1929. To the smart people who had disdained the exuberances in the second half of 1929, the new market level looked almost reasonable. The *New York Times's* curmudgeonly Alexander Dana Noyes allowed that the market might be oversold.[9]

Noyes might have restrained his enthusiasm. There were no more "crashes," but nearly all the economic indicators turned decisively down in the second quarter, and financial markets slipped into a state of catatonia, a slow-motion death crawl that finally bottomed out in mid-1932 with the DJIA at 41, just 11 percent of its 1929 high (see Figure 3.1).

FIGURE 3.1: DOW JONES INDUSTRIAL AVERAGE MONTHLY CLOSE

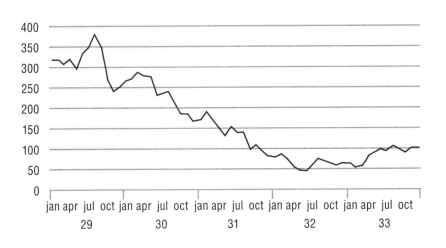

Source: Wigmore, *The Crash and its Aftermath*, Appendix Table A-19.

Industrial stocks were hit harder than service and retail stocks. But taking all New York Stock Exchange common shares together, the market was worth $82.1 billion in September 1929; by July 1932, values had collapsed to only $12.7 billion, or just over 15 percent of pre-Crash valuations.[10]

The market crash occurred in the seventh month of the term of the new president, Herbert Hoover. The subsequent economic collapse overwhelmed him, forever destroying his reputation. That is a pity, because in calmer times, he might have created a positive legacy of progressive policy-making.

Herbert Hoover was a force of nature. Raised in dour Quaker poverty, he was orphaned as a child and serially farmed out among a grim collection of distant relatives, from a sodhouse-dwelling plains farmer to a skinflint, sharpster uncle in Oregon. Very early, he learned to work prodigiously, to improve himself constantly, to trust his own apparently limitless abilities, and to push through any obstacle that got in his way. By sheer grit, plus the luck that often accompanies talent, he was accepted into the first class at the new Stanford University, and discovered geology. In 1896, at twenty-two, having grown a mustache and added thirteen years to his age, he won a commission to scout mines in the Australian outback—one-hundred-plus-degree weather, scorpions and other venomous varmints, and some of the world's toughest and most desperate men. He found a promising mine, engineered its purchase by his home office, and brought it to production, returning sixty-five times the investment.[11]

Hoover repeated that performance again and again. He had some flops, of course, but they were far outweighed by his triumphs, and he gained wide recognition as a genius mining engineer. From then until the outbreak of World War I, his life was spent in the world's most inhospitable places, on almost every continent, most of them as the head of his own international mining consultancy, nosing out new mines, or bringing failed mines into production. Since he usually took shares in the properties he rescued, he quickly became very wealthy. His wife, Lou Henry, whom he had met at Stanford and married after his first success in Australia, sometimes traveled with him, and their first son, Herbert Jr., had circumnavigated the world twice by the time he was two. As a practical matter, however, Hoover's two sons rarely saw their father when they were young, and were often without the presence of either of their parents. Both sons became successful engineers and investors. Herbert Jr. was undersecretary of state in the second Eisenhower administration, and often served as acting secretary during the illnesses of John Foster Dulles.

Hoover began to think of retiring while he was still a young man. He had distilled his professional lore into a college textbook, *Principles of Mining*, something of a minor classic, and had enough money to live in luxury for the rest of his life. He was not a religious Quaker, but had internalized the Quaker imperative of service, and felt that he could contribute to improving the lot of humanity. As it happened, Hoover was in London on the fateful day that Germany invaded Belgium in 1914. More than a hundred thousand American nationals found themselves caught in war zones, and began streaming across the channel into London. These were not poor people, but their assets were blocked on the continent, so they could not buy passage back to the United States. Hoover bulldozed his way into control of a fledgling committee to raise loans from local expatriates to finance their countrymen's passages home—along the way falsely claiming authorization of the American ambassador. In his mining career, Hoover had proved himself an extraordinary manager, and he displayed all of his talents in his humanitarian work—recruiting willing volunteers, furnishing them with precise instructions, then hard-driving both himself and his crews. Within about two months, the London strandees had almost all been repatriated, at the cost of $400,000, almost two-thirds of which came from private donors, and almost all of which was repaid.

Hoover was wrapping up his London affairs and about to embark for home himself when he got a call from the American ambassador: would he take on a mission to save up to a million Belgians from starvation? The Germans had displaced a large share of the Belgian population, and the British were enforcing an embargo on imports into the continent. The Americans hoped to mount a private effort to save the Belgians, with strong but unofficial American backing. Hoover was ready. Within days, he was raising a million dollars a week and ordering huge volumes of food, far beyond his current resources, much of it secured by his personal pledge, far in excess of his own fortune. Within just a couple of weeks, a shipload of food was on its way to Rotterdam.

Purely as a private citizen, Hoover negotiated with the heads of state and senior officials of Great Britain, France, Belgium, Germany, and the Netherlands. The German government gave him carte blanche to travel anywhere within their lines, and when a ranking German general tried to stop him, Hoover entrained to Berlin and had him overruled. Churchill detested him because he was compromising the British embargo; Senator Henry Cabot Lodge wanted to prosecute him for unauthorized negotiations with foreign powers—a serious offense—until Teddy Roosevelt warned Lodge that he was attacking a hero.

William Leuchtenburg, a Hoover biographer, writes:

> If a man without Hoover's daring had held his post, many thousands would have starved to death. An organization with no legal standing and no stable source of funds, the Commission for Relief in Belgium crossed national frontiers in the midst of the world's first global war, plunged into markets on two continents, and spent unheard-of sums. Nothing daunted Hoover. He seized control of railways, took over factories and warehouses, and commandeered five hundred Belgian canal boats. When the kaiser's armies occupied northern France, Hoover extended his realm there too. The CRB, said a British Foreign Office functionary, was "a piratical state organized for benevolence."[12]

Few people liked Hoover. He came across as an icy bully, utterly sure of himself, a fact machine, and almost always maddeningly right. British ministers are masters of deflection and demurral. Hoover would force himself into their presence, batter down their objections, and invariably get his way, which they greatly resented. His staff idolized him, for his energy, his equanimity in the face of hardships and danger, his utter fearlessness, and above all his clarity—the razor-like focus on the essential mission stripped to its bare particulars.

Hoover repeated essentially that same performance two more times, but on a larger scale. He was called back to the United States upon Wilson's war declaration and appointed "food czar," charged with feeding the troops, holding down prices, rationing domestic food, and managing the American food relief programs for Europe. Then, at the close of the war, he returned to Europe and ran a version of his Belgian relief program for the entire continent. Both those jobs came with wide authority, which he always exceeded. It is highly unlikely, for instance, that he had the right to trade Austrian locomotives for Galician eggs. But he did it, because it made sense, and no one dared tell him otherwise.

Hoover's casual assumption of godlike powers may have been a heritage of his mining experience. Managing a big mine in the prewar era entailed supervising large collections of hard men in remote areas without modern communications. The ideal manager necessarily had a deep knowledge of mining; immersed himself in the operation; made rapid, practical, and correct decisions; insisted on strict and unquestioning obedience; and was the final authority on everything. In other words, he was a lot like Herbert Hoover.

When Hoover returned to the United States in 1919, he may have been the most famous man in the world. Scores of high-level officials throughout the world carried grudges from his rough handling. There were murmurings that Hoover had overstated his accomplishments or given too little credit to his subordinates. But the achievements were real, and could be measured in millions of tons of food shipped around the globe, millions of people saved from starvation, and the near miraculous absence of scandal or fraud in all of his operations. It can also be measured in the grateful acknowledgments that flowed in from European potentates, and spontaneously from the people who had been beneficiaries. Hoover had his flaws, to be sure, but his performance had been magnificent. Experienced people, embittered by other well-meaning humanitarian interventions, were amazed. John Maynard Keynes, a man who had earned his cynicism, pronounced Hoover "the only man who has emerged from the ordeal of [the Versailles negotiations] with an enhanced reputation." Wilson's youthful, but politically sagacious assistant naval secretary, Franklin Delano Roosevelt, said Hoover "is certainly a wonder, and I wish we could make him President of the United States." His wife, Eleanor heartily agreed.[13]

There was no possibility of Hoover winning a major party nomination for the presidency in 1920, although it certainly crossed his mind. He had once joined a Republican club, but preferred to be called a "progressive." He foolishly allowed his name to be entered as a contender for the Republican presidential primary in California, against a native son, Hiram Johnson, and was roundly trounced for his effrontery. Given the unravelling of the late-stage Wilson administration, a Republican victory in the general election was an almost foregone conclusion, and Hoover eventually settled for secretary of commerce in the star-crossed and corrupt Harding administration.

As a commerce secretary, Hoover was almost comically hyperactive—anything to do with "commerce," he was sure, came under his authority. So he claimed the power to regulate airports, radio, and housing. Some of it he made stick: for example, by enforcing minimum lighting and runway standards for airports angling for US mail service contracts. His Bureau of Standards, "the largest research laboratory in the world" established a vast range of standards for weights and measures, highway safety, and model building codes. After a persistent campaign, he forced the steel industry to end its twelve-hour-workday schedules, and he mediated coal strikes. With his left hand, as it were, he ran a Russian food relief program, evolved a water management plan for western rivers, and pushed Colorado dam legislation through the Congress. His first year in office, he created the *Survey of Current Business*—a monthly compilation of business and financial statistics, which drew the envy of Keynes, the godfather of national economic reporting.[14] Most famously, when catastrophic floods devastated the Mississippi River valley in 1927, he replicated his virtuoso performances on the European continent, creating temporary housing for hundreds of thousands of people, raising funds (the federal government had none), and marshalling food supplies, as well as recommending comprehensive flood control measures.

Hoover's boss, through most of his tenure at the Department of Commerce, was "Silent Cal" Coolidge, the tireless preacher of smaller government and lower taxes, who had succeeded to the presidency on Harding's death in 1922, and won a full term in 1924. Their relationship was uneasy, to say the least. The larger-than-life Hoover draped himself all over Coolidge, once insisting on giving him fly-fishing lessons when Coolidge, who was no outdoorsman, had been cajoled by the press into an awkward attempt to fish with worms. Near the very end of his administration, Coolidge let slip his real opinion of Hoover, who was already a shoo-in to be his successor: "That man has offered me unsolicited advice for six years, all of it bad!"[15]

In the general election Hoover crushed the Tammany stalwart, Al Smith, an anti-Prohibition "wet" and a Roman Catholic to boot, picking up almost 59 percent of the popular vote and carrying the Electoral College by 444 to 87. He took up his duties in March 1929, with brimming hopes for a truly scientific, progressive administration, one that would seek to harness the best efforts of government, big business, and the voluntary sector to improve the nation's economic and social functioning.

The high point for Hoover's hopes came very soon after he took office, when he convened a group of leading demographers, economists, and social scientists to organize a committee on recent social trends. Their goal was to prepare a complete survey of Americans, "their economic well-being, their health and habits, their problems and hopes," which he planned to use to set a reform agenda for his second term. Two thick volumes were published in 1933 and 1934 containing thirteen monographs, ranging from population studies through specific topics like "Labor in American Life," "The Family," and "Arts in American Life."[16] But by that time Franklin Roosevelt was in the White House, and the aspirations of the Hoover administration and the pretensions of social scientists had been swept away by the global tsunami of the Great Depression.

Measures of national economic growth are usually presented in "real" numbers, stripping out the effects of price changes. Five percent nominal GDP growth, in a year when prices rise by 3 percent, is logged as 2 percent real growth. The economic collapse that commenced in mid-1929 was accompanied by a *downturn* in prices on top of the steep fall in GDP. From 1929 through 1933, measured annual GDP dropped by a crushing 45 percent, but that collapse had two components—a 26 percent drop in real output, and a 19 percent fall in prices (see Figure 3.2). Factoring out the change in prices, real GDP had recovered to its 1929 level by 1936, although that was hard to explain to the man in the street.

The name of Irving Fisher still lives in infamy. He was the famous Yale economist who confidently assured the world in 1929 that the stock market had reached "a permanently high plateau."[17] That lapse aside, he was one of the greatest of the moderns, arguably on a par with Keynes, and was one of the first to explicate the peculiar horrors of deflationary downturns. Debts outstanding do not adjust with changes in price levels. If both the price index and the wage index drop by half, workers' relative purchasing power doesn't change, but the weight of any preexisting debt will double. Deflation by itself isn't the problem, it is the mountain of unpayable debt that it leaves in its wake. Debt defaults cause a contraction of deposit currency, so the money supply shrinks and prices keep falling. The "swelling" dollar causes currency hoarding and further contraction. Or, as Fisher puts it in his 1932 book, *Booms and Depressions*:

> That the dollar disease—falling prices—is the main secret of great depressions is confirmed by the observations . . . that depressions last three or four times as long when prices are falling and are very short when, by some good fortune, an up-tide of prices intervenes.[18]

FIGURE 3.2: US REAL AND NOMINAL GDP, 1929–1937

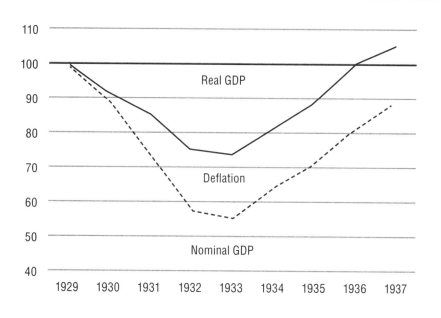

Source: BEA, NIPA Tables 1.1.5., 1.1.6, 1.1.9.

Fisher used the term "dollar bulging" to describe the *increase* in each dollar's purchasing power during a deflation. The flip side is that discharging a $1,000 home mortgage assumed in 1929 would require the purchasing power of $1,200 in 1933, even though most paychecks would have adjusted downward to reflect falling prices. Once underway, the deflationary process feeds off itself. Companies default on their debts, banks start reining in credit, production slows, and people are laid off.

The worst possible reaction to a deflationary depression, Fisher continues, is to "balance the budget," because it always entails reducing spending and/or raising taxes, either of which worsens the deflation, since it is extracting spending power from the economy. A 1932 Hoover tax increase came when "each dollar was already 60 per cent more burdensome to the debtor than in 1929." If the government had instead commenced borrowing and spending to reflate prices, it "would have lowered the *real* debts, public and private, by lightening the real dollar."[19]

The modern picture of a deflation is more complicated than Fisher's. Deflation increases the "real balances" of households; when prices fall, the cash in your cookie jar, and the national money supply, is worth more. But those happy effects are counterbalanced by the contractionary real burden of debt. In addition, if investors' expectations of future prices go down with no change in the interest rate, *real* interest rates will have risen. The Fed kept its interest rate low during the Depression, usually at or near 1 percent, but the real rate, taking into account the appreciating real value of the future payoff stream, was 10–12 percent or even higher. Investors were not fooled and real investment collapsed. In index numbers, gross domestic investment fell from 100 in 1929 to only 16 in 1932. Keynes, while agreeing with the Fisher deflationary story, points to its impact on investment as the real cause of the collapse.

Fisher's model of the monetary system was updated in the famous Milton Friedman-Anna Jacobson Schwartz *Monetary History of the United States* (1963). Total spending, and the price level, is a function of the money supply times its velocity, or annual turnover rate.* Friedman and Schwartz defined "high-powered money," or the monetary base, as gold, currency in the hands of the public, bank vault cash, and member bank deposits at the Fed. The deposit-reserve ratio was the money multiplier, since banks could lend multiples of their deposit base. Friedman and Schwartz's third variable of interest was the deposit-currency ratio. Before the advent of deposit insurance, people converted deposits into currency in times of crisis. While that increased the monetary base, the net effect was depressive because it lowered the volume of deposits subject to the money multiplier. Currency hoarding was rife in 1932 and 1933.[20]

Federal Reserve System rules required that member banks keep an average of about 10 percent reserves against their deposits. Such reserves, in the form of gold, cash, and good commercial bills, or, after 1932, government securities, were deposited with their respective federal reserve district banks, which in turn were required to hold 35 percent reserves against them. The Fed was not a passive player. If it actively supplied new reserves to the system, it could generate up to thirty times that much in new economic activity. (New Fed reserves will support approximately three times their amount in new member bank deposits, which in turn

---

* Velocity is often fairly stable, but can change rapidly. In the 1920s, velocity at New York banks doubled between 1925 and 1929, then collapsed to three-quarters of its 1925 rate in 1932.

could generate ten times the added deposit value in new lending.) That is the magic of the "money multiplier." And the Treasury and the Fed had the power to create as many new reserves as they pleased—for example, by running a budget deficit, financing it by selling debt securities to the Fed, and using them to support new deposits and more aggressive lending.[21]

Friedman and Schwartz are scathing in their treatment of the 1930s Fed, and suggest that the Fed could have arrested the deflation by injecting $1 billion or so of liquidity into the banking system. The time to do that was in 1930 when banks were displaying signs of weakness but before the deflationary momentum had really taken hold. They blame the failure to do so squarely on the Federal Reserve, and speculate that if Benjamin Strong, the savvy and charismatic president of the Federal Reserve Bank of New York had been alive—he died of tuberculosis in 1928—he could have substantially moderated the Depression's course.[22]

That is unlikely. It is far from clear that Strong was an inflationist, but even if he had been, he would have faced powerful opposition. The estimable banker Paul Warburg, for example, was convinced that easy money was the root of the crisis. Lester Chandler, an early historian of the Fed, calculated that in mid-1931, when the Depression was markedly deepening, only two district bank boards favored monetary easing, seven were completely opposed, and three were undecided.[23]

The deeply dug-in opposition to monetary solutions is illustrated by Oliver M. W. Sprague, arguably America's leading monetary expert. He was professor of banking and finance at the Harvard Business School and an adviser to both the Federal Reserve and the Bank of England. His 1910 *History of Crises Under the National Banking System* is a seminal work even today. The editors of the *New York Times* commissioned him to write ten long features in November and December 1933, an extraordinary allocation of editorial space that attests to Sprague's eminence. Sprague is very clear:

> I do not believe that the depression is primarily due to monetary causes, and . . . I hold that no monetary policy, however wisely formulated, is sufficient to bring about a trade recovery. We had sound money and no doubt about the security of the currency between 1929

and 1933. There was also during those years a plentiful supply of credit available at low rates and at intervals widespread confidence that prosperity was at hand; and yet the country drifted more and more deeply into depression. . . .

The essential problem, then, of trade recovery is to develop conditions under which industry will absorb the millions who are now out of work and find a continuing and profitable demand for a very much enlarged industrial output.

We already have a supply of money amply sufficient to support far more credit and currency than would be required with full employment, active business and a level of prices and money incomes far above those which obtained in 1926.[24]

From the modern perspective, the wrong-headedness seems striking, but is much less so from the vantage point of contemporaries. In the 1920s, Keynes was as yet little known in America—his *Treatise on Money* was published only in 1930—while Fisher's *Booms and Depressions* saw the light of day only in 1932. Practical bankers had long since internalized an informal collection of "sound banking principles" centered around a strong bias against deliberate inflation. (Just as *deflation* increases the burden of debt on borrowers, *inflation* reduces the value of loans on bank balance sheets. Farmers love inflation because it's easier to pay off their crop loans.)

The fear of inflation was not merely purblind, for it had centuries of history behind it: debasing the coinage was the surest sign of a failing king. Recent experience ringingly confirmed that ancient wisdom. The United States experienced a nasty deflationary crash in 1920–1921. The government deliberately did not reflate the economy, and there was a rapid recovery, followed by a sustained period of high-productivity growth. At about the same time, there was a depression in Germany, where the banking authorities and their masters in the government chose an opposite strategy. Instead of allowing the market to take its course, they reflated aggressively and created a legendary monetary disaster. In 1920–1921, the value of the Reichsmark (RM) fell from 320 DM/$1 to about 4 *trillion* RM/$1, not that anyone was really counting. Only a brave theorist could recommend a strategy of reflation; for an empiricist, the case was closed.

Timelines are compressed by historical memory. The American story therefore becomes: the stock market crashed, and the Great Depression ensued. But that's not how it appeared at the time. Professionals knew that the stock market was only a tenuous proxy for the real economy, which in 1930, seemed in pretty good shape. Yes, the big jump in automobile production in the first three quarters of 1929 was overdone, leaving the industry with at least an extra quarter's excess inventory. A slowdown, and a mild recession, was very likely in the cards, but there were still a number of positive indicators. The 1929 unemployment rate was down to only 2.9 percent, one of the lowest ever. Radio and talking pictures were still in a high-growth mode. Air travel was on the brink of a boom. Rural areas were still underserved by electricity. Older manufacturing cities had severe housing and infrastructure problems. Corporate profits were strong, and prices were well-behaved. A reasonable scenario looked like a modest slowdown to realign the real economy, followed by pickup in the financial markets.

And at first, that looked like what was happening. The indicators in the June 1930 *Survey of Current Business*, reporting April data, were below the unsustainable 1929 results, but felt like a pause, not a collapse. The *Survey* data are in the form of index numbers, taking average output for 1923–1925 as 100. In the red-hot spring of 1929, automobile production hit 188, but dropped off a cliff in November, December, and January (65, 36, and 83 respectively). By April 1930, however, production had recovered to 134, within a whisker of average production for all of 1929. Steel and pig iron had rebounded to their 1928 levels, although manufacturing as a whole had slipped to its weaker 1927 pace, and factory employment was down about 8 percent from 1929. The stock market seemed to be regaining some confidence: the index of industrial stocks had rallied to 279 in April, or just below the 286 average for April 1929.[25]

Hoover instinctively threw himself into heading off a recession, to the almost universal praise of businessmen. Starting in November 1929 and extending through most of 1930, he held rounds of meetings with businessmen, governors, mayors, private associations—whoever would listen—urging that businesses maintain wages and that states and cities accelerate their inventories of construction projects to stabilize spending and employment. Hoover has been criticized for not wielding the federal spending club, but that was a chimera. The federal government accounted for only about 4 percent of GDP, with much of it devoted to the military. The states and the cities were still where real spending power lay.

Hoover's grasp of the potential power of government spending to offset business downturns was proto-Keynesian, well before all but a narrow elite had heard of Keynes. His economic instincts, however, were waylaid by his scruples against expanding the federal government, his fear of inflation, and his emotional attachment to the gold standard. Beyond that, he had a cherished illusion that his successes in relief work stemmed from marshalling private resources, ignoring how much of his support came from allied governments.[26] None of his initiatives in coordinating private resources by businessmen, or by local governments, were successful. The best that can be said about his term in office was that he left behind a few promising interventional ideas, like the Reconstruction Finance Corporation, which was empowered to make federal loans to banks and businesses, that were later exploited, if only occasionally acknowledged, by the New Dealers.

T o the average person, the central reality of the Depression was the collapse of the job market. Cities were especially hard hit, since construction employment collapsed to less than 20 percent of its 1929 level, manufacturing employment fell by more than 40 percent, and hours worked were cut by 60 percent. In Chicago, a Census Bureau study found that 30.7 percent of male workers were unemployed in 1931. The toll was especially fierce among blue-collar workers: 40.4 percent of skilled workers were unemployed, 36.6 percent of semiskilled workers, and 57.2 percent of the unskilled. Proprietors, managers, professionals, and clerical workers fared much better—only 6.8 percent of clerks were unemployed in 1930, and 18.1 percent in 1931. In Philadelphia in 1936, 43.9 percent of unskilled blue-collar workers were still unemployed, and 29.2 percent of skilled and semiskilled workers. And the duration of unemployment continued to stretch. In Massachusetts in 1940, 62.6 percent of the unemployed had been out of work for more than a year. Detroit was especially hard hit because of its dependence on the automobile industry. The Ford payroll alone shrank from 128,000 in March 1929 to 37,000 by the summer of 1931.*[27]

The voluntary agencies that Hoover hoped would spearhead relief efforts were overwhelmed, forcing cities and states to assume financial responsibility for the growing armies of frightened people with paltry savings and little hope of getting another job. *Fortune* wrote in 1932 that "social agencies manned for the service of a few hundred families, and city shelters set up to house and feed a handful of homeless men were compelled by the

---

* Unemployment data were quite imprecise at this period. Definitions were still cloudy, and the numbers themselves were residuals of two much larger surveys—of the labor force participation rate and employment-to-population ratio. Small estimation errors in the large surveys can cause big swings in the residual calculation. Later scholarly estimates suggest that actual unemployment may have been three million or so higher than the *Historical Statistics* data cited above. (See Margo, "Employment and Unemployment," in the endnote for a good discussion of the data issues.)

FIGURE 3.3: PERCENT UNEMPLOYED IN UNITED STATES: CIVILIAN LABOR FORCE, CIVILIAN PRIVATE NONFARM LABOR FORCE, 1926–1941

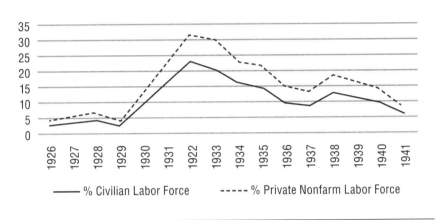

Source: *Historical Statistics*, Tables Ba 475–476.

brutal necessities of hunger to care for hundreds of thousands of families and whole armies of the displaced and the jobless." Hoover's response was to set up the President's Emergency Committee on Employment (PECE). The committee comprised a number of talented and sincere people, but it had no appropriation except for a small staff budget, and could be little more than a cheerleader for local efforts. Hoover even refused to consider an expanded federal public works program because he thought federal spending had already reached the limits of "financial prudence."[28]

National morale was an early casualty. Researchers in Chicago noted the despair of "middle-aged men, those between thirty-five and fifty-five, just at the time when their family responsibilities were greatest." "A man over forty might as well go out and shoot himself," one man wrote. There was a distinct tendency for employers to favor younger people, making some families dependent on their working-age children. Women had an easier time finding jobs than most men, because clerical and low-end service jobs, like cleaning, were not hit nearly as hard as factory or construction jobs, although the pay was lower.[29]

Time reported on "Doleful Detroit" in the summer of 1931:

Free lodging houses were opened by the city. Thousands of destitute families were put on the municipal relief list. The dole was advanced to

Pictures like this one of a smartly dressed man hawking a luxury car for $100 after being wiped out in the market crash were part of the iconage of the Depression.

its largest U. S. flowering. The fame of Detroit as a jobless haven spread and it was all the police could do to keep out the bums and tramps who flocked thither. Mayor [Frank] Murphy was hailed on speaking trips about the country as the only U. S. municipal executive who had really sponsored a practical, inclusive relief program. Last spring at the Progressive Conference in Washington he got a thunderous ovation from Senators and representatives who wanted the Federal Government to adopt the Detroit system on a big scale.[30]

Workers in extractive industries may have been hit even harder than urban manufacturing workers, since rural areas lacked even minimum support systems. Here is *Time* again, in that same summer:

As the summer wore on, on wore the sorrow of the Eastern soft coal industry. In West Virginia last week two renegade strikers, about to enter a mine in Putnam County, were killed by rifle fire. In Ohio a boy of 16 was fatally shot in a fight between workers and strikebreakers.

Acute suffering in Pennsylvania moved sad-eyed Governor Gifford Pinchot to appeal for Red Cross aid three weeks ago. American Red Cross Chairman John Barton Payne refused, regretted he could help only in disasters due to "act of God." Governor Pinchot sighed and went off fishing. The Press was full of horrid details of hungry Pennsylvania families awaiting eviction from squalid shacks; of small children, denied milk, eating dandelions.[31]

New York City had created a modestly effective relief agency during the 1920–1921 crash, and resurrected it in the summer of 1930. Within a month or so, the agency had employed more than 1,500 men doing part-time work in public parks, but with a budget of only $200,000, it was quickly tapped out. Seward Prosser, the head of Bankers Trust, agreed to head a committee of bankers and businessmen to finance relief efforts. They started with a goal of raising $150,000 a week to fund full-time jobs for 10,000 men at $3 per day for five months. When the first day's response was overwhelming, they doubled their fund-raising target, and quickly achieved it, mostly with large gifts. The Rockefellers put in $1 million by themselves. All told, they employed 38,000 people, with a peak of 26,000 in January 1931.

Prosser's committee was among the more successful of private-sector responses, but by early 1931 the tone in New York was turning nasty. There were fights in bread lines, people picked through garbage, the first apple sellers appeared on street corners. Demonstrating his tin ear, Hoover insisted that apple-selling attested to the power of American enterprise, and later claimed that many of the apple sellers "had left their jobs for the more profitable one of selling apples." By spring, the Prosser committee was running out of money. Private soup kitchens were feeding 85,000 a day—even though formerly employed people hated to be seen at soup kitchens. Prosser headed a successful legislative drive for government-financed relief, which was in place by the summer of 1931, although it was marred by petty corruption and political favoritism.[32]

For all their flaws, the relief efforts in New York were models of efficiency compared to what was going on in Chicago. The city had been effectively insolvent since the mid-1920s, and a committee of bankers had final say over its spending. But conditions were desperate; by the fall of

1931, there were 624,000 unemployed people in the city. And since Chicago was a major transportation hub, people were pouring into the city from rural areas. To make matters worse, following the polyglot pattern of Chicago's settlement, the city had proliferated small, usually undercapitalized, ethnically-oriented, mutual savings and insurance societies. By the time of Franklin Roosevelt's Bank Holiday of 1933, 166 of 199 of those smaller institutions had failed, taking the painfully accumulated savings of tens of thousands of families with them.[33]

Detroit may have been the worst-hit of major cities, as the automobile industry cut its vehicle production by more than half, while its revenues fell two-thirds in nominal terms (but about half in real terms). Senator James Couzens, formerly Henry Ford's right-hand man, tried to create a Prosser-like private relief agency, personally pledging $1 million, but the city's elite declined. A large share of the industry's workers lived in Detroit, but most of the plants were just outside the city limits, and so made minimal contributions to the tax base. When Henry Ford was approached for a contribution, he refused, insisting that "Endowment is an opiate of the imagination, a drug to initiative." Frank Murphy was the rare Irish politician who was not a crook, but his open-handed approach to the city's increasingly desperate unemployed quickly brought Detroit to the brink of insolvency. States were hardly richer than their major cities, and almost all had strict balanced budget laws, even as the tax base was dropping like a rock. Pressure was building within the Congress and among the public for a leading federal role in relief provision.[34]

The bread lines, the soup kitchens, the lines in front of relief agencies, and the squatter settlements that were spreading on city outskirts and in public parks offered a highly visible narrative for urban poverty, but rural areas may have been in even worse shape, although they mostly suffered out of sight.

Part of Hoover's childhood was spent on a prairie dirt farm, and he had a deep appreciation of the brutal uncertainties and bone-deep struggles of the farming life. American farmers had prospered during World War I, but global agriculture recovered quite quickly after Armistice Day, and American farmers found themselves badly overextended. Production and markets had returned to a better balance by the mid-1920s, but bumper crops at the end of the decade, especially in cotton and wheat, were playing havoc with agricultural prices. Paradoxically, large swaths of Midwestern and Southeastern farming country were hit with a years-long drought, so the farm sector was a starkly contrasting picture of either desertification—witness the massive dust storms immortalized by John Steinbeck in the 1930s—or silo-bursting overproduction.*

Hoover entered the White House with two priorities—agricultural policy and a tariff increase—and called for a special session to enact them. His Agricultural Marketing Act featured his characteristic mix of an activist federal policy, but with private-sector delivery. Pushing it through the special session was a stark demonstration of his power, as he disdainfully flicked away the special interests buzzing around the new law. The act followed a model much favored by agrarian progressives: the agricultural cooperative, like Wisconsin's very successful Land O'Lakes butter cooperative. Instead of individual farmers dealing with produce brokers, farmers sold their output to their own cooperatives, which then bargained with the buyers from a position of strength. The Federal Farm Board, chaired by the former chief of International Harvester, was empowered to lend the new cooperatives up to $500 million to buy and store produce.[35]

It was a fiasco. European economies turned down earlier than America's did, so export markets collapsed, even as one bumper crop after another buried the cooperatives' hopes of raising prices. In the summer of 1931, the Farm Board announced that the:

> government cotton report . . . provides total crop and carryover supply
> of more than 24,500,000 bales against probable world consumption of
> American cotton of 13,000,000 or possibly 14,000,000 bales. . . . Time
> has now come when cotton producers themselves must be called upon for
> immediate and drastic action. . . . Board suggests you immediately mobi-
> lize every interested and available agency including farmers, bankers,

---

* The "Dust Bowl" phenomenon was real in the sense of a decade-long 1930s environmental disaster, due to persistent drought and the lack of soil-conserving agriculture by small farmers. Outmigration increased sharply, but farmers were the least likely to migrate, and those that did mostly moved to adjoining areas. "Okie" migration to California was proportionally no greater than from other areas. Farmers who did move from the Dust Bowl in the main improved their economic position.

merchants, landowners and all agricultural educational forces to induce immediate plowing under of every third row of cotton now growing.[36]

Farmers naturally resisted such advice, and cotton slid to a "sickening" 4½ cents a bale. In hardly more than a year, the Farm Board wrote off $345 million of its $500 million revolving loan fund.

The situation was even worse in wheat:

> Disheartening to the Federal Farm Board were figures on the 1931 winter wheat crop, issued last week by the Department of Agriculture. Instead of reduced production, another bumper harvest. . . . As estimated by Government crop reporters on May 1, winter wheat would produce this year 652,902,000 bu. or 48,000,000 bu. more than last year and 105,000,000 bu. above the five-year average. The condition of the crop was 90% normal, a figure unequalled in a dozen years. . . . Plainly in the making was another thumping big wheat surplus to be piled on top of the 250,000,000 bu. of 1930 being carried by the Federal Farm Board.[37]

The Farm Board threw in the towel in the summer of 1931, dumping 257 million bushels of wheat on the market, crushing grain prices.

While farmers in one section of the country were smothered in abundance, farmers in the drought-struck regions could grow nothing at all. *Time* reported in 1931 that:

> 500 half-starved farmers and their wives raided the food stores of England, Ark. (pop. 2,408). Most of these hungry citizens were white; had been fairly prosperous husbandmen until last year. Their crops had been ruined. Their provisions were gone. Assembling in England with guns tucked in their clothes they demanded Red Cross relief. When this was not forthcoming because the supply of Red Cross requisition blanks had been exhausted, they threatened to loot the stores. One George E. Morris, attorney, tried to pacify them with a speech, was constantly interrupted by cries of: "We want food and we want it now! We're not beggars, we're not going to let our children starve." Women sobbed, children whimpered.[38]

A few numbers capture the violence of the transition. American farmers made modest, but real gains in the 1920s. From 1922 through 1929, the price index for manufactured goods fell by about 7 percent, while the farm products price index rose by the same amount. But farm prices collapsed in the first years of the Depression; by 1933 in constant 1929 units, it took 41 percent more farm output to buy the same unit of manufacturing output. Those ratios turned sharply after the New Deal support programs kicked in. By the end of 1933, the adverse farming terms of trade had improved to 1.2 farm units for one manufacturing unit, and by 1936, the ratio had dropped to 1.1:1.[39]

Hoover's second priority was an increase in tariffs, which in his mind was the second pillar of his agricultural policy—since dumping of overseas farm surpluses would undercut the farm cooperatives' ability to stabilize prices. Although Hoover did favor protective tariffs, he preferred them to be on the low side. He was also acutely aware that any tariff bill would trigger a riotous clamor of congressional special pleading. The linchpin of his proposal, therefore, was an expert trade commission with the power to change any tariff by 50 percent up or down. Congressmen were naturally bitterly opposed to losing control over the specific tariff impositions, but Hoover threatened to veto any bill without the Federal Trade Commission, and he got his way, although the legislation had to be held over for the 1930 congressional regular session.

The tariff bill finally passed on June 30 was the much-maligned Smoot-Hawley tariff that has often been accused of either triggering, or greatly worsening, the Great Depression. (One contemporary economist called it "an act of almost incredible economic folly.") American imports and exports both fell by about 40 percent in the two years after Smoot-Hawley took effect—but American GDP fell by 30 percent over the same time, so the collapse in trade was likely driven by the drop in incomes. A careful econometric calculation suggests that the Smoot-Hawley tariff caused a 5–6 percent increase in the relative price of imports, which would have reduced import volumes by about 4–8 percent. Since total imports were only about 4 percent of GDP, the impact was minor, probably within the margin of error for GDP calculations. The real impact on tariffs came from deflation, and had nothing to do with Smoot-Hawley. About a third of all tariffs were not ad valorem but were denominated in fixed-dollar terms, more or less as mortgages were. As prices dropped across the board, the fixed-dollar tariff levies raised many real import prices quite sharply, and reduced trade volumes about twice as much as Smoot-Hawley did.[40]

Hoover's presidency was effectively over by the end of 1931. He was booed when he attended a World Series game in October. There was a banking crisis (see below), and Hoover, as was his wont, called together a consortium of senior bankers to coordinate liquidity infusions. To Hoover's shock, the bankers were reluctant. They finally agreed to make an attempt, but only on the proviso that the federal government would step in if they failed, as they seem to have expected. When they did fail, Hoover created the Reconstruction Finance Corporation, empowered to provide long-term loans to banks and businesses. In principle, it was a good idea, and the Roosevelt administration made extensive use of it. When Hoover announced it, though, bankers were still in shell shock, and mostly used the loans to build up their reserves rather than to lend.

Through it all, Hoover remained steadfastly opposed to aid for the poor. Senator Robert Wagner said, "We shall help the railroad; we shall help the financial institutions, and I agree that we should. But is there any reason why we should not likewise extend a helping hand to that forlorn American, in every city and village in the United States, who has been without wages since 1929?" *Fortune* estimated that 34 million people had no income at all, stipulating that the count "omitted America's 11 million farm families, who were suffering in a rural Gethsemane of their own."[41]

Hoover's darkest moment was undoubtedly his fumbling of the "bonus marchers" convergence on Washington in the spring of 1932. Fumble it he undoubtedly did, but a recent Hoover biography paints a considerably revised picture of the incident, drawn mostly from primary sources. A Portland, Oregon, veteran's group, several hundred strong, made a pilgrimage to Washington in the hope of winning an early payment of a veterans' bonus due only in 1945. They steadily picked up additional marchers on the way, and by the time they arrived in the district, they were twelve thousand strong.

The proposal was passed in the House, but failed three-to-one in the Senate. (The country genuinely worried about the federal budget deficit. Most newspapers, and even the American Legion, were opposed to accelerating the payments.) A great portion of the veterans remained in Washington after the vote, probably because many of them had no place to go. The Washington police chief, Pelham Glassford, was an emollient presence, helping to arrange temporary living quarters, mostly with military equipment. (The army brass had nixed his request, but Hoover approved it over their heads, unbeknownst to Glassford.) Publicly, Hoover kept himself aloof, allowing the press and Glassford to infer that he was opposed to the whole enterprise.

By the end of July, the crowded camps had become pestilential and dangerous. Food and other donations were tailing off. The government had appropriated $100,000 for train fares home for indigents, without much effect. City officials decided they had to clear at least the downtown areas. There were confrontations and a melee. Glassford was knocked down twice by bricks, and another officer suffered a fractured skull.

Herbert Hoover's inability to connect with ordinary people was arguably a major cause of his failure as a president. When veterans marched on Washington to petition for early payment of their war-service bonuses, he maintained a cold distance in public, which eventually led to an unnecessarily violent resolution.

Twenty squatters surrounded four police officers in a confined space. The police shot one of them to death, and another squatter was seriously injured, as were three of the police.

The city requested federal troops. That was the first time Hoover became closely involved—after all, this was the summer of the party conventions. Douglas MacArthur, the chief of staff and a Hoover appointee, decided to lead the action himself—over the objections of Major Dwight Eisenhower, who thought it was a "highly inappropriate" role for the country's highest military officer. MacArthur wanted to declare martial law, because he was convinced that the marchers were radicals "with machine guns and other weapons" and that a Washington riot would "be a signal for a communist uprising in every major city." Hoover refused the request, limiting MacArthur's instructions to clearing federal property and returning the squatters to their camps. The biggest, and most unsightly, of the squatter camps was an 8,000-strong shanty-town on the muddy Anacostia Flats. Since it was not federal property, it was not included within MacArthur's remit. To make sure, during the day, Hoover twice renewed that order to MacArthur. MacArthur naturally ignored the president's orders, and fell upon the camp at night. No one was shot, as some press accounts had it, but the area was cleared with considerable roughness, including whacking with saber flats, and burning most of the tents and the squatters' pathetic belongings. MacArthur then reportedly apologized to Hoover and offered his resignation, doubtless in full confidence that it would not be accepted.

Surprisingly perhaps, the press reports and editorials supported the action. With his tin ear for public relations, Hoover still turned harshly on imaginary critics. He demanded a grand jury investigation of the alleged subversives and criminals in among the marchers. (No indictments were returned.) He also criticized Chief Glassford, because he led "mobs . . . to believe that the civil authorities could be intimidated with impunity because of attempts to conciliate by lax enforcement."

The more Hoover defended himself, the more the incident was used against him. It clinched the argument that despite all his talents, Hoover did not have the temperament for the presidency. Leave aside the fact that advance payments of the bonuses might have been a shot in the arm for the economy, since Hoover and the majority of the Congress clearly believed otherwise. But these were *veterans*, entitled to the presumption that they had served their country at great risk, and were now either in destitution, or on the brink of it. It was not the money, it was the lack of respect. Franklin Roosevelt, who had just been selected to run against Hoover in November said, "Well this elects me."[42]

───── V. THE BANKING CRISES OF THE GREAT DEPRESSION ─────

In their *Monetary History*, Friedman and Schwartz identified banking crises as a causal factor in triggering and prolonging the Great Depression. They identified four: the first occurred in the last quarter of 1930, and ended early in 1931. It involved a clutch of bank failures throughout the Southeast that ultimately spread to the very substantial Bank of the United States (BUS) in New York City, which had no connection with the federal government. A second crisis commenced in March 1931 and gathered momentum in the backwash from a banking crisis in Germany and Austria.

The third of the Freidman-Schwartz crises is dated from Great Britain's departure from the gold standard in September 1931, which led to sharp withdrawals from the United States (out of fears that the United States would also go off the gold standard). The fourth, and last, crisis dates from January 1933, when the stock of money fell precipitately, and there was a reversal in some hopeful 1932 indicators of recovery. As the crisis spread, state after state declared "bank holidays"—simply closing banks—to prevent a wildfire contagion. The motley state regulatory regimes, and the haphazardness of the rules for the various holidays pointed toward a dangerous fiasco, especially since it hit hardest in the awkwardly long interregnum between the Hoover and new Roosevelt administrations.[43]

The Friedman and Schwartz bank crisis story is one of their most plowed over. Spotting a "banking crisis" is like deciding whether Pluto is a planet or just a big asteroid. The *Monetary History* is a polemic, aimed at placing monetary issues at the center of macroeconomics, and its impact has been profound. But it was published a half-century ago, and scholars digging through its examples and case studies often come up with different conclusions. The bank crisis story is one of those instances, and there is now a near-consensus that all but the 1933 crisis were at most minor contributors to the Depression.

Bank crises can be categorized as either fundamental or contagion-driven. Fundamental failures are usually traced either to malign external forces like a crop-and animal-killing drought, or to management—they expanded too fast, had too little equity, or made foolish loans. True contagion-driven failures are rare, since they catch up solvent banks in a fear-driven run on banks in general. Over recent decades, a number of scholars—Charles Calomiris, Joseph Mason, Berry Wilson, Elmus Wicker, Barrie Wigmore, and Peter Temin—have mined the surviving loan books, accounting records, and local newspaper notices of the banks targeted in the *Monetary History* to divine their financial positions and to distinguish the fundamental failures from panic-driven ones.

The US banking system, in fact, was peculiarly prone to fundamental failure. Nine thousand banks failed between 1930 and 1933, but that was out of 27,000 banks. By contrast, Canada had four banks, each with branches throughout the land. Each was large, with a deep capital base, widely spread shareholders, and a diversified customer base, so bank failures in Canada were very rare. Most American states prohibited local branches of out-of-state banks, even through a locally incorporated subsidiary, and many maintained a strict unit-banking rule—no more than one office in the state. The absurd atomization of American banking was the work of the powerful agrarian lobbies. Farmers did not want to be at the mercy of distant urban behemoths for their banking. They wanted to bank with neighbors who understood farming cycles and would work with their customers in hard times. But that almost guaranteed that rural lenders would be thinly capitalized and failure-prone.

The economist Peter Temin has described the *Monetary History*'s banking crises as merely a continuation of a national shakeout of small banks. Between 1920 and 1933, 15,000 banks failed, half of them before 1930. Elmus Wicker's research shows that with a couple of possible exceptions, all of the banks failing in the first three of the *Monetary History*'s bank crises failed for fundamental reasons. In the first crisis, for example, many of rural banks fell in the wake of the collapse of an overleveraged financial conglomerate, the Caldwell Corporation, involved in banking, insurance, publishing, and other businesses. Local banks that held their bills and other securities were seriously hurt by their demise. A number

The American banking system was highly fragmented and failure-prone. A series of bank crises from 1930 through 1933 made images like this one a commonplace, especially in farm country.

of other rural banks in the Southeast failed because of severe drought conditions that ruined their customers. But in both the Caldwell and drought-region failures, there was no contagion of the kind associated with a classic "banking crisis." Although Friedman and Schwartz suggest that the rural bank failures triggered the collapse of the BUS, it is hard to show any important connections, and BUS's closure did not cause any disruption in the New York money markets. Its depositors subsequently recovered 83.5 percent of their money, albeit after a long wait.[44]

The second Friedman-Schwartz crisis, in 1931, is much the same tale. The failures were localized in industrial regions like Pittsburgh, Cleveland, Chicago, and Philadelphia, all of which had seen their business models shattered by mass factory unemployment. (See page 141, above, for the failure of Chicago's small language-centered banks.) The succession of bad news from Europe didn't help, of course, and currency hoarding*

---

* Currency hoarding lowers banks' deposits and so reduces the power of the money multiplier. Friedman and Schwartz criticize the Fed for not recognizing the impact of hoarding. But the impact of currency hoarding on the stock of money was first rose, which put pressure on the money supply. But with one or two exceptions, there were no panicky runs on solvent banks, and the banks that failed, like those in Chicago, were typically the doomed runts of the litter. The third Friedman-Schwartz crisis, that followed Great Britain's departure from the gold standard, came hard on the heels of their second one, and was triggered by European money traders selling dollars on the bet that the United States would follow England off the gold standard. When that didn't happen, the gold flows reversed. Hoover's new Reconstruction Finance Corporation (RFC) played a useful role in 1931, making some $643 million in loans to shore up struggling but solvent banks, although lending restrictions in its charter made it less helpful than it might have been. Hoover also pushed through much-needed legislation that substantially expanded the Fed's lending authority.[45]

The 1933 crisis was a different matter, and clearly qualifies as a panic, since it swept up solvent and insolvent banks alike. There was a wave of suspensions in Chicago in January, and in Idaho and Nevada in February. But the fulcrum of the panic was in Michigan. With the implosion of the automobile industry, the region's 1932 factory employment fell by about 70 percent. Deposits naturally fled the banks if only because people needed their money. Discussions with the state governor, the Fed, and the RFC on saving two flagship Detroit banks foundered in confusion. Neither the RFC nor the Fed was willing to take the lead in stabilizing the banks, and both pushed hard at the Fords to supply a new equity layer, which was refused. (The Fords later changed their mind, but the opportunity had passed.) The Michigan governor closed all the state banks on February 14, and extended the closure indefinitely on February 21. In the two and a half weeks before Roosevelt's inauguration, thirty more states declared bank holidays. The drama ended once the new president was inaugurated in March. One of his first acts, quickly ratified by Congress, was to declare a nationwide bank holiday, suspend gold payments, and create several important new channels for maintaining the liquidity of the banks.[46]

While the work of Temin, Wicker, Berry Wigmore, and others mostly settled the "fundamental versus contagion" question, a cottage

---

identified in the literature only in 1934, and would have taken rather longer to become part of a central banker's tool kit.

industry of economists, including Ben Bernanke, and especially Charles Calomiris, Joseph Mason, and Berry Wilson dug deeply into the available data and add considerable nuance to that conclusion. More important, they shed considerable light on *how* banking crises affect the economy.

A landmark 2004 paper by Calomiris and Wilson examined the behavior of New York banks from 1920 to 1940 in managing risk.[47] The authors defined three types of risk: capital risk, deposit risk, and asset risk. They suggested that a bank that raises its equity capital from a small group of insiders who are deeply informed on the business has less capital risk than a bank that depends on flighty public markets; insider capital would also likely be less dependent on dividends. Deposit risk, they argue, relates to the stability of a bank's deposit base: Is it all demand money or is it weighted to stickier term deposits? Is it tilted toward long-standing business relationship accounts or dependent on deposit rates? Asset risk relates to the proportion of loans to cash on the balance sheet, and the riskiness of the loans.

Calomiris and Wilson showed that over the twenty years examined, banks consistently tried to normalize their deposit risk at very low levels by managing their capital adequacy and their asset risk. In the boom years of the 1920s, they increased their asset risk—taking on more borrowers and new types of customers consistent with the exuberance of the times, and funded the loans by raising more capital. In other words, they increased both asset risk and capital but kept their deposit risk constant at a very low level. Conversely, in the 1930s, when risk-intolerant depositors greatly increased the likelihood of withdrawals, the banks responded by contracting their loan base sharply, and since they could not raise capital, cutting dividends to husband their funds. It took several years to recalibrate their loan and capital risks, but at the end point both capital and asset risk had been considerably reduced, while deposit risk had stabilized at about the 1920s level. Depending on individual banks' riskiness at the start of the process, the adjustments were more or less difficult, but the proof of the strategy is that almost no New York banks failed.

This is all very inside-baseball stuff, but it clarifies long-standing debates on the mechanisms of the Depression—whether it was fear of lending, the presence or absence of deposit insurance, or other factors that determined banks' behavior. In fact, bankers appear, first and last, to have focused on maintaining their deposits; to that end all the New York money center banks followed a similar pattern of reducing their capital and curtailing their lending throughout much of the 1930s.

The combination of debt deflation, falling prices, contracting banks, and the daily sights of the struggling unemployed inevitably affected morale. It was a setting in which the failures of two of the day's most admired businesses, rather like the failures of Lehman Brothers and AIG during the 2007–2009 financial crisis, was a grimly tolling "Nevermore," a funereal announcement that seemed to banish all hope. Samuel Insull's utility empire was put into receivership in April 1932, just a month after Ivar Kreuger, the famous "match king," put an end to his own life rather than face the demise of his global conglomerate.

—— VI. THE TWILIGHT OF THE GODS I: INSULL ——

S amuel Insull was never that interested in amassing a personal fortune. By the mid-1920s, the congeries of companies and properties that made up the Insull utility combine disposed of some $3 billion in assets, engaged in annual financing activities that routinely exceeded $500 million, and delivered to people in thirty-two states more electric power than was consumed in any other country in the world. Insull, indeed, had a claim to have invented his industry, much as John D. Rockefeller and Henry Ford invented theirs. An informal estimate of Insull's fortune in 1926, however, showed that he was not especially rich, with a net worth of about $5 million, including his home. Most of his $500,000 annual salary went to civic and charitable organizations, especially around Chicago.[48]

Insull's companies, at this stage, comprised four dominant entities—Commonwealth Edison, serving greater Chicago, possibly the most efficient electrical utility in the world; Peoples Gas, Light, and Coke Company, serving gas to the greater Chicago area; Public Service of Northern Illinois, a large regional; and Middle West Utilities (MWU), a giant holding company for hundreds of utilities extending from the East Coast to the Great Plains. MWU was built out with layers of subordinate, but very large, companies, like North American Power, Mississippi Valley Utilities, New England Power, and Central and Southwestern Utilities.

Insull kept control of his sprawling empire through the simple device of peopling the major subsidiaries' boards of directors with the same dozen or so men, usually with Insull himself in voting control. Besides Insull, the directors nearly always included his son, Samuel Jr.; his younger brother, Martin; two close financial advisers, Harold Stuart, his bond underwriter, and Walter Brewster, who handled stock issuances; plus a handful of key financial and engineering executives.

The holding company evolved as a favored form of organization because as an investment company, it did not fall within the reach of utility regulators. Eminently sensible regional power arrangements, for example, could not be accommodated by state-based regulation. But a holding company could assemble contiguous state-regulated companies in a pattern that made economic sense and contract to provide common generating, construction, and financial services. By the mid-1920s, as the basic utility infrastructure was being built out, the smart money was shifting from building competing operating companies, to buying and selling shares in holding companies.[49]

Insull had entered the holding company fray almost as an afterthought. His flagship Chicago and Illinois utilities were independent operating companies. But in his early career, he was often called upon by bankers to reorganize troubled utilities, and in 1902, to test the skills of Martin, he gave him one such assignment in Indiana. Martin turned out to be a brilliant, aggressive, if possibly risk-prone, manager, and by 1911 he had consolidated a swath of disparate companies into an attractive Midwestern franchise. Insull decided that he wanted to keep them, and a board member suggested the idea of a holding company. That gave birth to MWU in 1912, which by the mid-1920s, was the largest entity in the Insull group.

While the stacked pyramid of holding companies made excellent management and financial sense, it also opened the door to dangerous financial leverage. In Insull's case, by the time his pyramids imploded, his leverage (the ratio of borrowed money to cash equity) had ballooned to a highly dangerous 2000:1 (see the Appendix for details).

Insull had a mixed record as a holding company operator. On the positive side, his overhead charges were barely a tenth of those of other pyramids, like Electric Bond and Share Company, a Morgan controlled entity and a notorious cash stripper. (One of the attractions of holding company pyramids was that it was difficult for regulators to track the overhead fees through the multilayered corporate structures.) In the final days of his company, of course, when Insull was caught in a death-grip cash squeeze, he was as diligent as any other big operator in sniffing out pockets of cash to stave off his bankruptcy. Insull also gets credit for not—at least not until very late in the game—engaging in extreme pyramiding; even a very hostile post-Crash federal investigation commented that the use of pyramiding in the Insull group was "at a comparatively modest scale."[50]

On the other hand, Insull took full advantage of opportunities of the holding company structure to manufacture profits. Favorite gambits were trading illiquid securities between controlled entities at artificial values, accounting for stock or rights-based dividends, and depreciation accounting (see the Appendix for details).

Insull's tragic flaw may have been his infatuation with his legacy. He wanted to found a dynasty, even though his son, "Junior," a diligent and intelligent young man, was not of the same mettle as his father. A perfect retirement occasion came Insull's way in 1926, when he was sixty-seven. He had played a major role in laying out the plan for a modern British electrical grid, and was sorely tempted when the prime minister, Stanley Baldwin, invited him to return to his home country and head the effort to create the system. Junior had been ambivalent about committing to the company, and had Insull taken Baldwin's offer, he would have had to devise a more permanent, less family-oriented management structure. But first he consulted Junior, who told him that he now wished to inherit the dynasty.[51]

Insull was well aware that MWU was a cash sink. It required accounting gimmicks of all kinds to produce even a modest layer of reported earnings. Federal auditors found that its 1928 statements, for instance, were overstated by about $10.8 million. The biggest cash drain was the hefty dividends on a small mountain of preferred stock. Sometime in early 1929, Insull and Stuart developed a plan to refinance all the MWU outstanding preferred shares with a new security flotation of $145 million. That would buy out all of the preferred and provide an additional $20 million in free cash. There would be a preferred issue for $52.5 million, carrying a 6 percent dividend payable at the holder's option either in cash or rights to purchase common at highly favorable prices, and a common issue for $92.5 million, with all dividends in the form of stock purchase rights. This was very much a bull market offering, built on the premise that most investors would treat stock purchase rights as a superior currency to cash. If all investors chose the stock rights alternative, the cash flow savings would be $9 million a year.[52]

But there was a problem with the pricing. For the deal to work, the "highly favorable" price for converting the preferred to common had to be at least $200/share. But recent price slippage in MWU stock put them in a trading range well short of $200. (Investors presumably understood that MWU was a much dicier proposition than the three Chicago and Illinois flagship companies.) It was common practice in those pre-Securities Exchange Commission (SEC) days for investment bankers looking to sell an issue of common stock to first organize a pool to push up the share price. Insull's market operators therefore began a quiet purchasing and selling campaign under a variety of brokerage names, mostly with cash borrowed from banks. Within a month, MWU's stock price had jumped from 181 to 308. By comparison, the Dow Industrial index gained only 4 percent in that same month, while the Utilities index grew only by 6.5 percent. The rapid run-up in the share price generated its own momentum. Without any additional purchasing by the Insull pool, within another couple of weeks, the stock shot up to 364 by July 27. When Insull announced the refinancing a couple of days later, the stock hit a high of 492. A month later, when a broad distribution syndicate for the issue was announced, it went to 550.

The timing was awful. That glittering 550 price came in September 1929. Within a month, MWU shares slipped to $185. Heroic buying by the underwriting syndicate pushed them back to the 250–300 range. But the shares had been sold mostly by subscription, with monthly installment payments over a ten-or twelve-month period. As stock prices wavered, a number of subscribers defaulted, with their subscriptions being picked up by the syndicate, often with Insull companies stepping in as the buyer of last resort. Given the gyrations in the MWU stock price, of the shareholders who paid their subscriptions, nearly all opted for cash dividends. Add in the heavy bank debt incurred during the refinancing operations, and the whole exercise might well have increased the cash drain.[53]

The disappointing MWU refinancing was a double blow, for Insull was deeply worried about maintaining control of his companies. Sometime in 1928, Insull became aware that a shadowy combination of brokers and investors were building substantial positions in his three Illinois operating companies, which he considered an existential threat. With a little sleuthing, he learned that the combine was headed by Cyrus S. Eaton, a senior partner in Otis and Company, a Cleveland investment bank, as well as chairman of Continental Shares, a big investing and acquisition vehicle. Insull knew Eaton, but their relations were "never of a confidential character." He was a Canadian, forty-five years old in 1928, who had once run a modest gas utility for the senior John D. Rockefeller. He had taken a liking to the utility business, and moved to the United States to build a portfolio. Quiet and shrewd, by 1928 he controlled about $1 billion of gas and electric utilities, and had become enamored of the opportunities in the Chicago region. That same year, Insull and Eaton ran into each other on shipboard returning from London, and spent considerable casual time together. Since Eaton never mentioned his interest in Insull's businesses, Insull's threat antennae went on high alert.[54]

In earlier days, when Insull stock was still fairly closely held among customers and local investors, the tight insider director network made Insull's control position almost impregnable. But with a $3 billion capitalization, and national distribution of shares, a canny operator like Eaton could easily build a sufficiently large block of shares to cause no end of trouble. Insull's worries were magnified by his dynastic ambitions: a strong nonfamily ownership presence was likely to object to handing the company over to Junior.

Insull's defense strategy was to create a super holding company to acquire large blocks of shares in the Insull properties by buying them on the open market. Insull Utility Investments (IUI) was formed in December 1928. A year later, to fix a technical glitch,* Insull created a twin company, Corporation Securities Company (CSC) of Chicago, with the same mission. As Insull explained in his IUI announcement:

> I have felt for some time past that, in the interest of the various properties with which my name is associated, there should be some rallying point of ownership and friendship. So after consultation with my son and my brother, Mr. Martin Insull, and other members of my family, I decided to form an investment company to buy and hold securities generally, but more particularly to buy and hold the securities of the several companies with which my name is associated. . . . Such was the

---

* The IUI shares were subject to preemptive rights of existing shareholders to buy the new shares in proportion to their current holdings—an obvious oversight, since it could dilute insider control. CSC shares had no preemptive rights, and had the additional protection that voting rights were conferred by trust certificate upon named trustees for a term of years, whether or not the shares were sold. Later, as Insull's stock machinations became increasingly desperate, the two companies masked questionable operations through a kind of two-card monte—shifting shares back and forth between the two companies and subtly manipulating their values at each turn.

purpose for the forming of Insull Utility Investments, Inc. I wanted it, for all time, to be interested in the properties that it has been my privilege either to create, improve, or develop, and I thought I could trust the board of directors with the name of "Insull," that is of more consequence to me than anything else in the world.[55]

The IUI shares opened on the public exchanges in January 1929, almost perfectly timed for the wild run-up in the stock market. The Insull reputation was golden, and the new holding company looked like a money machine. By late summer, IUI shares had rocketed from $15 to $150. Between them, IUI and CSC took blocking positions ranging from 17 to 29 percent in the three Illinois operating companies, as well as a 28 percent share in MWU.[56]

Eaton waited until April 1930 before disclosing his intentions, using an intermediary, Donald McLennan, who was a cofounder of the Marsh & McLennan insurance combine, a friend of Eaton, and a director of Commonwealth Edison. By that time, Eaton had shifted most of his attention to steel: the previous December, he had announced the merger of a number of steel companies around the Great Lakes into Republic Steel, creating the third largest steel producer in the country. Insull was in London when McLennan made his probe, and after a great deal of cable traffic, Eaton, Insull, and their retainers met in early May 1930. Eaton, as Insull must have known, was under considerable pressure. He had been working assiduously to add the Youngstown Sheet and Tube Company to his steel combination, but Bethlehem Steel had just muscled its way in as a suitor, and Eaton needed to shore up his liquidity for a bidding war.[57]

Famously, Eaton opened the meeting by proposing a combination of the Insull and Eaton utility holdings. In Insull's account, "Mr. Eaton . . . assured me . . . that as long as I was in control of the management of the three operating companies, any stock that he represented would be voted for me." Insull's biographer, Forrest McDonald, based on the notes taken at the meeting, and extensive interviewing of still-living attendees, calls this an "offer . . . to consolidate all his holdings with those of Insull, under Insull's exclusive management, no strings attached." Even assuming that is what Eaton said, it is hard to believe. It is true that Eaton didn't manage any of his acquisitions, and that he genuinely admired Insull. But he was an activist investor, a prototype of, say, a Carl Icahn, and his hands-off promise would be good only so long as the companies prospered. Tom Girdler, Eaton's hand-picked chairman of Republic Steel, said that other steel company executives "were simply scared to death of Eaton."[58]

Insull wasn't interested in a combination, and offered to buy all of Eaton's holdings—160,000 common shares distributed among the three target companies, with just over half of them in Commonwealth Edison. The offer was for $56,000,000, or $350 per share, about a 12 percent premium to the current market. (Insull share prices held up well during the first stages of the crash.) Eaton wanted $400 a share, and threatened to create an investment banking syndicate to sell off the shares to any comers, which played on Insull's aversion to allowing the big New York banking houses gain a foothold in his business.[59]

Negotiations broke off at that point, but McLennan continued to advocate for a deal, and finally, in June, Insull agreed that he would purchase all of Eaton's stock, at the $56 million price, payable $48 million in cash and $8 million in the common stock of the two holding companies, IUI and CSC. Stuart was in London, and Insull pointedly did not inform him of the deal in advance, since he would have objected to any such commitment prior to locking up the financing. The terms were agreed on June 2, and the deal closed on June 9. IUI and CSC were each obliged for half the payments. While the stock transferred immediately, the cash was paid in three installments, $10 million on closing, $14 million on July 9, and $24 million on October 9.[60]

It took considerable scrambling to marshal the cash. Between them, IUI and CSC took out short-term bank loans to cover $7.25 million of the $10 million first installment. For the July 9 payment, IUI borrowed $28 million from an MWU $50 million gold note flotation, and used half of it for the Eaton payment, and most of the rest to pay off bank loans. The $24 million final payment due October 9, 1930, was daunting, since a first $10 million installment payment on the MWU gold note was coming due, and there were no more available MWU gold note proceeds.[61]

Insull tried to raise the final installment in the public markets, but a summer offering of 600,000 IUI common shares priced at a substantial discount fizzled. CSC ended up taking nearly half the issue, which avoided embarrassment, but produced no new cash. In August, Halsey,

Stuart and Company attempted to syndicate $40 million in CSC gold bonds, but the tepid market forced a reduction in the offering to only $30 million. To make up for the shortfall, Insull borrowed $10.25 million from a consortium of banks, including, to his chagrin, several New York banks. To scratch out more collateral for loans, Insull bulked up IUI's balance sheet with $16.6 million of Insull company shares, purchased from one of the group's employee benefit funds. The payment was at market value, but the consideration was a goulash of new IUI shares, "assumptions of obligations," and other paper, but only $5.9 million in cash.[62]

By such expedients, the final payment to Eaton was made on time. Eaton was a considerably richer man, while Insull was left under a severe cash strain. To make matters worse, the prices of Insull securities were dropping rapidly. Although Insull stocks had basically held their prices during the first half of 1930, the second half was a disaster. IUI and CSC taken together closed their years with an unrealized market value loss of more than $100 million. Euphoria briefly returned when good year-end earnings reports created a bounce-back to early 1930 prices. It was a mirage. Public utilities continued to outperform industrial companies, but as the Depression ground on, Insull shares were on a relentless downward slide.[63]

The long American boom that had started in 1923 had dimmed memories of difficult times. And Insull had had a smoother ride than most. Even during the banking crisis of 1907, he had ready access to the London money market. He hadn't blinked at the big cash commitment for the Eaton purchase because the public markets adored his securities. By late 1930, however, capital markets were firmly closing to even the most blue-chip borrowers—even to Insull.

MWU, IUI, and CSC went into receivership in April 1932. Between them, they had $84.1 million in bank debt, almost all of it in demand notes, and all of it requiring collateral of 150 percent of outstandings, or about $120 million. Since all three were holding companies, their primary assets were shares in other Insull companies. MWU held securities with a book value of $299 million, about three-quarters of it in Insull paper; the receivers marked its recoverable net worth down to $30.9 million. IUI's book value was $259 million, again almost all in Insull securities, which was marked down to $27.5 million. CSC had a book of $142 million,

FIGURE 3.4: ANNUAL US CORPORATE CAPITAL FLOTATIONS, 1926–1936

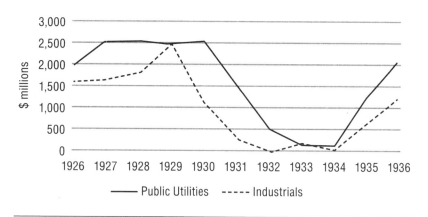

Source: Wigmore, *The Crash and its Aftermath,* Appendix Table A.26, 659–666.

which was valued at $13.3 million. Forrest McDonald seems to fault the banks for not seeing Insull through, but they had no choice—$84 million was a lot of demand loans, especially without collateral. The economy did not tick up until a full year after the Insull companies entered receivership; the public markets remained tightly shut until 1934, and didn't truly recover until 1936.[64]

A number of smaller Insull companies followed the big three into bankruptcy, but with few exceptions the operating companies survived handily. One study shows that of 120 Insull companies with securities held by the public, only 23 lost any appreciable amount of money, and most of them were intermediate holding companies or trading subsidiaries. Commonwealth Edison bonds, for example, never dropped below 90, and all were paid off on schedule. Even the great majority of the MWU operating companies—which, in the last days of Insull's struggle for solvency were stripped of almost all their cash or salable securities—survived intact without service interruptions or other calamities. The losers were primarily financial players and naïve investors. Power customers saw little disruption. A careful 1962 analysis suggests total losses to the public of about $634 million, or about a quarter of the 1929 capitalization.[65]

Insull would almost certainly have survived if he had resisted the Eaton purchase. Virtually the entire cash payment, whether at first or second remove, was financed by impatient demand-note bank debt. Fending off Eaton was also a prime motive for the formation of the two investment companies, IUI and CSC. Taken together, they issued $81 million in gold bonds and debentures and $206 million in various preferred and common shares. The bonds and debentures all defaulted after just a few payments, and the shares were pure water. Absent the investment companies, Insull might have followed a more cautious path in the MWU refinancing, spurned the Eaton probe, and managed his cash position more vigilantly. The Depression was hard on everyone, but the core of the Insull system was strong enough that it should have survived with its stellar operating record intact.

Insull was summarily removed from operating control of his companies in early June, not quite two months after the first receiverships. He quietly sailed to Europe, even as pressure built for criminal trials in the United States. Junior visited him in Paris in the fall, and suggested that he stay abroad in a country without extradition treaties until the blood-lust for his scalp abated. Insull chose Athens, where a court had ruled against extradition, and he spent much of a year laying out a modern electrical power plan for the government. The new Roosevelt administration pressured the Greeks to give them Insull, to the point where Insull embarked on a freighter to seek asylum elsewhere. At American prodding, however, the freighter made a "repair" stop in Istanbul, where the police took him into custody for extradition. When he was arrested in America, he couldn't make bail until friends passed the hat. [66]

Insull went on trial in Chicago in October 2, 1934. It lasted six weeks. Almost every offense charged involved detailed issues of accounting and disclosure, that even the prosecutor's team, not to mention the jury, often had trouble getting right. Charges that Insull had engaged in large-scale embezzlement hardly squared with the fact that he had almost no money; his entire fortune was in Insull holdings, and he probably lost more than any individual investor. The chances of conviction, however, still seemed good—juries were not in a mood to give tycoons a break. But on the first day of November, Insull took the stand and "wove a spell" around the jury, explaining what he had done in Chicago, the intriguing technical issues, the shift to steam turbines, his mastering of the economics of the business, his sadness at the ending. The case went to the jury two weeks later. As soon as they had been sequestered, the jurors took a poll and found that they were unanimously for acquittal. For form's sake they lingered in the jury room for two hours, so they wouldn't be accused of being bribed.

Insull had two more trials—one in Washington, DC, alleging embezzlement by him and Martin, in which they were quickly acquitted, and a federal proceeding, in which the judge directed a verdict for Insull after hearing the prosecutor's case. Insull returned to Paris, where he lived quietly and thriftily. In July 1938, he was found dead in a Paris subway, apparently the victim of a heart attack.

Insull was a great entrepreneur, and by no means a crook—though for 1920s financiers, noncrookedness was not a high bar. The intercompany churning of thinly traded securities to generate ersatz mark-to-market profits was deceptive, as was the skew of income statements toward noncash earnings. The understating of depreciation, or the shameless bulling of the MWU stock price to ease its refinancing were all crass attempts to mislead investors. Some of the accounting gambits were practiced so assiduously that they might have supported a common law charge of fraud. But the Insull group was hardly the only conglomerate that engaged in such practices—the Pecora hearings disclosed roughly similar practices at most of the major banks.[67] Accountancy was very much in a state of flux: the definition of generally accepted accounting standards had to await the New Deal security markets reforms. Quiet syndicates formed by insiders to bull share prices was something that gentlemen did. The Arthur Young accountancy had signed off on all of the gambits employed by the Insull group.

A final note of poetic justice. Cash-rich after his deal with Insull, Eaton engaged in a grueling two-year-long battle to become a top-tier player in the steel industry, and ended up losing everything. Continental Shares, his primary acquisition vehicle, was a publicly traded investment company; today we would call it a private equity fund. Founded in 1926, it was capitalized at $150 million, and was widely held. Eaton seems to have learned how to ruin a company at Insull's feet. Having overextended himself in his steel wars, Eaton resorted to heavy bank loans collateralized by his stock holdings. By June 1932, the Continental Shares stock price had fallen from $78 a share to just 25 cents, and the bank creditors wound it up some months later. In 1932, however, Eaton was only forty-nine, and unlike Insull, had time for a comeback. He quietly resumed his banking activities in 1938, and in 1961, *Fortune* listed him as one of America's top tycoons, with a multibillion empire in mining, steel, and banking, and a personal net worth of $100 million.[68]

Ivar Kreuger, the Swedish "match king," committed suicide on March 12, 1932, within a few weeks of the collapse of Insull's empire. Kreuger's death left his murky collection of hundreds of companies in dozens of countries to the tender mercies of receivers. The final report, prepared by the accounting firm Price Waterhouse, was scathing:

> We do not think more need be said about these published accounts except that the manipulations were so childish that anyone with but a rudimentary knowledge of bookkeeping could see the books were falsified. . . . Entries in its general books were palpably false, few entries even looking reasonable on the surface. [69]

Childish the Kreuger books may have been, but from 1918 until its collapse, Kreuger had raised $771 million, with the sources and dispositions at book value as shown in Figure 3.5.[70]

At fair market values, the Price Waterhouse team estimated that available assets were impaired by $250 million, or about 30 percent of its stated book value. As a Price Waterhouse partner explained it to a Senate investigating committee:

> Company A may show that it has received 200,000,000 kroner of earnings which are fictitious. Out of that it pays a dividend to another company. And that company receives it in cash, possibly, and has no good reason to doubt that it has perfectly good earnings in its hands. But when you trace the whole chain you will find that that 200,000,000 kroner is probably a return to it of 200,000,000 kroner that it paid for an investment in another company possibly as an income that comes out of another company as a dividend.[71]

FIGURE 3.5: IVAR KREUGER: CLOSING FINANCIAL POSITION, AT BOOK VALUE, 1932

Sources	$ [millions]
Stock and Bond Issues	566
Bank Loans and Credits	164
Revenues and Other	40
Total	771

Uses	
Interest and Dividends Paid	165
Kreuger Appropriations, Net	107
Marketable Securities	279
Subsidiary Operations	220
Total	771

The report revealed that "serious irregularities had extended back for at least 15 years," that "large sums of money had been appropriated and concealed," and that "fraudulent practices assumed large proportions in 1923 and 1924 and continued thereafter." Such frauds were possible, they concluded, only because of:

> (1) the confidence which Kreuger succeeded in inspiring, (2) the acceptance of his claim that complete secrecy . . . was essential to the success of his projects, (3) the autocratic powers which were conferred upon him, and (4) the loyalty or unquestioning obedience of officials, who were evidently selected with great care (some for their ability and honesty, others for their weaknesses).[72]

Ivar Kreuger was a strange compound of business titan and confidence man, and could have been a success in either persona. He was born in 1880 to a large Swedish family headed by a minor executive in a match factory. By the time he reached young adulthood, Ivar was physically imposing with an arresting personality, able to hold forth on almost any topic in five languages—and still come off as self-effacing. No one could have guessed that his easy charm was the product of many hours preparing material for social events, and studying the people he wanted to impress. The brilliance wasn't faked, but like a professional athlete, he assiduously polished his talents to the highest sheen and displayed them with the instinct of a showman. When conducting major business negotiations, Kreuger almost always appeared without lawyers or accountants, without papers or notes, exhibiting casual mastery of every nuance of a business, every number in a pile of balance sheets, waiting serenely as his counterparties fumbled through their files to stay abreast.[73]

He was a legitimate millionaire by his early thirties. After graduating from engineering school, Kreuger went to America to learn modern skyscraper engineering. Talking his way into a low-level position with Manhattan's largest construction company, he worked on the Macy's building, the Metropolitan Life tower, the Flatiron Building, and the Plaza and St. Regis Hotels, along the way spotting and fixing critical flaws in the building's designs and techniques. He moved to South Africa to work on the Carlton Hotel, then the world's largest building, and later briefly joined the Transvaal militia, before embarking on a "multiyear bender" through a large swath of the world. Returning to Europe, he formed a shoestring partnership with an architect, Paul Toll, in a highly successful design and construction business, working throughout Europe. Their major selling point was guaranteed on-time performance, with heavy penalties for failure. Toll was a fine architect and Kreuger a master salesman whose American experience had given him a thorough grounding in modern construction management. The business was a resounding success, and the two quickly built an international practice, including in the United States, where they built the prize-winning football stadium at Syracuse University.[74]

A Swedish banker, impressed with the success of Kreuger & Toll, offered to back them in any business of their choosing. Kreuger picked matches, while Toll opted out, choosing to work full time on the firm's construction business. Matches were something of a Swedish specialty because of their abundant forests, and Swedes had invented the strike-on-the box safety match. Employing tactics both fair and foul alike, including "sweetheart" deals with the government, Kreuger crushed his competition and created a Swedish match monopoly that at least appeared to be making a steady profit. His model, he frequently said, was John D.

Rockefeller's oil monopoly. Matches and oil, he argued were low-margin businesses that could become profitable if and only if one could control the entire market.[*][75]

Kreuger made a trip to the United States in 1922, to sound out the prospects of creating a US match monopoly, and was disappointed to discover that Americans did not favor monopolies. But he realized that no country could rival the United States in capital raising capacity, so he decided to raise American capital to finance match monopolies abroad. In conjunction with the investment banker Donald Durant, of Lee, Higginson, Kreuger worked out a strategy of raising money on Wall Street to finance cash-desperate governments in return for long-term match monopolies. It was sweet music to Lee, Higginson partners. Their firm was an old Yankee establishment that yearned after a presence in international lending, then dominated by the Morgan bank.[76]

Lee, Higginson arranged an informal road show for Kreuger, exposing him to a broad segment of the financial community—and he wowed them, with his vast frame of reference, with his diffidence and apparent modesty, with his intimate knowledge of European corridors of power, but most of all with the regular 25 percent dividend paid by his holding company, Kreuger & Toll, and the 12 percent dividend paid by his manufacturing company, Swedish Match. It was an easy step from there to a $15 million dollar gold debenture floated by a new company, International Match, controlled by Ivar Kreuger. It was money that Kreuger badly needed. Parts of the whopping dividends paid out to investors were paid from bank loans, and the banks were dunning him for repayment. His match operations were running losses, but he had hidden them in off–balance sheet "investment" accounts.[77]

Kreuger had carefully prepared for his American windfall by setting up a circle of companies in Sweden, Switzerland, and Liechtenstein,

---

* A "genius businessman" Kreuger may have been, but he was fundamentally mistaken about the commonalities between oil and matches. Rockefeller's dominance in oil was based on economies of scale. The capital required to build a global oil business was enormous, but it created great market efficiencies, allowing Rockefeller to steadily *reduce* the price of oil to a level where smaller companies could not compete. The capital required for a match factory, however, was modest enough that a regional player could compete as well as a national one—which is why match manufacturers needed a government franchise to make reliable profits.

and then creating a string of accounting entries to spirit the $12.2 million net proceeds of the American flotation into the dark recesses of a secret Liechtenstein entity—Continental Securities, with a single employee dedicated to doing exactly as he was instructed by Kreuger. Kreuger diligently avoided consolidating the accounts of his companies and spread financial reporting among multiple national jurisdictions. His cover was almost blown at the very start. Well before the American debenture sale, an accountant from the Swedish Bank Inspection Board had figured out what Kreuger was up to and wrote a damning report. Amazingly, the Swedish banks who were lending to Kreuger, and making substantial profits from his stream of dividends, collectively buried it.[78]

Match monopolies were old hat in Europe. France had created the first, in 1872, and at least a dozen countries had followed suit. Although Kreuger easily enamored American investors, in the real world in Europe he faced a host of entrenched politically connected competitors. His first breakthrough came in Poland. Its government was chaotic, and the finance minister was desperate for a western loan. The official terms of the Polish deal were that the government would grant Kreuger a match monopoly in return for a $6 million loan that carried an interest rate calculated to equal the royalties expected from the match monopoly.[79]

But there was also a secret deal, by which Kreuger promised to deliver the Polish government $25 million, at a usurious 24 percent interest. That deal was closed in July 1925, and it required that the $25 million be disbursed in two tranches, one of $17 million in October, and a second for $8 million the following July. The contract also provided that the match monopoly would be administered by a new Dutch company, Garanta, controlled by Kreuger, but with Polish representation. Garanta, like Continental Securities, was intended as a black hole, an invisible cash sink solely at his disposal. Kreuger had actually used much of his first Lee, Higginson underwriting to speculate on foreign currencies, and had done quite well. Later he had taken big losses, but covered them by transferring them to Garanta. That didn't help his cash flow, but it placed the misadventures beyond the reach of pesky accountants.

Even Durant, who usually acted as Kreuger's enabler, had problems with the second Polish deal, because Kreuger refused to show him the contracts or explain how they worked. But Kreuger's reputation as a financial magician was rising on Wall Street, in part because of use of groundbreaking financial instruments—securities that morphed between debt and stock, or had special dividend rights or conversion rights, or embedded options. They may have been mostly worthless, but investors loved them, especially when they didn't understand them. But they always included highly favorable terms for the issuer and its bankers. Just the kind of instrument that makes investment bankers smile. Durant swallowed his doubts, and yet another Kreuger placement, managed by Lee, Higginson, went on the market at a premium—and sold out in a trice. Poland got its $17 million first installment, and the thumpingly high interest payment was duly received every quarter at Garanta. Kreuger's legend grew.[80]

Durant was entitled to his doubts. For all he knew, Kreuger might have simply invented the second Polish deal and plunked the offering proceeds into the recesses of Garanta at his own disposal, using part of it for speculation and the balance to pay the interest, while counting on future raises to pay off the principal. By this time, Kreuger had thoroughly suborned the Ernst & Ernst accountancy manager who supervised the group's audits. He never pressed for detail on Kreuger's secret companies, and on his own motion occasionally changed financial reports to comport with previous claims by Kreuger.[81]

By 1927, Kreuger was a renowned mogul. His match operations extended around the world, and he was the major producer of match machinery. As International Match's stock price rose to the stratosphere, he used it as a cheap currency to buy businesses throughout the globe—in mining, real estate, timber and paper products; a big stake in L.M. Ericsson, the Swedish phone giant; even in the film industry. It was Kreuger who discovered Greta Gustafsson in a hat shop, and helped her become Greta Garbo. While he was something of a health nut, and abstemious in food and drink, he lived lavishly, with large apartments in major cities, always staffed and prepared for a flying visit. He liked fast cars and boats, and built a stunning headquarters in Stockholm named the Match Palace. After the early death of a childhood sweetheart, he never married, but apparently had discreet liaisons with several charming and talented young women.

But he never lost his confidence-man instincts. When Percy Rockefeller, one of old John D.'s nephews and a director of International Match, visited Kreuger in Stockholm, he was given a lavish party at the Match Palace with a substantial fraction of the European ambassadors in attendance. Rockefeller was duly impressed, and reported to fellow directors that Kreuger was "on the most intimate terms with the heads of European governments," and that they were "fortunate indeed to be associated with" him. The "ambassadors," however, were actors, carefully rehearsed to dazzle innocents like Rockefeller.[82]

If any single deal catapulted Kreuger into the global business stratosphere, it was the theft of French bond business from under the nose of the Morgan bank, who had treated European finance as a family heirloom. Raymond Poincaré had just been reinstated as the prime minister of France, and was desperate for money. France already owed the Morgans $100 million, at 8 percent interest. Poincaré and Kreuger were friends, however, and they worked out a plan for a massive $75 million loan from International Match with a forty-year life at only 5 percent interest, plus a stream of revenues from a new French match monopoly. The actual proceeds to the French would be $70 million, with $20 million coming from International Match reserves and $50 million from placing a typically innovative Kreuger hybrid bond. The securities Kreuger sold in America went out at 98.5, which gave him a $2.5 million margin over the money he delivered to France. In addition, at payoff, the French would owe $75 million, not $70 million, which was more potential margin for Kreuger. One hitch was that the French socialists objected to the monopoly—it would have disturbed a politically connected monopolist already in place. Kreuger nimbly changed it to a monopoly on match equipment sales in France, priced at a premium that would produce about the same income.[83]

Kreuger struck another blow at the Morgan empire in the summer of 1929, by committing to make a $125 million loan to Germany, subject to a fifty-year match monopoly and German participation in an international debt-restructuring process. Jack Morgan was shocked to see that Kreuger had winkled the biggest international financial transaction in history from under his nose. Germany promptly met all of Kreuger's conditions, and Lee, Higginson pointedly excluded the Morgans from the securities syndicate.[84]

Kreuger's German-linked bonds went to market in the fall, just as markets were turning unusually skittish. Durant was confident that

Kreuger-sponsored securities would always sell, because of the magic of the name, but he thought that any further placements would have to be delayed until the markets recovered. The Kreuger sale was closed on Wednesday, October 23, the day before Black Thursday—the first day of the dizzying crash in stock prices and the occasion of the ultimately unsuccessful intervention by Richard Whitney and the bankers' pool. The bankers in the Kreuger syndicate had a collective attack of angina. Although they had already received customer commitments for the securities, they expected widespread defaults. Kreuger-sponsored securities went out only on a "firmly underwritten" basis. The bankers had already written their checks, and would end up swallowing whatever amount was left unsold.[85]

Ironically, this was the same week that *Time* featured Kreuger on its front cover, reporting breathlessly that when two US visitors missed seeing "the countryside aglow with Sweden's famed roses," Kreuger invited them to one of his country houses, which displayed "everywhere rose-bushes in full bloom"—supplied just for the occasion from a Stockholm hothouse. The encomium ended with a quote from the match king: "There is not a single competitor with sufficient influence upon the different markets to cause us any really serious harm. No market is sufficiently significant to be of importance to us. The reason is that the whole world is our field."[86]

The stock market was closed the Friday and Saturday after Black Thursday—in the mostly paper-and-pencil accounting environment, the day's price swings had left a mountain of incomplete transactions to work through. To this point, Kreuger had been mostly incommunicado, while affecting a Zen-like calm with his closest associates. He broke his silence on Friday afternoon, with a cable to Lee, Higginson:

I am very sorry that our issue seems to have come at a very unlucky moment. We are very anxious that the syndicate . . . will not have reason to regret their action, and we are also anxious not to overload the American market with our paper. We have therefore arranged with a Swedish syndicate to offer to take over, on December 31, 1930, up to half the amount of such debentures as the American syndicate has acquired. This will be done at the acquisition cost to the American syndicate. We expect to receive notice no later than December 15, 1930, of the extent to which the American syndicate wishes to avail themselves of this offer.[87]

The bankers swooned. Durant announced the offer to the syndicate, adding that it "is without precedent . . . [and] shows conclusively the breadth of the man." Virtually all the syndicate members rushed to assure Durant of their intention of holding on to the securities, as Kreuger knew they would. The offer, indeed, should be in the Hall of Fame of market ploys. In effect, it was a free putback at their own price, and the offer was good for more than a year. Since the overwhelming sentiment on Wall Street was that the market would quickly recover, there was little risk in waiting, and a quick putback might cost them potential profits. The calmness, the "almost casual" way the offer was framed, added to the effect. Kreuger, investors believed, had nearly unlimited resources—how else could he outbid Jack Morgan for major country bond business? The syndication was for only $28 million, half of that, to the Kreuger of the carefully crafted legend, was chump change. In fact, at the end of 1930, when he was very hard up for cash, Kreuger had to pay $4.4 million in put settlements. Characteristically, he sent Durant $5 million to settle the accounts, and told him to hold the extra $600,000 for the time being, since he "didn't need it."[88]

Some bankers, not least at the Morgan bank, wondered how Kreuger could dispose of so much money. Yes, he controlled perhaps two-thirds of the world's match industry—his strategy of buying monopoly privileges from national governments had been very successful. But matches were a low-margin business, and his global sales were almost certainly less than $150 million. Stripping out misleading items, like "profits" that were just dividends paid by one company to the other, his match companies still reported $30 million in clear profits, which would have required a 20 percent headquarters margin on global sales, which should have been impossible. When pressed on the issue, Kreuger airily dismissed it. Of course matches didn't earn that much, he said, but both the match companies had large investment portfolios and had done very well on "speculations."[89]

Bravado aside, Kreuger was facing an August 1930 first installment of $50 million on his German loan, and however he scraped or scrambled, he could not come up with that much money. But there may be special gods who look after the truly bold. Poincaré lost his premiership amid an upheaval in the French government, even as France enjoyed a sudden economic boom. The new government decided to repay the Kreuger loan, all $75 million, in April 1930, earning Kreuger a $5 million profit—the difference between the $70 million proceeds to the French and their repayment obligation.[90]

With splendid business-as-usual aplomb, Kreuger delivered the promised $50 million to Germany, and announced, in addition, that Kreuger & Toll's dividend would be increased from 25 percent to 30 percent. A respected investment newsletter recommended Kreuger securities as "sound" with "possibilities of appreciation." *Time* magazine noted that Kreuger had a government loan portfolio of $315 million, and had just added seven new match monopolies to his stable.[91]

In fact, Kreuger's long string of successes was running out. The Price Waterhouse accountants, who performed the postmortem on Kreuger's financial empire, accused him of running a "Ponzi game." Frank Partnoy, the author of an outstanding Kreuger biography, took issue with that characterization, because the original Ponzi gambit was pure swindle. Charles Ponzi made no investments, but simply used proceeds from new investors to pay glittering returns to previous ones. Kreuger, Partnoy points out, had vast earning assets—highly productive iron mines, excellent factories for both matches and match-making equipment, vast timber holdings, extensive real estate in Stockholm, and major security holdings, including a controlling interest in the Ericsson telephone enterprise.

Kreuger's problem wasn't so much the scale of his assets as the inadequacy of his cash flow. The economist Hyman Minsky defined "Ponzi finance" as a state when a company's cash flows are such that it must either borrow or sell assets to pay *both* interest and principal on its debt. The name is justified because both the original Ponzi game and versions like Kreuger's require ever larger borrowings just to stay ahead of their debt service. Absent some dramatic windfall, the firm indulging in Ponzi finance must eventually fail.[92]

In Kreuger's case, the walls were closing in. He sold his controlling position in Ericsson to America's International Telephone and Telegraph (IT&T), dazzling the assembled bankers and advisers on the IT&T side with one of his patented solo-with-no-notes negotiating marathons. The proceeds were $11 million, which Kreuger desperately needed to meet an interest payment on one of his debentures. Some months later, however, the accountants for IT&T caught an important misstatement in Ericsson's cash reports—which Kreuger surely knew about—and Jack Morgan, IT&T's banker, nixed the deal, with considerable glee one imagines. Kreuger humbly agreed to return the $11 million. The strain on Kreuger was becoming evident. He had always been attentive to his health, getting regular exercise, cultivating calmness. Now he was drinking and smoking heavily, losing his temper, railing at his closest subordinates. He seems to have been acutely aware of his deteriorating mental and physical health, and went to great lengths to avoid personal meetings, often locking himself inside a personal inner sanctum he called his "silence room" for days at a time.[93]

His behavior after losing a hoped-for contract for a match monopoly shows his desperation. Kreuger had a trusted printer forge £21 million worth of Italian treasury bonds, and Kreuger himself forged the signatures of the Italian officials. He used them only once. In 1931, when he was badgering Lee, Higginson for yet another bond flotation, they asked for documentation of the "$77 million" in securities he claimed to have in one of his (by now semi-) secret companies. He invited an accountant into his vault, pulled open the drawer with the faux bonds, and got his deal done.[94]

By 1931, Kreuger had been playing a Minsky-style Ponzi finance game for a long time. While he had a great many businesses besides matches, the majority were commodity, low-margin businesses, like ore and timber. And some businesses, like his film enterprises, were complete losers. To maintain his pace of borrowing, his holding companies had to continue to pay eye-popping dividends. The shadowy bridge between the grotty world of his real businesses and the golden glow of his holding companies was assembled from a tissue of exaggeration, misrepresentation, glamor, and outright fraud. That bridge could stand only so long as the bull market reigned. By March of 1932, all hopes of early world recovery had fled, the cruel deflation in security markets had shut down the channels of Ponzi finance, and accountants were pressing for the details on Kreuger's forged Italian bonds. He was finished. Suicide may have seemed the most elegant way out.[95]

———

The contractionary shocks in the early 1930s in America were surely enough to cause a nasty recession. But to explain the extraordinary virulence of the Great Depression, we have to add the international developments that pushed the United States over the brink.

PART FOUR

Blood, Gold, and Unpaid Debts

─── I. ENTANGLEMENTS ───

T he 1920s boom in America was unique. It was the most autarkic of nations. There were no enemies on its continent and great oceans on its shores. It had vast natural resources, an ambitious and entrepreneurial population, and an outsize share of the world's money. It was the world leader in mass production manufacturing, in energy, in industrial research, and in the average education of its population. It was no mystery that with the war ended, Congress and the great majority of Americans wanted to shake off the dust of Europe and enjoy the blessings of "normalcy," frolicking in the world's first consumer paradise of cars, phonographs, radios, movies, packaged foods, exciting new music, and electric homes.

But the entanglements were not to be escaped so easily. Wilson had brought the country into the war, and Americans had seats of power in virtually all the negotiations for ending it. There were still American troops in Europe, and Americans wanted them home. They had approved of the reparations to be exacted from the Germans, and they wanted their own massive wartime lending to be repaid. And there were the murky questions of national boundaries, of restoring national defenses, of limiting German rearmament, and of specifying periods of occupations and inspections.

Resolving these issues took the entire decade of the 1920s, and beyond. The drawn-out process delayed the reestablishment of stable governments, empowered extremists, stoked paranoia and recriminations on the part of both right and left parties, and fed into the toxic brew of tribalism and race that ultimately exploded into another global paroxysm that dwarfed the "Great War."

The magic elixir for navigating weighty international impasses is always money, and in the aftermath of the war, with all the economies of Europe stagnant and staggering, the only money of interest was gold. Understanding the role of gold in this era requires understanding how nineteenth-century Britons managed their world empire.

The most astonishing construction of the Victorian era was what the historian John Darwin has called the British World System. It was not so much a conscious creation as an organic evolution of assumptions, institutions, and practices, maintained for the most part by private parties seeking private interests, within broad boundaries established by the government. Its physical expression was the system of long-distance sea lanes, monitored and protected by the Royal Navy, tied together by a vast port and shipping infrastructure and the world's deepest financial network. Like some huge but usually benign spider, Great Britain sat on top of a global web of trading relations stretching from Hong Kong, New Delhi, and New Zealand, to Russia, Central Europe, Persia, and Egypt, to Argentina, Brazil, and North America, as well as to nearly all the accessible dominions of Africa.

The Industrial Revolution of the eighteenth and early nineteenth centuries was almost exclusively a British phenomenon. As Great Britain gave over more and more of its economy to manufacturing, its exports shifted to finished textiles, steam engines, machine tools, and rolling stock, and its imports to basic commodities, like cereal grains, iron ore, and lumber. As its trade sector grew apace, it naturally became the global leader in accountancy, law, shipping, finance, and other high-end commercial services. The combination of a frugal government with its sizeable streak of adventurous, inventive, and entrepreneurial people led directly to the accumulation of immense amounts of capital.

Financial settlements were mediated by a deep network of city finance houses that bought and sold mostly sterling trade bills,* the majority of

---

* The "bill of exchange" was the effective currency of trade. Goods purchased in Hong Kong, say, would be paid for by a bill evidencing the amount owed and the terms of the purchase, usually specifying full payment when the goods were actually received. Mostly British banking houses bought and sold those bills at less than face value depending on the time to final collection and other risks of the transaction. Bills from

them with no British parties on either end of the transaction. At moments of temporary stringency, a rise in the London bill rate would quickly pull in investors from the United States and the continent to make up the shortfall. The top London finance houses also worked at the long end of the market, deploying the country's capital surplus in great exploits of project finance; building the world's canals, dams, water systems, and railroads; and reaping big upfront placement fees and long-term streams of interest and dividends. The proceeds of those global bond and stock placements were usually deposited in those same London banks, adding to the city's liquidity. Finally, if funds were really tight, the chancellor of the exchequer could always place paper with its Indian colonial adminis-tration, which typically had large trade surpluses (cotton, spices, tea) with the home country.[1]

In his classic 1873 tract, *Lombard Street*, Walter Bagehot, the long-time editor of *The Economist*, provided a veritable handbook of advanced nineteenth-century central banking. The management of a nation's gold reserve was a central concern. A trading nation like Great Britain must keep a sufficient reserve of legal tender, either gold or reserves of currency readily convertible to gold. The challenge to be met was that "foreign payments are often very large and very sudden . . . [a] bad harvest must take millions in a single year." The primary weapon in the central banker's armory, the "effectual instrument," in Bagehot's words, "is the elevation of the rate of interest:"

> Continental bankers and others instantly send great sums here, [to England] as soon as the rate of interest shows that it can be done prof-itably. . . . The rise in the rate of discount acts immediately on the trade of this country. Prices fall here; in consequence imports are dimin-ished, exports are increased, and, therefore, there is more likelihood of a balance in bullion coming to this country after the rise in rate than there was before.[2]

---

distant locales usually worked their way to London, where the final holder would collect the sum due from the merchant. The Bank of England was a major buyer of commercial bills, so its "discount rate" or rate of interest on bills, established the mar-ket rate. If the bank pushed up the discount rate, trade would suffer, and if it lowered the rate, economic activity usually increased.

The alleged automatic operation of the classic gold standard is the source of its allure. An episode of inflation, whatever its cause, devalues the local currency—it takes more currency units to buy a standard unit of goods. Trading partners at some point will spurn payments in currency and insist on gold. As gold reserves dwindle, authorities are forced to quash the inflationary momentum by raising interest rates or by using open market operations—selling securities to banks to mop up lendable cash. The process was first described by the Scottish philosopher and savant, David Hume, and dubbed the "price-specie flow mechanism." Some modern conservative politicians, who hope to shrink government, preach that the automaticity gained from a return to a classic gold standard would make the Federal Reserve unnecessary.

The "classic gold standard" actually prevailed for barely a century between the Napoleonic wars and World War I, with a period of admirably efficient operation of perhaps fifty years. The actual workings of Victorian-era finance, however, were quite different from Hume's hallowed price-specie flow mechanism. Although the pound sterling was nominally linked to gold, sterling, not gold, was the normal settlement currency both throughout the Empire and with most other trading partners. As the system matured, Great Britain almost always ran a merchandise trade deficit with the rest of the world, which it more than balanced by a vast flow of investment returns and other "invisibles" like shipping proceeds. None of this was happenstance. Senior civil servants, leading merchant bankers, and top cabinet members had a roughly accurate grasp of how the system worked, the benefits it conferred on the home country, and how it could go wrong. The gold standard was certainly a critical part of the system, but it was important mostly for keeping non-sterling peripheral countries in line. The list of "peripheral" countries would have included the United States, which for most of its history had to conduct its foreign trade with gold. By the prewar period, however, the dollar, which had been pegged to a specific gold parity since 1879, was gaining increasing acceptance in international commerce.[3]

Since London was awash in other people's money, the Bank of England had few liquidity concerns, and so carried only a "thin film of gold" in its reserves, running as low as 2–3 percent of the money supply. Such low cover occasionally caused problems, as in the 1890 collapse of the House of Baring. The Barings were caught with a large position in Argentinian government bonds that had been repudiated by a popular revolution. A failure of Barings would have shaken dozens of major city firms. Foreign and local deposits alike briefly fled the banking system, draining gold. When Russia let it be known that it was reviewing its own deposits, bankers feared for the convertibility of sterling. The crisis was resolved by large gold loans from France and Russia, plus a large additional French gold standby credit. The mere announcements of the loans was enough to quell the crisis and create time for officials to sort out the mess. Roughly the same sequence of events played out during the severe American banking flash-crisis of 1907—the gold standard was maintained because the major gold-using countries pulled together to ensure the Bank of England's continued liquidity.[4]

The apparent stability of the gold regime suggested that it would survive even the cataclysm of the world war. All of the belligerents except the United States left the gold standard during the years of active hostilities, and even the United States restricted the sale of gold. But it was taken for granted that when the fighting stopped, some simulacrum of the prewar system would be reconstructed, albeit with an American role more consistent with its great power. All statesmen understood that major wars had no happy endings: financial systems would be in disarray; trade relations would be disrupted; factories, roads, housing, and other infrastructure would be heavily damaged; populations would be dispersed and rootless. But those issues, it was assumed, would become more tractable once there was a shared and updated monetary machinery.

The hoped-for seamless return to the gold standard didn't happen, for many reasons. For one thing, countries had quite disparate recent histories of deflation and inflation, which colored their attitudes toward growth, and made it difficult to devise mutually agreeable exchange rates. There were also extreme imbalances of national gold holdings, which as a practical matter, had the same effect as actual gold shortages. The halcyon days of the British monetary dispensation had been eased by new mine openings that made gold relatively abundant. In the postwar period, however, the maldistribution of gold was exacerbated by falling production rates. Through the 1920s, average production was about 13 percent lower than in the immediate prewar period.[5]

Most discussions of gold, moreover, were quickly muddied by the quasi-religious significance attached to gold as the ultimate standard of value—which to the literal-minded was usually identified with the pre-war valuations. The wartime inflation had made a nonsense of those numbers. The US dollar gold parity, for example, was $20.67 per fine gold ounce, unchanged since 1879. That number had served until the start of World War I, in part because prices had been remarkably stable over most of that period. By the end of the war, however, maintaining the gold price at $20.67 was a gross understatement of its purchasing power, which persisted even after the US deflation of 1920–1921. Besides reducing the incentives for gold miners, the undervaluation increased the volume of gold required to meet central bank coverage ratios, at the same time as it raised demand for gold in the jewelry industry. Such considerations were merely theoretical when almost all countries were off the gold standard, but raised difficult questions once central banks began to contemplate its resumption.

The maldistribution of monetary gold was the most visible issue, but was very difficult to address, since it exposed fundamental contradictions among big-country central bankers.

As Figure 4.1 shows, the US share of monetary gold ballooned through the war and the deflationary episode of 1920–1921, before settling

FIGURE 4.1: MONETARY GOLD HOLDINGS, SELECTED COUNTRIES

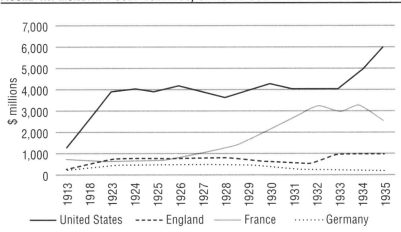

Source: Hardy, *Is There Enough Gold?*, 92–93.

at about $4 billion in 1924. There is a small, barely visible, dip following an episode of easing by Benjamin Strong, the president of the New York Fed, in 1924–1925—both to counter a modest US recession and to facilitate the British return to gold in 1925. There is a second dip following an episode of easing in 1927, again to counter a mild recession and to help the British stabilize their sterling/gold parity.[6]

Until his untimely death in 1928, Strong was the de facto leader of the Federal Reserve, not only dominating Fed economic policy making, but using his great financial leverage to assist the other major countries to return to a workable gold standard as well. While America's financial power naturally enhanced his stature, it was Strong's personal judiciousness and considerateness that made him a natural intermediary in keeping a prickly group of financiers moving more or less together and to similar ends at least most of the time. Altogether, it was one of the happier matches of talent to policy challenges in the annals of American finance. That he failed to achieve his international objectives testifies to the virtual impossibility of the project, given the witch's brew of hatred and revenge still smoldering on the continent of Europe.[7]

One of the major obstacles to "resumption," as the return to gold was called, was the overhang of international debt stemming from the war. To Strong's embarrassment, the United States was the world's dominant creditor and by no means an especially accommodating one. Men like Hoover, Strong, and Thomas Lamont, a senior Morgan partner and adviser to the Treasury, understood that a pettifogging US attitude toward European war debts could forestall a world recovery and risk a dangerous depression. But the American Congress and nationalist politicians like Calvin Coolidge, at least in public, expected cash-on-the barrelhead repayment in gold, ignoring America's already dominant share of the world's monetary gold supply. The issue of war debts was complicated by the heavy schedule of reparations imposed on Germany and its allies by the Treaty of Versailles, which France in particular was determined to collect, in part to help pay off its war debts.

An international conference, spearheaded by the British, assembled in Genoa in 1922, and while it did not reach a consensus, it aired some useful ideas. The United States did not attend in part because Strong did not want to be besieged by America's importunate debtors. Ralph

Hawtrey, the British Treasury's monetary expert, advocated converting the gold standard into a "gold-exchange" standard, by which countries would accept the pound and the dollar as gold reserve equivalents, which France naturally took as an insult. Strong let it be known that he was averse to a gold-exchange standard. Among other dangers, overseas buildups of dollar reserves could lead to runs on American gold, which did become a real problem in the 1960s. Several economists, including Keynes, Sweden's Gustav Cassel, and Irving Fisher, weighed in with various proposals for "managed" gold standards by which gold prices could be adjusted to reflect shifting economic realities. Such schemes gained little traction, however, against the objection voiced by traditionalists like Russell Leffingwell, a Morgan partner and former Treasury official, who argued that restoring prewar gold parities could not be a question of "expediency." The business instinct on gold parities, he went on, were based "on the sound principle that promises are made to be kept. . . . [T]here cannot be prosperity without confidence, nor confidence without a fixed measure of values and medium of exchange." But even Leffingwell conceded that the rule applied only to "any country which *can* restore its currency to pre-war mint parity."[8]

To return European countries to the gold standard, however, required sorting out the positions of the three major European powers—Germany, Great Britain, and France—each of which faced quite different challenges. Germany's may have been the most daunting.

III. GERMANY, 1919–1925: VENGEANCE, REPARATIONS, AND WAR DEBTS

The Treaty of Versailles was written entirely by the victors: the Germans were shown it only in its completed form and were given only three days to accept it—although that was extended a week. Germans felt aggrieved and angry—but they had invaded Belgium, a neutral state, and on their locust-like march through the country had wreaked atrocities against civilians, destroyed cherished cultural artifacts, and shipped much of Belgium's industrial machinery back to Germany. Then they fell upon France, killed a quarter of the country's young men and diligently destroyed its industrial infrastructure. Nor did Germany have any standing to object to reparations. They had imposed heavy reparations on France after the 1870–1871 war, and had recently imposed stinging indemnities on Russia and Romania following their victories on the eastern front.[9]

But the Germans were determined to pay as little as possible in the way of reparations and preferably nothing at all. The reparations question was necessarily entangled with the question of repaying the very large loans that the Allies owed to the United States and Great Britain. Great Britain, which was both creditor and debtor on the war loans, made a strong case for a general amnesty. Yes, the United States had sent massive amounts of dollars and goods across the Atlantic, but surely they had profited mightily from the war business.

At the Versailles conference, however, delegates floated such phantasmagorical numbers for German reparations, as high as $100–200 billion, that wise heads adjourned the reparations discussion to an expert working body. In the meantime, the Germans were compelled to make in-kind reparations, mostly transferring coal, railroad rolling stock, and industrial machinery. After nearly two years of discussion, the Reparation Commission came up with a total reparation figure of 132 billion gold marks, or roughly $33 billion—the "London schedule" (assuming gold

A powerful fist is shown squeezing a hapless German, as the victors use the Versailles process to force Germany to pay, what Germans insisted, were crippling reparations. The reparations, in fact, were no more than Germany had regularly exacted from territories that it had conquered.

marks at about four to the dollar). It was a fake number—consciously framed to satisfy the "*le Boche paiera tout*" thirst for vengeance on the part of the French and Belgians. The fine print divided the payments into three classes of bonds. The first two, an "A bond" and a "B bond," together with a $2 billion credit for German in-kind transfers, totaled $12.5 billion or about a single year's worth of German GDP. Both the A bonds and the B bonds carried explicit amortization schedules and stringent provisions for establishing sinking funds and other measures to assure payment. The C bonds, with a face value of 82 billion gold marks, or about $20 billion, had no such provisions; indeed, the fine print had so many escape hatches for Germany as virtually to preclude any payments at all. Poincaré commented in disgust, "L'État des payements avait surtout un caractère théoretique."[10]

The Germans made the required first $250 million payment on the London schedule in mid-1921, with borrowed money that was repaid with export earnings—but that was only because German customs stations were still under Allied occupation. Once the Allies turned over the customs posts, the Germans made only negligible cash payments, but they continued to make in-kind transfers, although typically with deficiencies in the range of 15–30 percent. The British made no secret that their priority was to restart the German economy to drive a European recovery, and consistently opposed serious enforcement of reparations. The French, acutely conscious of their demographic and industrial inferiority, were in mortal fear of just such a German revival; besides that, the German destruction of French coal and iron resources made it impossible to restart French industry without substantial transfers from Germany.[11]

French dyspepsia worsened in the spring of 1922 when the Soviet and German delegations to the Genoa currency conference repaired to the modest town of Rapallo a few miles distant, and hammered out a commercial and financial treaty. Ominously, that following January, when the French and Belgians invaded the coal-rich Ruhr industrial region to enforce reparations, Berlin and Moscow made joint protests, and the Soviets warned France that they would not tolerate further absorptions of German territory. The occupation itself was a near-disaster. German officials mounted a campaign of passive resistance even as Comintern agents fomented radicalism among the workers. There were waves of sabotage, which were put down violently by the French and Belgian occupation troops, and widespread deportations and abuses of women and children, including "hundreds of rapes," some of them quite brutal.[12]

In the meantime, Germany had descended into monetary chaos. As the reality of the Kaiser's abdication and Allied military victory sunk in, the 1918 "November Revolution," or "quasi-revolution," triggered a full year of upheaval: the old aristocracy fell back on their estates, bracing for a French-style revolution; workers' councils took over factories and even whole cities; marches, political demonstrations, and political-sectarian gun battles disrupted basic services. The social fabric held sufficiently, however, and a constitutional parliamentary democracy, the so-called Weimar Republic, was formed under a center-left socialist government. It immediately enacted a string of expensive reconstruction programs, began to pay property owners for losses from postwar territorial transfers, and legislated big boosts in social welfare provision—an eight-hour day, unemployment insurance, and generous pensions for veterans and war widows. The ambitious spending agenda implied huge budget deficits or major tax increases. Seats in the National Assembly were allocated by proportional representation,* which made it very difficult to push through meaningful revenue increases—so, by default, the government fell back on a strategy of large deficits and rapid inflation.[13]

The inflationary mechanism was simple enough. The Weimar treasury financed its spending increases with short-term notes that it sold to the central bank for currency. Although the central bank was autonomous, bank management cooperated with the policy of inflation. Since there was no limit to the amount of short-term paper the treasury could create and sell to the bank, there was no limit on the production of new currency. Revenue generated by printing new money soon exceeded revenue generated by taxes and fees. Since money was essentially free, a left-leaning government curried political favor by expanding its social provision.[14]

For at least the first year or so, many Germans made out very well from the inflation. German industrialists had been heavily leveraged at the war's end, and rejoiced as inflation blew away their debts. Exports soared, as the plunge in the Reichsmark secured Germany's position as the low-cost producer. Foreign investors, accustomed to Prussian punctiliousness in paying debts, snapped up German bonds. From 1920 through mid-1922, when prices first became totally unmoored, perhaps $1 billion flowed into the country, most of it from America. About half of it purchased real goods and the rest was lost in the inflation. Prior to that, however, the industrial revival had stabilized the mark at about 65 to the dollar, compared to the prewar dollar-gold parity of 4.2 marks. The rich cream of the recovery redounded primarily to the owners, but under the Weimar governments a decent portion of the drippings percolated down to workers, with the largest benefits tilted toward the lowest paid. The primary losers included landlords and other *rentiers*, as well as overseas investors, who saw the value of their assets wafted away like morning dew.

---

* Most of continental Europe used some form of proportional representation—allocating legislative seats according to the percentage of votes received by each party. Unlike the winner-take-all systems of Great Britain and the United States, it assures a voice for minority constituencies. Its characteristic failure mode is that the multiplicity of parties requires constant brokering to form one unstable coalition after another.

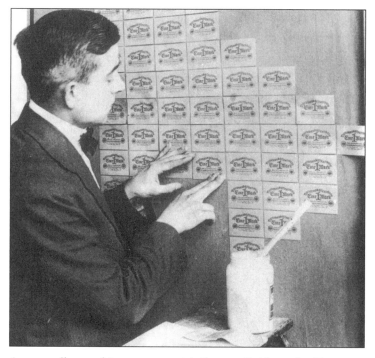

A man wallpapers his apartment with German Reichsmarks. They were made from high-quality paper and the hyperinflation made them much cheaper than ordinary wallpaper.

In 1920, Walter Rathenau, a future finance minister who was chief executive of Germany's largest electrical trust, openly extolled the power of inflation to increase exports and maintain employment. In fact, as the German financial press duly noted, the headlong depreciation of the Reichsmark against the dollar and pound was financially equivalent to a large interest-free capital infusion. By mid-1922, however, investors had taken fright, and the inflation had become destabilizing. Mounting civil disorder culminated in a wave of assassinations, including the murder of Rathenau in 1922. The Ruhr invasion the next year triggered a panicked flight from German debt and many creditors lost all of their stakes.[15]

Long-standing financial practices contributed to the hallucinatory character of the Weimar inflation. Many taxes, especially for the wealthy, were assessed long before they were due, so the longer taxpayers waited, the less their payments were worth, automatically ratcheting up the budget shortfalls. Crazy price misalignments resulted from pervasive price controls on food, rents, and many other basic items. The country tipped into hyperinflation in mid-1922, up by 1,000 percent. By 1923, the increases were exponential: in August 1923, an American dollar bought 630,000 marks; in November, it bought 630 billion marks, a millionfold inflation. The most impecunious Americans could live like byzantine potentates. The writer Matthew Josephson enjoyed a palatial apartment, with a full complement of servants, and every amenity at his beckoning. It cost a Texan $100 to hire the entire Berlin Philharmonic for an evening. At the same time ordinary Germans had been reduced to barter. Some sense of the dislocations can be captured by newspaper inflation guides. The example in Figure 4.2 applies to apartment rents, which were generally under rent control. Readers were advised to check frequently for updates.[16]

As inflation spiraled toward infinity, it was the German industrialists who finally blinked. Foreign finance had dried up, and riots and other disturbances were spreading through the country. Their first concession was to accede to the French terms in the Ruhr. A new Conservative government, led initially by Gustav Stresemann, an economist and experienced politician and lobbyist, took power on the express condition that he could rule by decree. Within a couple of months he had restored calm and set about fixing the currency. His chosen instrument was Hjalmar Schacht, a brilliant, audacious, and wealthy banker, whose talents were compromised by his overweening ego and tin ear for ethical issues.[17]

The appropriate job for Schacht would have been the presidency of the Reichsbank, but that appointment was not within the government's

FIGURE 4.2: NEWSPAPER POSTING OF APARTMENT RENTAL RATES, GERMAN HYPERINFLATION, 1923

Base Rent	30 RM
Administrative Supplement	30 RM
Current Maintenance	65,000,000,000 RM
Long-term Maintenance	65,000,000,000 RM
Total	130,000,000,060 RM

RM = Reichsmarks

power, and the current occupant, a gentlemanly civil servant, refused to step down. Instead, Schacht was designated the "commissioner of currency," charged with implementing an idea of Stresemann's of a scrip or faux currency, called a "Rentenmark," collateralized by German land. On the face of it, that was absurd, if only because a useful currency needed to be collateralized by a highly liquid and easily transferable asset. Schacht was doubtful, but agreed to give it a try. The Rentenmark was duly created as a legal tender, subject to a tight ceiling on supply, and it was announced that the government would be willing to exchange Rentenmarks for paper Reichsmarks. Setting the conversion price was left to Schacht, who turned the occasion into a powerful symbol of reform. He waited until the mark fell to 4.2 trillion to the dollar, and then set the price of a Rentenmark at 1 trillion Reichsmarks—4.2 Rentenmarks therefore equaled $1, just like the old gold marks. As luck would have it, on the very evening that Schacht fixed the Rentenmark conversion price, the civil servant who had blocked his ascendance to the presidency of the Reichsbank dropped dead, finally clearing the way for Schact's appointment.[18]

Within a few weeks, people were lining up to trade in their paper currency for the new Rentenmarks, stores reopened, long-hoarded goods were back on shelves, commerce returned almost to normal. As Schacht mopped up the sea of paper currency, Stresemann steadily whittled down the Reich's excessive social and reconstruction spending. As far as purely intra-German transactions were concerned, the economy started to tick along quite nicely, but the sleight of hand did little for Germany's external credit. Foreign lenders had been badly burned by Germany's adventures in currency despoliation, and refused any transactions not immediately settled in gold. Since Germany had very little gold, it could not make a lasting recovery without substantial gold credits, which could only come from the United States.[19]

The US Senate failed to ratify the Treaty of Versailles in March 1920. The official stumbling block was the famous Article X, requiring that signatories join the League of Nations and agree to join in wars declared by the League. If Woodrow Wilson had not been incapacitated by a massive stroke, he might have been able to push the bill through or find an acceptable compromise. But it would have made little difference. The country was thoroughly sick of wars, of international intrigues, of Bolsheviks and socialists, and of war profiteers. A year later, Harding and the Republicans took over the White House on the promise of returning to "normalcy." Europe and its travails be damned, not least because they were stiffing us on their war debts.[20]

European chanceries abounded with hard feelings toward America. Yes, the almost-too-late war entry by the United States had saved their bacon, and yes, the United States had provided loans to the Allies equivalent to a full quarter of annual prewar US GDP. That behavior was a sharp break from America's wary "no entanglements" policy, which dated all the way back to the founders. The intervention against the Germans was considered a one-off thing, caused by German attacks on US shipping. Now that the war was over, America's priorities were to clean up its financial books, squelch inflation, develop reasonable arrangements to collect on its loans, and get back to business. The average congressman was oblivious to or didn't care that much of the war lending had been recycled right back home, where it had fueled a mighty expansion of the United States's already formidable production apparatus. Or that the economies of all the belligerents had contracted during the war, except for that of the United States, which had grown half again larger. Or that the United States also controlled more than 40 percent of the world's monetary gold and was a cynosure for much of the world's "safe-haven" money.[21]

The usual story is that "Uncle Shylock" would not be moved, as epitomized by then-Vice President Calvin Coolidge's famous dismissal of loan forgiveness: "They hired the money, didn't they?" In reality, America's elite bankers and businessmen understood that Europe's finance and trading systems had to be returned to working order, post haste. As Strong had written to Treasury Secretary Andrew Mellon, "The financial advantage of collecting the debts is a consideration of minor importance to the country," compared to the benefits of a broad stabilization of major country monetary regimes. Despite his image as a conservative fossil, partly based on a years-later comment by Herbert Hoover,* Mellon had spent a lifetime in international finance, and was finely tuned to its nuances.[22]

Hoover, then the commerce secretary, and Charles Evans Hughes, the secretary of state, were quietly pushing for more American involvement in Europe's problems, and Hughes floated the idea of having a purely private "committee of experts" come up with some solutions. Montagu Norman, the head of the Bank of England, who had developed a good working relationship with Schacht and was particularly close to Strong, favored the idea. Raymond Poincaré, the French prime minister, whose ministry was still bogged down in the Ruhr invasion, was also desperate for practical solutions.

The challenge was how to shake some money loose from the Americans without the official involvement of the administration or Congress. America's private-sector investment banks could readily raise the required amounts from commercial investors; the problem was how to provide unimpeachable security in the absence of a US guarantee. The banks, led by J. P. Morgan with support from Kuhn, Loeb and Company, Dillon, Read and Company, and other American investment banks, were willing to try, with guidance from a committee of experts along the lines suggested by Hughes. The Coolidge administration gave a quiet nod of permission for American bankers to participate, and Morgan's Lamont was made point man.[23]

Neither the United States nor Great Britain was especially enamored of reparations, taking their cue from Keynes's best seller, *The Economic*

---

* Mellon may be best remembered for allegedly stating during the 1920s deflation that policy should be to "liquidate labor, liquidate stocks, liquidate farmers, liquidate real estate." That comment was attributed to Mellon many years later by Hoover in his memoirs. Hoover did not like Mellon, who was skeptical of interventionist policies in the Great Depression. I have found no independent evidence of his actually saying it.

Consequences of the Peace, with its dire predictions of the chaos that would follow enforcement of reparations on the scale approved by the 1921 London schedule. That arrayed the Anglo-Saxons against the French and Belgians, who had absorbed by far the greatest part of human and economic damage from the war, and who had most counted on reparations to finance their recovery. The French economy had enjoyed surprisingly good economic returns in the early 1920s but had hit a wall by 1924.[24]

The experts' committee members were officially advisers to the Reparation Commission.* Their remit was to develop a workable plan that was acceptable to investors, to speed a German recovery, and to achieve reasonable justice for the countries that been devastated by the German invasions. The committee had ten members and was chaired by Charles G. Dawes, a former Chicago banker who had served in France as a brigadier general with the American forces and had been the US budget director in the Harding administration. He was the perfect frontman for the delicate negotiations that lay ahead, because he had no difficulty in ignoring reporters—or roaring at them to get out of his way. The brains of the committee, however, was Owen D. Young, forty years old and already the chief executive of both General Electric and the Radio Corporation of America. The committee was filled out by two Englishmen, two Frenchmen, two Italians, and two Belgians.

The Americans held the balance of power on the committee, because everyone understood that nothing could happen without additional money, which could come only from American bankers. As Jack Morgan put it, he had no views on politics; his profession was "merely interpreting sentiment in financial markets"—in other words, he couldn't sell bonds unless they were backed by sufficient collateral and other provisions to secure the promised returns. The British naturally allied themselves with the Americans. One of the British members, Josiah Stamp, was a shopkeeper's son who had gotten a first in economics as a part-time student at the London School of Economics, went on for a PhD, became an expert

---

* There were actually two experts' committees, the "first committee" charged with advising on stabilizing the German economy, and a "second committee" charged with determining the amount of German capital exports to date. The state of German financial records made that impossible, so the second committee made a rough estimate and disbanded, filing a two-page report.

on taxation and incomes, a prominent businessman, and director of the Bank of England. In 1938, he was elevated to a peer of the realm as the first Baron Stamp. The report of the committee was drafted primarily by Young, working closely with Stamp on technical issues.[25]

Dawes and Young led the negotiations with the principals, mostly leaving the details of the bond indentures to Lamont. Since the British were at one with the Americans on almost every question, Dawes and Young focused on the French and Germans. Dawes had made many powerful friends in France during his wartime service, and was fluent, so he handled the French side. As a senior GE executive, Young had long interacted with the top ranks of the German industrialists, most of whom agreed to support at least the spirit of the undertaking. The leading German industrial magnate, however, Hugo Stinnes, was an important holdout. Stinnes was a near-legendary figure in Germany, with massive holdings in coal and coke, iron and steel, and much else, all supported by wide-ranging global trading and financial interests, the kind of figure that inspired classic *Timeese*:

> Hugo Stinnes. Crafty, potent, indurate, Herr Hugo Stinnes, coal magnate, multimillionaire, present "All-Highest" of Germany. . . . His aim is the control of the European steel industries, and, like all mysterious figures who move in the no-man's-land of international politics, he stands to win whichever side comes out on top.

As Young and Stinnes wound up a discussion that had carried into the wee hours, Stinnes pronounced himself "still unconvinced." Young shot back: "It is not for me to convince you, but rather you to convince me, as a Report is going to be made quite regardless of the attitude of any person or even the whole group of industrialists." The magnate got aboard the next day, after Young agreed to a minor technical clarification.[26]

There was a final flap over the committee's failure to set a definitive reparations number, which greatly irritated the French. The Germans complained almost as vociferously, but it was a pose—they had every interest in delaying the fixing of a number, so as to gain more time to whittle it down. The Americans and British refused even to make an attempt, given the recent chaos in the German economy—insisting in effect that the Dawes process would establish the boundaries of the possible and desirable, which would later inform a final settlement.

The *Report of the First Committee of Experts to the Reparation Commission* was released on April 9, 1924. It is a superb piece of work—calm, lucid, comprehensive, and fair. Benjamin Strong, after reviewing it at Young's request, wrote that it was "a masterpiece of ingenuity." The most telling accolade, however, came from Keynes, the violent critic of the whole idea of reparations. He wrote in *The Nation and Athenaeum* on April 12:

> The report is the finest contribution hitherto made to this impossible problem. It breathes a new spirit and is conceived in a new vein. It achieves an atmosphere of impartiality, and exhibits scientific workmanship and sound learning. Though the language seems at times that of a sane man, who, finding himself in a madhouse, must accommodate himself to the inmates, it never loses its sanity. . . . [I]t is an honorable document and opens a new chapter.[27]

The preamble of the *Report* set the tone for the whole:

> We have approached our task as businessmen anxious to achieve effective results. We have been concerned with the technical, not political problem presented to us. . . . The dominating feature of the German Budget is Germany's obligation to the Allies under the Treaty of Versailles. We are concerned with the practical means of recovering this debt, not with the imposition of penalties. . . . [A]t the same time it is no ordinary debt with which we deal, for Germany suffered no appreciable devastation, and her primary obligation is toward those who have suffered so severely through the war. . . .
>
> Finally convinced as we are, that it is hopeless to build any constructive scheme unless this finds its own guarantee in the fact that it is in the interest of all the parties to carry it out in good faith, we put forward our plan relying on this interest.[28]

Rather than attempt to compute Germany's "capacity to pay," Young looked for benchmarks from Germany's peers. Unlike the other belligerents, Germany did not impose heavy taxes to finance the war, instead relying far more on borrowing. (The government had assumed it would win the war and would repay the debt by looting its victims.) So an obvious first step was "commensurate taxation," bringing Germany's federal taxes to the average rate of the Allied powers and devoting the increment to reparations. Then there was the opportunity created by the German hyperinflation, which had extinguished virtually all preexisting German bonds. With industry virtually debt-free, and with a modernized plant, there was room for a large issue of conservatively funded reparation industrial bonds. The final major source of funds would be the privatization of the national railroad system, the most modern in Europe. Privatization would entail large bond and stock issues, with the bond proceeds devoted to reparations, and stock proceeds going to the government. A few other cats and dogs, like a temporary transport tax that was made permanent, rounded out the package.[29]

The inducements for the Germans to sign on was money—specifically a $200 million gold loan, with the lead syndication by Morgan, and with the promise of a ready takeup by the financial markets. $100 million would create a healthy gold reserve for the Reichsbank, and the remainder would fund a cushion for the German transition to a balanced budget and any initial shortfalls in reparations. Since it would take time to establish the new taxes and sell the bonds, the reparation payments would be phased in. During the 1924–1925 fiscal year, no payments would be required. A payment of $300 million would be required in the second year, which would be ratcheted up in roughly equal steps to $625 million in 1929–1930, which would become a steady state, encompassing Germany's entire annual obligation. In theory, those payments would extend for sixty-five years, but no one expected that this would be a permanent arrangement. The numbers all added up, and seemed well within the financial capabilities of the country. In the event of shortfalls, creditors had the right to apply the proceeds of specific sales and customs taxes to supply the deficiency.[30]

The plan took particular pains on the mechanics of payments. A special account would be set up in the Reichsbank, and all payments would be made to that account. The position of "agent-general for reparations" was created within the Reparation Commission, along with a transfer committee with five foreign members. The Germans were credited with the payments once they were deposited in the agent's account, and the transfer committee directed the distributions with an eye for avoiding disruptions to international money markets. Funds could be accumulated within the account up to a limit, if necessary, and could also be invested in Germany, with securities issued to the reparation beneficiaries. The agent would also maintain a constant review of the German budget and spending practices, and would make an annual report on Germany's financial and budgetary positions.[31]

Despite the accolades showered on the report, it still had to be approved by national legislatures. In Great Britain, the plan was adopted almost by acclamation. The French were stickier. Secretary Hughes made a tour of European capitals and leaned hard on the French, bluntly explaining that the Dawes plan was now "American policy. If you turn this down, America is through." The Morgan-syndicated gold loan was obviously the main point of the Dawes plan, but the bankers worried that the political risk could kill the issue. The most fraught questions were the occupation of the Ruhr and the Rhineland. After much hard bargaining by Lamont, and reams of transatlantic cables, they accepted a French promise to withdraw from the Ruhr at the end of 1925—which was honored—and to shorten somewhat the period for the Rhineland occupation. The Morgans had considerable leverage of their own: they had floated a short-term $100 million note to tide the French over a budget crisis, which the French needed desperately to convert into a long-term loan. The price for that was signing off on the Dawes plan. A few days after the plan was finalized, the French were rewarded with a $100 million twenty-five-year bond syndication. Even the relatively inexperienced French prime minister, Édouard Herriot, carried the Parliament with little trouble.[32] Lastly came the Germans. By then, the government strongly supported the Dawes plan, and each measure was carried by comfortable majorities. But the provision on railroad privatization required a two-thirds vote of the Reichstag, and the right-wing nationalist parties had enough votes to block it. It was finally passed after the chancellor, Wilhelm Marx, threatened to go to the country. The powers signed off on the plan on August 30. The loan went off successfully: American investors put up half the total, the British just under a quarter, and the French 6 percent, with the rest scattered through other European countries.[33]

The first permanent agent was S. Parker Gilbert, a lawyer in his early thirties and an assistant secretary of the treasury, universally conceded to be brilliant. The first few years of the Dawes plan almost justified the most extravagant hopes. German reparations were paid scrupulously. The major European nations all returned to the gold standard. The Germans effectively resumed gold payments once Schacht's Reichsbank received the proceeds of the Morgan-led gold loan. By 1925, Germany's national unemployment numbers had fallen from the very high levels of the immediate postwar period to well under a million—an estimated national rate of only about 4.5 percent, one of the best in Europe. Good feelings even spread to the point where Germany was admitted to the League of Nations by the Locarno Treaties in October.[34]

The good times, unfortunately, did not last. Part of the reason was the pervasive bad faith of the German statesmen and officers who participated in the postwar treaty implementation. For example, the Allies delivered the names of 895 men suspected of war crimes for trial in Germany. Very few trials were held, only twelve people were convicted, and only two, who had murdered women and children in lifeboats, received quasi-serious sentences of four years imprisonment each. They both escaped within two weeks and, allegedly, were never found.[35]

The German military ignored the Versailles disarmament mandates from the very start. Soon after the war ended, apparently without the government's knowledge, they had reached agreements with the Soviets both to transfer weapons technology and to establish German factories in Russian territory producing arms for both nations. The French had good data on government-subsidized weapons research and development at Krupp plants. Even German industrial investment was concentrated in the large-scale machine tools, steel works, and heavy equipment needed to support future armies. German tractors got bigger and heavier to anticipate the production of new-generation tanks. "Flying clubs" proliferated through Germany, eventually enabling Hitler to miraculously create a German air force almost as soon as he took power. Police forces and the multiplying paramilitary organizations like the Free Corps, the Civil Guard, and the Home Defense were trained to full military standards. Hans von Seeckt, the senior military commander, and his subordinates openly mocked the feeble Allied efforts to control the pace of rearmament. In the mid-1920s,

Seeckt claimed that he had a million men under arms, which was a gross exaggeration, but unsettling. Berliners joked about the worker in a baby carriage factory who stole an assembly to build one for his child, but it somehow always came out as a machine gun.[36]

The British government had detailed information on the German rearmament drive, but waved it off. Ramsay MacDonald said, "What can we expect? Would not we do the same thing here if we had been defeated, and . . . used with the same treatment?" The Royal Navy and Air Force busied themselves with planning defenses against *French* attacks on England. It was only the Army general staff that warned that Germany would "inevitably" clash with Great Britain, and that the German military would be "reconditioned, redisciplined, and thirsting for revenge" by 1935, when the last Allied troops would have withdrawn from the Rhineland.[37]

German financial ministers had a similarly dismissive attitude toward the payment of reparations. They became masters of playing off the British and the American bankers against the French, of winning early terminations of the Ruhr and Rhineland occupations, and in steamrolling the hapless Herriot to give up remedies against German reparation defaults. When Schacht arrived at the London conference where the final details of the Dawes plan were hammered into place, he cabled home with some delight that the British and the American bankers had imposed restrictions on the French protections that "almost go beyond the German claims." For his part, Stresemann in private conversations always emphasized that the reparation agreements could never be enforced. The early year payments were manageable, he argued, and it would be to Germany's advantage to act like a compliant power at first and to default when the later payments began to bite. Schacht had much the same view, and more than once noted that his objective was to cause reparations "chaos."[38]

Altogether, a generous reckoning of German reparation payments, in cash and in kind, is about $5.5 billion, paid over the dozen years 1919–1931. It amounted to about 2.7 percent of German GNP over that span. Except for the first cash payment, all the rest was financed by loans that were never repaid. In stark contrast, the 5 billion gold franc reparations imposed by Germany on France at the conclusion of the Franco-Prussian

War of 1870–1871 was fully paid off in only three years, or two years ahead of time. The French did it by mustering essentially all their national savings, and pushing down internal consumption to boost exports and repressing imports. War reparations may always be a bad idea, but given that history, one can sympathize with the French point of view.[39]

── V. ENGLAND, 1919–1925: CHURCHILL ── (SORT OF) CHOOSES RESUMPTION

T he interwar years were not kind to Great Britain. Before the war it was still the greatest nation in the world, the center of the global trading networks, the sagacious manager of the world's monetary system. Until the rise of the United States, Great Britain had been the path-breaking nation, the maker of the Industrial Revolution. No European nation was as free, as democratic, or gave as much scope to the individual. While it was nominally ruled by a languid upper class, Great Britain, unlike a France or an Italy, allowed room for energetic climbers in the middle; indeed, successful inventors and industrialists were often knighted or otherwise honored solely on their merits, irrespective of their birth or connections.

But the fate of first movers can be cruel. The 1880s marked the peak of the Victorian era, for by the end of that decade, American industrial output had already surpassed Great Britain's. By 1900, the American edge had grown to about a quarter larger, and by the eve of the war, a stunning 2.3 times larger. In 1860, Great Britain accounted for about 20 percent of world industrial output, and the United States only about 7 percent; by 1913, the American share was 32 percent, while Great Britain's had slid to 14 percent. For the total period from 1870 to 1913, American industrial output grew at a compound annual rate of 4.9 percent, Germany's at 3.9 percent, and Great Britain's at 2.2 percent. As for the other "great powers," France steadily lost ground to both Great Britain and Germany, while Russia was still at the threshold of modernity. On a per capita basis, America's industrial output grew sixfold from 1860 to 1913, compared to only 1.8 times in Great Britain. Only Germany among the major powers showed per capita growth rates (5.6 times) comparable to that in America, but the Germans started from a much lower baseline—prewar British per capita output was still about a third higher than Germany's.[40]

Loss of leadership in steel was especially painful for Britons. Steel was the foundation industry for the late-Victorian period, much as information technology is today. Military power, high-technology capital equipment, and mass production of consumer goods all depended on steel, and British steel had been the global benchmark for centuries. So when reports of massive, highly mechanized American steel factories began to circulate in the 1880s, they were met with disbelief on the part of British experts. It was not until the turn of the century that knowledgeable Britons actually investigated American practices. They found to their alarm that American steel and pig iron production was already more than British and German production combined, and because of extensive mechanization, American rail and rod mills routinely produced three times the output of British mills with fewer than half the men.[41]

D. E. Moggridge, a historian of the British return to gold, comments on the near-blissful ignorance of top British industrialists and political mandarins of the trouble they were in.

A country's current account is a statement of income on sales and loans to other countries. On its current account, as Figure 4.3 shows, Great Britain normally ran a deficit on its merchandise account—it imported more physical goods than it sold—but balanced that with a big surplus on its "invisibles"—shipping receipts, banking fees, investment

FIGURE 4.3: GREAT BRITAIN'S CURRENT ACCOUNT WOES

British Current Account Balances (£ millions)

	1913	1924	Change
Merchandise Trade	-134	-337	-203
Invisible Income			
Net shipping income	94	140	46
Net investment income	210	220	10
Net short interest and commissions	25	60	35
All other	10	-10	-20
Balance on Invisibles	339	410	71
Balance on Current Account	205	73	-132

Source: Moggridge, British Monetary Policy.

income, and the like. The British financial objective was to run a sufficient surplus on the current account to capitalize its global financial network, maintain its status as the premier global financial partner in all weather, and feed the golden stream of interest, dividends, and capital returns that kept the city financial machinery humming.

The current account data in Figure 4.3, however, should have sounded an alarm. The merchandise account was in total collapse, with a deficit that swallowed up nearly all of the returns on invisibles. That was scary enough, but if a diligent number-cruncher had dug into the sub-accounts, she would have found that of the thirteen markets tracked by British statisticians, only *one* showed any growth. That happened to be Central and Southeast Europe, perhaps the most vulnerable to a revivified German trade push—which was a top priority of the new Dawes plan.

There were also ominous trends on the invisibles account, strong as it looked at first glance. Nearly half the total receipts came from investment and other banking services, which were rapidly migrating to New York. The second largest item was shipping receipts, but the British merchant fleet had suffered considerable damage during the war, and the Scandinavians were winning substantial British business.

The current account is paired with the capital account, which is an investment account, recording inward and outward investments, loans, and other capital transfers. The capital account presented problems of its own. Superficially, it was in the black. The government and private lenders were creditors on loans of some £2.1 billion, about 80 percent on the government tab. That was financed primarily by borrowing, but also by selling securities, and collecting repayments of matured paper, leaving a net surplus of £55 million. If our number-cruncher dug a little deeper, however, she would notice that the country's biggest creditor was the United States, and its biggest debtors were default-prone France, Russia, and Italy—in other words, the national financial balance sheet was very shaky.[42]

Moggridge points out that the decision to return to a gold standard was assumed from the outset with hardly anything in the way of analysis. In 1918, as the war seemed to be nearing a favorable conclusion, a number of parliamentary committees were convened to plan the transition from a war footing. One committee, chaired by Lord Cunliffe, the governor of the Bank of England, was to plot a path to resuming the gold standard.

Virtually all the experts argued that Great Britain could not regain its status as a financial superpower until it stabilized the pound at the prewar conversion ratio of £1=$4.86. Converting at precisely the prewar rate was considered essential, since a nation without permanent standards could not serve as the world financial bellwether. Despite the consensus on the goal, witnesses were cautious on the timing. The wartime inflation in Great Britain had been much greater than in the United States, so the majority thought it could take a long time to realign the currencies. The British budget deficit was about two-thirds of total expenditure, there was a mountain of debt, much of it short-term, and because of the super-heated rate of wartime spending, the public was awash with cash.[43]

Over the next few years, however, the Treasury and the Bank of England, working together, made real progress on their financials. By 1920–1921, government spending had been cut by almost 60 percent, revenues had increased by more than a quarter, and the budget was in surplus. With sharp cuts in borrowing and a contracting money supply, wage indexes obediently fell. By 1922, the pound had risen from $3.40 immediately after the war, all the way to $4.63, close enough to start thinking seriously about resumption. Opinion spread that it would be a great boost to public confidence if the return to full resumption could be made at an early date.[44]

Benjamin Strong weighed in forcefully, writing that a failure to resume would be "too serious really to contemplate," and "would mean violent fluctuations in the exchanges, with probably progressive deterioration of foreign currencies vis-à-vis the dollar." A return to gold by Great Britain would also help Strong redistribute the huge buildup of gold in the United States, which he had to "sterilize"* to prevent its becoming an engine of inflation. Strong acknowledged that British prices for internationally traded commodities were about 10 percent higher than America's, roughly consistent with Keynes's estimate. So long as sterling wasn't directly linked to gold, the price differential could be accommodated in the exchange rates; alternatively if a fixed peg was desirable, the British

---

* Gold was high-powered money, and the floods of it into the United States could have caused the Fed to lose control over the money supply. So Strong matched each influx of gold by draining an equivalent amount of other high-powered money from the Federal Reserve banks.

could choose a sterling/gold rate sufficiently below the canonical $4.86 rate to equalize the $/£ average price for traded commodities. $4.30–$4.35 or so may have been about right.[45]

Neither Strong, nor Norman, nor any of their advisers showed much, if any, interest in fixing a lower dollar value for the pound—leaving aside a few nonmainstream economists like Keynes, Cassel, and Irving Fisher, all of whom regarded gold as a "barbarous relic." There was in fact a nearly irrefutable case for returning to a gold standard, if only because so many other countries were in the process of doing so. But the casual consensus on sticking with the prewar exchange rate was misguided: compounded of a thoughtless reverence for tradition and a thick-headed refusal to recognize the uncompetitiveness of British industry. Pundits pointed to excessive wages in mining and heavy manufacturing, which was certainly part of the problem. The harder challenge was the obsolescence of great swaths of British industry. What was needed was new management, new plant and investment, and only then, new pay scales and work rules. Civil servants nattered about "reorganizing industry," but it was hot air. The lords of British industry, beribboned and admired as they were, had no interest in scorched-earth industrial reform, while the trade unions, which had acquired immense political power, were firmly for the status quo.[46]

The return to gold had been put on a back burner by the inflationary chaos in Germany, the French invasion of the Ruhr, and spats over reparations and war debts. With the acceptance of the Dawes plan in 1924, however, the path to resumption began to clear. More clarity came in the October election, in which the Tories, by resounding majorities ushered out a short-lived Labour government. Labour feared the downward pressure on wages that would accompany the return to gold, while Conservatives were reflexive gold bugs, irrespective of the cost. Stanley Baldwin, the new prime minister, sprang a surprise with the appointment of Winston Churchill as chancellor of the exchequer. He was a lifelong Tory who had apostasized to the shrinking Liberal party, and Baldwin wanted to harness Churchill's talents for the new government. Although Churchill insisted that he knew nothing about finance, he plunged into the arcana of budgets and taxes with characteristic gusto.[47]

P. J. Grigg, who was the private secretary to five chancellors, including Churchill, and later a permanent secretary of war, has a left a memoir that documents the care and circumspection that Churchill put into his decision both to resume gold payments and to do so at the time-honored price. Early in the process, he created an "exercise" of detailed questions for each adviser to answer. Why, Churchill asked, was there such a fixation on employing a "rudimentary and transitional stage in the evolution of finance?" Why was the United States so "singularly anxious to help us do this?" Why were the advocates of resumption so dismissive of its harmful effects on the merchant and the worker, favoring instead "the special interests of finance at the expense of the special interest of production?" And why the rush, when the economy seemed to be performing rather well—why not wait a few more years, especially with such a safe majority?[48]

Otto Niemeyer, a senior Treasury official and one of Churchill's informal advisers, gave a classic answer: the gold standard decision was "probably the most important financial decision of the present decade," and Churchill would be criticized no matter what he did. But "governments of all political shades" were confidently expecting the decision, and there would be a price to pay if those expectations were dashed. A failure to resume gold payments, he warned, "would reverberate throughout a world which has not forgotten the uneasy moments of the winter of 1923; and would be more convinced than ever that we never meant business about the gold standard because our nerve had failed."[49]

Churchill's response to Niemeyer said, in part, "The Treasury have never, it seems to me, faced the profound significance of what Mr. Keynes calls 'the paradox of unemployment amid dearth.'" After paying his respects to the Treasury view, he concluded: "but the fact that this island with its enormous resources is unable to maintain its population is surely a cause for the deepest heartsearching." Churchill especially courted Reginald McKenna, a former chancellor and a friend of Keynes, who was the chairman of the Midland Bank, one of England's Big Five. McKenna had been defending the return to gold, but in what to Churchill seemed to be a "deliberately weak" manner.[50]

While Churchill pondered, Norman and Strong were laying the groundwork for the British resumption. The standard way a central banker lowers market prices is to engineer a recession. Strong helped by making London more attractive than New York as a destination for loose capital. New York money rates were generally higher than those in London, so through the spring of 1924, Strong started bringing them down from 4.5 percent to 4 percent on May 1, to 3.5 percent on June 12, and to 3 percent on August 8. At the same time, he began purchasing securities from the reserve banks—pumping up their cash holdings—creating a broad easing in the American money markets.[51]

Norman had less flexibility, because Great Britain was already in recession, but he managed to keep British rates firm and significantly higher than in New York, despite the effect on employment. Investors with money to park naturally gravitated toward London, and the inflow of cash helped push up the $/£ exchange rate. But Strong could carry on the easing only for a limited time. When he started pushing down rates, the United States was in a minor recession, which justified his actions for Fed watchdogs. By the spring of 1925, however, the US recession was clearly over, and Strong had to tighten up a bit, but by then he and Norman were coordinating almost perfectly, and so still managed to keep an attractive rate gap in favor of London. When they began the process, the $/£ rate had been in the $4.30s; by the summer of 1924, it had reached the $4.50s; and by April 1925, it had reached $4.84–$4.90. Bingo.[52]

To their credit, both Strong and Norman understood that they had been lucky as well as good. They knew that the pound's rise mostly reflected the market's bet that the old parity would be restored. But other global developments—in grain and meat products, gold and silver, and most agriculture prices—had conspired to push the monetary currents in a favorable direction. The downside was that achieving parity by such a benign alignment of the stars did not speak well of its sustainability. Strong, therefore, insisted on extra insurance, arranging a $200 million gold British credit at the Federal Reserve and brokering a line of credit from the Morgan bank for an additional $100 million.[53]

Nineteen twenty-five was the last year that Great Britain could remain off the gold standard without new enabling legislation. Conservatives were acutely aware of the Labour jeering that would greet any such attempt to extend the date of resumption. According to Grigg, the decision was made in the early spring—on March 17, in fact. That was the night when Churchill organized a dinner at his residence, pitting Keynes and McKenna on the antiresumption side, against Niemeyer and Lord

Bradbury, a former permanent secretary to the Treasury. Grigg was in attendance, and later wrote that after McKenna and Keynes had made a case for the negative, Churchill asked McKenna:

> "But this isn't entirely an economic matter; it is a political decision, for it involves proclaiming that we cannot . . . complete the undertaking which we all acclaimed as necessary in 1918. . . . You have been a politician; indeed you have been Chancellor of the Exchequer. Given the situation as it is, what decision would you take." McKenna's reply—and I am prepared to swear to the sense of it—was: "There is no escape: you have got to go back; but it will be hell."
>
> Which Grigg took to mean "the ayes had it."[54]

Roy Jenkins, Churchill's biographer and himself a former chancellor, described Churchill's plight:

> As the Gold battle unfolded there was a sense of even such a dominating minister as Churchill being swept downstream by the force of a compelling current, protesting but nonetheless essentially impotent. The Treasury was against him, the Bank was against him, the Select Committee . . . was against him. Baldwin . . . in fact, played no part in the decision, but would have been very unhappy had Churchill decided against Gold. The two tufts of ground—Keynes and McKenna—on which Churchill attempted to stand proved, for various reasons, unsatisfactory footholds. The momentum of conventional wisdom swept them away.[55]

When Churchill made his chancellor's presentation on April 28, which included the announcement of the return to gold, he said, probably correctly, "If we had not taken this action the whole of the rest of the British Empire would have taken it without us, and it would have come to a gold standard not on the basis of the pound sterling, but a gold standard of the dollar."[56]

Keynes memorialized the occasion with a newspaper series and a blistering pamphlet, *The Economic Consequences of Mr. Churchill*, dripping with sarcasm. For example, he notes that a high exchange rate would increase imports and discourage exports. The Bank of England therefore, to protect its gold, would be obliged to curtail British lending abroad, while at the same time attracting US lending to England by keeping its bank rate higher than New York's (as Strong and Norman did). "The efficacy of these two methods for balancing our accounts is beyond doubt," Keynes writes.

> Before the war our capacity to lend abroad was ... about £181,000,000 ... and even in 1923 . . . our net surplus [was] £102,000,000. Since new foreign investments bring in no immediate return, it follows that we can reduce our exports by £100,000,000 a year, without any risk of insolvency, provided we reduce our foreign investments by the same amount. So far as the maintenance of the gold standard is concerned, it is a matter of indifference whether we have £100,000,000 worth of foreign investment or £100,000,000 worth of unemployment.[57]

The pamphlet is a brilliant polemic, and was spot-on in forecasting the result of the new policy. It is, unfortunately, far stronger and much more focused than the evidence Keynes gave to the parliamentary committee charged with making a recommendation to the government. In that presentation, Keynes stressed the likelihood of American *inflation*, which would likely force the true parity rate higher than $4.86, possibly causing an inflationary surge of gold in London. Otherwise, he made long and seemingly off-point disquisitions on systems for licensing gold and his conception of price stability. Robert Skidelsky, Keynes's biographer, writes:

> The Committee could well conclude that Keynes expected parity to be regained, without deflationary exertion, in the not too distant future, by a rise in American prices. This was what the Committee, and most of the witnesses, believed anyway. . . . Keynes's testimony helped to crystallize the view that the pre-war parity could be regained and maintained without detrimental effect on the real economy.[58]

Keynes was at heart a controversialist, a master of stinging repartee. But writing seems to have energized him more than mere speaking before an official body. In this case, at least, writing the pamphlet led him actually to do some research. For example, almost all the evidence leading up to the gold decision mentioned a British price disadvantage, variously put at 10 percent by Keynes and others. But as the pound's value drifted upward on the exchanges, the price gap shrank dramatically, to only 2 or 3 percent, which seemed hardly worth worrying about.

In the pamphlet, for the first time, Keynes pointed out that the best data on price behavior come from price behavior of traded or "unsheltered" goods, which are subject to external price competition. He expanded the point in later testimony, estimating that the cost of sheltered goods increased England's cost of living as much as 18 percent higher than in its main trading partners. He also suggested that the most important sheltered good was labor, which sold at a high premium in England compared to the rest of Europe. Great Britain's trade unions were very powerful, with nationwide bargaining in their main trades, and no amount of monetary meddling could force them to lower wages just for workers in unsheltered industries. To make a $4.86 exchange rate stick would have meant pushing down *all* wages, which would have required a deep recession. (Keynes, with his academic's airy view of practicalities, suggested a "social contract" calling for a 5 percent pay cut for all wage earners, along with an additional income tax of a shilling in the pound for dividend holders.)[59]

Churchill seems not to have complained about Keynes's pamphlet. Warrior that he was, flesh wounds were part of the daily routine. For his sins, however, when the million-strong miners' strike exploded in May 1926, Churchill was made point man for the government. As in many extractive industries, mining was virtually the sole industry in the coal regions, with a culture and an ethos, and a militancy, of its own. British mining may have been further down the curve of obsolescence than any— most production was still by pickaxe, rather than by cutting machines, as in most advanced countries. With considerable reason, the mine owners were also widely regarded as the most "stupid" of bosses.[60]

To make British coal prices competitive at the $4.86 exchange rate, the owners attempted to impose both a 13 percent pay cut and a return to an eight-hour day, against the contractual seven hours. The miners walked out, and the national Trades Union Congress (TUC) called for a general strike, creating a paralyzing walkoff of virtually all of the country's unionized workers. When the printing trades struck, newspapers ceased to publish, and the government created its own paper—*The British Gazette*, managed primarily by Churchill, of course, who was in his glory. It took only about a week and a half for the TUC leaders to lose their nerve and leave the miners on their own. The hyperloyal workers in the coal districts maintained the strike for nearly a year, until many were at the point of starvation. The strike finally ended when the Baldwin government provided a public subsidy, allowing the owners to impose the pay cuts but with the taxpayers putting up the difference for the miners. Keynes had predicted just such an outcome—unable to reduce real costs, the country would resort to deficits and inflation. Churchill swallowed his defeat, for defeat it was, with good grace, and allowed to his intimates that by the end of the confrontation, his sympathies were almost entirely with the miners.[61]

The general strike of 1926, protesting the treatment of coal miners, fizzled out after just a few weeks, although the miners held out for nearly a year. Pictured are Londoners walking to work due to solidarity strikes in public transportation.

VI. THE FRENCH ROLLERCOASTER

L ike all the belligerents, France had financed its wartime expenditures by printing currency. By the time of the armistice, its wholesale price index was 3.5 times higher than the prewar index, and by mid-1920, it was 5.5 times higher. The French monetary system was still quite primitive. Much of its commerce was carried out in cash, often in gold coins, which consumers carefully hoarded in coffee tins and larders. Even reasonably-sized businesses settled accounts in cash rather than by checks. The currency to deposit ratio in prewar French banks was only 3:2, compared to 20:1 in the United States and 16:1 in Great Britain, so the money multiplier inherent in fractional-deposit bank payment systems was not nearly as important as in the Anglo-Saxon countries.[62]

The backwardness of French banking turned out to be an advantage. The country's households had deep pools of savings and little regard for the wartime paper currency, so the government could mop up the currency overhang by selling short-term below-market-interest bonds. It was a strategy that at first produced sparkling results. Alone among the European economies, France saw its pace of business pick up handily at the end of 1921, with solid growth and low inflation. In just two years the price level dropped by 43 percent. With $4 billion of borrowing to rebuild its devastated northern areas, French employment markets were buoyant.[63]

It didn't last. The franc appreciated from its postwar lows, and loose international cash flowed into France, adding to the bounce. Much like the left Reichstag coalitions, the French parliament, led by the socialist Aristide Briand, could not pass meaningful tax legislation. The huge reconstruction debt, most of it short-term, was secured only by the swamp-gas promise of reparations. Prices were soon rising at a near-hyperinflation rate, and the burgeoning tide of short-term debt was blood in the water for offshore speculators. Many knowledgeable observers suspected that the British, or the American bankers associated with the Dawes commission, or the Germans, were behind the attacks on the franc. The historian Stephen Schuker has confirmed that all of them *discussed* such actions, but none of them actually added to the trading pressure. The British Treasury was almost too eager to use its power over French finance—a F600 million gold loan was overdue, for instance, and they mulled whether they should seize French gold on deposit with the Bank of England, or simply call the loan, but the political ministers would not hear of it.[64]

The French temporarily came to their senses while the Germans were still wallowing in their piles of worthless Reichsmarks. The right-center Bloc National took power in early 1922 under wartime Prime Minister Raymond Poincaré, an experienced and trusted hand. It still took him until 1924 to push through the so-called *double-decime*, a 20 percent across-the-board increase in all taxes that brought the budget into approximate balance. The Morgan $100 million loan that played such a dominant role in the Dawes negotiations, topped up by a $20 million credit from Lazard, helped finance a classic bear squeeze, buying heavily in the forward franc market to punish the speculators betting on its fall. The franc quickly jumped by 40 percent. For his pains, Poincaré was turned out of office that spring, although not before he had the satisfaction of seeing the Germans call off the passive resistance to the French Ruhr occupation, which for the first time began to return a modest profit.[65]

The Bloc's brief rule was followed by another left alliance, the Cartel des Gauches, a highly unstable slurry of agendas that eventuated in a parade of governments, including that of Édouard Herriot, who was bullied by the Americans and British at the Dawes negotiations. One nine-month stretch starting in late 1925 saw no less than five cartel ministries and six finance ministers. The franc once more descended into freefall. Part of the problem was that much of the short-term debt was not being rolled over as budgets had assumed. (The French had long made a practice of selling below-market-rate debt to their own citizens, perhaps counting on their relative lack of financial sophistication.) But any minimally attentive investor would have been scared away by the chaos of French left-alliance finance. To quote the Belgian fright advertising in the French press: "[Y]ou cannot place confidence in French credit; disorder is everywhere. . . . Belgian banks are prepared to aid you in gathering your indispensable treasure for the difficult times ahead."[66]

But common sense was still alive in France. A cabal of moderate-left deputies began to push for financial stabilization in early 1926, and by summer had a bloc of about seventy deputies. Although many of them had voted against Poincaré in 1924, they spearheaded a draft to bring him back as the head of a National Union Government. Briand and Paul Painlevé, both talented and experienced members of the Cartel were tapped for foreign minister and minister of war, respectively. Poincaré served as his own finance minister. His record inspired confidence, as did the fact that both left and right were in substantial agreement on the agenda—balancing the budgets and cleaning up the short-term debt. Neither was difficult. The budget had never been far out of balance, in great part because of Poincaré's 1924 tax program. Judicious pruning and some modest taxes put the country's fiscal position in order. Even better, in the burst of enthusiasm for the new government, once-expatriated franc holdings were flooding back into the country, easing liquidity pressures.[67]

The evidence of a political consensus may have been as important as the specific policy moves. When the exchange rate moved up from F49 to the dollar in mid-1926 to F25 at year-end, the Bank of France chose to peg the franc to the dollar. Pegging was not the same as a return to the gold standard. Great Britain had pegged the pound to the dollar during the war, but it operated as a convenience. Nor did pegging put a brake on speculation, for markets assumed that a peg could easily be changed. But after two years of experience with the pegged rate, the government fixed the gold parity at the $1/F25 rate in 1928.[68]

It was an interesting decision, fraught with implications. In the first place, it was a full 80 percent devaluation from the prewar parity of $1=F5. Prices were much higher in 1928, of course, but on a purchasing power basis the new franc was undervalued by about 10–15 percent with respect to the pound and the dollar. That would be a major spur to French exports, even as it acted as a tariff to discourage French imports.[*] It also marked a dramatic conversion for Poincaré, who had usually been

---

[*] Assume a 15 percent undervaluation of the franc to the dollar: an American wishing to buy French wine first must convert her dollars to francs, and because of the undervaluation of the franc, she would get an effective 15 percent discount on the wine. A Frenchman importing American beef, however, would have to pay a commensurate premium to equate his francs to the seller's dollar price.

associated with advocates of full "revalorization," or a return to the pre-war parity, based on the same vacuous slogans that had driven the British to overvalue the pound in 1925. The aristocrats on the board of the Bank of France, like Baron Edouard de Rothschild and the steel magnate François de Wendel, fought a two-year struggle against devaluation, or at least one so steep. The primary driver of the decision was Émile Moreau, president of the Bank of France, who had the sense to follow the advice of two brainy economists, Charles Rist and Pierre Quesnay, who had fully absorbed the lessons of the British resumption. In private, when he was pressed to explain the devaluation, Moreau usually said that he would not repeat the mistakes of the British. For the next few years, in fact, the French economy was the golden-haired prodigy of Europe.[69]

—— VII. THE END OF COOPERATION ——

Benjamin Strong was on good terms with his central banking peers, and took pains to keep their problems in the forefront of his mind. He and Norman were particularly close, usually spending two vacations a year in each other's company, both for pleasure and for wide-ranging policy discussions. Norman had especially cultivated Germany's Schacht, ensuring that Schacht and Strong had a good relationship. Norman did not like the French, however, and on his first meeting with Moreau, he was patronizing and cold—insisting on speaking in English, for example, although Norman was fluent in French and Moreau had no English. Given the new strength of the French economy, Norman's behavior was stupid, and in good time Moreau made him pay for it.[70]

Sensing cross-purposes among the four banks, Strong decided to host a conference in the spring of 1927, just for the four of them, with no notes, and no official record. Moreau, wisely, was represented by Rist, who was comfortable in English. The meeting was hardly secret—Norman's visits to the United States were always covered in the press, in part because he loved to travel incognito but always used the same few aliases so the press would be sure to find him. It was indicative of the powerful role of Strong at the Federal Reserve that he did not clear the meeting with his nominal overseers in Washington, or invite anyone else to the sessions, although the whole group made courtesy calls in the capital afterward.[71]

The meetings themselves stretched over five days at an undisclosed location—actually the modest (twenty-room) mansion of a senior Treasury official, Ogden Mills, in the Great Gatsby region of Long Island. The agenda was built around a set of critical questions: Could monetary easing in the United States take pressure off the pound and the mark? Was the wide movement back to the gold standard causing global deflation? How to manage the very large buildup of foreign exchange at the Bank of France? And could France satisfy its growing desire for gold reserves by buying them from the United States, rather than London? (London was cheaper due to shipping costs but the United States, in Strong's view, had excessive gold reserves that he would prefer to redistribute.) Schacht hoped to press for reductions in reparations, but Strong explained that there was no possibility of that until after the next US election.[72]

The meetings were apparently cordial and helpful. The most important policy change was a modest easing by the Fed, comprising a half-point discount rate cut and a modest injection of new reserves over a period of less than six months. Although Strong's action may have been primarily motivated to ease pressure on Norman and Schacht, the American economy was also showing signs of a slump, so Strong had an independent justification for it. Pressure was eased in both London and Berlin, and the French did redirect their gold purchasing to the United States, then the world's most willing seller. The episode is still controversial, however, for many writers hold that Strong's easing triggered the stock market bubble and crash, even though the 1927 easing was clearly more modest than the one in 1924, which involved three staged half-point rate cuts, and a larger injection of funds over a longer period. Markets do work in mysterious ways, and flapping butterfly wings can apparently cause hurricanes. So it's impossible to prove that Strong's action did *not* cause a cataclysm, but it seems unlikely.[73]

The Long Island meeting may have been the high point in interwar central bank cooperation. Strong died on October 15, 1928, of a botched intestinal surgery only peripherally related to the tuberculosis that was already killing him. He was replaced after his death by George Harrison, a highly intelligent lawyer who had spent much of his career at the Federal Reserve. But Harrison was not a charismatic leader in Strong's mold. The Fed board in Washington had long wanted to shift policy power away from New York, and with Strong gone from the scene, they finally succeeded. The Washington board, unfortunately, was a distinctly mediocre lot, who succeeded in making the Fed merely a bemused bystander through most of the Depression.

But currency management, or mismanagement, was only a thread in a much larger tale of high politics. At stake was whether or not the European democracies, with the help of the United States, could establish a new order of prosperity and peace. The biggest questions before the world were how to assure the security not only of France and Belgium, but also of Poland, Czechoslovakia, and other nations to Germany's east, and how to help Germany reach its full economic and political potential while restraining its military and its revanchist nationalists. Those were issues of a gravity that required decisions by governments. Central bankers could contribute to those discussions, but they did not have starring roles, and often were at cross-purposes with each other.

Between 1925 and 1929, European politicians made a determined run at coming up with a new dispensation. The Dawes plan was a big part of that, for it created a rules-based framework for German financial management and a forum for discussing the neuralgic questions of reparations and debts. Andrew Mellon played a key role as well, quietly negotiating war debt settlements with all of the Allies. The British government believed it *should* pay the debts, but needed a schedule it could manage. An early payment reduced the $5 billion debt to $4.6 billion, which was scheduled over the next sixty-two years at concessional rates of 3–3.5 percent for a total reduction in the present value* of the debt of 35 percent. Mellon had gone well beyond his settlement authority from Congress, but he made it stick at home. He then proceeded, year by year, to settle all of the $10.8 billion in war debt spread among twenty countries. All of the deals were for sixty-two years. After Great Britain, the lion's share of the debt was owed by France, Belgium, and Italy, which received present value reductions, respectively of 65, 63, and 81 percent.[74]

The Locarno Treaties of 1925 offered a similar forum for resolving problems of boundaries, security, disarmament, and trade. They were mutual security pacts signed by Germany, France, Belgium, Great Britain, and Italy—each promising not to attack any of the others, with enforcement by the nonbelligerents. (The border disputes on Germany's eastern front, with Poland and Czechoslovakia, however, were not resolved.) Those first successes evolved into a "Locarno process" of quiet negotiations between Great Britain, France, and Germany, represented respectively by Austen Chamberlain, the long-serving Conservative foreign minister, Aristide Briand, the French foreign minister (and eleven-time socialist prime minister), and Germany's Stresemann. The issues on the table were German disarmament, the early end of occupation in

---

* The lump-sum single payment required to pay off the full obligation at the present time.

Germany, and a fresh, highest-level look at the question of reparations. Although there were frictions and some serious personal strains, for the most part the three managed to get along, and occasionally even to enjoy each other's company.[75]

Despite the good will, the Locarno negotiations stretched into 1929, straining everyone's patience. The fact that they produced only a half-loaf of useful agreements cannot be considered a failure. The French agreed to an early evacuation from the Rhineland, but only after they had substantially completed their Maginot Line of fortresses on the French border. Versailles specified France's right to occupation only up to 1935, so it was a wasting asset. In any case, the Allies never had enough troops in the Rhineland to turn back a full-scale German assault; they were there to sound the alarm for mobilization and fight a delaying action. The formidable system of forts on the French side could presumably serve the same purpose at less expense.[76]

─── VIII. GERMANY UNRAVELS ───

For the first year or so on the Dawes Plan, the German economy revived considerably on its new diet of the Dawes loans. But it did not take long for the underlying contradictions in the Dawes arrangements to become evident. When France paid its reparations to Prussia after the 1870–1871 war, they paid for them with export surpluses that they earned by repressing national consumption and restricting imports, which worked real hardship on the populace. Germany, by contrast, paid its reparations out of the new foreign loans. Predominately American and British loan proceeds were paid to the Reichsbank, credited to the reparations account, and paid out to primarily to France, Belgium, and Great Britain. That worked fine in the short term—indeed, the Dawes plan explicitly described the loans as a stopgap until the German economy recovered to the point where reparations could be paid from national income.

The German leadership, Stresemann, Schacht, and the economics minister Julius Curtius, were well aware of their position. While they didn't want to pay reparations, they didn't mind the Allies paying reparations to each other. The problem, especially for Schacht, was that Germany was accreting large, private, foreign debts that would have to be paid in gold marks. Default could have serious consequences, since the Dawes protocols gave the reparations committee extraordinary enforcement powers, such as seizing tax collections. The original German argument against reparations was the nation's postwar poverty. But there was a catch-22 in that argument. If Germany did repress growth to prove their incapacity to pay, their trade account would swing into the black as their imports fell, and the Allies would have the right to claim the German export surpluses as reparation payments.[77]

Schacht had nightmares besides the reparations conundrum. All the foreign money flowing into Germany looked like an engine of inflation. The smoothness of the initial Dawes loan placements had acted like a AAA bond rating, and brought funds, both long and short, flooding into the country. Part of the attraction was the very high Schachtian discount rates. (The discount rate was *lowered* to 9 percent in 1925.) Industry was clamoring against the financial stringency, the government budgets were running substantial surpluses, and the economy actually contracted through most of 1925 and 1926.[78]

The combination of repressive German bank rates and floods of foreign-sourced liquidity sloshing around the banking system cost Schacht control of the money supply. By early 1927, he was forced to drop discount rates down to just 5 percent. But he was determined to force rates back up, which he proceeded to do with his characteristic mix of cleverness and ham-handedness. In December of 1926, he had prevailed upon the government to end the exemption from capital taxes for foreign bond purchasers, which stopped the foreign cash inflows in their tracks. Then he turned to the stock market, which he regarded an engine of speculation. In what has been called an "excessively brusque action," he forced sharp reductions in bank margin lending, under threat of loss of rediscount privileges. The banks complied, but the Berlin banks made a dramatic joint announcement that precipitated a severe market crash. The consequent flight of gold and foreign exchange from Germany forced a rise in the German discount rate to such an extent that Schacht had to acquiesce in a restoration of the capital tax exemption for foreign bond purchasers. (Subsequent research makes a strong case that there was no bubble in German stocks.)

Then, in February of 1927, Germany floated an enormous bond issue, possibly the biggest German bond issue ever to that point, with distribution limited to Germans. The bond issue was the brainchild of Peter Reinhold, the finance minister. The target principal amount was 500 million gold RMs, with 300 million distributed by a syndicate of eighty German banks and 200 subscribed for by state companies. The loan drew a great deal of criticism, both from Schacht, who feared that such a huge amount of money in the hands of the government could only be wasted, and even more from Parker Gilbert, the reparations agent. In a report for the half-year ending in June 1927, Gilbert showed the booking of the 500 million RMs, while noting that only 373 million had been realized from the flotation (German budget practices in this period were to book all planned receipts, with later fine-print deductions of shortfalls).*[79]

---

* In his report, Gilbert went on: "The effect of all this procedure is to present the

As much as anyone, Gilbert forced the reopening of the Dawes plan because of the slippage in the German budget performance. In 1927, for instance, an extremely generous unemployment benefits program sailed through the National Assembly without any funding provision. Gilbert warned that the reparations agenda would never be cleared up unless Germany started to "act to save itself, instead of looking to foreign loans and credits as a means of avoiding the disagreeable job of internal reform." Owen Young was drafted to chair a Dawes-like committee to develop a proposal. Mellon and the Coolidge administration blessed the undertaking, although stipulating that the American government had no official involvement with it.[80]

The Young panel's sessions were bumpy. Although both the Germans and the Allies had agreed in principle to establish some smaller, but significant, reparations schedules, it took months of wary circling before anyone produced hard numbers. The Germans seem to have convinced themselves that the Allies had realized what an obstacle to recovery the reparations had become, while the Allied representatives were willing to entertain some reductions in return for tightening the screws on German performance. It did not help that a Labour government took office in Great Britain and Chamberlain was replaced by Philip Snowden. He was an unusually irascible and contentious man, and tied up the conference for months straining pettily to capture more payments for Great Britain. The German side, unfortunately, was represented by Schacht, who was as disruptive as Snowden. When the final deal was cut, he refused to sign it, indulging in histrionic displays until he was ordered by Stresemann, in effect, to shut up and sign it before the Reich collapsed.

The Germans had reasons to be disappointed with the revised reparations schedule, since it was only about a fifth smaller than the Dawes payments. Stresemann wearily assured his colleagues that the Reich would collapse financially without new money, and the "Young plan," as

---

financial position of the Reich in a most artificial light. These outstanding revenues, consisting principally of loans to be issued, do not represent effective revenues whereas the outstanding expenditures represent actual authorizations to spend, which in large part are already committed. This system of accounting, in other words, permits budget surpluses to be shown which do not actually exist and which will only come into existence in the future to the extent that loans are actually placed. Expressed in another manner, the budget surpluses shown can often be realized only through borrowing."

it was called, would be reopened just as the Dawes plan was. The reparations agent was replaced with a new organization, the Bank for International Settlements (BIS), to process and distribute the payments. The BIS still exists today, because as Young and others perceived, and as its name implies, it became a useful clearing house for netting and settling international payments.* Once the deal was agreed in January 1930, the bankers floated a $300 million loan, two-thirds of which went to reparation creditors, with the rest to German budget relief. It was to be the last reparation payment. Nobody mentioned that the so-called "final" reparation schedule was well within the boundaries of German affordability posited by Keynes in his *The Economic Consequences of the Peace*.[81]

For all the real progress, there was a still sour edge to the winding up of the Locarno process. It had taken far too long, too much had been left undone, promises made in apparent good faith had not been kept. Again and again, negotiators who thought they had political clearance for their commitments were reversed because of power shifts at home. Snowden's last-minute antics embittered the French and the Belgians. The death of Stresemann shortly after the final agreements had been signed removed perhaps the central figure in the process, one of the last of the moderate Germans.

The years from 1924 to 1929 have been called the "golden age" of Weimar. But few people seemed to realize how precarious the German financial position had become. The country seemed prosperous, with real GNP growth of 5.6 percent from 1925–1929. But in retrospect the signs of a slump were visible as early as mid-1927, when the country began to run an export surplus. It wasn't because exports had risen; rather, it was because imports were falling faster than exports, suggesting an important weakening of spending, especially in investment and government spending. The economic historian and Weimar specialist Theo Balderston makes a strong case that the fatal fault lines lay in the German financial system. There was an extensive array of yawning pitfalls: investors were nervous about the rising reparations under the Young Plan; there had

---

* Interbank payments clearing is the process of aggregating the debits and credits between banks in a network in order to transfer only netted amounts. Especially in the gold standard days, a central netting and clearing mechanism greatly economized on the use of monetary gold.

been sharp unfunded spending increases in the Reichstag, suggesting a loss of discipline; the failed 1927 bond issue highlighted the enduring incapacities of German banking; and the right-wing shift in German politics possibly presaged an early repudiation of the entire post-Versailles treaty apparatus. All of those worries were dwarfed by the bedrock flaws in the German banking system, which had still not been fully recapitalized after the Great Inflation. About 40 percent of their deposits were short-term and foreign-owned and could disappear in an eye-blink.[82]

Gilbert's final report released in 1930 was caustic:

First and foremost, there has been no effective recognition of the principle that the Government must live within its income. Revenues have been ample . . . [and] would have been adequate to meet all legitimate requirements of the Reich, and even to provide a reasonable margin of safety, if only a firm financial policy had been pursued. For the past four years, however, the Government has always spent more than it received and at times, especially during 1929–30, it has made commitments to spend even more than it can borrow.[83]

It wasn't a pretty picture. The budget was out of control and public debt was rising rapidly. During the 1929–1930 fiscal year, debt increased by 16 percent, two-thirds of it short-term floating debt, most of it callable. German authorities later complained that their problems didn't

FIGURE 4.4: GERMAN FISCAL FOLLIES, 1924–1929[84]

	Balance on Current Account	Balance on Capital Account	Net
1924	-1,664	2,919	1,255
1925	-3,045	3,135	90
1926	39	607	646
1927	-4,244	3,792	-452
1928	-3,192	4,132	940
1929	-2,469	2,304	-165
Totals	-14,575	16,889	2,314

Source: Balderston, "Origins of Economic Instability," Table 1.

commence until 1928, when the American stock market sucked up American liquidity, cutting off its primary funding source. That wasn't true (see Figure 4.4). Germany was running big trade deficits (the current account), while at the same time receiving very large, often unsecured, capital infusions from starry-eyed investors (the capital, or borrowing account). The total of reparations paid over the entire period of the Dawes plan was less than the proceeds from international loans. In other words, the Germans paid the reparations by borrowing from the war's victors, and rubbed it in by defaulting on the loans.

IX. THE GOLDEN JIHAD

The forebodings were only worsened by a semimessianic drive by the French to force a gold-based deflation on the rest of Europe. Rather like some born-again evangelists, the conversion came after a period of riotous monetary dissipation, and was carefully cushioned by the 80 percent devaluation of the franc, well under the free market rate. In effect, the French gold parity was a tool to transfer wealth from France's trading partners. The French dogmatism, moreover, was laced with more than a dash of revenge-seeking against both Germany and Great Britain. Throughout the post-Versailles process, there had been a subtle pairing of the United States and Great Britain acting together to monitor how France and Germany worked out their war settlement. In the Locarno meetings, Chamberlain behaved as if Great Britain had no dog in the fight, usually intervening only when things got off track. But his opinion counted because he was still joined at the hip with America, who controlled the money. Germany and France, in effect, were at the kids' table, while the parents who dominated global finance quietly pulled the strings. That would be bad enough, but to French eyes, the adults consistently resisted placing limits on Germany, while diligently undercutting the years of French efforts to construct a reliable bulwark against being run over by a resurrected and reenergized German war machine.

But worms can turn. After Poincaré and Moreau pegged the franc to the dollar in 1926, they adopted a financial program much like the one the IMF imposed on repentant emerging market countries in the 1990s—balance budgets, reduce taxes, and pay off debt. Their twist was that they refused to consider foreign exchange as a reserve, insisting only on gold, francs, and high-quality commercial paper, a view that Benjamin Strong had shared. The French Monetary Law of 1928 converted the peg into the officially supported price for the new gold franc, while fashioning a stone corset for policy makers. The preference for not counting foreign exchange in the French reserves, for example, became a commandment.[85]

Experts considered that the franc had been valued at about 15 percent below its true purchasing power, while *The Economist* calculated that internal French prices were as much as 25 percent lower than in the rest of the world. Spreads like that precipitated a flood of hot money into France, seeking to profit from the imbalance. Under the old gold standard rules, such an influx would have triggered French inflation, removing the profit opportunity. But the Bank of France maintained price stability by sterilizing the inflows (offsetting them by withdrawing equivalent amounts of system liquidity). At first, that just increased the inflows, which the French deterred by selling back the foreign currencies to their home banks and insisting on gold.[86]

From the end of 1926 through mid-1928, the French gained $335 million in new gold and about a $1 billion in foreign exchange. Over the next three years it reduced its foreign exchange holdings by $350 million, but increased its gold holdings by $1.16 billion, raising its share of world monetary gold from less than 8 percent to more than 20 percent. During that time, there were no dramatic changes in American gold holdings, which fluctuated around 40 percent of the world total. Altogether, from 1926 until the world gold crisis of April 1931, the French absorbed $1.47 billion in gold while the United States took only an additional $290 million. By 1932, the French were actually drawing even with the United States in gold holdings—$3.5 billion for the United States and $3.2 billion for France, an absurd ratio for a country with a manufacturing output only 15 percent the size of that of the United States.[87]

The obsessive accumulation of gold on the part of the French had mixed political and doctrinal motivations. The politics were straightforward. Moreau must have enjoyed making a diary entry recording how the Bank of England finally understood that the French could knock them off the gold standard at any time. High French monetary circles also must have taken pleasure watching Schacht futilely struggling to ward off default as the French methodically pressured his limited supplies of gold. At the same time, the French were probably sincere in their commitment to maintaining the supremacy of gold as the global measure of value. The withdrawal of gold from world markets led to a vast contraction in available money and drove down most world prices near to those of France. The Bank of France celebrated the event, noting that "world prices have become fairly well adapted to the rate at which the franc was fixed in 1928." And again, "among the group indexes the index of imported commodities declined more than did the index of French commodities," suggesting that it was the French prices that were correct. Rist also expressed satisfaction with the price movements, complaining that there would have been "a general decline in the price level earlier if efforts had not been made from all sides to stimulate consumption artificially and to maintain it at a level superior to that corresponding to real income. It is there, in our view, that it is necessary to seek the specific origin of the present crisis." In the same vein, Rist complained that Federal Reserve easing only "obscured the impending decline in prices and . . . hindered the deflation of credit." After 1929, the deflation of credit was pretty much untrammeled. Between 1928 and 1930, British industrial prices fell by 27 percent, the price of goods imported into France fell as much as 40 percent, while internal French prices fell only by 4 percent.[88]

Deflation has consequences beyond the glow of moral satisfaction it produces in its advocates. As Irving Fisher and Maynard Keynes had long since pointed out, deflation is the scourge of debtors, since the principal value of a loan doesn't change when prices and wages fall. But nor is a serious deflation a boon for creditors, since past a certain point, debtors will simply default and bring the creditors down with them. The French-engineered price collapse in Europe did just that. Over the spring and summer of 1931, virtually all the major countries departed the gold standard. The primary axis of contamination ran from Austria to Germany to Great Britain.

The first victim was Austria's largest bank, the Kreditanstalt, part of the Rothschild financial network, with a blue-ribbon business clientele. Like many Germanic banks, the Kreditanstalt took equity positions in its clients as well as lending to them. Given the financial disruptions in postwar Europe, the Austrian government had enlisted the bank's aid in workouts of troubled lenders, most of them small. But in 1929, the Kreditanstalt had agreed to rescue its largest competitor out of bankruptcy, making its balance sheet bigger than that of all the rest of the Austrian joint stock banks combined. Worse, the bank's portfolio was seriously mismatched, with long-dated troubled assets funded with volatile, short-term liabilities. As the loan portfolio continued to deteriorate, the government made secret cash infusions to keep the bank afloat, which must have been known within Vienna's elite. But it was still a shock when in early May 1931 the officers admitted that they had run through almost all of the bank's capital, and still were exposed on $100 million of short-term liabilities in favor of the US and European nationals. A run on the Kreditanstalt quickly turned into a run on Austrian banks. The government stepped in again with an equity infusion for the Kreditanstalt, and the Austrian National Bank (ANB) took over large swaths of its paper.[89]

Austria was a country of only seven million people, and the Kreditanstalt was still relatively small potatoes. But the name and the connections drew the spotlight. The apparent takeover by the government and the ballooning short-term credits provided by the ANB looked like the first stage of a determined inflation. Most European banks were walking on a knife's edge. Superficially, they were brimming with deposits, but an unusually high share of them, in the range of $3 billion, was hot money drawn by the continent's high rates but ready to jump at the hint of danger. The ANB had begun the episode with a strong reserve position for a country its size. But once a run started, its reserves dropped by a third within just a few weeks. Seizing the chance to weaken a German ally, the French quietly encouraged their banks to repatriate their deposits in Austria.[90]

Seeking protection, the ANB cobbled together a $15 million credit line from the Bank of England, the Federal Reserve, and the BIS, but it took three weeks, well into June. By that time, the run had intensified, and the ANB was in desperate need of another $20 million. France volunteered to provide it, subject to the condition that Germany and Austria drop plans of forming a customs union, which they had announced two months before. (In the nineteenth century such arrangements had been a step toward unifying Prussia and smaller German states. Versailles had strong provisions against German territorial additions.) Austria indignantly refused, and Norman provided the money from the Bank of England. But he conditioned the loan on a stand-still agreement sharply limiting depositors' ability to move their money out of the country. In the eyes of traders, stand-stills were tantamount to leaving the gold standard. The Austrian government fell, and markets were distorted, although, technically, the Kreditanstalt did not fail.[91]

Stand-still agreements were like a virus—once used, they spread like swine flu. If Austria froze deposits, the offshore depositors were at greater risk of defaulting on their non-Austrian obligations. The Berlin stock market dropped steeply, and wild rumors swept through the German financial community. The Reichsbank lost $250 million of gold and foreign exchange in just three weeks. Later research suggests that it was the *German* depositors who were the first movers in pulling out their money, and there are multiple reports of wealthy Germans hauling suitcases of money over the Dutch and Swiss borders. The panic eased on June 24 when Hans Luther, a former finance minister who had replaced Schacht at the Reichsbank, put together a $100 million credit line from the Bank of England, the Federal Reserve, and the BIS.[92]

By that time, Lamont had begun lobbying President Hoover to declare a moratorium on war debts and reparations. While Hoover was vetting Lamont's proposal with his cabinet, the conservative German chancellor, Heinrich Brüning, trying to gain control of the Reich's budget deficits, announced a major austerity package, including new taxes and substantial benefits cuts. In the same announcement, he complained bitterly about the Young plan and "the intolerable reparation obligations" and "tributary payments" being exacted from Germany. Henry Stimson, Hoover's secretary of state, took umbrage at Brüning's tone, warning that it would trigger capital flight from Germany and undercut Hoover's still secret moratorium.[93]

Two weeks later, after extensive consultations with the Congress, and with Germany hemorrhaging gold, Hoover announced that the United States would forego a year's principal and interest on $245 million of war debts, provided the Allies suspended $385 million in reparations. Incredibly, as it seemed to outsiders, the administration teams putting together the package had diligently consulted everyone except the French, by far the largest reparations creditor. But it was not an oversight; Hoover feared that the French would block his proposal, so he and Stimson chose to surprise them. The entire French nation was outraged. Treasury secretary Mellon was in France on a vacation and was hurriedly dispatched to Paris to patch things up, which he did, after three weeks and some minor technical adjustments, a delay that was costly.[94]

By the time the moratorium was officially announced, a major German textile conglomerate had failed, exposing the Danat Bank, one of Germany's largest. An immediate panicked run on the Danat forced Luther to run through his entire credit line by July 4. Luther somehow kept the Reichsbank afloat, although in violation of its gold and exchange reserve requirements. On July 8, Luther told the other major central banks that he needed a new credit line of at least $500 million, and ideally $1 billion, to stop the rot. The bankers were skeptical. Their information suggested that it was German nationals, not foreign depositors, who were causing the run. There was also a loose consensus that the sums Luther was looking for needed approval from their respective governments.

That was impossible: French aid would come only with stringent political conditions; the British wanted all reparations and similar conditions dropped; the Americans were willing to countenance a one year moratorium, after which the agreed payment schedules would once again be enforced. At a London meeting of July 20–23, the bankers and government representatives agreed only to organize a study group. Like Austria, Germany did not officially go off the gold standard, but maintained a pretext of functioning by freezing all international accounts—in effect, living off other people's money, as they had been doing for some time.[95]

By mid-1931 Great Britain's Labour government had been in power for two years, and was tearing itself apart. The prime minister, Ramsay MacDonald, and his chancellor, Snowden, were diligently following the hard path required to wrench the country's finances into conformity with its overvalued pound. For their pains, they had seen industrial output decline by about a fifth and the unemployment rate double to about 22 percent. Arthur Henderson, the foreign minister and a leading figure in the TUC, accused the government of punishing ordinary workers to satisfy the whims of its overpaid financial industry. Great Britain was clearly in trouble. Its short-term liabilities were at least $2 billion, supported by only a fourth or fifth that amount in gold reserves. It had succeeded in reducing imports, but had cut its exports even more. It had cut its overseas capital investment, but had seen its invisibles trade and earnings from overseas investments fall even more—precisely vindicating Keynes's sarcasm in *Consequences of Mr. Churchill* that "so far as the maintenance of the gold standard is concerned, it is a matter of indifference whether we have £100,000,000 worth of foreign investment or £100,000,000 worth of unemployment."[96]

The July attacks on the Danat bank quickly spread to the pound. Sterling fell beneath the gold export point, and within two weeks, Great Britain had lost a quarter of its gold and foreign exchange reserves, at a time when the German stand-stills had barred access to $300 million of British deposits. Financial authorities in France, Belgium, Switzerland, Holland, and Sweden all pulled assets out of London. It didn't help that the government released the final version of the parliamentary *Macmillan Report*, an analysis of the country's fiscal situation, for it had the first revelations of the country's immense overhang of short-term liabilities. Rumors flew.

The government responded with platitudes. Norman collapsed, and left for a months-long recuperation in Canada. Parliament adjourned.[97]

Harrison and Clément Moret, Moreau's successor at the Bank of France, assembled a credit line of $250 million in July, each putting up half. Its effect was diminished by haggling over the process for disbursing funds. At about the same time, Snowden announced the current year's budget deficit would be well over $600 million—the biggest since 1920— and would be even larger the next year.[98]

Great Britain burned through the $250 million in less than a month. Snowden produced a new, rigorously austere budget, which split the Labour party and brought down the government. But the king asked MacDonald to stay on as prime minister and organize a national government comprising mostly Conservatives and Liberals. Snowden was also retained as chancellor. Harrison worked diligently with the Bank of France and came up with a $400 million rescue package, half from a private flotation by a Morgan-led banking consortium, while the French supplied its share 50:50 from a private flotation and a public offering.[99]

At the end of the day, the British commitment to gold may have been undone by a *Yertle the Turtle* event. As all Dr. Seuss fans know, Yertle was forced to hold up a huge tower of turtles, but when he burped, the whole construct collapsed. On September 15, the Admiralty announced that five hundred sailors at the Royal Navy base at Invergordon, Scotland, had refused to man their ships after learning of Snowden's pay cuts. The men had held an orderly meeting in a field, and later they "could be seen dancing on the decks of one battleship, and from all the ships came sounds of men singing and shouting." Their grievance was twofold. Men who had enlisted in the early years of the war received "permanent pay" of a $1-per-day equivalent, while newer men received a lower rate. The chancellor had not only broken the "permanent pay" pledge, but had made much steeper percentage cuts in the lower pay scales than for top officers. The nation was shocked, although the Admiralty had the good sense to announce an investigation into the men's complaints. In parliament, Winston Churchill cursed the gold standard, and Viscount John Sion, a senior and respected Liberal, called for the adoption of a tariff—a particularly radical notion in dogmatically free trade England. In his history of the period's central banking, Stephen V. O. Clarke writes "[T]here can be little doubt that the so-called mutiny . . . precipitated the final onslaught against sterling."[100]

By September 16, almost half of the new $400 million line had been committed to the defense, but with little visible effect on the markets. By September 19, the Bank of England's gold and foreign exchange exceeded its most pressing liabilities by only $20 million. By that point, the defense of sterling had consumed $1 billion over the space of two months, completely overshadowing Snowden's first balanced budget. Sir Ernest Harvey, the bank's deputy governor, who was acting for Norman, called Harrison in New York on the 19th to warn him that England was planning to go off the gold standard on Monday, the 21st. Harrison proposed alternatives, but Harvey had no interest. Harrison's memorandum records: "I said it seems a great pity to let it go and asked whether there was anything we could do within reason. Harvey replied that he thought we had already done a great deal and that he saw nothing else which we could do to help, that there was no alternative left."[101]

The blow to global confidence from the British departure was palpable. American bank failures rose by 86 percent in the second half of 1931, and defaults on foreign dollar bonds increased seventeenfold. The decline in industrial output accelerated, and industrial country unemployment reached new highs. World exports fell by about a third in 1932. Overall volumes were just two-fifths of those in 1929.[102]

———

France enjoyed a much easier Depression than the rest of Europe until about 1932, when their beggar-my-neighbor policies caught up with them. First of all, the deep decline in European production and purchasing power destroyed their export markets—specialty foods and wines, perfumes, and tourism. European prices mostly fell to the range of those in France, destroying the special advantage of the undervalued franc. And since the commodity gold price was no longer a constraint on most of France's trading partners, franc prices could be readily undersold. French unemployment spiked in 1932 to 15 percent, and industrial production dropped by 25 percent. From that point to the run-up to the war, the French economy simply stagnated.[103]

Germany and the United States are generally conceded to have endured the most serious depressions. In Germany, where unemployment rose to the 40 percent level, ragged crowds of former workers and their families were reduced to beggary. The destabilization paved the way for the rise of Hitler, who imposed a command economy focused on military production and financed by a radical suppression of consumer demand. By the mid-1930s, Germans were virtually fully employed living at a spartan but sustainable level. Most were happy to make the trade. Reparations had been repudiated, and Hitler was driving to a near autarkic economy.[104]

At a 1932 conference in Lausanne, Switzerland, Great Britain, Germany, and France agreed to suspend reparations, provided that the United States would suspend collection of its war debts—which Congress refused. The following year, Hitler repudiated the entire Versailles framework.

In 1933, in the United States, a new president, Franklin D. Roosevelt, attempted to inaugurate what his publicists called a "New Deal."

PART FIVE

Roosevelt, Reflation, and Recovery

I. WORLD MONETARY & ECONOMIC CONFERENCE

Representatives of sixty-six of the officially recognized sixty-seven nations of the world descended upon London in mid-June 1933 to gather in the Hall of Fossils of the city's new Geological Museum. "Statesmen of every color," *Time* magazine enthused, "babbling every language and brimming with every economic creed . . . sat down like schoolboys behind green metal desks for the World Monetary & Economic Conference, [the] most crucial gathering since Versailles."

Time's hyperbolic assessment of the conference's importance reflected the hopes of its organizers, foremost among them British Prime Minister Ramsay MacDonald, the former Labour prime minister who was now the leader of a national government dominated by Conservatives. The king himself, George V, welcomed the delegates and proceeded to boggle the translators and charm non-Anglophone delegates by switching easily between French and English in his address. MacDonald delivered a grim keynote: "The world is being driven on a state of things . . . in which the life revolts against hardships and the gains of the past are swept away for forces of despair. . . . [A] purely national economic policy in this modern world is one which by impoverishing other nations, impoverishes itself at the expense of others. . . . Nationalism in economics is the deathknell of . . . prosperity."[1] The conference organizers had set an absurdly ambitious agenda—to reach agreements on lowering trade barriers, commencing disarmament, resolving issues of war debts and reparations, returning major trading countries to the gold standard, and adopting a common view on issues of reflation and deflation. None of them was achieved. Disarmament was an impossible dream. The American Congress would not budge on war debts and reparations. Great Britain was committed to unwanted trade protections. Wise men were badly split on issues of deflation and reflation, while France was determined to force the rest of the world through a deflationary gauntlet to the old gold parities.

Conference planning had started long before the election, and Mac-Donald had carefully coordinated his plans with then-President Hoover, an enthusiast of conferences. Roosevelt was skeptical, dutifully praising the objectives without endorsing any specific policies. As it happened, the sheer fact of the conference and its intense early media coverage forced Roosevelt to clarify his attitudes toward gold and inflation, which he then almost casually proceeded to impose on the rest of the world. Roosevelt was not an economic naïf. He was born amid great wealth. As a young boy, he had been schooled in France and Germany, and was fluent in both languages. Leading money men were regular guests at Roosevelt family gatherings. At Harvard, while he was no scholar, he had taken several economics courses, taught by luminaries like Oliver M. W. Sprague, adviser to both the Federal Reserve and the Bank of England, and author of the late-1933 ten-part *New York Times* disquisition purporting to map the path to recovery. While Roosevelt respected leading bankers, academics, and businessmen, he was not overawed by them.[2]

Roosevelt's first actions drew the approval of the money men. Huge swaths of the country's banks were shuttered on the day he took office. He called an emergency session of Congress for March 9, asking for a national banking holiday in order to ascertain the solvency of America's banks, along with a conservative reform program—much of it from Hoover's Treasury—to allow the Reconstruction Finance Corporation (RFC) to invest in the preferred shares of sound banks in order to strengthen their capital. Most of the country's banks reopened the following Monday. There were some panicky moments when reports filtered into the White House that long lines were forming outside most banks, followed by whooshes of relief when it turned out that the lines of people were coming to redeposit their funds.

Still, among the day's policy aficionados Roosevelt was viewed as a politically gifted lightweight. During the campaign, Walter Lippmann wrote that Roosevelt "is a pleasant man who, without any important qualifications for the office, would very much like to be President." That impression was fostered in part by his congenital agreeableness—he smiled encouragingly through encounters with friend and foe alike—but also because of his skittering, intuitive way of thinking. Henry Stimson, a later secretary of war, once said that following the President's train of thought was "very much like chasing a vagrant beam of sunshine around an empty room." That is not a bad description of one of Roosevelt's most portentous early policy decisions—to take the country off the gold standard.[3]

In the long interregnum between the presidential election and the inauguration, Hoover was at his most bullheaded—essentially on a mission to convert Roosevelt to his fundamentalist version of the gold standard. Roosevelt was at first studiously noncommittal when Hoover badgered him to make joint policy statements on banking and monetary policy, but was finally forced into uncharacteristic rudeness to cut off the conversations.[4]

Since Hoover's fingerprints were all over the London conference, it was not a natural priority for Roosevelt. But as he and his advisers cast about for a monetary lever to elevate commodity prices, they hit on the London conference as a vehicle for reaching an international consensus on reflation. Their first move was to arrange for a postponement of the conference opening until June, since the White House team, although they knew they wanted higher prices, had not settled on a clear path to achieve them.[5]

Roosevelt's monetary policies are best understood through the lens of the congressional farm bloc. It was possibly the country's most influential special interest, and in 1933 its constituent industry was in desperate trouble. Opening the American prairies to intensive industrial agriculture was one of the great economic successes of the last quarter of the nineteenth century. American farmers received another huge boost when World War I disrupted competing agriculture supply chains. Farmers invested frantically to take advantage of the opportunity, and were badly overextended when the war suddenly ended and their traditional competitors came roaring back. The deflation immediately after the war ballooned the real debts of farmers who had borrowed to expand their operations during the boom. One study showed that in the first half of the 1920s, the average farm owner received less income than his hired men.[6]

The recovery of America's agricultural competitors intersected with solid increases in farm productivity. Farmers had been mechanizing since the advent of the McCormick reaper in the 1860s, and were among the first to take advantage of the internal combustion engine. Henry Ford took special pains to ensure that his Model T was adapted to deep-country conditions—with independent wheel suspensions to straddle rutted rural roads, rugged parts, engine layouts designed for easy repair, and kits to help farmers repurpose the Model T as a tractor. By the mid-twenties, Ford tractors were a profitable sideline. By the 1930s, the advent of the tractor consigned ten million horses and mules to slaughter and freed up the twenty-three million acres of farmland devoted to their fodder. Although there were many exceptions, farmers with larger properties, who had mechanized and adopted modern cultivation techniques, were relatively prosperous in the late 1920s. It was the smaller, less scientific farmers who were in the deepest trouble, the paradigmatic flotsam of a technology transition.[7]

Agricultural economists track the farm "parity ratio"—the ratio of the indices for prices paid *to* farmers over the prices paid *by* farmers. In 1917, when American food was sustaining most of Europe, the ratio was 120 in favor of farmers. By 1921, it had fallen to only 80, but recovered to an average of 90 through the rest of the 1920s. The apparent disadvantage to farmers would have been somewhat mitigated by the falling prices and quality improvements of mass-produced manufactured goods, like automobiles, washing machines, and radios. Despite the parity gap, successful farmers were probably still seeing improvements in their standard of living.[8]

But farm prices took a nosedive in 1930. From midsummer of 1929 to the month that Roosevelt took office, the farm price index dropped by two-thirds—primarily the result of perversely favorable weather, but possibly also progress on mechanization. The mountains of unsold grain and cotton that pushed the Hoover farm cooperatives into insolvency crushed farmers' parity ratios—from 92 in 1929, which farmers had complained about, all the way down to 58 in 1932. Gross farm incomes were halved.[9]

Unlike manufacturers, it was hard for farmers to exit a market. They generally lived on their farms, and were deeply invested in their land, their equipment, their animals, and their crops. Even the largest farmers were too small to influence their market. When granaries and meat lockers were overwhelmed with unsellable product, the rational farmer would just produce more, no matter what the price, since he had already absorbed the sunk cost. The waves of bank failures in the early 1930s were overwhelmingly in rural areas. The American political system systematically overrepresents rural areas, and did so even more in the 1930s than now. So when Franklin Roosevelt thought about monetary policy, it was primarily in pursuit of raising commodity prices and saving rural America.[10]

The Agricultural Adjustment Act (AAA) was passed by both houses of Congress and signed by the president after he had been in office less than a month. Its declared policy was:

> to establish and maintain such balance between the production and consumption of agricultural commodities, and such marketing conditions therefor, as will reestablish prices to farmers at a level that will give agricultural commodities a purchasing power with respect to articles that farmers buy, equivalent to the purchasing power of agricultural products in the base period.[11]

The law was a complex blend of debt relief for farmers, financial incentives to reduce plantings, and federal purchasing to push up prices. The act carried an appropriation of $100 million, to be used to defray all expenses, including benefit payments to farmers, but also provided a "processing tax" to be levied on the first processors of any commodity slated to receive benefits under the act.[*][12] The bill had few fans in the Congress, mostly because of its complexity, and even its supporters understood that it would take a long time to work. So Roosevelt and one of his favorite "Brain Trusters," Raymond Moley, investigated the possibility of jacking up commodity price levels through monetary policy, with considerable input from Henry Morgenthau, an old friend and gentleman farmer from New York, whom Roosevelt had drafted to chair the new Farm Credit Administration.

The Congress got involved in early April, pairing the AAA bill with the Thomas Amendment, named after its sponsor, a reflationist Oklahoma senator, Elmer Thomas. The amendment empowered the president

---

* The processing tax was declared unconstitutional in 1935, but the funding was replaced by general revenues.

to raise prices by any of a menu that included large-scale purchasing of government securities, issuing up to $3 billion in greenbacks, expanding the use of monetary silver, or devaluing the dollar. The original bill *required* the president to take one or more of those actions, and Roosevelt considered it a victory that the final bill had left it to his option. But the message was strong, and Roosevelt privately let it be known that he had been converted to the devaluationist camp. When that leaked in mid-April, the dollar took a steep fall, prompting celebrations in the White House and the Farm Belt. Roosevelt then secured legislation forbidding most private ownership of monetary gold and embargoing its export to prevent a flight of monetary gold from the Treasury. The practical effect was that the United States was no longer on the gold standard. If foreigners couldn't get paid in gold, they would be forced to protect themselves by bidding up paper dollar prices. And, indeed, commodity and stock market prices rose rapidly for the next several months.[13]

Those events occurred as MacDonald and Édouard Herriot, leader of the French Radical party and a three-time prime minister, were separately en route to visit Roosevelt in preparation for the world economic conference. They might as well have stayed home, for Roosevelt had lost interest when he learned that forgiveness of the American war loans was one of the conference's top priorities. He didn't feel strongly about the issue, but there wasn't a chance that the Congress would have stood for it. Roosevelt did give lukewarm support to a plan floated by his monetary experts to stabilize the dollar-pound-franc cross-rates, incorporating a 15–25 percent American devaluation. Neither Herriot nor MacDonald was willing to agree to such an arrangement, leaving it to the conference meetings in June.[14]

Roosevelt appointed a large and diverse American delegation to the conference, which was nominally led by Cordell Hull, the new secretary of state, with little policy guidance from the White House. The first order of backroom business was to negotiate a currency stabilization agreement between the British, the French, and the Americans. The chair of the monetary committee was James M. Cox, a former governor and congressman from Ohio—Roosevelt had been his running mate when Cox was the Democratic presidential nominee in 1920. Herbert Feis, a historian and economist, was an adviser to the Treasury along with James Warburg, an influential banker and a scion of the Warburg bank.

Roosevelt's former professor, Harvard's Sprague, had been enlisted as a technical adviser to the conference working group—he and Warburg may have been the most vociferous advocates for a stabilization agreement at almost any cost. Within just a few days, the three country teams agreed on a stabilization plan. Superficially, it looked like the plan Roosevelt had signed off on at the Washington meetings, but the fine print included show-stopping provisions, like promising never to invoke the Thomas Amendment powers, and setting an uncomfortably high level for the stabilized dollar. When news of the agreement hit the press, commodity prices and the stock market duly crashed, and Roosevelt quickly rejected it. The official communique to the conference said, "The American government feels that its efforts to raise prices are the most important contribution it can make, and that anything that would . . . possibly cause a violent *price recession* would harm the conference."[15]

In retrospect, it's easy to see how Roosevelt's position was evolving. At the right price levels, a British-French-American stabilization was a fine idea, but there was an immense gulf between the rock-hard deflationist position of the French and the reflationary yearnings of the British and Americans. Nor did Roosevelt see any urgency. The British, most of the Commonwealth, and the French, had all dropped the gold standard for periods of years, without any dreadful consequences. The United States needed time to think through its objectives, particularly since Roosevelt was convinced that getting the right prices was the main thing. Stabilizing too early could only handcuff his policy making.

At that point, Moley decided he should go to the conference, as Roosevelt had urged him to. He first met with the president, who was on a sailing vacation, for any last-minute instructions. According to the historian Arthur Schlesinger Jr., they were mostly about not visibly upstaging Hull. Hull, however, was a wily politician, who viewed Moley as a self-important meddler. As he later wrote, he decided "to give him all the rope he might want and see how long he would last." It took only a few weeks.[16]

Moley arrived at the conference just after Roosevelt's stiff reaction to the original stabilization agreement had touched off a sharp fall in the value of the dollar and a correspondingly sharp rise in American commodity prices. The dollar's fall against gold put great pressure on the "Gold Bloc,"—Belgium, the Netherlands, Poland, and Switzerland—that had adopted the French hardline deflationist monetary stance. As their currencies rose against the dollar, all of the deflationist countries' exports collapsed, and they feared being forced off gold. Desperately, they pleaded for a stabilization agreement to preserve their commitment to gold.

What they asked for, Moley thought, was utterly innocuous—merely affirmations from the United States that they were committed to an eventual return to a gold standard with fixed exchange rates. Spooling out all the rope that Hull had supplied, Moley took over the project. Sure of his own judgment, he deftly worked out a conforming agreement, cleared it with other key Roosevelt advisers, including the deflationists Dean Acheson, the undersecretary of the treasury, and Lewis Douglas, the director of the budget, and scheduled a Downing Street press announcement, with MacDonald presiding, *before* he cleared it with the president.[17]

Roosevelt was appalled, and quickly returned a firm rejection. That note was only for his own team, who would have normally crafted a careful message for public dissemination. But the next day, while steaming home from his sailing vacation on a naval ship, Roosevelt sat down and wrote an open letter to the entire conference, but more directed to his own team, that the United States would support stabilization only *after* achieving adequate reflation.

In press parlance, it was a "bombshell" deriding exchange stabilization and the gold standard as "old fetishes of so-called international bankers . . . a specious fallacy, a tragic catastrophe." The better goals, he went on were:

> to plan national currencies with the objective of giving to those currencies a continuing purchasing power which does not greatly vary in terms of commodities and need of modern civilization. Let me be frank in saying that the United States seeks the kind of dollar which a generation hence will have the same purchasing and debt paying power as the dollar value we hope to attain in the future. That objective means more to the good of other nations that a fixed ratio for a month or two in terms of the pound or the franc.*

---

* Note that Roosevelt's statement implies a commodity price base for the dollar, rather than gold. That was a favorite device of Irving Fisher, and Keynes flirted with it as well. Roosevelt may have picked it up from Morgenthau, but it suggests the eclecticism of his policy search.

Most serious analysts were derisory, but by no means all. John Maynard Keynes in his newspaper column pronounced the president "magnif-
icently right." Winston Churchill, still ruing his 1925 fixing of a too-high
parity for the pound, offered his congratulations and gratitude. "The
American Navy," he said, "has come over, as they did in the Great War,
and although separate from us is steaming along the same course."[18]

The markets reacted just as Roosevelt might have hoped. The dollar
fell by 8.1 percent against the pound, and 9.4 percent against the franc.
Commodity prices, which tend to be priced internationally, rose accord-
ingly. The farm price index, which was Roosevelt's main target, jumped by
48 percent between March and July of 1933. But when there was no immediate follow-up from the administration, commodity prices flattened out.
Morgenthau then reintroduced the president to a Cornell agricultural
economist, George F. Warren. Morgenthau had chaired a New York
State Agricultural Advisory Commission when Roosevelt was governor.
He had been very impressed by Warren, one of the commission's experts,
and had included him in a number of meetings with the governor.[19]

Warren is often portrayed as something of a crank, peddling economic snake oil of a kind that the amateurish Morgenthau and Roosevelt
were particularly susceptible to. He and a former graduate student, Frank
A. Pearson, had spent more than twenty years working up statistical
compendia of rural production and prices, which they gradually extended
both backward in time and laterally to nonagricultural commodities.*
Along the way, Warren became convinced that there was a close inverse
association between commodity prices and the price of gold: when the

* The "Warren-Pearson Indices" are still used by the US Department of Commerce
  for prices of pre-1914 commodities. Most criticism, as Keynes pointed out in a positive review of one of the Warren-Pearson books, centered on the reliability of the
  early-period data, which they tried to refine by statistically based inferences from
  other data, like freight loadings. Keynes admired their diligence, but thought they
  might have used greater caution in applying the results. The gold historian, C. O.
  Hardy, pointed out that for an English series covering the seventy-five years preceding
  the war, the proposed correlations were definitely right for only twelve of the years,
  definitely not correct for twenty-two years, and "roughly right" for forty-one years.
  Given the time spans and the data mining difficulties, "roughly" or "definitely" right
  for fifty-three of seventy-five years, or 71 percent of the time, might still be interesting information. Warren was also drafted by the US Department of Agriculture to
  develop the base 1910–1914 parities for the AAA.

price of gold fell, usually because of new discoveries, commodity prices rose and vice versa. It was a claim that seems to have particularly offended bankers and economists.

Elmus Wicker, a leading authority on the Federal Reserve, stated flatly in 1971 that, "Whatever the statistical shortcomings of the data or its interpretation, the observed relationship between the supply of gold, the growth of physical volume of production, and the price level is without causal significance." The great economist and student of crises, Charles Kindleberger, was similarly caustic, although he grudgingly agreed that because of "serendipity," and despite the fact that "Roosevelt and his closest advisors . . . often had no clear idea what they were doing," in the end "the policy may have been a good one."[20]

As it became clear that Roosevelt was paying attention to Warren—the two men had a number of private meetings—the president's official economic advisers became alarmed. At the pleading of Acheson and Warburg, Roosevelt convened an economic policy group that met without Warren, who was in Europe. Wicker deplores the fact that no one attacked the weaknesses in Warren's proposals, the most glaring of which was that the alleged relationship did not hold through most of the 1920s. Roosevelt had charged the Acheson-Warburg group to show him how to raise commodity prices. Instead, they wrote a report recommending international cooperation—in effect, the strategy of the recently trashed Monetary and Economic Conference. One can imagine the glaze spreading over the president's eyes. Warren, almost by default, became a key revaluation advisor.[†21]

In October, Roosevelt and Morgenthau began a cautious experiment to raise the price of gold by placing bids through the RFC, which was authorized to purchase commodities. Before actually making any purchases, on October 22, Roosevelt had a fireside chat, announcing to the country that

---

† Kindleberger's critique is similar to that of Roosevelt's committee. He wrote that "Once it is agreed that it is important and necessary to raise world prices, two means are available." The first is for "the countries of the world to embark simultaneously on programmes of government spending . . . carefully articulated . . . [so] each country's exports grow as fast as its imports," or "for all countries of the world to devalue in terms of gold, simultaneously, and in the same proportion." But those were alternatives, he conceded, that were "impossible in 1933."

"ever since last March the definite policy of the Government has been to restore commodity price levels." To do that would require revaluing the dollar. "I would not know, and no one else could tell, just what the permanent value of the dollar will be," but it was time the country took "firmly in its own hands the control of the gold value of our dollar."[22]

The first purchase was delayed for several days by Acheson's truculent foot-dragging, effectively his act of hara-kiri. An angry Roosevelt announced Acheson's resignation to the press without warning him. Acheson, ever unflappable, showed up at the swearing-in of his successor, delighting the president with "the best act of sportsmanship I've ever seen." Acheson was brought back into the administration in 1941 as an assistant secretary of state, both a tribute to his obvious talents and no doubt to his sportsmanship—both Roosevelt and Acheson were Groton boys who had learned the rules of right behavior from its long-time headmaster, Endicott Peabody.[23]

Morgenthau, Roosevelt, and the chairman of the RFC, Jesse Jones, met frequently to set the gold dollar prices. The first purchase was at $29.01 on October 21, and by the end of the year, prices had crept up to $34.06. At that point, Roosevelt decided to fix the price at a round $35, just short of a 60 percent increase over the old price of $20.67 per fine ounce. One important detail was what to do with the $2.8 billion profit from the revaluation of the US gold reserves. It was finally decided to transfer the reserves from the Federal Reserve to the US Treasury, with most of it earmarked as a stabilization fund, in effect a war chest to fend off future attacks on the currency.[24]

The early returns from the gold-buying activity, in fact, had been disappointing. The dollar price of gold drifted up in rough conformity with the RFC's prices, and American exports showed modest improvement, but there was no substantial improvement in commodity prices— indeed prices fell in parts of November and December. The problem was that traders were confused by the unpredictable changes in the dollar's value—it made them cautious, rather than bullish. Once the president announced that the experimentation was over, however—that $35 was the final number—a strong commodity boom got underway. American exporters started shipping the orders they had delayed until the currency was settled; importers that had overbought to lock in lower prices

FIGURE 5.1: US ALL-FARM PRICE INDEX

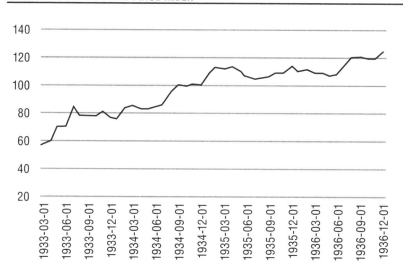

Source: FRED.

reduced their buying programs; currency traders that had sold dollars covered their positions and took their profits.[25]

It was more than fifty years after Roosevelt's action on the dollar before economists recognized the benefits of devaluing a currency in an economic crisis. Currency depreciation had been classified with trade restrictions as beggar-my-neighbor policies—designed to shift incomes to the country imposing the change—and therefore were universally dismissed or condemned by orthodox opinion. While both strategies usually stimulated the economies of the initiating countries, retaliatory actions by other countries, it was thought, typically reduced incomes all around. Two landmark papers by Barry Eichengreen and Jeffrey Sachs showed that, unlike trade restrictions, currency devaluations did not necessarily have adverse consequences. It all depended on the policy details: in principle, a properly managed devaluation could have win-win outcomes for all. For example, if Country A devalues, its imports will become expensive, its exports will boom, and as its businesses revive, incomes will rise. It's easy to see that those policies could hurt its trading partners, but with careful management, the stimulus in Country A will create more opportunities for its trading partners and trigger a virtuous circle of growth.[26]

To get the most out of a devaluation, it is critical that the monetary benefits are used to promote growth. The United States, recall, earned a $2.8 billion markup profit when it raised the price of gold. That could have been pumped into bank reserves to juice up spending, or if the private sector was too shell-shocked to borrow, it could have funded an infrastructure program without a tax or debt increase. Instead it was plunked into a stabilization reserve that was almost never used. In fact, all of the major devaluations, from the 1931 British one on, appear to have considerable beggar-my-neighbor effects, although they were mitigated to the extent that other countries eventually devalued as well.[27]

The United States didn't entirely waste its opportunity. The initial devaluation prompted a flood of gold into the country, $650 million worth, mostly from traders that had bought gold in anticipation of its revaluation and were now switching back into dollar instruments. But the river of gold continued to flow, as fears of Hitler's increasing sway over Germany triggered waves of flight capital. Gold was high-powered money, so it directly increased American spending power. It obviously would have increased it more, as Eichengreen argues, if the Fed had multiplied the gold trove by using it to support currency issuance and deposit expansion.[28]

Finally, a historical footnote: in the first of their two landmark papers, Eichengreen and Sachs tip their hats to George Warren and Frank Pearson for being the first to "document the relationship between exchange depreciation and relative price levels and outputs." Warren may have been disappointed that the relationship was not as mechanical as he supposed, or as his pre-1914 data had suggested, but it was there nonetheless, and Roosevelt's "milk farmer," as Acheson called him, made a real contribution to the recovery.[29]

⸻ III. CREATING THE "NEW DEAL" ⸻

No one ever accused the Roosevelt first-term program of consistency, nor would he or any of his advisers have made such a claim. In a commencement speech at Oglethorpe University, in the spring of 1932, Roosevelt told the graduates:

> The country needs and, unless I mistake its temper, the country demands bold, persistent experimentation. It is common sense to take a method and try it: If it fails, admit it frankly and try another. But above all, try something. The millions who are in want will not stand by silently forever while the things to satisfy their needs are within easy reach.[30]

The landslide election victory essentially gave him a free hand, a writ to reshape the government and its mission as he chose. To be sure, the troglodyte wing of the Republican party detested "that man in the White House," but they had been discredited by the market crash and the Depression. Although the South was solidly Democratic, its congressional bloc eventually came to oppose many of the administration's initiatives that appeared to empower black Americans—and generally got their way. Roosevelt, however, drew considerable benefit from the fact that his most serious early political opposition came from the left. Whenever recalcitrant congressmen deplored the radicalism of his program, he could paint a dire picture of what the *real* radicals would do if the New Deal foundered.

Mainstream Roosevelt supporters comprised an unwieldy mix of progressive intellectuals, blue-collar workers, small farmers, and social activists of all kinds, many of whom, like Harry Bridges, the great union organizer, were later targeted by Joe McCarthy's 1950s Communist hunters. There were a few charismatic individuals, however, who grasped the inherent power of the new mass media at least as well as Roosevelt did. They were supportive of the administration in the early days, but soon morphed into an informal opposition, for reasons both of principle and pique.

Charles Coughlin was the "radio priest," who turned a weekly broadcast from a church in Detroit into a national phenomenon. In the year before Roosevelt took office, Coughlin called for doubling the price of gold to expand the currency and fuel greater spending. He vaulted into national prominence as a witness in the trial of executives of two big Detroit banks whose imminent failure had helped trigger the nationwide wave of bank closings. Although Coughlin was an incurable sensationalizer, the executives' crass self-enrichment justified some extremism. (A bank examiner called their behavior "putrid.") By the end of the year, Coughlin was getting 10,000 letters a day—to the point where the postal service gave him his own post office. A flood of small donations financed a media empire, with national radio links, a newsletter, and books. A first edition of his broadcasts quickly sold a million copies. During the first few years of his prominence, Coughlin was warm in his praises of the president, and Roosevelt paid him the honor of a private hour-long meeting. But Coughlin grew disappointed with Roosevelt's progress, and even more with the lack of attention he received from the White House. Within a few years, he had become a dangerous opponent with a marvelous personal megaphone.[31]

Then there was the "kingfish," Louisiana's redoubtable Huey Long. Long's DNA was deeply entwined with that of his home state, and its political machinery worked like an extension of his brain. He was a demagogue, a shrewd mix of flamboyant buffoonery and cold calculation in service of his own ascendancy. But Long also delivered for the common man. In his first term as governor, he started an impressive highway building program, funded textbooks for all schools in the state, and passed a more progressive tax code. But a proposal to tax every barrel of oil refined in the state aroused the wrath of Standard Oil, the traditional muscle in Baton Rouge, the state's capital. An impeachment movement was quickly organized, but Long, exercising his entire demagogic kit bag, carried all before him, cementing his dominance in Louisiana. When term limits prevented him from retaining the governorship in 1932, he engineered both his election to the US Senate and his replacement in Baton Rouge by a loyal retainer. And a few years later, he finally got his oil tax.[32]

Long was materially helpful to Roosevelt at the 1932 Democratic convention, but Jim Farley, Roosevelt's political guru, restricted his involvement in the campaign, only to be startled by the pro-Roosevelt voting shifts that regularly followed a Long speaking appearance. For a while in 1933, Long's heavy drinking and vulgar clowning eroded his support at home, but he straightened up, dried out, and crushed any budding resistance. He also began to build a Coughlin-style media empire, and in 1934, in a brilliant stroke of branding, began his Share Our Wealth program—confiscatory taxes to ensure that no one retained more than $1 million of net earnings, with the proceeds going to a modest guaranteed nest egg for each child and minimum federal income support for the needy. Long was a diligent organizer who soon had in place a formidable system of local Share Our Wealth Clubs, which to Farley's suspicious

From left to right: Huey Long, Fr. Charles Coughlin, and Francis Townsend, for a short time in Roosevelt's first term became forceful advocates for strongly redistributionist government policy. Over time many of the policies they called for have become part of the American safety net.

eye looked like a serious grassroots political organization.[33] Coughlin and Long loosely coordinated with each other, and in 1935, they forged a similarly loose alliance with Francis Townsend, a sixty-six-year-old California doctor who was pushing a plan to provide every person over sixty years of age a monthly federal pension of $150, the equivalent of about $2,600 today. When a hazy array of radical farmer and labor groups appeared to coalesce in support of a Coughlin-Long-Townsend political party, the White House became genuinely alarmed at its potential to destabilize the 1936 election.[34]

Nothing of the sort happened. Long was assassinated in September 1935, shot in the Louisiana State House by the son-in-law of a judge whom he had squeezed out of office. (Long may well have survived in the hands of even moderately competent surgeons.) Without his presence, the network of Share Our Wealth clubs dissolved. As for Coughlin, he became increasingly extreme and, especially after 1938, grossly anti-Semitic. He and Townsend, plus a core group of their followers, organized the Union Party to run a nearly unknown North Dakota congressman, William Lemke, for president in 1936—who was utterly swept away in a historic Roosevelt electoral tidal wave.

Long, Coughlin, and Townsend were tapping into a rich vein of discontent. Workers were treated badly in the 1920s, even leaving aside the absence of job security, abusive shop foremen, long hours, and lack of overtime. Factory productivity growth was extraordinary, but as Figure 5.2 shows, workers got very little of it. The lack of income growth in worker households was made up by working longer hours and by borrowing, as consumer credit became steadily more available through the decade.

Nor by any means were the programs the three men espoused complete nonsense. Coughlin's gold price target of $41.34 an ounce was the same as George Warren's, and wasn't that far from Roosevelt's choice of $35 an ounce. Townsend's pension plan, of course, adumbrated Social Security. Long's Share Our Wealth plan was never a serious option, but the American tax code turned decidedly confiscatory in wartime, just as it did in World War I. This time, however, when the war ended, the tax code *stayed* confiscatory (a 75–90 percent top bracket) well into the 1970s. That paid for countless postwar infrastructure and human resource investments. The all-important GI Bill of Rights financed college or other

FIGURE 5.2: RATIO HOURLY MANUFACTURING PAY PER UNIT OF OUTPUT IN THE UNITED STATES, 1919–1941

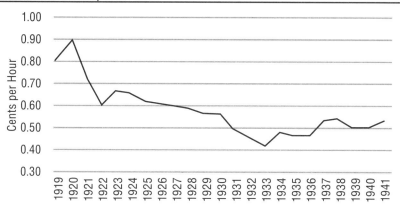

Source: Historical Statistics of the United States, Table Ba4361; and Kendrick 1961, Table D-2.

post–high school training for 7.8 million returning veterans, or nearly half of all servicemen and women. Veteran home mortgage guarantees practically created the suburbs.

Much of the spending, directly or indirectly, came out of the pockets of the rich. In 1928, the top 1 percent of taxpayers received about 24 percent of taxable income, or about the same share as they have absorbed through most of the 2000s. But the Roosevelt tax skew toward the upper bracket payers stayed in place well into the 1970s, and through all that time, the share of taxable income flowing to the top 1 percent of earners averaged just 10 percent, and the annual growth in taxable income was roughly the same across all income quintiles.* CEOs were wealthy men with nice houses in normal neighborhoods, not Sultan-of-Brunei-scale royalty with globe-girdling servanted estates. "Inequality" was not a political catchphrase, because most people felt that they were steadily improving their lot. That, too, was part of the Roosevelt legacy.[35]

---

* In 2015, the increment in the pretax income going to the top 1 percent at a share of 20.3 percent compared to the previous normal of 10 percent was $1.3 trillion—*every year.* That's more than total annual Social Security payments, twice as large as the defense budget.

The New Deal programs were a pastiche of income transfers, price and market interventions, and permanent regulatory initiatives. The first programs to get into operation were focused on creating jobs, like the Civilian Conservation Corps (CCC) and the Federal Emergency Relief Administration (FERA), which included welfare payments for the unemployable destitute. The Civilian Works Administration (CWA) was a four-month program in the winter of 1933 that employed over four million people at competitive pay rates. Additional income transfers, like unemployment insurance, public assistance programs, and Social Security, took longer to phase in since they often required state-managed operating structures or, as in the case of Social Security, an entire new federal bureaucracy.

A second thread encompassed programs to change market outcomes in pursuit of specific price, wage, or other policy objectives—the agricultural bill, with its programs to reduce output in order to maintain prices, and the National Industrial Recovery Act (NIRA), to accomplish similar objectives in industry, are the primary examples. Farmers got their price supports, and industrial workers got fair labor standards protection, a federal minimum wage, and greatly enhanced bargaining rights. Finally, there were four new permanent regulatory bodies, following the model of the Interstate Commerce Commission, the most important of which was the new Securities Exchange Commission.[36]

Given the blur of activity and the sheer variety of the initiatives, scholars have long clashed over the benefits, if any, the country reaped from the exercise. Over the past couple of decades, however, scholars have been amassing detailed data on the major programs, and find that they had real, if mixed, results. But before we look into the details, there are two important general points.

There is a widely accepted misconception that Keynesian fiscal policy—running deliberate government deficits to add to spending

FIGURE 5.3: CHANGES IN FEDERAL LIABILITIES (PERCENT GDP), 1930–1939[38]

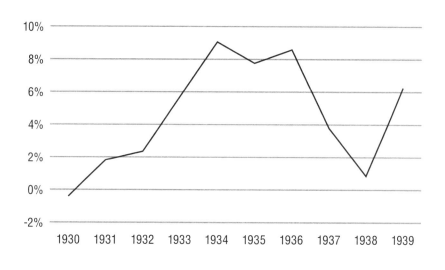

Source: Eggertsson, "Great Expectations."

power—was not a factor in the recovery. As an early scholar put it, "fiscal policy . . . seems to have been an unsuccessful recovery device in the thirties—not because it did not work, but because it was not tried." While it may not have been the main factor, it was not trivial. Figure 5.3 shows the year-to-year increase in federal liabilities, both budget deficits and off–balance sheet borrowings like the RFC's from 1930 to 1939. By the standards of the day, they were quite large. Most such outlays were subsequently repaid—as was most of the "bailout" spending during the recent Great Recession. It's the stimulative effect at a time of economic crisis that matters. Hoover also engaged in off-budget stimulus spending after 1930, but at a much lower level. For Hoover, moreover, the deficits were unintentional—he did his best to fund them with tax increases, but could never catch up to the fall in GDP.[37]

Secondly, there is a striking vein of research that suggests that the main factor in the recovery was Roosevelt himself—and it's not nearly as far-fetched as it sounds. It has long been a puzzlement that the economy picked up sharply in the *month* that Roosevelt finally assumed the presidency. There was no obvious reason for it—no sudden increase in the money supply, no fall in real wages that might explain a turnaround. The traditional explanation was that at some point, a collapsing economy will revert to its mean. As Kindleberger put it, "the fact that gross investment has a limit of zero is useful in explaining that the depression had to end. At some point gross investment turns up again and the accelerator principle comes back into its own."[39]

But that explanation doesn't comport with the facts. Manufacturing inventories were still very high relative to sales in 1933, so investment was far from hitting the "limit of zero." Nor did Roosevelt's gold devaluation entirely explain the upturn, since it wasn't fully effective until January 1934. The New Deal legislative program was passed with record speed, and included major new policy experiments, like the AAA and the NIRA, but it would be a while before they had much effect.

Peter Temin and Barrie Wigmore, in a 1990 paper, proposed a "policy regime change" as the explanation, working its magic through a change in expectations. Hoover relied mostly on jaw-boning in the early days of the collapse, especially asking industry to maintain wages. His most promising initiative was the RFC, although it was trammeled with restrictions that limited its effectiveness. As the crisis worsened, however, he took to blaming the Europeans, and adopted a strong deflationist policy—balancing the budget, protecting the gold parity, imposing steep tax increases, and grimly proclaiming that the government could do little except try to squeeze all the excesses out of the economy.

Temin and Wigmore do not argue that the public understood the details of the new administration's policies, but only that they grasped that Roosevelt's approach would be completely different. Roosevelt bided his time during the long post-election interlude, not attacking Hoover, but refusing to ally himself with the Hoover agenda. In his first weeks in office, he openly trumpeted his reflationist agenda with the bank holiday, the floating of the dollar, the suspension of gold exports, and his "bombshell" message to the Monetary and Economic Conference. The reaction of conservative media underscored the radical nature of the changes. The *Commercial and Financial Chronicle* called it "a step backward toward the darkness of the Middle Ages," while the head of the Chase Bank wailed that the devaluation was "an act of economic destruction of fearful magnitude." The wave of new legislation, large appropriations for the AAA, the open embrace of deficit spending, and a new, and more cooperative, chairman of the Federal Reserve who promptly eased credit were all part of the show. And it helped that some financial luminaries, including Jack Morgan, supported the president's policies. The stock market was gleeful. Industrial stocks doubled in the first four months after the inauguration, and the production of investment goods more than doubled by the fall of 1933.[40] Such developments, all in all, seemed dramatic confirmation of the Roosevelt campaign song, the Tin Pan Alley favorite, "Happy Days Are Here Again."

The economist Gauti Eggertsson has created a general equilibrium model* for both the deflationist "Hoover policy regime" and its replacement Roosevelt regime. Economic modeling of this sort is still a work in progress—if only because results are often suspiciously consistent with the political dispositions of the modeler. If nothing else, however, Eggertsson's work provides details for a plausible path to the Temin and Wigmore thesis. A paper by the economist Christina D. Romer rounds out the picture by identifying the fuel that extended the hyperfast recovery after the Roosevelt reflation—the huge flood of gold into the United States. A key to the effectiveness of the gold influx is that it went to the Treasury, not to the Federal Reserve, which based on past behavior would have sterilized it. Gold is high-powered money, and the monetary base swelled by about 10 percent a year in 1934–1937. It is probably not a coincidence that the economy grew by nearly the same rate through that period.[41]

---

* Properly, a dynamic stochastic general equilibrium (DSGE) model. It is a mathematical optimizing tool that, in theory, can incorporate all the policy-relevant variables in an economy. It is dynamic because it links agents' choices, outcomes, and expectations intertemporally; it is stochastic, because it is designed to calculate the impact of random "shocks," which can be positive or negative; and it is a general equilibrium model because all markets clear and are in equilibrium after each period. So-called new Keynesian DSGE models assign a significant role for expectations in determining current behavior.

I n early April 1933, Fiore Rizzo and three other young men pulled up in a taxi at an army recruiting station in lower Manhattan. The taxi fare was 65 cents, but the four had only 50 cents between them, so an army captain put up the difference. Rizzo was nineteen and single, from a family of thirteen children. He had been unemployed for a year, and his father had been unemployed for three years. By chance, he was the first registered recruit for the Civilian Conservation Corps.

Rizzo had a brief physical, took an oath, signed a form authorizing the government to pay his family $25 of his $30 a month pay, and was shipped off to an upstate training center for two weeks' of training and conditioning. From there he would be assigned to a six-month stint in the National Forests planting trees, clearing brush, working roads, building fire controls, and fighting insect pests. The CCC director expected Rizzo to be assigned to Tennessee because it was "already warm there." "Most of the men called," he said, "will be off the bread line. The work will not be intensely laborious—but it will be work. . . . There will be no military features in connection with the camps."[42]

The CCC was part of a package of work relief and income grants that were a focus of the Roosevelt Hundred Days legislative program. The fact that it was up and running in little more than a month after the inauguration is impressive, and was possible only because Roosevelt had the sense to turn the job of creating and administering the camps to the army. Colonel George Marshall set up seventeen of them. It may have been Roosevelt's favorite program—he made a point of visiting the camps whenever his schedule took him by one, and he mused about making it a permanent establishment. He was a conservationist by inclination and by family ties. As governor of New York, he created a forestry and tree-planting program with slots for 10,000 unemployed men.[43]

Thirteen hundred CCC camps were up and running by mid-June, and by mid-July, they had enrolled and deployed 300,000 men. Altogether

2.5 million went through the camps, most of them staying for six months to a year, with the high point of enrollment at 500,000 in July 1935. There were usually some dropouts among each new batch, because of the strangeness of the surroundings and the quasi-military discipline, but most enrollees seem to have viewed it as a life-changing experience— many had never been out of their neighborhood, much less lived in a forest. They also learned simple trades, like driving a truck, laying stones, and mixing concrete. Exit interviews were mostly positive—"I weighed about 160 pounds when I went there and when I left I was 190 about. It made a man of me all right." And "if a boy wants to go and get a job after he's been in C's, he'll know how to work."[44]

CCC was a great showpiece, but the more pressing requirement was for financial relief for unemployed families. The Hundred Days legislative program included both the Federal Emergency Relief Agency (FERA) and the Public Works Administration (PWA). FERA was run by Harry Hopkins, perhaps Roosevelt's best manager. (Winston Churchill later dubbed him "Lord Root of the Matter.") FERA had great flexibility—it could give "direct relief," effectively the dole, but "work relief" was the priority. Most work relief was for low-end jobs—"leaf-raking" in common parlance, with frontline management from local governments. Work relief paid stipends that were about half the pay normally received by low-end workers, and was much preferred over the dole.[45]

The fall of 1933 was the first of the New Deal, but it was the fourth year of the Great Depression. Unemployed workers and their families were demoralized, and some were joining "unemployment leagues," many of them organized by Communists, like Louis Budenz. Hopkins lobbied Roosevelt to let him run a short-term winter program, of approximately four months, to hire four million people for work projects at full civilian pay. Starting virtually from scratch in mid-November, he had 2.6 million people on the CWA payroll by mid-December, and four million by mid-January. (He apologized profusely for missing his target.) About a third of his workers repaired or surfaced roads, but others built or improved 40,000 schools, cleaned up parks, dug sewer lines, and cleared industrial canals. The evidence is that much useful work was completed, but given the sheer numbers of people engaged, there was a great deal of wasted effort, and complaints of men getting paid for leaning on shovels all day. (The prominence of shoveling, however, stemmed from a Hopkins policy decision. The main purpose of work relief was to create work, so Hopkins banned most modern machinery from the work sites. Sewers were dug by hand because it took longer.)[46]

Hopkins was imaginative—hiring 3,000 artists and writers to ply their trades as CWA workers, and paying for 50,000 laid-off teachers to return to their schools. The speed of the launch was conducive to political interference and corruption, much to Hopkins's chagrin, and he hired army officers to clean up his processes. A senior West Point officer, however, was greatly impressed: "Mr. Hopkins's loose fluidity of organization was justified by the results achieved. It enabled him to engage for employment in two months nearly as many persons as were enlisted . . . during our year and a half of World War mobilization." The officer's praise was warranted: for all the pratfalls, FERA and CWA distributed more than

Roosevelt's right-hand man, Harry Hopkins, was a brilliant organizer and performed prodigies creating millions of jobs for the unemployed. In truth, much useful work was done, and the employment programs were life savers for millions of families.

$23 per US resident in the year beginning July 1933, equivalent to almost 3 percent of the 1929 GDP, and more importantly, over 5 percent of the depressed 1933 GDP.*[47]

The other major public works spending program was the PWA, run by Harold Ickes. Both Roosevelt and Ickes insisted it was not a relief program, but rather an investment in high-quality public infrastructure. Since there were only a few shovel-ready projects at the start of the program, it took a while before there were visible results, and the delay was extended by Ickes's insistence on personally reviewing each contract. (Because of the slow start, Hopkins was able to fund his CWA with unused PWA funds.) Hoover had greatly accelerated public work grants to state and local governments, and had also accelerated the Army Corps of Engineers' river and harbor works, but Roosevelt and Ickes ratcheted up the Hoover commitments by several notches. The PWA, in fact, made a major contribution in shoring up the country's public investment—highways, sewage and water systems, power plants, schools and other public institutions, docks and tunnels, ships for the US Navy, and the biggest public program of them all, the Tennessee Valley Authority. During its life, PWA spent an annual average of $3.50 per US resident, not including three years of spending an additional 41 cents per capita on public housing.[48]

Roosevelt's honeymoon period lasted for perhaps a year and a half. He had come into office with thumping majorities in both houses of Congress, amid widespread fear that the country was coming apart. By the spring of 1934, although the Depression was far from ended, there were clear signs of recovery. Industrial production was up by almost half over the previous spring, and over the full year, the economy racked up 10.8 percent real growth. Unusually, the 1934 mid-term congressional elections, instead of trimming Roosevelt's majorities actually added to them, giving him a two-thirds majority in both houses. Possibly because of their big majorities, however, the new Congress was more obstreperous.

---

* It is almost inconceivable that a comparable program could be launched so rapidly today, which speaks not only to the desperation of the unemployed, but to the leanness of government and business. For reference, the Empire State Building broke ground in March of 1930 and was fully open in only thirteen and a half months, even with an exterior that required ten million hand-laid bricks.

Southern and Midwestern Democrats were closer to the business view of federal spending than they were to Roosevelt's. Most state governors were happy to see increased relief spending, but almost all of them wanted more control, and all of them had been offended by Hopkins's insistence on his right to approve or veto projects, to allocate funds, or, as he chose to do in seven states, to federalize uncooperative state relief administrations. The Southern congressional coalition, in particular, always hypervigilant against breaches in the post-Reconstruction regime of white dominance, was upset at Hopkins's racial blindness in distributing aid.

New Deal historians talk about the "First" and "Second" New Deal, with the break somewhere in late 1934. The relief programs were significantly reorganized, with a common theme of limiting federal discretion. FERA was disbanded, and there was a major reorganization of the income relief components. Four programs—OAA, or assistance to poor elderly; AB, or Aid to the Blind; and ADC, or Aid to Dependent Children; plus UI, or unemployment insurance—were handed over to state administration, although the lion's share of the funding was still federal, with funding allocations by strict legislative formula. The Works Progress Administration (WPA), the new name for Hopkins's work relief programs remained federally administered, since it was due for an early shutdown. OASI, or Old Age and Survivors' Insurance—the basic senior retirement program—of course, was entirely federal.[49] Roosevelt, over the protests of friends on the left, insisted that both Social Security and unemployment insurance be funded with contributions both from workers and employers. When an economist warned of the deflationary dangers of a new payroll tax, Roosevelt retorted that it wasn't about economics:

> [T]hose taxes . . . are politics all the way through. We put those payroll contributions there so as to give the contributors a legal, moral, and political right to collect their pensions and their unemployment benefits. With those taxes in there, no damn politician can ever scrap my social security program.*[50]

---

* Economists agree that, irrespective of the employer/employee sharing formula, the entire Social Security payment comes from the payroll account. But Roosevelt was surely right that the visibility of the employee contribution has made Americans fiercely protective of the program.

────── VI. THE REST OF THE NEW DEAL: A ROUNDUP ──────

The National Industrial Recovery Act (NIRA), in Roosevelt's mind, was a twin of the Agricultural Adjustment Act, since each was intended to exercise active oversight of prices, markets, and modes of competition. Its preamble stated its objectives, which were something new under the American sun:

> to provide for the general welfare by promoting the organization of industry for the purpose of cooperative action among trade groups, to induce and maintain united action of labor and management under adequate governmental sanctions and supervision, to eliminate unfair competitive practices, to promote the fullest possible utilization of the present productive capacity of industries, to avoid undue restriction of production . . . [and so on and on].[51]

That is a classic statement of the aspirations of 1920s-vintage progressive reformers, with its roots in the "scientism" of turn-of-the-century philosophers and social scientists, like Henry Demarest Lloyd and Charles Horton Cooley.[†] John Dewey predicted that when the methods of physical science were "progressively applied to history and all the social sciences, we can anticipate no other outcome than increasing control in the ethical sphere."[52] The twenty-five-year-old Walter Lippmann, in his *Drift and Mastery* (1914) cheered the advent of "the new science of administration," by which "experiments conducted by experts" would resolve age-old business problems. Lippmann's discussion of "mastery" anticipates the NIRA almost point for point:

---

† *The Education of Henry Adams* is a fine, self-mocking account of the author's encounter with the triumphalist aspirations of the new social sciences.

Technical improvement must be for the whole industry, the labor market must be organized and made stable, output must be adjusted to a common plan. The appearance of federal organization seems to suggest a possible compromise in which the administrative need for decentralization is combined with the social demand for a unified industrial policy.[53]

It was a pleasant fantasy, but in its real-life incarnation, the NIRA was a hopeless mess. Hiram Johnson, a California politician, in the process of losing a struggle against alcoholism, was the wrong choice for the job. Big businesses dominated the process of setting industry "codes" on pricing and competition, gleefully organizing trusts with impunity. Small businesses complained that the bigger players were systematically eviscerating their markets. Unions had been badly weakened in the 1920s, and were simply ignored until they took advantage of the NIRA's union-protective clauses to mount waves of strikes. The Supreme Court's 1935 decision against the NIRA's constitutionality was greeted almost with relief.* New specific legislation—the National Labor Relations Act and the Fair Labor Standards Act, were enacted in due course, while the Federal Trade Commission once more returned to its trust-busting mission. The one stimulative accomplishment of the NIRA was the pay codes; real wages improved substantially after 1934.[54]

Price Fishback and John Wallis have constructed a table of average annual New Deal spending per capita on the base 1930 population in 1930 dollars (see Figure 5.4). The per capita/per year protocol in constant dollars also allows a convenient apples-to-apples comparison with the Hoover administration.[55]

The New Deal relief grants, which included both work relief and welfare grants, constituted about 41 percent of the average total annual per

---

* *Schecter Poultry v. United States* was nevertheless a major blow to the administration's legislative strategy, for reasons that had nothing to do with the NIRA. The court ruled that a Brooklyn poultry packer, most of whose chickens came from out of state, escaped federal regulation since "when the poultry had reached the defendants' slaughterhouses, the interstate commerce had ended, and subsequent transactions in their business, including the matters charged in the indictment, were transactions in intrastate commerce," which obviously would greatly circumscribe federal reach over commerce. After Roosevelt unveiled his "court packing" plan in 1937, one of the Schecter justices, Owen Roberts, reversed himself in a later quite similar case.

FIGURE 5.4: APPLES-TO-APPLES COMPARISON, ROOSEVELT AND HOOVER SOCIAL SPENDING (PER YEAR, PER CAPITA, 1930 DOLLARS)

	FDR 1934–1939	HH 1930–1933
Relief Grants	46.94	0.12
Veterans Aid	22.20	10.42
Public Works Grants	8.15	3.50
Public Works Loans	1.37	0.00
Agricultural Grants	6.56	0.14
Agricultural Loans	9.47	1.27
Miscellaneous	20.16	10.24
Totals	114.85	25.69

Source: Fishback and Wallace, "What Was New," Table 10.2.

capita spending. The next highest figure for both Roosevelt and Hoover was aid to veterans. The New Deal total includes the veterans' bonus, which was passed by the Congress over the president's veto. Actual outlays were about half again higher than shown in Figure 5.4, because the program was also credited with repayments of veterans' previous loans against their bonuses. The Hoover veterans' amount mostly comprised such loans. The "miscellaneous" category in the Hoover column was dominated by RFC lending, primarily to banks and railroads, while about half the Roosevelt total consisted of mortgage lending by the new Home Owners' Loan Corporation (HOLC), which refinanced home mortgages, usually on extended terms with low interest rates. HOLC financed more than a million homes, with a life-of-program cash loss of $53 million, or about 2.7 percent of the $3 billion of lending. Its books were closed in 1951, and it is usually considered one of the more successful New Deal programs. Agricultural grants and loans and public works grants and loans, in that order, rounded out the major spending programs.[56]

Within the past couple of decades, scholars have performed a number of detailed econometric studies of the impacts of specific New Deal programs, with the main findings summarized here.

Home Owners' Loan Corporation (HOLC) The debt-fueled 1920s housing boom was brutally reversed early in the Depression. Average home prices fell by 30–40 percent, and as unemployment spiked to a previously unheard-of 25 percent, the HOLC was created to mitigate the impact on homeowners "in hard straits largely through no fault of their own." The HOLC was created to purchase troubled mortgages from lenders and to replace them with direct federal loans with easier payment schedules. In the 1920s, housing finance was usually provided by specialized lenders who required a 40–60 percent down payment, five years of steep interest payments, and a balloon payoff of the principal at the end of the term, usually by a refinancing. In addition, in most conurbations "building and loan societies" provided loan terms closer to those of modern loans—with flat amortization of interest and principal—to members who had amassed enough savings for a 20–30 percent down payment. HOLC loans generally had 15-year level payment amortizations at 5 percent interest, about 1–2 percent lower than a building society loan, and much less than the rates charged by specialized mortgage lenders.[57]

The HOLC loans had an average principal of about $3,000, with the bulk of the refinancings in 1934. All of them were troubled loans. The typical refinancing replaced a loan that was two years in default of payments, with tax delinquencies stretching out even longer. Many states had legislated foreclosure moratoria, and even if they hadn't, the resale market was so desolate that lenders saw no point in foreclosing. An indication of the depths of the housing market is that HOLC turned down nearly as many applications—800,000—as the million it approved. If nothing else, therefore, the HOLC made a major cash infusion to a broad range of lending institutions.

HOLC terms were generous: they often valued a home value at the pre-Crash price, and added reconditionings and tax delinquency pay-offs to the primary mortgage. By 1936, 39 percent of their portfolio was nonperforming, and they ultimately foreclosed about half that number. Between 1936 and 1940 HOLC owned and sold off some 2 percent of the nonfarm dwellings in the country.

Price Fishback and his colleagues, in a 2010 paper, attempted to measure the housing market benefits of HOLC. Roosevelt officials had, logically enough, evaluated HOLC by regressing (measuring the relationship between) increases in home values and home ownership with local HOLC expenditures. The results were positive—impressively so. The stunner was that an extra $1 per capita in HOLC expenditures was associated with a $51 increase in home values.

It was a mirage. Statistical analysis has made huge strides since the 1940s, and simple regressions are no longer conclusive, unless the analyst separates all the factors that may bear on a result. The apparent HOLC results were skewed because loans were disproportionately distributed to areas with higher home values and ownership rates. Deeper analyses suggest that HOLC may have been associated with *declines* in home values and ownership levels and reductions in rents and increases in rentals, although the correlations are weak. There were, however, substantial positive results in counties with less than 50,000 people: HOLC spending was associated with increases in home values and home ownership at a 10 percent level of statistical significance. Those results make intuitive sense: rural areas generally had poor access to full-service financial institutions, so HOLC loans would have filled a real need.

After the last HOLC loan was paid down in 1951, and the agency closed down, the Treasury estimated its losses at about $78 million, which the Fishback group says could have been as high as $100 million, or about 3 percent of the amount lent, although the cash losses were only about half as much. That seems a small price to pay for a critical infusion of cash into credit markets. Investment had collapsed in 1933 and 1934, so there could be no concerns about crowding out more productive lending. The possibility of a death plunge in the housing market was all too real, so solely for its preventive effects, HOLC must be counted as a good investment.

Welfare, Work Relief, and the AAA Another Fishback-led paper examined the impact of the administration's relief spending, including both welfare payments and pay for work relief under various New Deal programs—FERA, WPA, PWA, and CWA, as well as programs sponsoring public roads and public housing. A number of neoclassical economists were convinced that such spending might actually decrease employment.[58]

The Fishback team analyzed the effect on retail sales in every county that received the various forms of direct relief and work relief, as well as the benefits of the AAA, using an arsenal of modern statistical techniques to filter out false signals. The results for the relief programs were unambiguous. One dollar of public relief or work relief raised retail sales in 1939 by 44 cents. Since retail sales on average consumed nearly half of household incomes, that suggests that one dollar of relief spending raised local incomes by about 83 cents.

Counties receiving AAA funds on average showed the opposite result, since most of the AAA grants were designed to take crops out of production. It was the *landowners*, after all, who were the object of concern for the farmers' lobbies. Production limits raised farmers' incomes at the price of reducing incomes for farm laborers and sharecroppers. The loss of incomes at the lower end of local populations apparently matched, or slightly outweighed, the incomes gained by farm owners. For good or for ill, that is, both the relief spending and AAA grants accomplished what they set out to do.

A follow-up study looked specifically at the notion that the relief programs reduced private employment opportunities. Using panel data from forty-four cities, the analysts showed that in the First New Deal (1933–1935), the increase in relief programs *increased* private employment, doubtless because of their impact on local spending power. The impacts were different during the Second New Deal, 1936–1939, however, because the contexts had shifted. Direct relief (welfare) programs had been turned over to the states, but the WPA programs were still run out of Washington. The more important change was that, by 1939, real economic growth had returned per capita GDP back to its 1929 level. Companies were hiring, and unemployment, although still too high, was considerably lower. And the analysis bears out the complaints of employers that WPA employment made it more difficult to fill positions. That would have surprised the WPA managers, for their jobs deliberately paid about half the wage available in private employment, and a WPA worker could be terminated for refusing a private job offer. The explanation, apparently, is that private sector jobs were still viewed as uncertain, with a constant possibility of layoffs. As one WPA worker put it: "Why do we want to keep these jobs? Well . . . we know all the time about persons on direct relief . . . just managing to scrape along. . . . My advice, buddy, is better not take too much of a chance. Know a good thing when you got it." In other words, the risk of being laid off and having to resort to welfare, with lower stipends than the WPA, was not worth it. We'll come back to the unemployment conundrum below.[59]

That same study also looked at the allegations that the Roosevelt administration was buying votes with its relief programs. Harry Hopkins had, if only allegedly, but still famously, disclosed the Roosevelt formula for success: "We shall tax and tax, spend and spend, and elect and elect." The analysts found, however, that program distribution was matched closely to need. Severely impacted Democratic areas did not get notably more aid than similarly impacted Republican areas, although it was true that local relief spending was higher in election years. An older study, however, by Gavin Wright, showed that, in principle, there was a game-theoretic approach to influence voting while still maintaining the focus on seriously impacted areas. The trick was to supply additional funds when Democratic majorities were in flux, and modest amounts of extra federal money might help achieve a critical majority. In the 1936 and 1938 elections, there was indeed evidence of such fine political tuning of the outlays. With Jim Farley's hand on the political steering wheel, it would have been almost disappointing not to find any manipulation.[60]

There were a number of ancillary positive effects of federal relief in poor areas. A relief infusion of $2 million was associated with a reduction of one infant death, one suicide, 2.4 deaths from infectious diseases, and one death from diarrhea. A 10 percent increase in work relief saved 1.5 property crimes, although a 10 percent increase in private employment had a much larger effect, virtually one to one.[61]

The New Deal was always a messy operation. It had to be—there was no consensus on what had gone wrong, and even less on what to do about it. But the deflation gauntlet had been so demoralizing and destructive

No peacetime president had ever spent the immense amounts that Roosevelt did in attempting to reverse the Depression. When Roosevelt prematurely pulled back on the spending, the economy crashed almost immediately, and recovery came only when most of the programs were revived.

that throwing money at the problem was not a totally crazy idea. And throw money the New Deal surely did. From 1934 through 1936, federal debt as a share of GDP rose from 16 percent to 40 percent. Despite the oft-told tale that Keynesian stimulus was barely tried in the Depression, the official budget deficits, plus the off–balance sheet borrowing of entities like the RFC and the HOLC, brought the annual increase in federal liabilities during 1934–1936 to an average 8.5 percent of GDP, a powerful kick. Monetary policy also played a major role, from the dollar devaluation and the Treasury's permissive attitude toward monetizing gold inflow from Europe and Japan. The results were clear—a three-year real growth rate of 8.7 percent.[62] Then, in mid-1937, something happened.

Harvard University's *Review of Economics and Statistics* for 1937 could have been draped in black crepe:

> The year 1937 opened with high industrial activity, sharply advancing commodity prices, and strong security markets, which gave superficial indication of prosperity and perhaps approaching boom; and it closed with the severe contraction of output, sharp reduction in prices, and acute weakness in security markets which frequently mark the initial stage of severe depression. . . . Full appraisal of the causes of the downturn, and its extraordinary severity, is difficult or impossible . . . But a basic and decisive weakness of the situation was that the entire recovery since 1933 had developed largely in circumstances which rendered it exceedingly vulnerable. A revival induced mainly by stimulating consumer purchasing power could generate no sustaining momentum. . . . At colossal cost, we have tested whether stimulated purchasing power can produce recovery; 1937 teaches that conditions had not been generated which could maintain prosperity when the reduction of stimulus—inevitable sooner or later—began.[63]

The downturn was extremely steep. Scholars differ as to whether it was the second or third worst in US history, after the Great Depression itself. It was about as sharp as the downturn in 1920–1921, and twice as steep as at the outset of the Depression. Between May 1937 and the trough in June 1938, industrial production fell by 32 percent, employment by 22 percent, and stock prices by 40 percent. The year-to-year drop in quarterly GDP, although less volatile than industrial production, was still a very steep 11.3 percent (see Figure 5.5). The psychological impact of the downturn was much the worse, since it was a complete surprise.[64]

The 1937 crash—no other word can describe it—was entirely self-inflicted. At heart, Roosevelt was a Dutch fiscal conservative and wasn't

FIGURE 5.5: US INDUSTRIAL PRODUCTION, MARCH 1933—JANUARY 1940 (MARCH 1933=100)

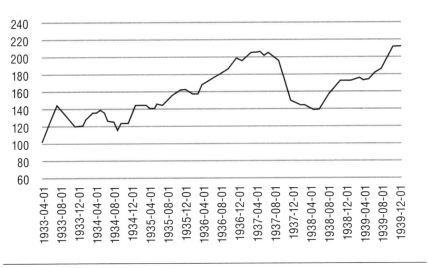

Source: FRED, Table G-17.

comfortable with the prospect of long-term deficits. Roosevelt was genuinely worried about the rising levels of federal spending, and in his 1936 campaign, he made a special point of returning to balanced budgets. He was strongly reinforced by Morgenthau, the skittish Treasury secretary who, along with many enlightened businessmen, was nearly in a state of panic over runaway deficits. Wholesale prices had jumped in 1937, and to fiscal managers of the 1930s, who had seen the damage done by runaway inflations in Germany and France, alarm bells were sounding.

Roosevelt's budget message to the Congress in April 1937 was framed around the necessity for frugality—"for eliminating or deferring all expenditures not absolutely necessary," with no passes given to the "emergency" programs of the original New Deal measures. Few programs were slated for elimination, but sharp cuts were planned for virtually all. The underlying message was that the New Deal had won, the economy had been enjoying near-record growth, employment was rising, factories were starting to hum, and agricultural earnings were looking quite healthy. The 1937 budget (for the fiscal year ending on June 30, 1937) cut the deficit from 5.1 percent to 2.4 percent. The 1938 budget was actually balanced within a tenth of one percent. Then, mystifyingly, everything fell apart.[65]

Time magazine weighed in with a long leading article in September:

When brokers cleared their desks fortnight ago, hustled out of town for the Labor Day weekend, the market had been falling steadily for three weeks. Supposedly it had fully discounted both war in China and a sudden wave of pessimism over fall business prospects. But the day sun-browned brokers returned from their holiday, a first-class European crisis burst on the front page. . . . When the closing bell bonged that day 385 stocks had touched bottom for 1937, and all three Dow-Jones stock averages had reached new lows for the year. . . . European stockmarkets showed no similar apprehension. Markets in Paris and London declined but never approached a break.

For two days after the Tuesday break the market seemed ready for a healthy rebound. Then, without war-scare, labor trouble, Washington slams or serious business news, the market nose-dived again. In the widest break since Oct. 17, 1930, on a volume of 2,320,000 shares—some three times the average daily trading for the past few months—463 stocks set new lows. In the words of old Alexander Dana Noyes, financial editor of the *New York Times*, the ready rationalizers of the market's behavior were "completely nonplussed."

By numerous industrial indices August was the best eighth month of any year since 1929. The Department of Commerce estimated last week that the 1937 national income would reach $70,000,000,000— 12% ahead of last year and highest since 1930. . . . [Yet] another wave of selling hit the Exchange, sending prices crashing for the third time in seven days. Declines from the day's high to the day's low were reminiscent of November 1929.

Wall Street came to the inevitable conclusion that it was all the fault of the New Deal. . . . Purpose of restriction on inside trading, like that of all the New Deal's securities regulations, was to make the market safe for the true investor. Violent and unjustified fluctuations were to be ended. Wall Street last week was asking whether the result, ironically enough, was to make the fluctuations more violent and unjustified than ever.[66]

But there was much more going on, much of it deflationary. For one thing, the 1936 Congress, over Roosevelt's veto, had authorized full payment of the veterans' bonus in 1936. The total amount was $1.7 billion, of which $1.4 billion had been cashed. The 1937 fiscal year therefore started with a big drop in national spending. Roosevelt also pushed through a steep tax increase, almost doubling the bite on upper-income taxpayers that took effect in 1937. That came on top of the first year of Social Security tax collection—$1.6 billion extracted from employers and workers, with benefits not to be paid until 1942 (later moved ahead to 1940). Then the Federal Reserve Board decided to reduce the level of banks' excess reserves, which, thanks to the gold inflows, had ballooned to about $2 billion worth. In principle, those reserves could support thirty times that amount of new lending, which monetary alarmists viewed as an inflationary landmine. From 1936 through 1938, the Fed doubled reserve requirements in three separate steps, which Friedman and Schwartz viewed as a significant monetary tightening.[67]

On top of that, Roosevelt imposed a new tax on net business earnings not distributed as dividends, with tax rates on a steep sliding scale based on the percentage of undistributed earnings. (The idea was that investors would invest dividends more intelligently than self-centered corporate executives.) Roosevelt had proposed it as a replacement for the corporate income tax, but Congress passed it as an additive tax, which he went along with. Then the National Labor Relations Act, better known as the Wagner Act, reinvigorated the union movement. There were a number of strikes in 1935 and 1936, and wages for industrial workers rose by about 10 percent. Neoclassical economists have also argued that Roosevelt's court-packing drive, his criticisms of businessmen as "economic royalists," his tax increases on the wealthy, created a "regime change" in Temin's and Wigmore's sense that was inimical to investment. Finally, the Federal Reserve and the Treasury agreed that to reduce the inflationary pressures, the Treasury would sterilize the still-strong gold inflows from Europe and Asia.[*68]

---

* Once the gold price was stabilized in January 1934, the Treasury replaced the Federal Reserve as the custodian for American gold. Up until then, the Fed had made a practice of "sterilizing" gold inflows by offsetting them with new liabilities so base money would not be increased. The Treasury's practice was to pay for gold inflows with drafts drawn on the Fed, which it replenished with new gold certificates. As the Treasury spent down those replenished funds, the monetary base was increased

To the modern eye, it might amaze that the country's policy makers were not aware of all those deflationary bombs. But it wasn't entirely their fault. In the 1930s, a national economy was still a hazy and shifting entity, like a galactic gas cloud. Basic concepts like GNP hadn't been invented yet. The Census Bureau had long tracked business activity, and Herbert Hoover, when he was secretary of commerce, began to publish monthly activity data, but no one pretended that it was comprehensive. It was only in the 1930s, in great part because of the shock of the Great Depression, that the economist Simon Kuznets and the National Bureau of Economic Research were engaged by the government to prepare a comprehensive set of national income accounts. By the mid-1940s, the completion of national product and expenditure accounts enabled the creation of complete GNP accounts.

Monetary theory had also been around for a century at least, but its importance wasn't fully elucidated until the famous Friedman and Schwartz *Monetary History*, which was published in 1963. Many of the basic concepts of monetary policy had been noted by Keynes, Fisher, and others, but the greater part of the Friedman-Schwartz conceptual apparatus was a post-World War II development. Seemingly obvious facts, like the difference between real and nominal interest rates, were not yet part of the official 1930s conversation.[69]

Roosevelt's initial reactions to the 1937 crash were reminiscent of Hoover's in 1930. In October, he told his cabinet, "I have been around the country and know conditions are good. Everything will work out if we just sit tight and keep quiet." That initial bravado quickly dissipated. Morgenthau, at the Treasury, noted that "The White House has the jitters," which Morgenthau was certainly contributing to. A few days after the stock market slide, he wrote the president, "I have had to come to the conclusion that we are headed right into another depression." A Fed advisory committee warned darkly of "another major depression. . . . Plants are closing down every day. Thousands and thousands of production workers are being laid off every day. . . . Such movements gather their own

---

by the same amount as the new gold inflow. When the Treasury decided to sterilize the inflows, it paid for the gold with drafts on the Fed as before, but deposited the resultant certificates into an inactive Treasury account and repaid the Fed out of its current balances, thus avoiding net money creation.

momentum and feed upon themselves." In early 1938, when the economy was sliding at an alarming rate, Harold Ickes confided to his diary, "It looks to me as if all the courage has oozed out of the President. He has let things drift. There is no fight and no leadership."[70]

The recession lasted for just about a year, from the summer of 1937 to the summer of 1938. What turned it around was a resumption of government stimulus. The most important action was ending the sterilization of gold. The sterilization had started in November 1936, and over its life it sequestered about $1.4 billion of gold. $300 million of that was released in September 1937, but for technical reasons, not as a conscious stimulus. Perversely, the sharp US downturn also slammed shut the foreign gold pipeline—traders had seen Roosevelt resort to a gold revaluation before and feared he might do so again. In April 1938, the Treasury desterilized the remaining gold, and spent it down, or "monetized" it, over the next year. Worryingly, the gold flow from Europe did not resume immediately—once burnt, twice shy, perhaps—but the Nazi move on Czech Sudetenland in the fall of 1938 panicked wealthy Europeans, and the gold flows picked up briskly. By this time, gold accounted for about 85 percent of the US monetary base.[71]

For his part, Roosevelt finally cast aside his pose as the prophet of balanced budgets. Hopkins, recovering from stomach cancer, sent him a note showing that unemployment had risen by 2.5 million since the previous summer. Marriner Eccles, the Federal Reserve chairman and perhaps the only committed Keynesian in the administration, had protested the budget balancing fervor from the start, and was a strong internal voice for more stimulus. The WPA and PWA had shelves of already-designed projects, and the RFC had plenty of bonding capacity in its financial arsenal. Congress shed its fear of spending and meekly pushed through $2 billion in direct spending, $1 billion in direct project lending, plus an additional $1.5 in RFC borrowing. The total stimulus, counting the newly desterilized gold, ran to nearly $6 billion. Assuming the spending was pumped into the economy over a period of eighteen months or so—Hopkins was master of getting money out fast—the stimulus effect would have been about 4 percent of GDP, which would make a difference. Add to that the resumption of large gold inflows from abroad and the strong growth pickup for the rest of the decade is fully accounted for. (That number also tracks with the stimulus bulge calculated by Eggertsson (see Figure 5.3).[72]

Modern research has also elucidated which of the alleged deflationary agents were important in inducing the downturn and which weren't. The current consensus seems to be that the Social Security tax was of little significance. Tax proceeds were used to purchase government securities to be deposited in a trust fund. Holders of the government debt, in other words, received cash for their securities, which they could spend or reinvest as they chose. Recent experience, however, suggests that the consensus is wrong. Wealth and income were about as concentrated in the 1930s as they are now. Any process that funneled money from paychecks to buy bonds from wealthy people had to be contractionary. (The trust fund arrangement was dropped in 1940 and the system was put on a pay-as-you-go basis.)

The Fed's focus on excess reserves, however, was probably of little consequence, despite the criticisms of Friedman and Schwartz. The level of excess balances was so large that the reserve increases did not restrict banks' ability to lend. After the 1933 banking crisis, most banks maintained high levels of precautionary liquidity, and with interest rates so low, idle balances were not a drag on earnings. One or the other reserve districts, especially New York, experienced brief episodes of tightness, but they could be explained better by local policy decisions than by the Fed's actions.*[73]

Another chip in the 1936 Roosevelt legislative package—the tax on net undistributed earnings—turned out to be a bad idea and was repealed after two years. The tax particularly weighed on smaller, entrepreneurial, technically advanced companies. Because they were small, they had to pay prohibitive fees of 25 percent and up to tap public markets, so it was economically efficient for them to use their earnings for research and development instead of returning them to shareholders. It is probably true that the tax increases on the very wealthy reduced their propensity to invest. Similarly, it is likely true that the worker strikes and wage increases were

---

* Despite stated worries about the inflationary potential of large excess reserves, the primary motive for the Fed's action was to take back monetary controls usurped by the Treasury. The conventional Fed monetary tools, controlling the level of reserves through the discount rate and open market operations, were useless if the banks carried large idle balances. The Fed was quite circumspect in implementing the reserve rules, and stayed in close contact with the Treasury throughout.

seen as elements of a "regime change" by businessmen, whose feelings of besiegement may have hastened the onset of the 1937 crash.

Businessmen must have quickly learned to swallow their anxieties, however, for the wage hikes and the regulatory initiatives were still in effect when very rapid growth resumed in mid-1938—even in the face of a new and very aggressive antimonopoly drive. The neoclassical economist Lee Ohanian argues that regime-change-type effects are evidenced by the "weak" 1933–1940 recovery. But that is a strained description, to say the least. From 1933 through 1940, a period that includes the 1937–1938 recession but ends just before the upsurge of wartime spending, the economy turned in a seven-year average real growth rate of 7.2 percent, the fastest peacetime growth in history. By way of comparison, it was much faster than the 5 percent annual growth rate in the eight years from 1921–1929, which includes the double-digit growth coming out of the 1920–1921 crash.[74]

IX. THE UNEMPLOYMENT CONUNDRUM

Nineteen-twenty-nine was a boom year, with durable goods, especially, running ahead of their markets. It is also the first year for which the Department of Commerce later produced official GDP figures, so it is the benchmark for measuring the downturn. The steep descent of real GDP ended in 1933, with a four-year real drop of more than a quarter. The economy recovered to its real 1929 level in the three years from 1933 through 1936—a 36 percent gain from the 1933 low point. Per capita GDP caught up to 1929's level in 1939, and by 1940, per capita real GDP was 10 percent higher than in 1929. After an extreme drop, in other words, the GDP numbers suggest a brisk recovery. But the long unemployment lines belied those data.[75]

FIGURE 5.6: US UNEMPLOYMENT AND WAGES, 1929–1940[76]

	Lebergott	Darby	Wage Index (1940=100)
1929	3.2%	3.2%	69.4
1930	8.7%	8.7%	75.7
1931	15.9%	15.3%	83.2
1932	23.6%	22.9%	80.8
1933	24.9%	20.6%	79.5
1934	21.7%	16.0%	84.3
1935	20.1%	14.2%	80.4
1936	16.9%	9.9%	81.1
1937	14.3%	9.1%	85.5
1938	19.0%	12.5%	93.9
1939	17.2%	11.3%	97.3
1940	14.6%	9.5%	100.0

Source: Margo, "Employment and Unemployment," Table 1.

The difference between the Lebergott and Darby unemployment data is simply that Darby counts workers on government relief programs as employed, while Lebergott counts them as unemployed, which was the Census Bureau practice. Unemployment figures for this period, in any case, have large margins of uncertainty. No government agency conducted surveys of the unemployed like the modern *Current Population Survey* does. Instead, unemployment was taken as the residual of two other databases—the labor force participation rate and the employment-to-population ratio. Very small variations in either of the two source databases may generate major differences in the residual. The data from this era are also likely to harbor major sampling errors—big companies were consistently oversampled, for instance—and definitions and counting conventions were still evolving.[77]

The primary conundrum, however, is the behavior of real wages. A hoary postulate of classical economics is that employment moves in the opposite direction from the real wage. If the real wage is higher than the market-clearing rate, employment will fall (and unemployment will rise) until wages adjust to balance demand and supply. If real wages are too low, conversely, job openings will go unfilled until employers adjust wages up.* So the puzzle of the 1930s is, with a reserve army of the unemployed equivalent to a quarter of the labor force, most of them with respectable recent work histories, why didn't wages fall?[78]

The traditional answer, notably from Keynes, was "sticky wages." That made intuitive sense in England, where the postwar Labour governments had won near-blanket union coverage in major industries with national bargaining protocols conducted by professionals on both sides. National bargaining by itself provided a pro-wage momentum, reinforcing the stated political objective of raising the income of the working classes.[79]

But the United States was not England. Unions had strong support within the Roosevelt administration, but most large employers were unalterably opposed to them, a position that commanded considerable

---

* In his famous MacMillan Committee testimony, Keynes pointed out that the "Treasury view" following the tenets of classical economics was that "unemployment, except of a merely transitory character of which one need take no serious account, is an impossibility."

sympathy among conservative Democrats, especially in the South. Unionism, however, had become a transcendent cause, with its own songs and folk heroes, much like the 1960s civil rights movement. After the demise of the NIRA, legal protections for workers were enshrined in the National Labor Relations and the Fair Labor Standards Acts.

But the panoply of new protections was not self-enforcing. It took several years to establish rules of decision, and progress was slowed by a host of hostile congressional investigations. Consider the epochal confrontations in the automobile industry, especially the multiyear effort by Walter Reuther's United Auto Workers (UAW) to organize the Ford plants. The company resorted to hiring thugs to intimidate workers, and Reuther and his top aides absorbed a fearful beating at the Rouge River plant in 1937. The company's lawyers fought a grim phrase-by-phrase battle against the new National Labor Board's authority, and Ford even agreed with the old-line, and corrupt, American Federation of Labor (AFL) to sponsor a second auto workers' union with company support. Reuther's union finally prevailed in 1941 by huge margins, much to Ford's chagrin. By the end of the war, the industrial unions were recognized in big plants throughout the country, and big companies were professionalizing their employee relations and bargaining functions. But the notion that in the 1930s, employers were greatly trammeled by a "sticky wage" tradition, does not comport with the facts.[80]

An early NBER effort, however, sheds light on how big employers managed their workforces during the Crash. Frederick C. Mills was a researcher engaged in the Kuznets GDP project. His specialty was prices, and he put together a data set of monthly manufacturing unit output and sales prices for the years 1929–1934. Multiplying sales and prices produces manufacturing gross revenues. Figure 5.7 combines those data with contemporary manufacturing payroll data collected by the National Industrial Conference Board (NICB), including nominal and real hourly and weekly wages, average worker hours employed, and the total payroll.[81] I've adjusted the Mills data, however, to take into account a discrepancy between his data and that of the Census Bureau. Mills and the NBER use quoted prices rather than final prices in their pricing data bases. Mills points out the size of the discrepancy, which he attributes to depression-driven price-cutting, but also notes a number of other factors, like

FIGURE 5.7: COMBINED US MANUFACTURING PAYROLLS AND GROSS REVENUES, 1929–1934

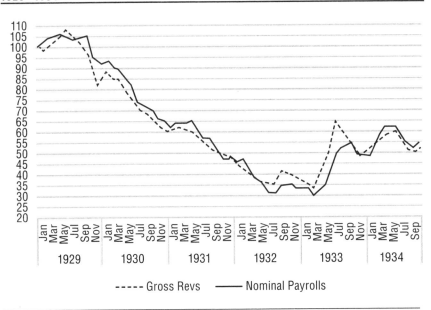

Source: Mills, "Changes in Pricing"; and Beny, *Wages, Hours*.

skimping on part quality, substituting less expensive models, and other factors. To be sure my numbers are conservative, however, I adjusted the data to assume that all of the discrepancy is from price-cutting.

Employers' behavior seems quite rational. Most employers were optimistic in late 1929 and early 1930, and seem to have delayed drastic manning cuts. Once they changed their outlook in 1930, wages were tightly linked to the falling profile of revenues until late 1933, when the Roosevelt wage legislation came into play.* Businesses managed their payroll by cutting hours of those employed, cutting workforces, and cutting nominal wages, in that order. It's not likely that they were trying to track real wages. This was, after all, a time when even the Federal Reserve ignored real interest rates. Instead they appear merely to be trying to keep their expenses within their available revenues.

---

* Note that the source data are in index numbers, 1929=100, so they show only relative changes of the two variables, with no information on their absolute values, although business profits were high in the late 1920s, and Figure 5.2 suggests that workers were getting a dwindling share of the pie.

There were practical limits that dictated the sequence of cuts. At the outset, it probably made sense to emphasize cuts in hours before employees, since shift times could be varied from day to day. But running a plant with many short-hour shifts could quickly become inefficient. And too-short shifts had their own problems: a report on the steel industry indicated that the 1932–1933 average steel worker earnings were below the "minimum health and decency" standard for a family of four. Finally, in complex industries, there would necessarily be essential operations that required a minimum of skilled men.

Figure 5.8 compares the 1929 averages for nominal and real hourly pay, hours worked, and total payrolls to the average for 1932, and to the nadir of this series, which came in March 1933. It also demonstrates the great advantage of staying employed during the Depression. Factory workers who kept their jobs through 1932 had an effective real wage 20 percent lower than in 1929, after accounting for the increased purchasing power of a dollar. Employers, of course, kept their books on a nominal basis, and the reductions in average actual pay and hours worked in 1932 would have reduced nominal payrolls to about 60 percent of the 1929 amount. Since payrolls were cut to only 30 percent of the 1929 level, manufacturers must have cut their work forces in half. In the big factory towns, like Detroit, there would have been little alternative employment, leaving family heads to the lean pickings of the dole or WPA projects.

FIGURE 5.8: CHANGES IN HOURS, REAL AND NOMINAL WAGES, AND EMPLOYMENT IN MANUFACTURING, 1929–1933 (1929 = 100)

	Nominal Hourly Earnings	Real Hourly Earnings	Total Hours Worked	Total Payrolls
1929	100	100	100	100
1932 Avg	83	109	73	30
	-17%	9%	-27%	-70%
March 1933	76	109	67	29
	-24%	9%	-33%	-71%

Source: Beny

FIGURE 5.9: US DURABLE MANUFACTURERS' PRODUCTION, PRICES, AND GROSS REVENUES, 1929–1934 (1929=100)

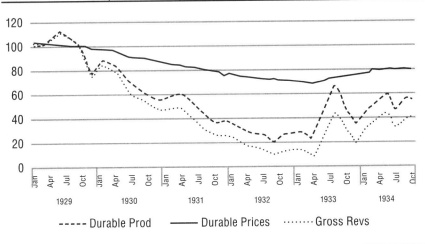

Source: Mills, "Changes in Pricing."

Interestingly, the Mills data also suggest that there was a strong "sticky *price*" phenomenon operating among the durable manufacturing sector during this period.[82] (See Figure 5.9.)

There is anecdotal evidence supporting the existence of sticky prices. *Time* reported in October 1932 (note the date; it was already well into the third year of the Depression):

> Prosperity, depression and a threatened investigation by the Government were unable to change the price of steel rails for a decade. Billets might go up (to $36 a ton in 1929) and billets might go down (to $26 last week), but the price of steel rails mysteriously remained at $43 a ton.
>
> Last week Myron Charles Taylor, chairman of United States Steel Corp., invited a group of railroad presidents . . . to lunch with him in his company's private dining room. He told them how concerned the steel industry was with the lack of orders from their industry, especially at the lack of rail orders. The rail-roadmen suggested that if the price of rails were a little lower they might be interested.

The very next week, all the steel companies reduced their rail price by $3 a ton, or 7 percent, producing, if not a flood of orders, at least a temporary bump-up.[83]

FIGURE 5.10: COMPARISON OF US DURABLE/NONDURABLE DEPRESSION PRODUCTION AND PRICING STRATEGIES

Low Points	Durables		Nondurables	
	Index No.	Date	Index No.	Date
Prices	68	Apr 1933	41	Mar 1933
Production	21	Sept 1932	69	Jul 1932
Revenues	9	Apr 1933	37	Mar 1933

Source: Mills, "Changes in Pricing."

Nondurable manufacturers, as it happens, followed an opposite strategy. Instead of holding prices, they cut them, maintained higher production, and earned more than twice the level of revenues. See the comparison of low points (Figure 5.10) for each branch of the industry.[84]

The fact that manufacturing industries as a group adopted practices that split along durable and nondurable business lines suggests that there were business reasons for the choices. The inventory risk of durables and nondurables may have been quite different; perishable nondurables, for example, would tend to have short shelf lives. But the *Time* article quoted above suggests the prevalence of cartelized pricing in heavy manufacturing—a legacy of Elbert Gary's long reign at US Steel.

The classical economic "law" that employment moves inversely to real wages was born in an era when great segments of society worked at routine jobs. Assuming a minimum set of physical skills and comprehension, laborers were laborers. The industrial revolution, however, spun off multiple new classes of artisans. When the United States was acquiring the technology for mechanized spinning and weaving, a skilled and ambitious artisan like the young Samuel Slater could emigrate from England, settle in a mercantile town like Providence, and rather quickly become rich. A generation or so later, textile mill mechanics were well paid—usually at the top of the blue-collar pyramid—but were no longer a scarce commodity.[85]

The advent of giant steam engines enabled much larger factories and forced capital deepening, which pushed up the wages of the most-skilled manual workers and increased the employment of white-collar workers— typically more highly educated, at ease with symbolic information, and more highly paid. Well into the early twentieth century, literate and numerate high school graduates commanded substantial pay premiums. The advent of AC wholesale electricity enabled yet another revolution in manufacturing, which Ford was the first to implement. Recall that in 1914, the first year the industry produced more than 500,000 cars, Ford produced nearly half of them, with only one-fifth the workers of his competitors.

The "Middletown" researchers who analyzed the mores, manners, and economic practices of the city of Muncie, Indiana, reported that Fordism had taken hold in the traditional Middletown manufacturing enterprises. Muncie's plants mostly sold into the automobile industry in the 1920s; they were benefiting from the rocketing sales and were under great pressure to keep up technically with their customers. A generation before, Muncie's manufacturers had employed skilled workers, who had completed formal apprenticeship programs and made all or substantial elements of a workpiece. Under Fordism, factories were staffed by operators who loaded machines and turned them on and off, or executed a small number of repetitive manual tasks. They could usually be trained within a few hours or, at most, a week or two, and the best Fordist lines produced parts that didn't need special fitting. But the people running Muncie's plants were not Henry Fords. A reasonable estimate is that it took about twenty years to implement full-bore Fordism in a major plant: it required great discipline in the setup, and fanatical attention to detail. It is likely that in Muncie most of the parts manufacturers did the job only partway, enough to qualify for contracts but without the tireless zeal to weed out all the diseconomies.[*]

Kenneth Roose, who wrote the first book-length account of the 1937 recession, noted with puzzlement that during the 1930s factory construction fell precipitately, while machine purchases rose quite dramatically.[†]

---

[*] I can't prove this, of course. But in the 1980s, I worked as a valuation consultant for buyout firms, with a particular focus on manufacturing. It was a period when America's factories were being decisively outperformed by German and Japanese competitors. Few of the companies selling their manufacturing units had any idea how poorly they were run.

[†] Roose treats residential and business construction together. By 1937, they were less than a third of the peak quarterly rate in the 1920s. His text suggests without quite stating that they moved down roughly at the same rate. Producer durable equipment, however, enjoyed "a vigorous expansion" bringing them back to the 1929 level by 1936, and almost 20 percent above the 1929 peak by the second quarter of 1937.

In fact, that is direct evidence of the continued march of Fordism. Factories became single-floor, compact structures, with machines laid out to create the most efficient routes and travel times of workpieces. None of that was possible before the advent of purchased AC electricity. In steam-driven plants, machines were segregated by the heaviness of the belting, and multifloor layouts allowed driving multiple classes of machinery from a single drive. AC-drive plants became cleaner, brighter, and quieter. Roose's puzzle, in other words, was the natural result of the continuing Fordist transition: factory construction costs were substantially reduced, but almost all of the machinery had to be replaced.[86]

Over the last couple of decades, there has been a welcome trend in economics to dig beneath aggregate data for the significant microdata that may determine events. Timothy Bresnahan and Daniel Raff have focused on such microdata in a series of studies that document the violent Depression-era shakeout in the automobile industry. Plant closings followed a clear pattern—in general, smaller plants closed and the larger ones survived. Discontinued plants on average were about half the size as the surviving plants and accounted for a third of the job losses. Some Big Three plants (Ford, GM, and Chrysler) were mothballed, but reopened as business picked up. Labor productivity fell somewhat at the surviving plants, suggesting some "labor hoarding"—retaining senior more highly paid men, while dismissing younger, less-skilled workers. White-collar workers were more protected; only about 25 percent were let go, compared to 50 percent of blue-collar workers.

As the market picked up after 1933, productivity responded dramatically. By 1935, vehicle production had doubled, while blue-collar employment had increased only by half, and white-collar employment was virtually unchanged, although overall productivity was still not quite at the blowout 1929 level. The number of plants had not increased from their 1933 low, but on average they were much bigger than their pre-Depression predecessors. In effect, the modern automobile industry—dominated by a few very large oligopolistic firms—took shape in the crucible of the Crash.[87]

The economist Richard Jensen, in a well-known paper that complements much of the Bresnahan-Raff work, points to the "efficiency wage" as a major factor in the persistent unemployment figures. Efficiency wage principles may well have influenced the Ford-Couzens decision to jump to the $5 pay standard in 1914. Their company was growing by leaps and bounds, but the discipline of a highly mechanized manufacturing operation system was a hard one, and turnover was a growing, and expensive, problem. While the company was very profitable, factory indiscipline may have been perceived as a real threat to future growth. While the record supports a belief that Ford and Couzens wanted to share their profits with the workers, they could have done that without doubling the wage. It was a bold decision and paid off magnificently.[88]

Jensen stresses that the day's workers were not a homogeneous collective. Just as there were too-small, insufficiently rationalized, and essentially doomed auto manufacturers at the outset of the Depression, so there were workers who lacked the temperament, or the smarts, or the discipline to make their way in a modernized work environment—Jensen calls them the "hard-core." Barriers to hiring such people were doubtless raised by the minimum wage and other provisions of the NIRA, and after its demise, successor legislation like the National Labor Relations Act and the Fair Labor Standards Act.[89]

Before 1930, with the near-total lack of a social safety net, people had to work and generally accepted the market wage. Data from 1885 to 1930 suggest that only 10–20 percent of the workforce had been unemployed for more than six months. In 1930, only about 1 percent of the workforce had been unemployed that long. But once the Crash hit, unemployment spread rapidly and, Jensen suggests, created a distinct tiering of the ranks of the unemployed. Part 3 recounts the astonishing unemployment levels in the big factory cities. Rural unemployment was probably at least as bad, but was less visible and mostly not counted.[90]

Employment, however, was very fluid. Even in the very depths of the Depression, factories hired a million workers every three or four months. But they were no longer hiring the next body in the shape-up. Each hire would be interviewed and questioned on his work history, pay rates, and personal habits. A sorting process to distinguish competent workers from warm bodies was gradually taking hold throughout industry. These were also practices that Ford had pioneered twenty years before, when he implemented his $5-per-day regime. The very existence of such studies evidences the professionalization of personnel management and the emergence of explicit sorting procedures that pushed the least capable workers to the end of the hiring queue.[91]

The impact of Depression-era unemployment varied widely among industries. The construction and manufacturing industries were the worst hit. In 1933, almost three-quarters of construction workers and 40 percent of manufacturing workers were jobless. The two industries were still hard hit in 1938, with 55 percent and 28 percent joblessness, respectively. With such numbers, relief work was a godsend, and, as we have already seen, there is evidence that the long-term unemployed settled into their lot, despite the rules that the assignments were supposed to be temporary. Supervisors bargained with WPA workers that if they took an available private job, they could return to the WPA slot if they were let go. In one documented instance of a mass termination—783,000 workers in August 1939—57 percent were back on relief within a year. It is interesting, too, that the wives of unemployed men not on relief were apt to find private employment, while the wives of men on relief were less likely to do so.[92]

There is no single answer to the question of why Depression-era unemployment was so intractable. Embattled companies upped their investment in machinery and husbanded their best workers, squeezing out whatever pips of productivity they could find. More explicit hiring standards inevitably left an indigestible lump of disqualified applicants that would grow or shrink depending on shifts in aggregate demand. The very long periods of unemployment that became routine in the 1930s must have inculcated the expectations of failure and attitudes of shiftlessness associated with "hard core" unemployment. The solution, however, came quickly—fifteen million men were called into service in 1940–1941, military contracts turned on the lights in disused plants, and seven-day, twelve hours a day factory shifts were suddenly routine.

The economist Alexander Field has recently made the striking claim that it "was not principally the Second World War that laid the foundation for postwar prosperity. It was technological progress across a broad frontier of the American economy during the 1930s."[93] Yes, the years 1929–1933 saw a crash in effective demand, the collapse of heavy manufacturing, and a devastating hollowing out of labor markets. Simultaneously with those disasters, however, the working economy was turning in one of the best records in total factor productivity (TFP) in the country's history—even better than the spectacular growth record in the 1920s. The concept of TFP sprang from the 1950's research of two well-known "growth economists," Moses Abramovitz and Robert Solow, who reconstructed economic databases for the nineteenth and early twentieth centuries. They found they could explain most nineteenth-century growth by summing the contributions of changes in the inputs of labor and capital (e.g., new plants and machinery). In the first quarter of the twentieth century, however, growth was consistently *higher* than suggested by the identifiable inputs. Solow called the unexplained growth factors the "residual." TFP, then, was revised to include inputs of labor and capital plus the residual, which was assumed to capture the invisible technology-enabled improvements in the use of the inputs. That residual began to shrink in the second half of the twentieth century, and is now nearly undetectable, which is raising some alarm among policy experts.[94]

The twenties was an extraordinarily productive decade, but its advances were almost entirely explained by the growth in manufacturing TFP—an amazing 5.12 percent a year from 1919–1929. In the thirties, with much of the factory productivity revolution already in the bank, manufacturing TFP dropped to 2.76 percent—which is still a very strong number. Capital investment played only a minor role in the thirties, and the TFP gains came from two broad categories of progress. First, as we have seen in the automobile industry, smaller, older plants were forced to

FIGURE 5.11: US PRODUCTIVITY GROWTH, 1929–1941

Sector	TFP % Growth, 1929–1941	1941 % Share of PNE*	% Share of Total PNE TFP Growth
Manufacturing	2.76	42.4	50.7
Transport & Public Utilities	4.50	12.3	23.8
Wholesale & Retail Trade	2.33	22.2	22.5
Other**	0.22	23.1	3.0

* PNE = private nonfarm economy
** Mining, construction, finance, insurance and real estate
Source: Field, Great Leap.

close, raising the average productivity of them all, and second, manufacturers raised their scientific game. Despite the black clouds that still hung over the entire economy, industry made major investments in research and scientific manpower in the thirties. Total research and development employees in American manufacturing rose from 6,250 in 1927, to 11,000 in 1933, to 27,800 by 1940. Specific advances in manufacturing technology during the decade included improving the thermal efficiency of engines; reusing waste gases and other detritus; development of plastics, tungsten, and carbon alloys; and a host of other individually modest research-based advances.[95]

With manufacturing productivity merely very good in the 1930s, other sectors had to jump ahead to make up the shortfall.

The "private nonfarm economy" excludes the government and farm sectors, since they do not lend themselves to TFP measurement.* About a third of the spectacular TFP gains in transport and utilities were concentrated in trucking and warehousing. The wildfire growth of the automobile industry in the 1920s pointed ineluctably toward a colossal national traffic jam, until infrastructure investment, much of it financed by the government, built out a national highway bridge and tunnel system. That

---

* Farm productivity varies with the weather, and the outputs of government and many types of service workers don't lend themselves to productivity measures. In the case of a kindergarten teacher, for example, would larger class sizes be an index of productivity?

connecting system of highways enabled the first modern trucking industry, the consummate tool to speed deliveries to the world's first nation of
consumers. The second-best sector contribution to transport and utilities TFP was the railroads, as their integration with short-haul trucking
vendors created what must have been the most flexible haulage industry
in the world. The final major contributor in the transport and utility sector was the electric power industry as it continued to ride up the golden
ladder of scale efficiencies, filling in the blank spots in their local service
areas and prospering from the ubiquitous and thickening web of consumer electrical necessities. The final sector to show rapid TFP growth
was wholesale and retail distribution, a natural twin of transport and
utilities. Note that its 2.33 percent is the lowest of the three most productive sectors, but since its share of the economy was almost twice as large as
the transport and utility sector, the two sectors made very similar contributions to the economy's dynamism.[96]

Field's research casts a new light on the conventional story that World
War II "ended the Depression." For sure, the flood of war spending was
a massive "demand shock" that quickly mopped up the Depression-era
excess workers. But there is little evidence of a wartime "supply shock"
that created the infrastructure to both win the war and power America's
postwar success. While the war accelerated some specific technologies—
like airframes, antibiotics, and munitions—the disruptions caused by
rapid-fire national mobilization and demobilization, along with other
wartime distortions, probably outweighed the positive developments.
The strong post-war economy, Field argues, was the legacy not of the war,
but of the combination of high productivity gains in manufacturing—
spectacular in the 1920s and still strong in the 1930s—plus the crucial
1930s capacity increases in industrial R&D, transportation, communications, public utilities, warehousing, and distribution, much of it financed
with public funds. America's world-class productive capacity was not, in
the main, created in wartime; it was already there, awaiting conversion to
new purposes.

PART SIX

The Geology of the Collapse

——— I. THE LEGACY OF WAR ———

I t is hard to conceive of the Great Depression absent World War I. Presumably, if Austria-Hungary had behaved as most diplomats expected and not mobilized, the Sarajevo crisis would have been papered over as multiple other such crises had been, and millions of casualties and trillions in economic losses would not have occurred. But the "if" in that sentence is a very large one. Great Britain's Victorian dispensation was surely entering its dotage. Germany, France, Russia, Japan, and other rising states were determined to expand their boundaries, whether in Europe or in colonies abroad. German industry, especially, was decisively outperforming Great Britain's and the rest of Europe's in almost every category, and was determined to expand its footprint, whether on the continent or abroad. But more than merely mercenary considerations were in play. There was an engrained metaphysics of war, an atavistic "Idea" of war as a purifying flame, a ratification of the quality of one's racial stock, an essential step to the realization of national destinies. The philosopher William James, a pacifist, in order to emphasize the difficulties of the pacifist cause, extolled the virtues of war:

> Patriotism no one thinks discreditable; nor does anyone deny that war
> is the romance of history . . . and the possibility of violent death the
> soul of all romance. . . . It is a sort of sacrament. Its profits are to the
> vanquished as well as the victor . . . it is an absolute good we are told,
> for it is human nature at its highest dynamic.[1]

And so the war came. Rivers of blood were shed. Millions of men died in pestilential trench mud. Industrial and cultural edifices were turned to ashes. National treasuries were emptied. Whole populations displaced.

To make matters worse, the "Spanish flu" pandemic arrived in Europe some months before the armistice. It was almost certainly carried by American soldiers and was dubbed the "pale rider" of the troop ships.

The European version of the disease was far more virulent than the one in America, and the disruptions of war—poor nutrition, crowded refugee camps, unhygienic field hospitals—helped it spread like wildfire.[2]

Travelers' reports painted a grim picture. A number commented on the evident undernourishment of German children, but many blamed it on the Germans. "[The country] makes political capital out of her undernourished children," one wrote, even as they rerouted food supplies to a wildly profitable black market. Germans, he went on, were a nation of *"scheibers,"* who refused to live by the rules. While he was "deeply touched" by the sight of the children, he was disgusted at the two hundred all-night restaurants in Berlin "filled with revelers reveling in their own stolid fashion and eating vast quantities of forbidden food while the rest of the nation converses glibly of starving children."[3]

Other veteran travelers to Germany were surprised at the condition of Berlin, a once slumless city that had now become a "slum *en bloc,*" with beggars exposing their mutilated limbs and streets filled with "unshaven men and ill-washed women," along with "loosely organized soldiers who roamed the city at will." American travelers were surprised at their friendly reception in Germany, although others realized it was just in contrast to the German hatred of the French. Most Germans seemed anxious to press their war narrative on visitors: "we won the war—on the field of battle, such a war as never before waged against a nation in history . . . our line never cracked." The loss was due to the "arrival of the Americans, starvation due to the naval blockade, a military command gone 'stale'," and the realization that "the whole world [was] against us."[4]

Travelers to Vienna, one of the world's most elegant cities, found it in a pitiable state: "The Peace Conference stripped Austria of everything she needs in order to exist. . . . She can't buy coal, she can't buy food, she can't buy raw materials. . . . She is cold and starved and helpless and hopeless." But the locals revered Herbert Hoover, whose relief operations were keeping the city on survival diets. An Austrian official said Hoover was "the most humane, the best-informed, the most practical, and the biggest-brained man not only in the United States, but in the world today."[5]

Some travelers engaged in a kind of battlefield porn—special tours to the battle sites and trenches that ran through northern France and Belgium. The desolation at Ypres awed visitors: one described a mangled tank as "a most pathetic animal . . . more human than any other kind of machinery . . . lying amid the blackened stumps and seas of mud."[6]

An American traveler who had lived for twenty years in Germany and France was surprised at first at the number of young French women working in jobs usually held by men, until he realized it was a conse-quence of the war's fearsome toll on young men. He found less explicable the booming business at theaters, cabarets, and casinos: the "hotels as spacious and luxurious as ever; the restaurants . . . as glittering and gay," but he gradually realized that just beneath the surface, the "European continent [was] a seething hell of hate: life is oppressed by a pall of vindic-tiveness and mutual distrust."[7]

All of the tangled threads that twisted together to create the catastro-phe of the Depression originated in Europe and can be traced through the choices made by the governments of the United States, Great Brit-ain, Germany, and France. Those choices, however, wrongheaded as they often were, were made in the context of large global forces that ensured that their consequences were often as bad as they could possibly be.

The Great Depression was an international catastrophe. The "advanced countries" of the world, sixteen countries in Western Europe and North America, taking 1929 as a base of 100, saw their real national output drop by 17 percent. Prices and trade volumes each fell by about a quarter. At the Depression's trough in 1932, nearly a third of all workers were unemployed. The real downturn in output in the United States was especially severe—26 percent between 1929 and 1933—although it started from a higher base. While there is still much to be understood about the Depression, it was the product of three different but related forces.[8]

The first was the deflationary momentum created by the major-country* push for gold-based currencies at prewar parities. The downward price pressure was generated simply because market prices in almost all economies had floated well above the target parities.

The second was the global agricultural glut of the 1930s. As we saw in Part 3, the Hoover administration's farm programs were overwhelmed by splendid bumper crops at a time of global excess production. But the problems were even worse in most other agrarian countries, which were typically far more dependent on agriculture.

And the third was the collapse in world trade, which was the product of, but additive to, the effects of the first two.

To take them in order: As we have seen, a clear majority of highly experienced economists, finance ministers, investment bankers, and financial academics favored a return of the pound, the mark, and the franc to their traditional relationship with gold. That was not crazy, as it

---

* When Great Britain returned to the gold standard in 1925, most of the smaller European countries followed, but most of them did so at devalued exchange rates, some at just a tiny fraction of the prewar parity. The point of their "resumption," however, was just to peg the value of a currency to a strong outside standard as a point of stability. Small-country currencies were rarely accepted in international trade.

is sometimes made to appear. Throughout history, rulers had destroyed their realms by debasing their money. (The word *sincere* is derived from the Latin for "without wax," echoing the times Roman emperors shaved their coins and filled them out with wax.) The admirable Benjamin Strong, with his superior grasp of central banking, was as committed as any to maintaining the gold standard at its traditional parity. Russell Leffingwell of J.P. Morgan had put the reasoning succinctly: if you borrow money, you should pay it back with coin of the same value.

It was particularly easy to reach an anti-reflation consensus, for it was less than a decade since Weimar Germany had provided an object lesson for the ages. The German inflation, in fact, had been started intentionally, with considerable agreement among the political parties. For the first couple of years it was quite successful. Germany's exports were high, and its unemployment rate was the lowest in Europe. Then some ineffable moment passed, and it was out of control.

Among the wise men of finance, devaluation was only slightly less foolish than an outright repudiation. A sound currency was one that was *constant*. Economic growth was always desirable, but not at all costs. If public deficits were mounting, and traders getting skittish, you didn't *devalue*. Responsible ministers pulled in their horns, reined in the spending, and began to steer under a better star. Strong made his position crystal clear in a much-quoted letter memorializing a meeting with Montagu Norman, his British counterpart:

> Mr. Norman's feelings, which in fact, are shared by me, indicated that the alternative—failure of resumption of gold payment—being a confession by the British Government that it would impossible to resume, would be followed by a long period of unsettled conditions too serious really to contemplate. It would mean violent fluctuations in the exchanges, with probably progressive deterioration of the values of foreign currencies vis-à-vis the dollar; it would provide an incentive to all of those who were advancing novel ideas for nostrums and expedients other than the gold standard to sell their wares; and incentives for governments at times to undertake various kinds of paper money expedients and inflation.[9]

Nineteen-thirty may have been the year of transition to global deflation. Great Britain was struggling to push down its export prices to competitive levels, but with little effect. Heinrich Brüning had taken over as the Reich chancellor to staunch the hemorrhaging of the federal budget and to build back the country's gold reserves. The French monetary law of 1928 had locked in both the undervalued gold price of the franc and the ban against counting foreign exchange in the monetary base. It took a while before the financial community understood what a powerful deflationary engine that created. The undervaluation of the franc naturally drew foreign exchange to France, which to the French looked like an engine of inflation. So the French began to redeem their foreign exchange holdings for gold, and sterilized the gold. The Bank of France managers, Moreau, Rist, and Quesnay, knew exactly what they were doing. In 1927, after meeting with a senior official of the Bank of England, Moreau wrote in his diary that the English official did not conceal the "distress or anxieties caused to the Bank of England by the brutal revelation of the power of the Bank of France upon the London market."[10]

For its part, the Federal Reserve mostly sat on its hands. To the majority of the governors, the downturn looked like the inevitable result of an out-of-control liquidity binge that had also caused a dangerous stock market bubble. Luminaries like Oliver Sprague preached that the world economies would right themselves once world prices had fallen to the level of "industrial equilibrium." A respected and long-serving Fed governor, Charles Hamlin, told a group of New England bankers that "the Federal Reserve was designed to break up the vicious circle under which a speculative orgy accompanied every forward step of industry," and claimed that the present downturn was a sign of the Fed's success. Passivity reigned.[11]

———

The world agricultural crisis was a second major contributor. Charles Kindleberger suggested as much in his 1973 *World in Depression*, but it did not stimulate much in the way of full-blown research. In a wide-reaching 2001 article, Jakob Madsen argued that the deflationary pressure generated by the mania for gold still did not fully account for the

FIGURE 6.1: COLLAPSE OF FARM PRICES

AGRICULTURAL PRODUCTION AND REVENUES, 1929–1932 (1929=100)

	1929	1930	1931	1932
Production	100	100	106	99
Wholesale Revenues	100	85	64	48

Source: Mills, *Prices in Recession.*

extraordinary drop in world income, and he indicted the Depression-era worldwide agricultural glut as the missing villain of the piece. The United States clearly suffered from a farming price collapse, but it was far worse in the rest of the world. Although the United States was one of the world's largest agricultural and raw material exporters, those industries were not as important in the American economy as they were in most other industrialized countries. The dominance of Americans in Depression studies may be the reason that the agricultural crisis is not generally highlighted as a primary cause of the downturn.[12]

American farmers did suffer mightily in the Depression. Frederick Mills, a star NBER researcher in the 1930s and 1940s, compiled the changes in farm production and revenues (see Figure 6.1).

Farmers' terms of trade worsened at the same time. Manufacturers were suffering, too, in 1932, but they had much more control over their production. Measured in February of 1933, Mills calculated that farmers' pricing power had deteriorated about a third more than the deterioration in the rest of the economy.[13]

Madsen points out that in the sixteen advanced countries in his sample, 31 percent more workers were employed in agriculture than in manufacturing, and they accounted for more than a third of the entire workforce. Removing the United States, the United Kingdom, and Germany from the sample, 54 percent more workers were employed in agriculture than in manufacturing, and agriculture employed 46 percent of the workforce.[14]

Worldwide, farmers had much the same wartime experience as those in the United States. Incomes leaped during the war, so farmers responded by expanding aggressively, only to find themselves in a vise when the war ended and European supply chains rebuilt themselves. Giovanni Federico (see Part 2) has made a convincing price-based case that American farmers, after a couple of tough years, stabilized themselves and made reasonable livings in the last half of the twenties. American farmers, however, would have made much greater use of technology, such as Ford tractors, to expand their production and reduce required workers. Few other countries, except possibly Canada, would have made such adjustments. Still, as the Mills data show, American farmers were very hard hit after 1930.[15]

The sheer size of the agricultural sector ensures that any large-scale shifts in income or production, especially ones that are sudden, are likely to have profound effects on the rest of the economy. And they did so in the 1930s. Falling farm incomes shifted both income and investment away from the farm sectors. There were radical drops in the value of farmland—American farmland values fell 40 percent from 1928 to 1933, with the greater part of the fall *before* the stock market crash—suggesting that the industry was following an internal logic of its own. Such steep losses reverberated through bank balance sheets, triggering the doleful consequences of a Fisherian debt deflation—rising real debt loads and real interest costs. Waves of farmer bankruptcies wreaked havoc on rural banks. Most farm commodities were traded internationally, so the glut triggered round after round of cut-throat pricing. The thirties were therefore a heyday of tariffs and quotas, which channeled income away from farmers to governments, or outright subsidies, which reversed the flow. Perversely, many American tariffs were denominated in fixed dollar amounts, so the relative burden of the tariffs increased as prices fell. Finally, since farmers were generally poorer than industrial and services workers, they spent more of their incomes, so by itself, the shift of farm income to other sectors reduced national spending.[16]

Madsen included a number of simulations of the GDP and other consequences of the observed developments in his sample countries from 1929 to 1932. Because of the very small number of data points (sixteen countries over four years), the modeling required formidable statistical manipulations. Suffice it to say that the effects he reports are large but are consistent with a commonsense assessment of the vast damage inflicted on what was then the world's largest industry.

The third global force conducing toward Depression was the collapse in world trade. Between 1929 and 1933, the gold value of world trade shrank by 65 percent, and trade volume fell by a quarter. The decline was driven both by the general fall in national incomes and by an explosion in protectionism. In principle, import substitution by a protectionist country should increase the protectionist's income. In practice, protectionist moves, especially from a major country, generate offsetting retaliations that result in a standoff in relative trading positions, but at a lower level of output—a lose-lose all around.[17]

The United States was a particular offender due to its powerful agricultural lobby. The Fordney-McCumber tariff of 1922 put up quite a high tariff wall, generally a 38.5 percent charge on the value of the dutiable import. Understandably, in the heat of the postwar struggles over reparations and war debt repayment, the tariff drew quite hostile receptions from American trading partners, and over time considerable retaliation.

The Smoot-Hawley tariff, passed in 1930, was a priority of Herbert Hoover in reaction to the agricultural glut. Hoover wanted a modest tariff limited to agricultural products, but lost a bidding war with the Congress that both expanded coverage and raised the levies. Protectionism, coming from the richest and most productive nation in history, again drew much criticism and adverse comment. The average Smoot-Hawley levies were about 20 percent, but were on top of the already high Fordney-McCumber levies.[18]

The British, after they had left the gold standard, passed two tariff laws—the Abnormal Importation Act (1931) and the Import Duties Act (1932) that imposed a tariff of just 10 percent levy on most traded goods. Shortly after that, the Treasury pegged the value of the pound at $3.40, a rate that went a long way toward solving the British productivity problems. Another Madsen paper, analyzing the trade patterns of seventeen advanced countries, found that the nominal value of trade fell by more than half between 1928 and 1932. But the profile of trade changed hardly at all. Countries traded with their normal counterparties and traded the same goods, just at lower volumes and lower prices.[19]

Although the efficiency losses of the trade collapse seem obvious, it is difficult to place a number on them. The drop in the measured value of trade wasn't caused primarily by tariffs, since most of it can be accounted for by deflation and the real fall in national incomes. A complicating factor (see Part 3) is that a number of American products had fixed-dollar tariffs instead of a percentage of the import price. In a period of runaway deflation, the burden of fixed dollar tariffs was greatly magnified. Another wild card was introduced by nonmonetary trade barriers, such as the quotas that France imposed on more than a thousand products in 1931 and 1932.

Douglas Irwin and Jakob Madsen have each tried to allocate the impact of protectionism, using quite different methods. Working with an American data base, Irwin found that two-thirds of the decline in trade was due to falling national incomes, with the remaining third split 2:1 between the "debt deflation" effect of fixed-price tariffs and pure protectionism. Madsen, applying statistical models with his 17-country data base computed that falling world incomes accounted for 14 percent of the decline in trade volumes, while discretionary tariffs, deflation-induced tariff increases, and nontariff barriers accounted for further contractions of 8 percent, 5 percent, and 6 percent, respectively, for a volume drop of fully a third.[20]

Barry Eichengreen and Douglas Irwin have shown a distinct pattern of trade policy management that related to a country's adherence to the gold standard. Countries that left the gold standard early, like Great Britain and its sterling bloc, imposed far fewer trade restrictions than those that remained on gold. A country that had left the gold standard did not need to impose tariffs, because the pricing could be adjusted in the exchange rates. With no deflationary pressure weighing on their currency, they could reflate and boost their trade and national income, instead of imposing dead-weight trade barriers.[21]

—— III. THE DETAILS ——————————————

A lone among the participants, the United States had a good war. Its casualties were fairly light. War lending vaulted its banks into the top tier of international finance. War production fattened its export earnings. The twin impact of conscription and full-blast operation of its factories brought unemployment to the vanishing point. With European agriculture moribund, farmers in the United States vastly expanded their production—as did farmers in Australia, Argentina, and other commodity producers.

After the short and sharp 1920–1921 recession, real growth took off. For the eight years from 1921 through 1929, the economy clocked in a healthy 5 percent real rate of growth. But that was the least important part of the story. The twenties in America were a glorious decade when a cornucopia of new products and technologies stamped themselves on the brains of Americans, radically changing their outlooks, their lives, and their ambitions. A byproduct of that transformation was that the country became very rich: by war's end, almost without noticing it, it had nearly quadrupled its prewar gold trove.

The 1929 stock market crash was a loud announcement that the economy had overheated. It did not cause the Depression. The outward aspect of the American economy at the start of 1929 was that of a sleek and smoothly humming machine, but a peek under the hood might have raised some doubts. Economists have been doing lots of poking for nearly a century now, and have identified a number of warning flags.

For instance, Americans had enjoyed a rather remarkable binge in consumer debt, which has been thoroughly dissected by Christina Romer, Frederic S. Mishkin, Martha Olney, and Christopher Brown, among others. Around 1929 households were pulling back sharply on consumer durables, presumably because the market crash had raised their anxieties and weakened household balance sheets.[22] More portentous than consumer debt, however, was the very large run-up in home mortgages. The total outstandings were $27.5 billion in 1930, or 30 percent of the 1930s GDP.* The housing market collapsed in the early 1930s; nationwide the loss in value was about a third. Little help came from the federal government until 1935 and the advent of the Home Owners' Loan Corporation (HOLC), which was after a recovery was already well underway.[23]

Developments in financial services undoubtedly also played a part in the downturn. Modern scholarship has considerably modified the Friedman and Schwartz hypothesis that 1930s banking failures precipitated the Depression. But work by economists such as Charles Calomiris, Ali Anari, Alexander Field, and Ben Bernanke has shown that suspensions of banks can immobilize reserves and shrink the money supply. Winding up a failed bank in the 1930s took an average of *six years*. Failed banks also disrupt credit intermediation, as customers acclimate to new lenders and vice versa. The 1928 and 1929 stock market boom also locked up an inordinate amount of cash in deadweight broker transactional accounts.[24]

Then there is the hoary theory that too much of the national income flowed to the richest, which is certainly true. Workers increased their incomes in the 1920s, but mostly by working more hours, even as output per hour rose sharply. At the same time, the share of pretax income flowing to the top 1 percent was the highest ever recorded, although just a couple of decimal points ahead of that recorded in 2006. The 2000s, of course, also saw a boom in consumer credit, so the average earner could maintain an accustomed level of spending, with notably unhappy results.[25]

The lists above demonstrate that the economy was vulnerable. But put them all together, and add in the quarter of excess automobile production in 1929, and you still don't get a Great Depression—a nasty recession undoubtedly, certainly more than a "correction" as in 1924, but not Hoovervilles and men selling apples in the streets.

---

* Total private mortgage debt was $41.3 billion; the number above strips out farm mortgages and residential mortgages held in corporate names. The ratio of household mortgage debt to GDP today is 53 percent. Given the fact that the home mortgage finance industry had been a major factor in the economy for barely a decade, the growth is impressive. The day's economic managers likely had little idea of the time bomb they were sitting on.

O f the three European major countries, Great Britain emerged from the war ostensibly in the best shape. It was both a debtor to the United States and a creditor primarily to France and Belgium. British statesmen hoped that the United States would join with them in renouncing reparations payments in return for the forgiveness of all war debts. Quite likely, that would have paved the way for an orderly financing to restore Belgium and France, and, presumably with stringent disarmament conditions, lending to put the German economy on its feet. The deep-seated German sense of grievance over the way the war ended still may not have been completely assuaged, but without reparations to rub into the psychic scabs, the clawing sense of injury may have faded much faster.

Simple and reasonable as that sounds now, there was no chance of it happening. The United States was the only country with the wherewithal to sponsor so generous a solution, and neither the Congress nor the country would have stood for it. Charles Kindleberger's disappointment that the United States could not act as the "hegemon" as it did after World War II was misplaced. America was still an adolescent nation: powerful and clumsy, unsure and suspicious. A generation later, the role of hegemon felt natural. In 1919 the trousers just didn't fit.

Nor, sadly, was the former hegemon, Great Britain, able to step into the gap. For all its deep experience in global politics and its great financial acumen, its day as *the* world power was over. Its halting recovery in trade is indicative: British trading volumes in 1924 were £212 million lower than in 1913, a huge slippage. And it got worse. Taking 1924 as an index base of 100, export volumes in Western Europe had climbed to 134 by 1929; Great Britain's had crawled back to just 109.[26] All of its traditional industries were in a serious state, union pressures were unrelenting, its management class was one of the worst in Europe. The heedless return to sterling at the traditional parity was the final nail in the coffin.

———

G ermany, by contrast, appeared to be almost in blooming health. In the mid-twenties, it had recovered from its great inflation and was abiding by the Dawes plan. In a 1927 review, the great Swedish economist Bertil Ohlin wrote that, after a shaky start, the Dawes regime had stabilized wholesale prices, improved the country's trade performance, and was making real headway against unemployment. But it was a mirage; Germany was on the road to collapse and would bring the rest of Europe and the world down with it.[27]

Great events are usually overdetermined. The critical reality of postwar Germany was its utterly toxic politics. The ambiguous surrender, after German troops had been hailed as "conquerors" as they marched into Berlin, called forth recriminations and conspiracy theories of all stripes. The November 1918 "half revolution" initiated some ten months of internecine violence before an unstable socialist coalition established a shaky government at Weimar. The violence abated but did not end. The assassination of two respected finance ministers—Matthias Erzberger and Walter Rathenau—conveys a sense of the disorder.

Germany had no money to speak of at the war's end, but they still had credit—lending markets were in a bullish mood and decided that the motley assemblage at Weimar would exercise the same fiscal rectitude as its Prussian forebears. Loans came flooding in, which governments squandered on sweeping social legislation and subsidies, while omitting the provision of any tax revenues. The deficits were funded by untethered issuance of paper Reichsmarks, and within the blink of an eye in economic time, the German currency floated from the solid clay of earth toward the Kuiper Belt.

After the Stresemann-Schacht 1924 currency reform broke inflation and revitalized the internal German economy, the Reichsbank was recapitalized with proceeds from the Dawes loans, allowing a couple of years of recovery and relative stability. It was at that point that the source of reparations payments was supposed to shift from external loans to proceeds from German taxes and bond issues, secured by railroads and heavy industry, which were nearly debt-free by virtue of the hyperinflation.

In principle, Germany could have paid the reparations. The final version of the Dawes plan brought the total liability very close to, indeed probably less than, the total that Keynes had pronounced as reasonable in his *Economic Consequences*. But the politics of the day made such speculations irrelevant. Just as there was no possibility of the United States acting as a benevolent global hegemon in 1919, there was no possibility of Germans voluntarily paying reparations with their own money.

The casualness of German public finance was matched by the deplorable condition of Germany's major banks, particularly in the aristocracy of German banking, the six Berlin *Grossenbanken*, or "the great Berlin banks." They had emerged from the inflation with only a fifth of their prewar capital, but nonetheless expanded rapidly and increased their risks to boost their earnings. Scarily, 42 percent of their deposits were for the accounts of foreigners. The Danatbank that failed in 1931 was only the worst of the lot.

Bad as the state of the Berlin banks was, German politics was even worse. Unable to pass a budget, the Reichstag president, the eighty-four-year-old Paul von Hindenburg, appointed a new chancellor, Heinrich Brüning, a leading figure in the Prussian Catholic Centre Party, to get public spending under control. Brüning produced a draconian budget, which was passed only after von Hindenburg called a snap election, the fateful poll in 1930 that made the Nazis the second most powerful voting bloc in the Reichstag.

Brüning, however, cut an impressive figure. A tour of the world financial centers drew raves from the financial press and generated healthy price appreciation for the Young plan bonds. Even the French, with a new government under Pierre Laval, with Aristide Briand as foreign minister, both of them interested in a démarche to Germany, declared an interest in lending to Germany.

At that point politics intervened. The investment bankers syndicating the loans had a territorial spat that slowed the process. Then Brüning, at his patron von Hindenburg's insistence, included a new pocket battleship and other armaments in his supposedly bare bones budget, deeply embarrassing Laval and Briand. Von Hindenburg also announced that he was exploring a customs union with Austria, which looked like, and was quite likely intended to be, a first step toward a merger of the two countries, which was forbidden by Versailles.

And then Brüning's budget fell apart. Although it had appeared reasonable when it was announced, German incomes were falling far more rapidly than expected, and mandatory unemployment and other benefits were soaring. By that time Brüning's string had pretty well played out.

Markets then learned that the Reichsbank's bailouts of Danatbank and other bleeding great banks had brought it close to breaching its legal gold cover. The president, Hans Luther, shut the gold window. Fire sirens ululated through trading rooms. Göring and the Nazis were in full cry. Generals prepared troops for civil unrest. There is considerable evidence that the panicked flight of money was led predominately by Germans, rather than foreigners. Stories abounded of wealthy Germans toting suitcases of money to the Netherlands and Switzerland. Americans reportedly took heavy losses.

The Reichsbank's repudiation naturally transferred the pressure to Great Britain, which had $300 million stuck in the German financial tundra. After burning up its own reserves and several very large external loans through August and early September, Ernest Harvey, Montagu Norman's deputy at the Bank of England, made the decision to stop making gold payments as of September 21, 1931.

The French were the last still standing. But the field they had won was stripped bare. They managed to keep most of the gold bloc countries together for a few more years. But they were finding it expensive, since the deflation they had been forcing on the rest of Europe was destroying the French pricing advantage from their undervalued franc.

———

The deflationary winds blowing from Europe had turned into a hurricane. The collapse in agricultural prices, the prostration of trade, the Fisherian debt deflation that set bankers everywhere scurrying for cover, the precipitate collapse in manufacturing output, it all swept over America—the country that had the farthest to fall, and indeed, fell the farthest. Friedman and Schwartz speculated that the creation of $1 billion of new money in 1930, when the economy was still teetering on the brink of collapse, could have arrested the downturn. They're probably right, but virtually all the contemporary experts *knew* that would just make things worse. It took a political lightweight, with an appetite for experimentation, to prove that the experts were wrong—at least this time—and even Franklin Roosevelt lost his nerve in 1937.[28]

Dreadful as the Depression was, however, it paled against the fact that Germany had withdrawn behind its mental fortresses and was gearing up for what Churchill called the Second Part of Europe's new Thirty Years' War.

IV. A POSTSCRIPT TO THE READER

I'm an historian with a professional background in finance. I'm not an economist, although I am comfortable with most of the literature and have read hundreds of papers in preparing this book. A number of star economists—see the Acknowledgments—were quite generous with their time in responding to my questions, pointing me to sources, and clarifying ideas. The economists who have been in the forefront of Depression studies have done prodigious work in digging into the musty crannies of bank files, diaries, legislative investigations, and similar sources that make history come alive and often call into question long-accepted maxims. Yes, employment is usually an inverse function of the real wage, but not always, even in the absence of government interference. Businesses have multiple values that are reflected in their hiring practices, economists have learned, and they have developed a catch-all concept called the "efficiency wage" to sweep in all the exceptions.

The focus on empirical work, along with the enormous advances in computer power, has stimulated the development of new statistical tools that can turn a spotlight on hitherto unexpected relationships. Alex Field's demonstration that the transactional balances in brokers' accounts during the late-twenties stock market boom significantly reduced the available money supply is a good example. Depression studies also lend themselves to rich narratives, such as Thomas Ferguson's and Peter Temin's small masterpiece "Made in Germany," their account of the last days of Weimar. One of its great virtues is to recognize the importance of *contingency*—the fact that history is "one damn thing after another." The short-lived Laval-Briand government in France may really have been willing to shovel some of its vast gold hoard into Germany before von Hindenburg and the German nationalists killed it with their pocket battleships and Austrian customs union.

Charles Calomiris is one of the few economists who explicitly puts contingencies front and center. He writes, for example, "Because the financial system is path-dependent, disturbances to the allocation of wealth and the viability of financial intermediaries . . . cannot in general be reversed" by retracing your steps, for the damage has already been done. Remedial action might alleviate the harm, but you can't run the tape backward and restore the status quo ante. Calomiris has also commented on Depression-era Fed policy that "one cannot expect the Fed to have learned the lessons of the Great Depression before it happened."[29]

Theo Balderston, an economist and historian who specialized in Weimar studies, may have said it best:

> [T]he insights of economic theory should not be overrated. Economic theory is the attempt to imagine rational relations between data in relation to what *has* taken place. The imagination is always influenced by the knowledge of what happened later—and by the prevailing economic "paradigm." We forget the infinity of other unimagined rational relations that could "explain" the data, let alone temporary irrational derangements. Neither the simple economics used here, nor any logically superior macroeconomics of present or future, can leap the chasm that divides us from the minds of the historical actors. . . . The sombre connection of the history studies in this book and the Nazi catastrophe should make the historian ready to doubt what he thinks he knows.[30]

The idea of a mental *regime* or a *paradigm* is a powerful one, and is especially applicable in Depression studies. Time and again, the researcher sees highly intelligent people make serious mistakes because they were unwitting prisoners of an idea. The prime example, of course, is the almost slavish adherence to the gold standard, which was for many discerning folk a moral issue. Especially when dealing with the gold standard episode, many economists cannot resist poking at the "ignorance" of the day's policy makers.

But that's unfair: history doubtless has far more examples of inflationary movements destroying economies than deflationary ones. Consider the experience of the 1970s. In his first term as president, Richard Nixon found himself stuck in a "stagflation"—with unemployment and interest rates rising at the same time. With the 1972 election looming, Nixon did a Roosevelt—floated the dollar, slapped on wage and price controls, and earned a landslide victory. When he was finally forced to remove the wage and price controls, inflation flared out of control. President Carter and his hapless Fed chairman, G. William Miller, flooded the world with "petrodollars." By the end of the decade, the price of a barrel of oil spiked as high as $568, inflation was running almost 14 percent a year, and the long bond market was a distant memory. With Ronald Reagan's strong backing, Paul Volcker embarked on a deflationary squeeze over two agonizing years that a Heinrich Brüning or Émile Moreau or Oliver Sprague would have been proud of. It took a Fed discount rate of 19 percent and three-month Treasury bills paying 20 percent before the fever broke.

Wall Street blossomed, and a new mental *regime* took shape—"The Great Moderation," compounded of a faith that deregulation, rational expectations, and a mix of neoclassical and monetarist economics, was creating a new nirvana, called "complete markets." It is the kind of frictionless, perfectly clearing economy that neoclassical economists dream about. Its special feature is that any asset or risk position can be seamlessly converted into a contingent claim—that is, a financial derivative. Alan Greenspan and later, yes, Ben Bernanke, blinded by theory, bought that proposition, and so allowed the rickety towers of overpriced debt instruments, erected on foundations of fraud and wishful thinking, to mount skyward higher and higher until it all came tumbling down.

Should they have known better? Of course, in retrospect it's obvious that if traders are playing with the house money, they will be tempted to take large risks. When the rewards can run into the tens of millions, and the worst outcome is just getting fired, the choice is pretty easy. The implicit premise of the Great Moderation was an assumption that all financial players would work for the best long-term outcomes of their institution, even if they could make pots of money by putting their own interests first. "Naïve" hardly covers the case.

But there were warnings. An investment partnership called Long-Term Capital Management (LTCM), run by one of Wall Street's most successful traders, with the participation of two professors who had won Nobel prizes for their insights into capital markets, found itself badly overextended in 1998. The Fed, under its chairman, Alan Greenspan, arranged a bailout by Wall Street banks, which was appropriate because the firm had built a portfolio of $100 billion on an equity base of

$1 billion, and was about to generate losses that could have prostrated half of the Street.

Some in the Congress criticized Greenspan's involvement in such a rescue, but he stressed:

> Had the failure of LTCM triggered seizing up of markets, substantial damage could have been inflicted on many market participants, including some not directly involved with the firm, and could have potentially impaired the economies of many nations, including our own.[31]

But just a few years after that, at a Chicago investment conference, Greenspan said:

> Critics of derivatives often raise the specter of the failure of one dealer imposing debilitating losses on its counterparties, including other dealers, yielding a chain of defaults. However, derivative markets participants seem keenly aware of the counterparty credit risks associated with derivatives and take various measures to mitigate those risks.[32]

In effect, so long as you're willing to risk the occasional crash of "the economies of many nations," you should put your trust entirely in the self-surveillance of the finance industry. That is an error that matches any by a Depression-era financial regulator.

Alan Greenspan retired from the Fed in 2002, so he wasn't in office when the Great Recession hit the entire world—the "economies of many nations" that Greenspan had invoked in 1998. Ben Bernanke was, though, and except for a year serving on the President's Council of Economic Advisers, had been serving on the Fed since 2002. He was also a notable proselytizer of the Great Moderation and the complete markets paradigm.

We were fortunate that Bernanke was a leading scholar of the Depression, which gave him an admirable tool kit for repairing the damage. Conceivably no other Fed chairman, without his particular experience in Depression studies, could have done as well, and we should be grateful for his service. But his record will forever be blackened by his failure to see the crash coming, victim of his own blinding mental *regime*.

——ACKNOWLEDGMENTS——

A number of economists who have specialized in Depression studies generously allowed me to abuse their time. Alex Field read an early draft of the book and saved me from a number of errors. I also learned much from interviews and follow up questions with Peter Temin, Barrie Wigmore, Barry Eichengreen, Charles Calomiris, Richard Jensen, and Rob Johnson.

Peter Goldmark and Richard Freeland were unusually close readers, and I profited from multiple suggestions from each. Others who read all or parts of a bulky manuscript and made helpful suggestions include Alan Silberstein, Claude Singer, Jamie Stewart, Chris Reid, Jon Weiner, and Andrew Kerr. Tom Gelinne checked my math throughout. My daughter-in-law, Jenn Morris, helped me recover pricing data from old NBER newsletters. Lisa Mataloni of the federal Bureau of Economic Analysis, a model civil servant, fielded a number of questions on the details of the NIPA accounts.

I have long enjoyed my association with Peter Osnos, both before and after his founding of PublicAffairs. Clive Priddle edited with a light touch and still greatly sharpened the manuscript. Melissa Raymond, the production wizard, turned in another bravura performance. Deborah Heimann was an unobtrusive, but thorough, copy editor. Pete Garceau and Jack Lenzo did the terrific jacket and text design. Jane Robbins Mize researched and assembled the illustrations.

For some years now, I have greatly benefited from the New York Public Library's MaRLI program that provides access to its own and several other New York academic libraries for independent researchers. It is an essential air supply for writers.

And as always, my love and gratitude to my wife, Beverly, who has seen me through yet another book with her trademark affectionate good humor.

PHOTO CREDITS

Page 11   © IWM (Q 5935)

Page 15   National Archives (LC-B2- 4956-10)

Page 27   Science, Industry & Business Library, The New York Public Library, Astor, Lenox and Tilden Foundations

Page 36   From the Collections of The Henry Ford. Gift of Ford Motor Company

Page 56   Courtesy of the author

Page 74   National Archives (44-PA-531)

Page 111   Prints & Photographs Division, Library of Congress, LC-USZC4-7880

Page 139   ullstein bild / Granger, NYC—All rights reserved

Page 146   Smithsonian American Art Museum. Gift of Charles Isaacs and Carol Nigro. 2007.37.1

Page 151   Farm Security Administration-Office of War Information Photograph Collection, Library of Congress, LC-USF34-042264-D

Page190   Daily Express, London. 1919

Page 193   Photo Researchers, Inc / Alamy Stock Photo

Page 216   World History Archive / Alamy Stock Photo

Page 259   Heritage Image Partnership Ltd / Alamy Stock Photo

Page 268   National Archives (69-N-19626)

Page 278   UniversalImagesGroup / Contributor

APPENDIX
MILKING THE INSULL STRUCTURE

THE LEVERAGE GAME

In general, the larger an electrical utility's service area, the more efficient its operations, since there were very large operating economies of scale. This conflicted with state-based regulatory regimes, which limited a utility to service a particular state. The holding company was a practical solution. A utility holding company could create a power complex to serve regions of different states, as dictated by geography, and then sell power to local state-based subsidiaries. While that made excellent economic sense, the holding company model opened the door to highly leveraged, abusive, pyramid structures.

Assume a local operating company, AZ Power, with a capitalization of $12.5 million, earning a net of $1 million for an 8 percent return on capital. Half of the capitalization is funded by long-term 5 percent bonds, a quarter by 6 percent nonvoting preferred stock, and the rest by a single class of voting common. The investor positions, at standard rates, are represented in Figure A.1.

The bondholders are first in the queue to get paid, followed by the 6 percent preferred shareholders. The 5 percent interest coupon on the

FIGURE A.1: AZ POWER WITH STANDARD RATES

	Investments	Operating Company Interest & Dividends
Operating Company Capital	12,500,000	
5% Bonds	6,250,000	312,500
6% Nonvoting Preferred	3,125,000	187,500
Voting Common	3,125,000	
Operating Earnings at 8% on Capital	1,000,000	

$6.25 million in bonds and the 6 percent dividend on the $3.125 million equals $500,000 altogether. With net operating income of $1,000,000, the common shareholders will have increased their wealth by $500,000—a nice, and fairly safe, 16 percent return. Insull's flagship companies, like Commonwealth Edison, often did better than that. Note that the common holders have taken most of the risk, so they deserve higher returns.

Now assume a holding company (HC1) enters the scene, and purchases all the common stock of AZ Power, paying the market price of $3.125 million. HC1 finances half of the purchase price, or $1,562,500, with a new issue of 7 percent nonvoting preferred, and half with cash. The operating company still makes $1 million, and still must pay $500,000 to the bondholders and the original 6 percent preferred. Then it must pay an additional $109,375 to the owners of the new 7 percent preferred. But that leaves $390,625 for the $1,562,500 in common shares, for a 25 percent return on equity. Note that HC1 need not be an outsider of the original deal. The founders of AZ Power may have simply decided to take back some of their cash.

Repeat that step four more times: HC2 buys HC1's common equity, funding half the purchase with new 7 percent preferred, and the rest in cash, then HC3 buys out HC2's common, with the same financing method, and so on (see Figure A.2). The company at top of the pyramid, HC5, will make $296,875 on just $97,656 equity, a 304 percent return. Most importantly, although HC5's $97,656 in equity is only 0.8 percent of the operating company's total capitalization (97,656/$12.5 million), it owns *all the voting stock*. The chain of holding companies not only can

FIGURE A.2: A FIVE-TIER HOLDING COMPANY PYRAMID ATOP A STANDARD UTILITY OPERATING CAPITAL STRUCTURE

(Each Successive Holding Company Purchases Previous Outstanding Common with One-Half Cash and One-Half 7% Preferred)

	7% Preferred Shares	Operating Company Annual Interest	Operating Company Annual Dividends	Additional Preferred Dividends to HC1	Additional Preferred Dividends to HC2	Additional Preferred Dividends to HC3	Additional Preferred Dividends to HC4	Additional Preferred Dividends to HC5	Book Value Common	Income to Common	Return on Equity	Common % of Capital
HC5	97,656	312,500	187,250	109,375	54,688	27,344	13,672	6,836	97,656	296,874	304%	0.8%
HC4	195,313	312,500	187,250	109,375	54,688	27,344	13,672		195,313	302,735	155%	1.6%
HC3	390,625	312,500	187,250	109,375	54,688	27,344			390,625	316,406	81%	3.1%
HC2	781,250	312,500	187,250	109,375	54,688				781,250	335,938	43%	6.3%
HC1	1,562,500	312,500	187,250	109,375					1,562,500	390,625	25%	12.5%
Operating Company		312,500	187,250						3,125,000	500,000	16%	25.0%

FIGURE A.3: SAME PYRAMID WITH 5 PERCENT ON EQUITY

	7% Preferred Shares	Operating Company Annual Interest	Operating Company Annual Dividends	Additional Preferred Dividends to HC1	Additional Preferred Dividends to HC2	Additional Preferred Dividends to HC3	Additional Preferred Dividends to HC4	Additional Preferred Dividends to HC5	Book Value Common	Income to Common	Return on Equity	Common % of Capital
HC5	97,656	312,500	187,500	109,375	15,625	0	0	0	97,656	0	NA	0.8%
HC4	195,313	312,500	187,500	109,375	15,625	0	0		195,313	0	NA	1.6%
HC3	390,625	312,500	187,500	109,375	15,625	0			390,625	0	NA	3.1%
HC2	781,250	312,500	187,500	109,375	15,625				781,250	15,625	NA	6.3%
HC1	1,562,500	312,500	187,500	109,375					1,562,500	15,625	1%	12.5%
Operating Company		312,500	187,500						3,125,000	125,000	4%	25.0%

create outsize profits on minimal equity positions, but also can lock in control for a very small group of investors, with them putting up only a minimum of cash.[1]

Of course, squeezing down the common equity greatly increases the risk. Assume that same structure but, due to some misfortune, a 5 percent equity return at the operating company, which is hardly inconceivable. The available cash would cover the amounts due to the bondholders, the senior preferred, and HC1 preferred, leaving only a 1 percent dividend for the common. If there were an HC2 layer, holders would get a sliver of their dividend, leaving nothing for the common nor for any of the additional layers of preferred.

Note that in the Insull conglomerates, the successive holding companies were almost always formed by insiders. The directing boards were typically the same as in all the other Insull properties. The advantages of the pyramid structure were, among other things, that the additional 7 percent preferred was good collateral for more lending, as financing standards got easier (and sloppier) through the 1920s. The extremely high profits to common also made great window dressing for subsequent flotations. Congressional hearings on the Insull structures suggested that MWU's actual leverage was 2000:1—$1 in common stock controlled $2,000 in assets.[*]

As the Eaton deal squeezed the Insull cash flow, the conglomerate raised cash by selling, or using as collateral, great volumes of securities in highly leveraged entities. When the bankers finally put a stop to that, the pyramids collapsed, and the company was insolvent.

VALUATION AND DEPRECIATION SCAMS

As the Insull holding companies' layers proliferated, it opened opportunities for intra-company stock trading at inflated prices. Let's say

---

[*] The layered utility holding companies of the 1920s and 1930s resemble in many ways the collateralized debt obligations (CDOs) that played such a prominent role in the 2008 financial crash. Holdings were highly stratified, with very high returns and very high risk accruing to the most junior tranches. In both cases, basically sound financing concepts were stretched to the breaking point in pursuit of profits and control—and inevitably they broke.

that the fourth holding company in the structure laid out in Figure A.4 chose to sell some of its stock to another Insull company. Since almost none of the intermediate holding company stocks traded on exchanges, the managers had considerable freedom in assigning values—possibly the original share price, or its book value based on a multiple of its most recent earnings, or the management's judgment of its intrinsic worth. It was common for one side of the transaction to book the sale at the highest plausible price while the other side used the lowest price to manufacture profits from the air.

The Insull companies also had a poor record in maintaining depreciation reserves, thus overstating operating income and net worth. The Internal Revenue Service (IRS) rules and best accounting practice for long-term assets, like power plants, were to take a 3 percent charge on original costs to reflect the diminished value of the asset. Many utilities, however, following Thomas Edison's lead, made best-estimate reserve decisions each year, which predictably tended to mirror their available cash. An analysis of Middle West Utilities (MWU)'s earnings in 1928 disclosed that it was reserving only 1.02 percent of the plant book values, compared to an average of 1.99 percent for three other major utilities. One major subsidiary of MWU, for instance, Central and South West Utilities (CSWU), reserved $4.5 million for depreciation between 1927 and 1931, when the IRS standard would have called for $21.4 million.* In those same years, CSWU claimed to have a $6.9 million net earned surplus, when proper depreciation accounting would have shown that the company not only did not earn a surplus, but also funded $10 million of the dividend payout from its capital (see Figure A.4). Such accounting dodges could not be hidden forever. In this case, the bill came due in 1932, when MWU's receivers in bankruptcy wrote off mountains of obsolete capital assets.[2]

---

* The depreciation reserve is not a cash reserve but is an accounting charge to reflect the wear-and-tear cost to an asset. When the electrical utility industry was in its rapid-growth mode, the thirty-year-depreciation standard was probably far too long, since a plant had to be constantly upgraded to keep up with the growth in demand.

FIGURE A.4: HOW ACCOUNTANTS MANUFACTURE EARNINGS

CSWU 1927–1931

	Actual (millions)	Standard (millions)
Depreciation	4.5	21.4
Cash Dividends	17.8	17.8
Surplus	6.9	-10.0
Total	29.2	29.2

——NOTES——————————————————

ABBREVIATIONS

Full Citations are noted once below. All instances in the Notes themselves are the short form:

Historical Statistics of the United States, Earliest Times to the Present: Millennial Edition, edited by Susan B. Carter, Scott Sigmund Gartner, Michael R. Haines, Alan L. Olmstead, Richard Sutch, and Gavin Wright. (New York: Cambridge University Press, 2006).

Short form: *Historical Statistics*

U. S. Department of Commerce, Bureau of Economic Analysis, *National Income and Product Accounts.*

Short form: *NIPA*

St. Louis Federal Reserve Bank, Federal Reserve Economic Data

Short form: FRED

Federal Trade Commission, "Utility Corporations: Report of the Federal Trade Commission to the Senate of the United States, Pursuant to Senate Resolution No. 83, 70th Congress, 1st Session, on Economic, Financial, and Corporate Phases of Holding and Operating Companies of Electric and Gas Utilities," multiple volumes.

Short form: Utility Corporations

Stock Exchange Practices: Hearings Before the Committee on Banking and Currency, Pursuant to Senate Resolutions, No. 84 and 248, United States Senate (1932–1934)

Short form: Pecora Commission

Report of House Committee on Interstate and Foreign Commerce, Pursuant to H. Res. No. 59, 72d Cong. 1st Sess. (1932) and H. J. REs. No. 572, 72d Cong. 2d Sess. (1933), Report on the Relation of Holding Companies in Power and Gas Affecting Control.

Short form: Public Utility Holding Companies

PRELUDE

1. For the politics of the war, I used primarily Christopher Clark, *The Sleepwalkers: How Europe Went to War in 1914* (New York: HarperCollins, 2012), esp. 488–554; and Margaret MacMillan, *The War That Ended Peace: The Road to 1914* (New York: Random House, 2013), esp. 575–631. For the events of the war, I used primarily John Keegan, *The First World War* (New York: Random House, 1998); and Peter Hart, *The Great War: A Combat History of the First World War* (New York: Oxford University Press, 2013). The kaiser's scene is from Keegan, *First World War*, 123.

2. L. C. F. Turner, "The Significance of the Schlieffen Plan," in Paul M. Kennedy, ed., *The War Plans of the Great Powers* (London: George Allen & Unwin, 1979), 191–221; Churchill quote at 205.

3. Ibid.

4. Keegan, *First World War*, 31–39.

5. Turner, "Significance," 210, 212, 204.

6. John Maynard Keynes, *The Economic Consequences of the Peace* (New York, NY: Harcourt, Brace & Howe, 1920), 10–12.

7. Norman Angell, *The Great Illusion: A Study of the Relation of Military Power to National Advantage*, 4th American ed. (New York: G. P. Putnam's Sons, 1913), 17–19.

8. Niall Ferguson, *The Pity of War: Explaining World War I* (New York: Basic Books, 1999), 100, 33.

9. Ibid., 92–93, 137; and Wayne Dowler, *Russia in 1913* (DeKalb, IL: Northern Illinois University Press, 2010), 18–50.

10. Ferguson, *Pity of War*, 89, 91.

11. Paul M. Kennedy, "The First World War and the International Power System," *International Security* 9, no. 1 (Summer 1981): 18–19.

12. Ferguson, *Pity of War*, 293–296.

13. The narrative follows Keegan, *First World War*, and Hart, *The Great War*.

14. Battle casualties from "Top 10 Deadliest Battles of World War I," TopTenz, accessed August 1, 2016, www.toptenz.net/top-10-bloodiest-battles -of-world-war-i.php.

15. Ferguson, *Pity of War*, 295.

16. Sally Marks, "Mistakes and Myths: The Allies, Germany and the Versailles Treaty, 1918–1921," *Journal of Modern History* 85, no. 3 (September 2013): 632–659, 635; and Edward M. Lamont, *The Ambassador from Wall Street: The Story of Thomas W. Lamont, J.P. Morgan's Chief Executive* (Lanham, MD: Madison Books, 1994), 124.

17. Sally Marks, "Mistakes and Myths," Ebert quote on 634.

18. Etienne Mantoux, *The Carthaginian Peace, or the Economic Consequences of Mr. Keynes* (New York: Charles Scribner's Sons, 1952), 90–91; and "Viewpoint: 10 Big Myths about WWI Debunked," BBC News Magazine, February 25, 2014, www.bbc.com/news/magazine-25776836.

19. Margaret MacMillan, *Paris 1919: Six Months That Changed the World* (New York; Random House, 2001); the Fourteen Points are on 495–496. And Arthur Ray Leonard, ed., *The War Addresses of Woodrow Wilson* (Boston, MA: Ginn & Company, 1918); the "no annexations" quote is in a speech Wilson delivered, "The Four Principles of Peace," Address to the Congress, February 11, 1918, 102.

20. MacMillan, *Paris 1919*, 463–478.

PART ONE: AMERICA DISCOVERS THE MODERN

1. For the Fitzgeralds and their coterie, the novels may be the best sources. *This Side of Paradise, The Beautiful and the Damned, The Great Gatsby, Tender Is the Night*, and the fragment, *The Love of the Last Tycoon*, are all available in multiple editions, as are various collections of Scott's short stories. Zelda's novel, available in reprint, is *Save Me the Waltz* (New York: Scribner, 1938). The quote from *The Beautiful and the Damned* is from the "Collector's Edition" (New York: Collectors Library, reprint 2013), x. It has the original cover depicting the actual Scott and Zelda. In addition to the Fitzgeralds' own writing, the portrait here draws on Nancy Milford, *Zelda, A Biography* (New York: Harper Perennial, 1992); Judith Mackrell, *Flappers: Six Women of a Dangerous Generation* (New York: Farrar, Straus and Giroux, 2013); Amanda Vaill, *Everybody Was So Young: Gerald and Sara Murphy, A Lost Generation Love Story* (Boston, MA: Houghton Mifflin, 1998); and Lucy Moore, *Anything Goes: A Biography of the Roaring Twenties* (New York: Overlook Press, 2010).

2. Milford, *Zelda*, 66.

3. Moore, *Anything Goes*, 64.

4. Sarah Laskow, "Will the Real Great Gatsby Please Stand Up?" Smithsonian. com, May 6, 2013, http://www.smithsonianmag.com/ist/?next=/arts-culture /will-the-real-great-gatsby-please-stand-up-53360554/; and Catherine Bailey,

The Secret Rooms: A True Story of a Haunted Castle, a Plotting Duchess, and Family Secrets (New York: Penguin Books, 2012), 419–420.

5. For the narrative of electricity's development, I mostly follow Jill Jonnes, *Empires of Light: Edison, Tesla and Westinghouse and the Race to Electrify the World* (New York: Random House, 2003). For technical developments, Louis C. Hunter and Lynwood Bryant, *A History of Industrial Power in the United States, 1780–1930*, Vol. 3, *The Transmission of Power* (Cambridge, MA: The MIT Press, 1991); and Harold C. Passer, *The Electrical Manufacturers, 1875–1900: A Study in Competition, Entrepreneurship, Technical Change, and Economic Growth* (Cambridge, MA: Harvard University Press, 1953). The details on the Niagara power complex are from Edward Dean Adams, *Niagara Power: History of the Niagara Falls Power Company, 1886–1913* (Niagara Falls, NY: Priv. printed for the Niagara Falls Power Company, 1927), 2 vols. The quote is from the preface to Adams, *Niagara*, I: ix.

6. Adams, *Niagara*, II, 85.

7. Jonnes, *Empires of Light*, 110.

8. My major sources for this section are Allan Nevins and Frank Ernest Hill, *Ford: The Times, The Man, The Company* (New York: Charles Scribner's Sons, 1954), the first volume in their three-volume biography; Steven Watts, *The People's Tycoon: Henry Ford and the American Century* (New York: Alfred A. Knopf, 2005); and Ford's autobiography, Henry Ford with Samuel Crowther, *My Life and Work* (Westport, CT: Greenwood Publications, 2010) originally published in 1922. On Ford's manufacturing from the Model T onward, the best source is David A. Hounshell, *From the American System to Mass Production: 1800–1932: The Development of Manufacturing Technology in the United States* (Baltimore, MD: Johns Hopkins University Press), 217–261, for the period covered here. For machine wonks, the *locus classicus* on Ford's shop methods during its growth period is Horace Lucien Arnold and Fay Leone Faurote, *Ford Methods and the Ford Shops* (New York: The Engineering Magazine Company, 1915). There is also an excellent eleven-part series on Ford machining practice by Roger H. Colvin, in *American Machinist*, 39 (1913). Both the Arnold-Faurote and Colvin treatments are in the public domain and pdf copies may be downloaded from Google Books. The Ford quote is from Watts, *People's Tycoon*, 119.

9. Watts, *People's Tycoon*, 42.

10. Nevins and Hill, *Ford: The Times*, 248n.

11. Nevins and Hill, *Ford: The Times*, Appendices, 644–649.

12. Ibid., 324.

13. Arnold and Faurote, *Ford Methods*, 77–83, 122, 327–329, 113–116, 138–139.

14. Hounshell, *From the American System*, 259.

15. See the discussion in "The Five-Dollar Day" in Nevins and Hill, *Ford: The Times*. On p. 530, they detail some of the shop management problems, but suggest that they had been mostly resolved before the $5 per day decision. The evidence they cite, however, comes from 1916, a full two years after the announcement of the new pay plan. A more convincing account is Daniel M. G. Raff and Lawrence H. Summers, "Did Henry Ford Pay Efficiency Wages?," *NBER Working Paper no. w2101* (December 1986), 8–10; available at SSRN: https://ssrn.com/abstract=344867

16. Nevins, 644–649, 488.

17. The details in this section are drawn, in addition to those cited below, from: Frederick Lewis Allen, *Only Yesterday: An Informal History of the Nineteen-Twenties* (New York: Harper & Row, 1986) a reprint of the original 1940 edition; Donald L. Miller, *Supreme City: How Jazz Age Manhattan Gave Birth to Modern America* (New York: Simon & Schuster, 2014); Bill Bryson, *One Summer: America, 1927* (New York: Doubleday, 2013); Edward White, *The Tastemaker: Carl Van Vechten and the Birth of Modern America* (New York: Farrar, Straus, and Giroux, 2014); and David E. Kyvig, *Daily Life in the United States, 1920–1940: How American Lived Through the Roaring Twenties and the Great Depression* (Chicago, IL: Ivan R. Dee, 2004); and Judith S. Baughman, ed., *American Decades: 1920–1929*, "History of American Journalism, the 1920s," at http://history.journalism.ku.edu/1920/1920.shtml.

18. Allen, *Only Yesterday*, 164–167.

19. Isabel Wilkerson, *The Warmth of Other Suns: The Epic Story of America's Great Migration* (New York: Random House, 2010), 161–163.

20. Ibid., 163–164.

21. Ibid, 271–273.

22. Ibid., 276–277.

23. The discussion of Prohibition is drawn from Mark Edward Lender and James Kirby Master, *Drinking in America: A History* (New York: The Free Press, 1982), 124–167.

24. Alcohol consumption data were compiled by the Rutgers Institute for Alcohol Studies and are reprinted in the Appendix of Lender and Master, *Drinking in America*. For a fuller discussion, see, John C. Burnham, "New Perspectives on the Prohibition 'Experiment' of the 1920s," *Journal of Social Studies II* 2, no. 1 (Fall, 1968): 51–68; Jeffrey A. Miron and Jeffrey Zweibel, "Alcohol Consumption During Prohibition," *The American Economic Review* 81, no. 2 (May 1991): 242–247; Jack S. Blocker Jr., "Did Prohibition Really Work?

Alcohol Prohibition as a Public Health Innovation," *American Journal of Public Health* 96, no. 2 (February 2006): 233–243.

25. Kyvig, *Daily Life in the United States*, 97.

26. Catherine Keyser, *Playing Smart: New York Women Writers and Modern Magazine Culture* (New Brunswick, NJ: Rutgers University Press, 2010), 61.

27. Lewis Mumford, "Magnified Impotence," *The New Republic*, December 22, 1926; James H. Collins, "Panic!" *Scientific American*, September 1925—both collected in "The Twenties in Contemporary Commentary," in Becoming Modern: America in the 1920s—Primary Source Collection, National Humanities Center—America in Class, 2012, available online at http://americainclass.org/sources/becomingmodern/.

28. Robert S. Lynd and Helen M. Lynd, *Middletown: A Study in Modern American Culture* (New York: Harcourt & Brace, 1929).

29. Ibid., 75.

30. Ibid., 33–34.

31. Ibid., 34.

32. Ibid., 162–163.

33. Christopher Brown, "Consumer Credit and the Propensity to Consume: Evidence from 1930," *Journal of Post-Keynesian Economics* 19, no. 4 (Summer, 1997): 617–638, 620–621.

34. Lynd and Lynd, *Middletown*, 256, 255–256, 257.

35. Ibid., 266–267, 258, 145.

36. The Scopes trial is covered in nearly all histories of the period. Most earlier histories followed the account in Frederick Lewis Allen's *Only Yesterday*, which was drawn primarily from newspaper accounts and is wrong in many details. The account here is based primarily on the trial transcripts, "The Scopes Trial Transcripts" 8 vols., The Clarence Darrow Digital Collection, Law Library, University of Minnesota, http://darrow.law.umn.edu/trials.php?tid=7. Michael Hannon, "The Scopes Trial (1925)" (May 2010) is a comprehensive, thesis-length synthesis based on the most recent sources. I also used Edward J. Larson, *Summer for the Gods: The Scopes Trial and America's Continuing Debate Over Science and Religion* (New York: Basic Books, 1997); and Louis W. Koenig, *Bryan: A Political Biography of William Jennings Bryan* (New York: G.P. Putnam's Sons, 1971). Quote "big sensation" is from Koenig, *Bryan: A Political Biography*, 60.

37. Koenig, *Bryan: A Political Biography*, 605, 645; Hannon, "The Scopes Trial," 30. For the footnote on Fundamentalism, Larson, *Summer for the Gods*, 20ff.

38. Larson, *Summer for the Gods*, 93.

39. "The Scopes Trial Transcripts," Vol. IV, 141.

40. Ibid., Vol. V, 176.

41. Ibid.; and Koenig, *Bryan: A Political Biography*, 645.

42. Koenig, *Bryan: A Political Biography*, 656.

43. Larson, *Summer for the Gods*, 200.

44. Koenig, *Bryan: A Political Biography*, 656.

45. Allen, *Only Yesterday*, 205, 206; and Larson, *Summer for the Gods*, 235–237.

46. Karl Pearson, *The Grammar of Science*, 3rd ed. (London: Black, 1911), 15.

47. James T. Kloppenberg, "Democracy and Disestablishment: From Weber and Dewey to Habermas and Rorty," in Dorothy Ross, ed., *Modernist Impulses in the Human Sciences, 1870–1930* (Baltimore, Johns Hopkins University Press, 1994), 68–90, at 84.

48. Dorothy Ross, *The Origins of American Social Science* (New York: Cambridge University Press, 1991), 238.

49. Joseph Wood Krutch, *The Modern Temper: A Study and a Confession* (New York: Harcourt, Brace & Co., 1929), 200, 39, 166–167, 170.

50. Walter Lippmann, *A Preface to Morals* (New York: The Macmillan Company, 1931), 22, 24, 27, 326.

PART TWO: "ONE HECKUVA BOOM"

1. Theodore Rosengarten, *All God's Dangers: The Life of Nate Shaw* (Chicago, IL: University of Chicago Press, 1974), 248–250. For the sharecroppers' union, see Michael Kief, "The Alabama Sharecroppers Union," *Encyclopedia of Alabama*, http://www.encyclopediaofalabama.org/article/h-2477.

2. Rosengarten, *All God's Dangers*, 256.

3. The White House, Office of Management and Budget, *Historical Statistics*, Table 1; see http://www.whitehouse.gov/omb/budget/Historicals; and *Historical Statistics*, Tables Ca213 and 214, inflation calculation by the author.

4. Statistics here and below from Hugh Rockoff, "Until It's Over, Over There: The U.S. Economy in World War I," NBER Working Paper 10580 (June 2004).

5. Allan Nevins and Frank Ernest Hill, *Ford: Expansion and Challenge, 1915–1933* (New York: Charles Scribner's Sons, 1955) 65–67.

6. Rockoff, "Until It's Over."

7. Leonard P. Ayres, *The War with Germany: A Statistical Summary* (Washington, DC: United States Government Printing Office, 1919), 134.

8. Allan H. Meltzer, *A History of the Federal Reserve, Vol. I, 1913–1951* (Chicago, IL: University of Chicago Press, 2003), 87–91; *Historical Statistics*, op. cit.

9. James Grant, *The Forgotten Depression: 1921, the Crash That Cured Itself* (New York: Simon & Schuster, 2014) is a lively, if tendentious, account of the period. Inflation and growth data are from *Historical Statistics*.

10. Meltzer, *A History of the Federal Reserve*, 97.

11. *Moody's Industrial Manual* (New York: John Moody and Co.): 1920 and 1921 for the respective companies.

12. US Department of Commerce, *Survey of Current Business*, no. 17, January 1923, 2–4.

13. *Historical Statistics*, op. cit, calculation by the author.

14. The account here, except as noted below, is drawn primarily from Forrest McDonald, *Insull* (Chicago, IL: University of Chicago Press, 1962) and Harold L. Platt, *The Electric City, Energy and the Growth of the Chicago Area, 1880–1930*, (Chicago, IL: University of Chicago Press, 1991).

15. McDonald, *Insull*, 88–90.

16. Ibid., 108–113.

17. John C. Zink, "Steam Turbines Power an Industry," *Power Engineering*, August 1, 1996, http://www.power-eng.com/articles/print/volume-100/issue-8 /features/steam-turbines-power-an-industry.html.

18. Platt, *The Electric City*, 108–114. For an excellent description of Insull's methods of rationalizing power supply, with exhibits, see Samuel Insull, "*Public Utilities in Modern Life, Selected Speeches, 1914–1923*," William Eugene Keily, ed., "Production and Distribution of Electric Energy in the Central Portion of the Mississippi Valley," 263–303.

19. Platt, *The Electric City*, 109–124.

20. Platt, *The Electric City*, shows the Barton ad between 110–111.

21. McDonald, *Insull*, 204–205.

22. Lawrence R. Gustin, *David Buick's Marvelous Motor Car: The Men and the Automobile That Launched General Motors* (Detroit, MI: Buick Gallery and Research Center, Alfred P. Sloan Museum, 2006), 17–40, 55–57. The development of the "valve-in-head" engine is a serpentine tale, with many participants; for a full account, see ibid., 67–72.

23. Lawrence R. Gustin, *Billy Durant: Creator of General Motors* (Ann Arbor, MI: University of Michigan Press, 2008), 42–88, on Buick, 149–152, 206–208.

24. Ibid., 72.

25. Ibid., 85.

26. Ibid., 92–96.

27. Ibid., 112–113.

28. Ibid., 134–141; David Farber, *Everybody Ought to Be Rich: The Life and Times of John J. Raskob, Capitalist*, (New York: Oxford University Press, 2013), 103–106.

29. Gustin, *Billy Durant*, 147–163.

30. Farber, *Everybody Ought to Be Rich*, 103–108; for a recent journalistic version, Andrew Engel, "The Original GM Bailout" *BloombergViews*, March 6, 2012.

31. Gustin, *Billy Durant*, 179–193.

32. Gustin, *Billy Durant*, 204–215; Farber, 172–183.

33. Sloan, *My Years with General Motors* (Garden City, NY: Doubleday, 1963), 154; the Durant and immediate post-Durant years occupy most of Part One of his book. See also David Farber, *Sloan's Rules: Alfred P. Sloan and the Triumph of General Motors* (Chicago, IL: University of Chicago Press, 2002), 51–105; Allyn Freeman, *The Leadership Genius of Alfred P. Sloan: Invaluable Lessons on Management, and Leadership for Today's Managers* (New York: McGraw-Hill, 2005), 11–48; and Daniel G. Raff, "Making Cars and Making Money in the Interwar Automobile Industry: Economies of Scale and Scope and the Manufacturing Behind the Marketing," *Business History Review*, 65, no. 4 (Winter 1991), 721–753, 741–742, 752.

34. All financial data from *Moody's Industrial Manuals* for the various years.

35. Sloan, *My Years*, 162.

36. Nevins and Hill, *Ford: 1915–1933*, 407–408, 416–417.

37. Data on market size and production for GM and Ford from Sloan, *My Years*, 151n, and Appendix: "General Motors Corporation, Unit Sales of Total Cars and Trucks by Division;" and Allan Nevins and Frank Ernest Hill, *Ford: Decline and Rebirth, 1933–1962*, (New York: Charles Scribner's Sons, 1963), Appendix 1: "Ford Motor Company Production Report, 1903 Thru 1955."

38. For the main story of the model change, see Nevins and Hill, *Ford: 1915–1933*, 429–431, 437–458, 466.

39. Ibid., 454.

40. Ibid., 459–460.

41. Ibid., 457.

42. Charles R. Morris, *The Dawn of Innovation: The First American Industrial Revolution* (New York: PublicAffairs, 2012), 252–258, (for Colt); Warren D. Devine, "From Shafts to Wires: Historical Perspective on Electrification," *The Journal of Economic History*, 43, no.2 (June 1983): 347–372.

43. Harold F. Williamson, Ralph L. Adreano, Arnold R. Daum, and Gilbert C. Close, *The American Petroleum Industry: The Age of Energy, 1899–1950* (Evanston, IL: Northwestern University Press, 1963) 329–330.

44. *Moody's Industrial Manuals*, 1923 and 1930.

45. Thomas J. Misa, *A Nation of Steel: The Making of Modern America, 1865–1925* (Baltimore, MD: Johns Hopkins University Press, 1995), 213–222, 242–247,

quote at 170. Also see Kenneth Warren, *Big Steel: The First Century of the United States Steel Company, 1901–2001* (Pittsburgh, PA: University of Pittsburgh Press, 2001) 123–132.

46. *Moody's Industrial Manuals,* 1929.

47. Giovanni Federico, "Not Guilty? Agriculture in the 1920s and the Great Depression," *The Journal of Economic History,* 65, no. 4 (December 2005), 949–976; *Survey of Current Business,* March 1930, 3 "Crops"; Harvester profits from *Moody's Industrial Manuals,* 1922, 1928, 1929.

48. FRED, "Index of Farm Prices of Crops for the United States" and "Index of Prices for Meat Animals in the United States"; and Harold Barger and Hans H. Landsberg, "Agricultural Productivity," in *American Agriculture, 1899–1933: A Study of Output, Employment, and Productivity* (Cambridge, MA: NBER, 1942), Table 38, 247–288.

49. Paul S. George, "Brokers, Binders, and Builders: Greater Miami's Boom of the Mid-1920s," *The Florida Historical Quarterly,* 65, no. 1 (July, 1986): 27–51, at 27–29.

50. Ibid., 27, 29.

51. Ibid., 35–36.

52. Ibid., 37, 38–39.

53. Ibid., 48–49, 40–42, 45–47.

54. Alexander J. Field "Uncontrolled Land Development and the Duration of the Depression in the United States," *The Journal of Economic History,* 52, no. 4 (December, 1992): 785–805. For the "short block" in the footnote, ibid., 798.

55. Ibid., 790, 791–792.

56. Ibid., 791–792.

57. John Kenneth Galbraith, *The Great Crash, 1929* (Boston, MA: Harcourt Houghton Mifflin, 2009), 70, 169.

58. Barrie A. Wigmore, *The Crash and Its Aftermath: A History of Security Markets in the United States, 1929–1933* (Westport, CT: Greenwood Press, 1985), 4.

59. Ibid., 26–27..

60. Federal Reserve Board, "Banking and Monetary Statistics of the United States, 1914–1941," Table 48, p. 142; Table 137, p. 489; Table 139, p. 494.

61. Galbraith, *The Great Crash,* 79; Vincent Carosso, *Investment Banking in America: A History* (Cambridge, MA: Harvard University Press, 1970), 346.

62. J. Bradford De Long and Andrei Shelfer, "The Stock Market Bubble of 1929: Evidence from Closed-end Mutual Funds," *Journal of Economic History,* 51, no. 3 (September, 1991): 675–700; Peter Rappoport and Eugene N. White, "Was There a Bubble in the 1929 Stock Market?" *Journal of Economic History,* 53, no. 3 (September, 1993). The two authors extended their model in Peter

Rappoport and Eugene N. White, "Was the Crash of 1929 Expected?" *American Economic Review*, 84, no. 1 (January 1994): 271–281. But see Tung Liu, Gary J. Santoni, and Courtenay C. Stone, "In Search of Stock Market Bubbles: A Comment on Rappoport and White," *Journal of Economic History*, 55, no. 3 (September 1995): 647–654, who argue that in 1919–1920 similar call loan spreads had no such effect; that an econometric analysis suggests that there was no radical break in the interest rate profiles, and that the timing of the call loan spikes does not correlate with the events of the crash. Gerald Sirkin, "The Stock Market of 1929 Revisited: A Note," *Business History Review*, XLIX, no. 2 (Summer 1975): 223–231; but see Ali Kabiri, "'Theory Anchors' Explain the 1929 NYSE Bubble," Special Paper 218, LSE Financial Markets Group Paper Series (January 2013). Kabiri points to specific erroneous theories for evaluating shares in the late 1920s that produced a substantial overvaluation of shares.

63. Meltzer, *A History of the Federal Reserve*, Chart 4.4, 253.

64. *Survey of Current Business*, July 1929, 12, 16.

65. Ibid., August 1929.

66. Ibid., September 1929; Wigmore, *The Crash and Its Aftermath*, 12.

67. FRED, "Industrial Production Data Series, 1919–2015;" Stephen G. Cecchetti, "The Stock Market Crash of 1929," January 1992, manuscript submitted for entry in *The New Palgrave Dictionary of Money and Finance*, access online at www.people.brandeis.edu/~cecchett/Polpdf/Polpo5.pdf.

68. Wigmore, *The Crash and Its Aftermath*, 4–5.

69. Galbraith, *The Great Crash*, 171.

PART THREE: THE CRASH IN THE UNITED STATES

1. "Bankers v. Panic," *Time*, November 4, 1929.

2. Barrie Wigmore, *The Crash and Its Aftermath: A History of Securities Markets in the United States, 1929–1933* (Westport, CT: Greenwood Press, 1985), 6–12.

3. Federal Reserve Board, "Banking and Monetary Statistics of the United States: 1914–1943," Washington, DC, Table 141, 497–498.

4. *Spectator*, 27, September 1929, p. 2.

5. Wigmore, *The Crash and its Aftermath*, 10–11.

6. Ibid.; and Michael Beschloss, "From White Knight to Thief," *New York Times*, September 13, 2014.

7. Wigmore, *The Crash and its Aftermath*, 25.

8. Ibid., 25, 31–32.

9. Ibid., 129–131, Appendix Tables A-19.

10. Ibid., Appendix Tables A-20.

11. Except as indicated, the narrative of Hoover's early career follows William E. Leuchtenburg, *Herbert Hoover* (New York: Times Books, 2009), 2–79.

12. Ibid., 26.

13. Ibid., 44, 47.

14. John Maynard Keynes, *A Treatise on Money*, 2 vols. (Mansfield Center, CT: Martino Publishing, 2011—reprint of Harcourt Brace 1930 edition), Vol. 2, 353–355.

15. Leuchtenburg, *Herbert Hoover*, 64.

16. Wesley C. Mitchell, *Recent Social Trends in the United States: Report of the President's Research Committee on Social Trends*, 2 vols. (New York: McGraw-Hill, Vol. I, 1933, and Vol. II, 1934). I have read them through, and there is a great deal of interesting information, often along the lines of the materials by the Lynds in Muncie, who also contributed to these volumes. Hoover had already lost his presidency by the time it was published.

17. John Kenneth Galbraith, *The Great Crash, 1929* (New York: Houghton Mifflin Harcourt, 2009 reprint edition), 70.

18. Irving Fisher, *Booms and Depressions: Some First Principles* (New York: Adelphi Company, 1932), 27.

19. Ibid., 104–105.

20. Ibid., 122–125, Table 13, 192.

21. Ibid., 129–129, 132.

22. Milton Friedman and Anna Jacobson Schwartz, *A Monetary History of the United States, 1867–1960* (Princeton, NJ: Princeton University Press, 1963), 50–53 (for footnote), 392, 308–309, 411–414.

23. Lester V. Chandler, *American Monetary Policy, 1928–1941* (New York: Harper & Row, 1971), 144.

24. Oliver M. W. Sprague, "Problems of Recovery," *New York Times*, no. 1, November 29, 1933, and no. 8, December 22, 1933.

25. All the data in this paragraph are from the *Survey of Current Business* (various issues).

26. Charles Rappleye, *Herbert Hoover in the White House: The Ordeal of the Presidency* (New York: Simon & Schuster, 2016), 196–197.

27. Irving Bernstein, *The Lean Years: A History of the American Worker, 1920–1933* (Chicago, IL: Haymarket Press, 2010 reprint edition), 317, 300; Lizbeth Cohen, *Making a New Deal: Industrial Workers in Chicago, 1919–1939* (New York: Cambridge University Press, 2nd ed., 2008) Table 14, Loc. 5020; and Robert A. Margo, "Employment and Unemployment in the 1930s," *Journal of Economic Perspectives* 7, no. 2 (Spring 1993): 41–59, 42.

28. Bernstein, *The Lean Years*, 301–304; *Fortune* quote on 302.

29. Cohen, *Making a New Deal*, 5063–5064.

30. "Doleful Detroit," *Time*, July 20, 1931.

31. "Labor: Below Animal Standards," *Time*, August 3, 1931.

32. Bernstein, *The Lean Years*, 292–295.

33. Ibid., 296–298; and Cohen, *Making a New Deal*, 4790.

34. Bernstein, *The Lean Years*, 300, 289.

35. Leuchtenburg, *Herbert Hoover*, 83; and Glen Jeansonne, *The Life of Herbert Hoover: Fighting Quaker, 1928–1933* (New York: Palgrave Macmillan, 2012), 57–61. For note on Dust Bowl, see Jason Long and Henry E. Sun, "Refugees from Dust and Shrinking Land: Tracking the Dust Bowl Migrants, *NBER Working Paper w22108* (March 2016).

36. "Husbandry: Cotton Crisis," *Time*, August 24, 1931.

37. "Husbandry: Again Bumper," *Time*, May 18, 1931.

38. "Husbandry: Simply Got Hungry," *Time*, January 12, 1931.

39. Frederick C. Mills, *Economic Tendencies in the United States: Aspects of Pre-War and Post-War Changes* (Cambridge, MA: NBER, 1932), 336, 340, calculations by the author; and *Prices in Recession and Recovery* (Cambridge, MA: NBER, 1936), 296.

40. The data are from Douglas Irwin, "The Smoot-Hawley Tariff: A Quantitative Assessment," *The Review of Economics and Statistics* 80, no. 2 (May 1998): 326–334. Mario J. Crucini, "Sources of Variation in Real Tariff Rates: the United States, 1900–1940," *The American Economic Review* 84, no. 3 (June 1994): 732–743 was the first to draw attention to the impact of deflation in increasing the weight of fixed-dollar tariffs. Barry Eichengreen, "The Political Economy of the Smoot-Hawley Tariff," NBER Working Paper No. 2001 (August 1986) makes a case that, while the effect of Smoot-Hawley was small, it was likely to have been expansionary. The "incredible folly" quote is on page 64. The best-known argument for a substantial negative effect from the tariff is Allan H. Meltzer, "Monetary and Other Explanations for the Start of the Great Depression," *Journal of Monetary Economics* 2 (1976): 455–472. Meltzer argues that the tariff interfered with the price-specie flow mechanism, thus interrupting international price adjustments.

41. Leuchtenberg, *Herbert Hoover*, 132, 133.

42. The short summary of Hoover's presidential demise follows Leuchtenberg, *Herbert Hoover*, 124–146, quotes at 132, 133, and 138; and Rappleye, *Herbert Hoover in the White House*, 346–351, 367–381, quotes at 374, 379.

43. Friedman and Schwartz, *A Monetary History*, 308–352.

44. Peter Temin, *Lessons from the Great Depression* (Cambridge, MA: MIT Press, 1989), 47–52; Elmus Wicker, *The Banking Panics of the Great Depression* (New York: Cambridge University Press, 1996), 32–38; and Charles Calomiris and Joseph R. Mason, "Causes of U.S. Bank Distress During the Depression," NBER Working Paper No. 7919 (September 2000), an econometric analysis that confirms Wicker.

45. Charles W. Calomiris, "Bank Failures in Theory and History: The Great Depression and Other 'Contagious' Events," NBER Working Paper 13597 (November 2007), 3–7.

46. Ibid., 11–15.

47. Charles Calomiris and Berry Wilson, "Bank Capital and Portfolio Management: The 1930s 'Capital Crunch' and the Scramble to Shed Risk," *The Journal of Business*, 77:3 (July 2004) 421–455.

48. Forrest McDonald, *Insull* (Chicago IL: University of Chicago Press, 1962), 274–275; and Thomas P. Hughes, "The Electrification of America: The System Builders," *Technology and Culture* 20, no. 1 (January 1979): 124–161, at 139–153.

49. Hughes, "The Electrification of America," 153–161.

50. Utilities Corporations, No. 72A, 619, 155; the MWU overhead charges were computed by the author from the income statements in Utilities Corporations, No. 38, Exhibit No. 5, 606–607.

51. McDonald, *Insull*, 274–276.

52. Utilities Corporations, No. 72A, 571, 555–556.

53. Utilities Corporations, No. 72A, 580–583.

54. Samuel Insull, *The Memoirs of Samuel Insull: An Autobiography*, edited by Larry Plachno (Polo, IL: Transportation Trails, 1992), 188–189, 192; and Marcus Gleisser, *The World of Cyrus Eaton* (Kent OH: Kent State University Press, 2005), loc. 471–473.

55. Public Utility Holding Companies, 1–2, and Insull, *The Memoirs*, 189, 191–192.

56. McDonald, *Insull*, 281–283.

57. Gleisser, *The World of Cyrus Eaton*, loc. 479–566; and McDonald, *Insull*, 289.

58. Insull, *The Memoirs*, 192–194; McDonald, *Insull*, 287; and Gleisser, *The World of Cyrus Eaton*, loc. 529.

59. Insull, *The Memoirs*, 195–197.

60. Ibid.

61. Ibid., 196.

62. Ibid., 196–198.

63. Ibid., 198–199.

64. Financial data for MWU, IUI, and CSC from the respective reports of the receivers: Utility Corporations, No. 50, 846–847; 757; and 1112–1114. For CSC detail and Eaton transaction, see Public Utility Holding Companies, 483–505.

65. Arthur R. Taylor, "Losses to the Public in the Insull Collapse," *The Business History Review* 36, no. 2 (Summer, 1962): 188–204.

66. The account here is drawn from Insull, *The Memoirs*, 232–269; and McDonald, *Insull*, 305–339.

67. Pecora Commission, Final Report.

68. Gleisser, *The World of Cyrus Eaton*, Loc. 772–808.

69. Pecora Commission, "A.B. Kreuger & Toll Group of Companies—Final Report Dated November 28, 1932—Price, Waterhouse & Co., Stockholm," 1260–1265. Kroner converted to dollars by author, at 26.8 cents/$1.

70. Ibid.

71. Ibid., Testimony of George O. May, 1268.

72. Ibid., 1261, 1263.

73. Except as indicated, the portrait of Kreuger follows Frank Partnoy, *The Match King: Ivar Kreuger, the Financial Genius Behind a Century of Wall Street Scandals* (New York: PublicAffairs, 2009).

74. Ibid., 31–32.

75. Ibid., 33–35.

76. Ibid., 37–41.

77. Ibid., 43–45, 50–54.

78. Ibid., 54–55.

79. Ibid., 70–74.

80. Ibid., 79–83

81. Ibid., 59–69, 103.

82. Ibid., 116.

83. Ibid., 103–111.

84. Ibid., 136–140.

85. Ibid., 140–143.

86. "Business: Monopolist," *Time*, October 28, 1929.

87. Partnoy, *The Match King*, 143–144.

88. Ibid., 144, 163.

89. Ibid., 154–155.

90. Ibid., 156–157.

91. Ibid.; and "Sweden: Glorified I.O.U.s," *Time*, April 28, 1930.

92. Hyman Minsky, "The Financial Instability Hypothesis," Working Paper No. 74, The Jerome Levy Economics Institute of Bard College (May 1992), 8.

93. Partnoy, *The Match King*, 164–165.

94. Ibid., 160, 164.

95. Ibid., 190–191.

PART FOUR: BLOOD, GOLD, AND UNPAID DEBTS

1. John Darwin, *The Empire Project: The Rise and Fall of the British World System, 1830–1970* (New York: Oxford University Press, 2009), 117–120, 144–145.

2. Walter Bagehot, *Lombard Street: A Description of the Money Market* (London: Dodo Press, undated), 23; and Allan H. Meltzer, *A History of the Federal Reserve: Vol. I, 1913–1951* (Chicago IL: University of Chicago Press, 2003), 48–51.

3. Barry Eichengreen, *Golden Fetters: The Gold Standard and the Great Depression, 1919–1939* (New York: Oxford University Press, 1996), 46–49; and Darwin, *The Empire Project*, 114–122.

4. Eichengreen, *Golden Fetters*, 50.

5. H. Clark Johnson, *Gold, France, and the Great Depression, 1919–1932* (New Haven, CT: Yale University Press, 1997), 50.

6. Charles O. Hardy, *Is There Enough Gold?* (Washington, DC, The Brookings Institution, 1936), 92–93.

7. Stephen V. O. Clarke, *Central Bank Cooperation, 1924–1931*, (New York: Federal Reserve Bank of New York, 1967), 85–90, 124–134.

8. Johnson, *Gold, France*, 45–58, quote at 58.

9. Margaret MacMillan, *The War That Ended Peace: The Road to 1914* (New York: Random House, 2013), xvii–xviv; Niall Ferguson, *The House of Rothschild: the World's Banker, 1828–1999* (New York: Penguin, 1998), see 204–219; MacMillan. *Paris 1919*, 161.

10. Sally Marks, "Reparations Reconsidered: A Reminder," *Central European History* 2, no. 4 (December, 1969): 356–365. The Poincaré quote is on 361.

11. Sally Marks, "The Myths of Reparations," Central European History 11, no. 3 (September, 1978): 238, 238n26, 240n34, and 241n38. The details of the borrowing are in David Felix, *Walter Rathenau and the Weimar Republic: The Politics of Reparations* (Baltimore, MD: The Johns Hopkins Press, 1971), 83–84.

12. D. G. Williamson, "Great Britain and the Ruhr Crisis, 1923–1924, *British Journal of International Studies* 3, no. 1 (April, 1977): 70–91, on the animosity between the British and the French; Conan Fischer, *The Ruhr Crisis, 1923–1924* (New York: Oxford University Press, 2003): 139–147, quote on 144, for French abuses; and Marks, "The Myths," 250.

13. Carl Ludwig Holtfrerich, *The German Inflation, 1914–1923: Causes and Effects in International Perspective* (New York: Walter de Gruyter, 1986), 231–243, 76–79.

14. Ibid., 164–172.

15. Johnson, *Gold, France*, 87–88; Liaquat Ahamed, *Lords of Finance: The Bankers Who Broke the World* (New York: The Penguin Press, 2009), 120–124; Felix, *Walter Rathenau*, 28, 168–169, 173–174; and William C. McNeill, *American Money and the Weimar Republic: Economics and Politics on the Eve of the Great Depression* (New York: Columbia University Press, 1986), 23, 47.

16. Ahamed, *Lords of Finance*, 120–124. The figure is adapted from Eric E. Crowley, *Hyperinflation in Germany: Perceptions of a Process* (Aldershot, Hants, England: Scolar Press, 1994), 73–74.

17. Ahamed, *Lords of Finance*, 127–129, 181–187.

18. Ibid., 187–190.

19. Ibid.

20. MacMillan, *Paris 1919*, 488–492.

21. Meltzer, *A History*, 84; and *Historical Statistics*, Table Ca214. American wartime and immediate postwar lending to its allies was $9.7 billion compared to a 1913 GNP of $36.25 billion. By 1918, nominal American GDP had roughly doubled, while the index of real growth had moved from 100 to 157. From Hugh Rockoff, "Until It's Over, Over There: The U.S. Economy in World War I," NBER Working Paper no. 10580 (June 2004), Table 4.

22. Ahamed, *Lords of Finance*, 142; Lester V. Chandler, *Benjamin Strong, Central Banker* (Washington, DC: The Brookings Institution, 1958), 276. Alleged Mellon comment is in Herbert Hoover, *Memoirs Volume 3*, 30–31.

23. Ahamed, *Lords of Finance*, 197–215; and Josephine Young Case and Everett Needham Case, *Owen D. Young and American Enterprise* (Boston, MA: David R. Godine, 1982), 274–287.

24. John Maynard Keynes, *The Economic Consequences of the Peace* (New York, NY: Harcourt, Brace & Howe, 1920), 135. Keynes calculated that a maximum reparation that Germany could be responsible for was somewhere between $8–$15 billion; Johnson, *Gold, France*, 74–75; Ahamed, *Lords of Finance*, 214; and Stephen A. Schuker, *The End of French Dominance in Europe: The Financial Crisis of 1924 and the Adoption of the Dawes Plan* (Chapel Hill: University of North Carolina Press, 1976) is a day-by-day account, predominately from the French point of view.

25. Schuker, *End of French*, 294; Case and Case, *Owen D. Young*, 274–287.

26. Case and Case, *Owen D. Young*, 286; and "The Ruhr: March 17, 1923," *Time*, March 17, 1923.

27. Strong quote in Chandler, *Benjamin Strong*, 271; Keynes in Case and Case, *Owen D. Young*, 290–291.

28. *The Report of the First Committee of Experts to the Reparations Commission*, April 9, 1924, reprinted in Federal Reserve Bulletin, May 1924, 351–417, quote at 355. The full report is available at fraser.stlouisfed.org/scribd /?toc_id=64276&filepath=/docs/publications/FRB/1920s/frb_051924 .pdf&start_page=31#scribd-open.

29. Ibid., 359–366.

30. Ibid., 365 (converted to $).

31. Ibid., 366.

32. Schuker, *End of French*, offers the most detailed account, 289–359.

33. Case and Case, *Owen D. Young*, 308.

34. Robert L. Hetzl, "German Monetary History in the First Half of the Twentieth Century," Federal Reserve Bank of Richmond, *Economic Quarterly* 88 no. 1 (Winter 2002): 1–35, 19 Table 1; and Jon Jacobson, *Locarno Diplomacy: Germany and the West, 1925–1929* (Princeton, NJ: Princeton University Press, 1972): 3–44.

35. Felix, *Walter Rathenau*, 9.

36. George F. Kennan, *Russia and the West Under Lenin and Stalin* (Boston MA: Atlantic Monthly Press, 1960–1961), 208–223; Richard Pipes, *Russia Under the Bolshevik Regime* (New York: Alfred A. Knopf, 1993), 427–435; MacMillan, *Paris 1919*, 481; and Felix, *Walter Rathenau*, 11, 135–136.

37. Schuker, *End of French*, 249–250, 253–254.

38. Ibid., 265–266, 318; and Stephen A. Schuker, *American "Reparations" to Germany, 1919–1933: Implications for the Third World Debt Crisis* (Princeton, NJ: Princeton University Press, 1988), 46.

39. Schuker, *American "Reparations,"* 106–109; Niall Ferguson, *The House of Rothschild: The World's Banker, 1849–1999* (New York: Viking Penguin, 1998), 204–217; and Michael Gavin, "Intertemporal Dimensions of International Economic Adjustment: Evidence from the Franco-Prussian War Indemnity," *The American Economic Review* 82, no. 2 (May 1992), 174–179.

40. Paul Bairoch, "International Industrialization Levels from 1750 to 1980," *Journal of European Economic History* 11, no. 2 (Fall, 1982): 269–333, and Stephen N. Broadberry and Douglas Irwin, "Labor Productivity in the United States and the United Kingdom during the Nineteenth Century," NBER Working Paper no. 10364 (March 2004). The 1870–1913 growth rate calculations are from

W. Arthur Lewis, *Growth and Fluctuation, 1870–1913* (London: George Allen & Unwin, 1978), 17–18. S. B. Saul, *The Myth of the Great Depression, 1873–1896* (Basingstoke, Hampshire: Macmillan, 1985), also includes a great deal of comparative data, generally consistent with Bairoch, but with a variety of additional nuances.

41. For a general history, see D. L. Burn, *The Economic History of Steelmaking, 1867–1939: A Study in Competition* (Cambridge, England: University Press, 1940).

42. D. E. Moggridge, *British Monetary Policy: The Norman Conquest of $4.86* (Cambridge, England: University Press, 1972), 30–36.

43. Ibid., 17–21.

44. Ibid., 24–26.

45. Clarke, *Central Bank Cooperation*, 74–75 (Strong quotes); and Chandler, *Benjamin Strong*, 291–331, and see 281–285 for a lucid Strong memo on the practical issues of establishing the exchange rate of disparate currencies.

46. Moggridge, *British Monetary Policy*, 28–29; and see Peter Termin, *Lessons from the Great Depression* (Cambridge MAS: MIT Press, 1989), 12–16.

47. Moggridge, *British Monetary Policy*, 37–51.

48. P. J. Grigg, *Prejudice and Judgement* (London: Jonathan Cape, 1948), 180–186; and detailed questions, Moggridge, *British Monetary Policy*, 65–66, with full text of questions on 260–262.

49. Moggridge, *British Monetary Policy*, 67.

50. Ibid., 75–77.

51. Clarke, *Central Bank Cooperation*, 85–88.

52. Ibid., 88–90.

53. Ibid., 93–96; Chandler, *Benjamin Strong*, 308–321. Neither line was drawn upon.

54. Grigg, *Prejudice and Judgement*, 184, 182.

55. Roy Jenkins, *Churchill: A Biography* (New York: Farrar, Straus and Giroux, 2001), 400–401.

56. Robert Skidelsky, *John Maynard Keynes: The Economist as Savior, 1920–1937*, Vol. 2 (London: MacMillan, 1992), 200.

57. John Maynard Keynes, "The Economic Consequences of Mr. Churchill," reprinted in *Essays in Persuasion* (Classic House Books, 2009), 132–147, at 138.

58. Skidelsky, *John Maynard Keynes*, 200–203, quote at 193.

59. Ibid., 200–201.

60. Jenkins, *Churchill*, 405; and "History: General Strike of 1926," BBC, bbc.co.uk/schools/gcsebitesize/history/mwh/britain/generalstrikerev4.shtml.

61. Jenkins, *Churchill*, 408–412.

62. Johnson, *Gold, France*, 33; FRED, "Index of Wholesale Prices (France)."

63. Johnson, *Gold, France*, 74–75.

64. Eichengreen, *Golden Fetters*, 172–175; Schuker, *End of French*, 95–100.

65. Eichengreen, *Golden Fetters*, 173–178.

66. Johnson, *Gold, France*, 81–82.

67. Ibid., 122–28; and Eichengreen, *Golden Fetters*, 182.

68. Eichengreen, *Golden Fetters*, 182–183.

69. Ahamed, *Lords of Finance*, 261–269.

70. Ibid., 259–261.

71. Ibid., 295–299.

72. Clarke, *Central Bank Cooperation*, 124.

73. See ibid., 124–125; Eichengreen, *Golden Fetters*, 213–214; and Meltzer, *A History*, 256–257 for the evidence against the likelihood that the 1927 easing policy was destabilizing, and Ahamed, *Lords of Finance*, 298–300 for the argument that it was destabilizing. The attack on Strong is the less credible because it was mounted originally by Adolph Miller, the chairman of the Washington Board, who had been mounting a guerilla campaign to undercut Strong's position and move international policy to the Washington board. Miller is widely viewed as among the weakest of Federal Reserve chairmen.

74. David Cannadine, *Mellon: An American Life* (New York: Knopf, 2008), 290–291; Schuker, *American "Reparations,"* 91.

75. Jon Jacobson, *Locarno Diplomacy*, 68–76.

76. Ibid., 104–110.

77. McNeil, *American Money*, 100–103.

78. Ibid, 122–123.

79. Theo Balderston, "The Beginning of the Depression in Germany, 1927–1930: Investment and the Capital Market," *The Economic History Review*, New Series 36, no. 3 (August, 1983), 395–415, 406–410.

80. Schuker, *American "Reparations,"* 60. For note, see S. Parker Gilbert, *Report of the Agent General for Reparation Payments*, IV. The German Budget, June 10, 1927; net.lib.byu.edu/~rdh7/wwi/1918p/rep27/repartc.htm.

81. Jacobson, *Locarno Diplomacy*, 250–276; Case and Case, *Owen D. Young*, 430; and for the text of the Young plan, see www.pca-cpa.org/hague1930ocfe.pdf?fil_id=388i.

82. Theo Balderston, "German Banking Between the Wars: the Crisis of the Credit Banks," *The Business History Review*, 65:3 (Autumn 1991), 554–605, 564.

83. "Report of the Agent General for Reparations, May 21, 1930," *Federal Reserve Bulletin*, November 1930, 694–737, quote, 697.

84. Theo Balderston, "The Origins of Economic Instability in Germany, 1924–1930: Market Forces versus Economic Policy," *VSWG: Vierteljahrschrift für Sozial-und Wirtschaftgeschichte*, 69:4, 488–514, 490.

85. Johnson, *Gold, France*, 135–136.

86. Ibid., 131.

87. Ibid., 142–144.

88. Ibid., 147.

89. Eichengreen, *Golden Fetters*, 267–269; and Ahamed, *Lords of Finance*, 404–406.

90. Eichengreen, *Golden Fetters*, 264–267; Ahmed, 406.

91. Ibid., 269–270.

92. Harold James, "The Causes of the German Banking Crisis of 1931," *The Economic History Review*, 37:1 (February, 1984), 68–87, 76–78.

93. Ahamed, *Lords of Finance*, 408–410.

94. Charles Rappleye, *Herbert Hoover in the White House: The Ordeal of the Presidency* (New York: Simon & Schuster, 2016), 261.

95. Clarke, *Central Bank Cooperation*, 193–194; and Ahamed, *Lords of Finance*, 414–418.

96. Clarke, *Central Bank Cooperation*, 201–202; and Eichengreen, *Golden Fetters*, 280.

97. Clarke, *Central Bank Cooperation*, 204–209.

98. Ibid., 208–213.

99. Ibid.

100. "Disorders in British Navy Follow Economy Pay Cut; Manoeuvres Are Cancelled," *New York Times*, September 26, 1931; and Clarke, *Central Bank Cooperation*, 214.

101. Clarke, *Central Bank Cooperation*, 215–216.

102. Ibid., 218–219.

103. Kim Quaile Hill, *Democracies in Crisis: Public Policy Responses to the Great Depression* (Boulder, CO: Westview Press, 1988), 37, Figure 3.3.

104. Peter Temin, "Socialism and Wages in the Recovery from the Great Depression in the United States and Germany," *The Journal of Economic History*, 50:2 (June, 1990), 297–307.

PART FIVE: ROOSEVELT, REFLATION, AND RECOVERY

1. International: "The World Confers," *Time*, June 19, 1933.

2. Eric Rauchway, *The Money Makers: How Roosevelt and Keynes Ended the Depression, Defeated Fascism, and Secured a Prosperous Peace* (New York: Basic Books, 2015), 71–91.

3. Quotes from Frank Freidel, *Franklin D. Roosevelt: A Rendezvous with Destiny* (Boston, MA: Little Brown & Co., 1990), 68; and Eric Larrabee, *Commander-in-Chief: Franklin Delano Roosevelt, His Lieutenants, and Their War* (New York: Simon and Schuster, 1988), 644.

4. Rauchway, *Money Makers*, 34–35.

5. Arthur M. Schlesinger Jr., *The Coming of the New Deal, V. 3 of The Age of Roosevelt* (Boston, MA: Houghton Mifflin Company, 1959), 203–212.

6. Lester V. Chandler, *America's Greatest Depression, 1929–1941* (New York: Harper & Row, 1970), 53–66, is a compact and data-rich summary; the study on farmer incomes is cited in Bernard F. Stanton, *George F. Warren, Farm Economist* (Ithaca, NY: Cornell University, 2007), 296.

7. Chandler, *America's Greatest Depression*, 56.

8. Chandler, *America's Greatest Depression*, 54; and Lloyd D. Teigen, *Agricultural Parity: Historical Review and Alternative Calculations* (Washington, DC: US Department of Agriculture, Economic Agriculture Report No. 571, 1987).

9. FRED, *Index of Prices Received by Farmers, All Groups for the United States 1900–1914 = 100, Monthly, Not Seasonally Adjusted*; and Chandler, *America's Greatest Depression*, 57–59.

10. Domenico Delli Gatti et al., "Sectoral Balances and Long Run Crises," paper presented to the International Economic Association, Beijing, July 8, 2011, 14–16.

11. Public Law 73–10, H.R. 3835.

12. Ibid.

13. Schlesinger, *Coming of the New Deal*, 195–203.

14. Barry Eichengreen, *Golden Fetters: The Gold Standard and the Great Depression, 1919–1939* (New York: Oxford University Press, 1995), 332.

15. Schlesinger, *Coming of the New Deal*, 213–218; Eichengreen, *Golden Fetters*, 333.

16. Schlesinger, *Coming of the New Deal*, 218.

17. Ibid.

18. Ibid., 219–224.

19. Sebastian Edwards, "Academics as Economic Advisers: Gold, the 'Brains Trust,' and FDR," NBER Working Paper 21380 (July 2015), 35; Stanton, *George F. Warren*, 353–358.

20. Elmus Wicker, "Roosevelt's 1933 Monetary Experiment," *Journal of American History* 57, no. 4 (March 1971): 864–879, at 876; and Charles P. Kindleberger, *The World in Depression, 1929–1939*, 40th anniversary ed. (Berkeley: University of California Press, 2013), 228, 230.

21. Wicker, "Roosevelt's 1933," 877–878. For Warren's prominent role—he was on the cover of *TIME* magazine—see Stanton, *George F. Warren*, 404–440.

22. Rauchway, *Money Makers*, 83–84.

23. Schlesinger, *Coming of the New Deal*, 241–242.

24. Rauchway, *Money Makers*, 89–90.

25. Eichengreen, *Golden Fetters*, 345–347.

26. Barry Eichengreen and Jeffrey Sachs, "Exchange Rates and Economic Recovery in the 1930s," *Journal of Economic History* 45, no. 4 (December, 1985): 925–946; and "Competitive Devaluation and the Great Depression: A Theoretical Assessment," *Economics Letters* 22 (1986): 67–71. Quote is from Eichengreen and Sachs, "Exchange Rates," 925.

27. Eichengreen, *Golden Fetters*, 345–347.

28. Ibid.

29. Eichengreen and Sachs, "Exchange Rates," 927n8.

30. "Address at Oglethorpe University, May 22, 1932," in *The Public Papers and Addresses of Franklin D. Roosevelt, Vol. 1, 1928–32* (New York: Random House, 1938), 639.

31. Alan Brinkley, *Huey Long, Father Coughlin and the Great Depression* (New York: Vintage Edition, 1983), 111–127.

32. Ibid., 22–31, 69.

33. Ibid., 79–80.

34. Ibid., 222–230.

35. "Education and Training: History and Timeline," US Department of Veterans Affairs, www.benefits.va.gov/gibill/history.asp; and Emmanuel Saez and Thomas Piketty, "Income Inequality in the United States, 1913–1998," *Quarterly Journal of Economics* 118, no. 1 (2003): 1–39, Table A3 (tables and figures updated to 2015 in Excel format, June 2016). The calculation in the footnote is the author's. I removed transfer payments from the GDP personal income figure, and applied the Saez-Piketty percentage to the remainder.

36. Price Fishback and John Joseph Wallis, "What Was New About the New Deal?" in Nicholas Crafts and Peter Fearon (eds.), *The Great Depression of the 1930s: Lessons for Today* (New York: Oxford University Press, 2013), 290–327, is a crisp summary.

37. "Not tried" quote in Christina D. Romer, "What Ended the Great Depression," *Journal of Economic History* 52, no. 4 (December, 1992): 757–784, 758; and Alexander J. Field, "Economic Growth and Recovery in the United States, 1919–1941," in Nicholas Crafts and Peter Fearon (eds.), *The Great Depression of the 1930s: Lessons for Today* (New York: Oxford University Press, 2013), 358–394, 374.

38. Gauti B. Eggertsson, "Great Expectations and the End of the Depression," *American Economic Review* 98, no. 4 (2008): 1476–1516, 1482.

39. Kindleberger, *World in Depression*, 193.

40. Peter Temin and Barrie A. Wigmore, "The End of One Big Inflation," *Explorations in Economic History* 27, no. 4 (1990): 483–502, quote at 483.

41. Eggertsson, "Great Expectations," 1501; and Christina D. Romer, "What Ended."

42. Relief: "Rizzo Goes to Work," *Time*, April 17, 1933.

43. Schlesinger, 337–340.

44. Ibid.

45. Ibid., 266–268, Ron Cynewulf Robbins, "Roosevelt's Bracken: Harry Hopkins, 'Lord Root of the Matter,'" *Finest Hour*, 146 (Spring 2010), www.winston churchill/publications/finest-hour/60-finest-hour-146.

46. Schlesinger, *Coming of the New Deal*, 269–271.

47. Ibid.; Fishback and Wallis, "What Was New," 298. Calculations by the author.

48. Fishback and Wallis, "What Was New," 308.

49. Ibid., 306.

50. Freidel, *Franklin D. Roosevelt*, 150.

51. Public Law No. 67 (H.R. 5755), June 16, 1933, Section 1.

52. Dorothy Ross, *The Origins of American Social Science* (New York: Cambridge University Press, 1991), 219–256. Dewey quote at 252–253.

53. Walter Lippmann, *Drift and Mastery: An Attempt to Diagnose the Current Unrest* (New York: Mitchell Kennerley, 1914), 44.

54. Freidel, *Franklin D. Roosevelt*, 136–138. *Schecter* quote in note: A.L.A. Schecter Poultry Corp. v. United States 495 (1935). Court Syllabus, Holding (1).

55. Fishback and Wallis, "What Was New," Table 10.2, summations by author.

56. Ibid., 296–304, 308–313, 316–319.

57. This section relies on Price V. Fishback, Alfonso Flores-Lagunes, William Horrace, Shawn E. Kantor, and Jaret Treber, "The Influence of the Home Owners' Loan Corporation on Housing Markets During the 1930s," NBER Working Paper No. 15824 (March 2010), quote at 6.

58. Price V. Fishback, William C. Horrace, and Shawn Kantor, "Did New Deal Grant Programs Stimulate Local Economies? A Study of Federal Grants and Retail Sales During the Great Depression," *Journal of Economic History* 65, no. 1 (March, 2005): 36–71.

59. Todd C. Neumann, Price V. Fishback, and Shawn Kantor, "The Dynamics of Relief Spending and the Private Urban Labor Market During the New Deal," *Journal of Economic History* 70, no. 1 (March 2010): 195–220, quote at 200.

60. Ibid.; and Gavin Wright, "The Political Economy of New Deal Spending: An Econometric Analysis," *Review of Economics and Statistics* 56, no. 1 (February 1974): 30–38.

61. Fishback and Wallis, "What Was New," 304.

62. Eggertsson, "Great Expectations," 1482; NIPA Table 1.1.6.

63. W. L. Crum, R. A. Gordon, and Dorothy Westcott, "Review of the Year 1937," *The Review of Economics and Statistics* 20, no. 1 (February 1938), 43–52, at 43. Kenneth D. Roose, *The Economics of Recession and Revival: An Interpretation of 1937–38* (New Haven, CT: Yale University Press, 1954) is data rich and intelligent, but dated.

64. Francois R. Velde, "The Recession of 1937—A Cautionary Tale," *Federal Reserve Bank of Chicago: Economic Perspectives* (4Q 2009), 16–36; industrial production drop calculated by author, from FRED, G-17, "Industrial Production and Capacity Utilization;" drops in employment and stock valuations from Velde, "Recession of 1937," 17; quarterly GDP data from the interpolated data developed by Robert J. Gordon and Nathan S. Balke, in Robert J. Gordon, ed., *The American Business Cycle: Continuity and Change* (Chicago, IL: University of Chicago Press, 1986), appendix B, Historical Data, 794–795.

65. Alan Brinkley, *The End of Reform* (New York: Random House, 1995), 28. Deficits from FRED, FYFSGDDA188s.

66. Business & Finance: "Crash! Crash! Crash!," *Time*, September 20, 1937.

67. Velde, "Recession of 1937"; Herbert Stein, *The Fiscal Revolution in America* (Chicago, IL, University of Chicago Press, 1969), 100–107; and Milton Friedman and Anna Jacobsen Schwartz, *A Monetary History of the United States, 1867–1960* (Princeton, NJ: Princeton University Press, 1963), 517–526.

68. Velde, "Recession of 1937," 19; Friedman and Schwartz, *A Monetary History*, 544; and Robert Higgs, "America's Depression Within a Depression, 1937–1939," Foundation for Economic Education, October 22, 1910. https://fee.org/articles/americas-depression-within-a-depression-193739/.

69. United States Department of Commerce (US DOC), BEA "GDP: One of the Great Inventions of the 20th Century," *Survey of Current Business* (January, 2000): 1–9.

70. Brinkley, *End of Reform*, 29, 30.

71. Douglas A. Irwin, "Gold Sterilization and the Recession of 1937–38," NBER Working Paper 17595 (November 2011).

72. Brinkley, *End of Reform*, 82–85, 97–101.

73. Charles W. Calomiris, Joseph Mason, and David Wheelock, "Did Doubling Reserve Requirements Cause the Recession of 1937–38: A Microeconomic Approach," NBER Working Paper 16688 (January 2011).

74. Charles W. Calomiris and R. Glenn Hubbard, "Internal Finance and Investment: Evidence from the Undistributed Profits Tax of 1936–37," *Journal of Business* 68, no. 4 (October, 1995): 443–482; and Field, "Economic Growth," 358–359, at 374. GDP growth calculations by the author from NIPA 1.1.6 and *Historical Statistics*, Table Ca213.

75. NIPA Table 1.1.6.

76. Robert A. Margo, "Employment and Unemployment in the 1930s," *Journal of Economic Perspectives*, 7, no. 2 (Spring, 1993), Table 1. The "Lebergott" column is the official Census Bureau version; for the Darby version, see Michael R. Darby, "Three and a Half Million U.S. Employees Have Been Mislaid: Or, an Explanation of Unemployment, 1934–1941," *Journal of Political Economy* 84, no. 1 (February, 1976): 1–16.

77. Ibid., 43–44.

78. Keynes quote in footnote from Donald Moggridge, ed., *The Collected Writings of John Maynard Keynes, Vol. XX: Activities 1929–1931, Rethinking Employment and Unemployment Policies* (London: MacMillan and Cambridge University Press, for the Royal Economic Society, 1981), 130.

79. For the flavor of British labor relations in the interwar period, see Roy Jenkins, *Churchill: A Biography* (New York, NY: Farrar, Straus, and Giroux, 2001), 403–417.

80. Irving Bernstein, *The Turbulent Years, A History of the American Worker, 1933–1940* (Chicago, IL: Haymarket Press reprint edition, 2010), 646–671, 569–571, 754–751.

81. Frederick C. Mills, "Changes in Pricing, Manufacturing Costs, and Industrial Productivity, 1929–1934," NBER Bulletin No. 53, December 22, 1934, 7; and Ada M. Beny, *Wages, Hours, and Employment in the United States, 1914–1936* (New York: National Industrial Conference Board, Inc., 1936), Table 2. (Note: I recovered the Mills data from charts in the cited newsletter. Mills did not consistently publish his monthly data, usually citing them only to mark start and end points of price movements. The charts in the cited newsletter were clearly based on monthly data, although they were hard to read and the Xerox pages were distorted. I engaged a computer graphics professional to produce rectified, blown up versions, on graph paper, so I could read off the monthly data.

82. Mills "Changes in Pricing," 7.

83. Business: "Steel Accedes," *Time*, October 31, 1932.

84. Mills, "Changes in Pricing," 7.

85. The discussion here draws from Lawrence F. Katz and Robert A. Margo, "Technical Change and the Relative Demand for Skilled Labor in Historical

Perspective," NBER Working Paper 18752 (February 2013). I have also written on the early American textile industry and white-collar revolution in Charles R. Morris, *The Dawn of Innovation* (New York: Public Affairs, 2012), 89–107; and *The Tycoons, How Andrew Carnegie, John D. Rockefeller, Jay Gould, and J.P. Morgan Invented the American Supereconomy* (New York: Henry Holt, 2005), 187–215, respectively.

86. Roose, *Economics of Recession*, 181.

87. Timothy F. Bresnahan and Daniel M. G. Raff, "Intra-Industry Heterogeneity and the Great Depression: The American Automobile Industry, 1929–1935," *Journal of Economic History* 51, no. 2 (June 1991): 317–331, Tables 2, 3, and 4. For essential background of the lengthy diffusion of Fordism, see Daniel M. G. Raff, "Making Cars and Making Money in the Interwar Automobile Industry: Economies of Scale and Scope and the Manufacturing Behind the Marketing," *Business History Review* 65, no. 4 (Winter 1991), 721–753; and "Representative Firm Analysis and the Character of Competition: Glimpses of the Great Depression," *American Economic Review* 88, no. 2 (May 1998), 57–61.

88. Richard J. Jensen, "The Causes and Cures of Unemployment in the Great Depression," *Journal of Interdisciplinary History* 19, no. 4 (Spring 1989): 553–583; and Daniel M. G. Raff and Lawrence H. Summers, "Did Henry Ford Pay Efficiency Wages?," NBER Working Paper No. 2101 (December 1986).

89. Jensen, "Causes and Cures," 555.

90. Ibid., 564–565.

91. Robert A. Margo, "The Microeconomics of Depression Unemployment," *Journal of Economic History* 51, no. 2 (June 1991): 333–341, Table 1.

92. Jensen, "Causes and Cures," 564; and Margo, "Microeconomics of Depression," Table 1 and 340.

93. Alexander J. Field, *A Great Leap Forward: 1930s Depression and US Economic Growth* (New Haven, CT: Yale University Press, 2001), 1.

94. Ibid., 20.

95. Ibid., 54–56.

96. Ibid., 58–63.

PART SIX: THE GEOLOGY OF THE COLLAPSE

1. William James, "The Moral Equivalent of War," in Robert McHenry, "William James on Peace and War," *Encyclopedia Britannica Blog*, March 22, 2010, http://blogs.britannica.com/2010/03/william-james-on-peace-and-war/.

2. James E. Hollenbeck, "The 1918–1919 Influenza Pandemic: A Pale Horse Rides Home from War," *Bios* 73, no. 1 (March, 2002): 19–27.

3. Jeffrey N. Dupeé, *Traveling Europe Between the Two World Wars* (Lanham, MD: University Press of America, 2013), 21.

4. Ibid., 26–27, 17.

5. Ibid., 20.

6. Ibid., 22.

7. Ibid., 30–31.

8. Nicholas Crafts and Peter Fearon, "Depression and Recovery in the 1930s: An Overview," in Crafts and Fearon, eds., *The Great Depression of the 1930s: Lessons for Today* (New York: Oxford University Press, 2013), 1, 3.

9. D. E. Moggridge, *The Return to Gold, 1925: The Formulation of Economic Policy and Its Critics* (Cambridge, England: Cambridge University Press, 1969), 24.

10. H. Clark Johnson, *Gold, France, and the Depression, 1919–1932* (New Haven, CT: Yale University Press), 133.

11. Allan H. Meltzer, *A History of the Federal Reserve, Vol. I, 1913–1951* (Chicago, IL: University of Chicago Press, 2003), 277–279.

12. Charles Kindleberger, *The World in Depression, 1929–1939*, 40th anniversary ed. (Berkeley, CA: University of California Press, 2013), 83–107; and Jakob B. Madsen, "Agricultural Crises and the International Transmission of the Great Depression," *The Journal of Economic History* 61, no. 2 (June 2001): 327–365.

13. Frederick C. Mills, *Prices in Recession and Recovery* (Cambridge, MA: NBER, 1936), 98–99.

14. Madsen, "Agricultural Crises," 328.

15. Giovanni Federico, "Not Guilty? Agriculture in the 1920s and the Great Depression," *The Journal of Economic History* 65, no. 4 (December 2005): 949–976.

16. Madsen, "Agricultural Crises," 331–335.

17. Crafts and Fearon, "Depression and Recovery," 21.

18. Ibid., 21–24.

19. Jakob B. Madsen, "Trade Barriers and the Collapse of World Trade During the Great Depression," *Southern Economic Journal* 67, no. 4 (April 2001): 848–868, 850–851.

20. Douglas A. Irwin, "The Smoot-Hawley Tariff: A Quantitative Assessment," *Review of Economics and Statistics* 80, no. 2 (May, 1998): 326–334, 329; Madsen, "Trade Barriers," 862–863. (I used the rounder numbers in the Abstract, however.)

21. Barry Eichengreen and Douglas Irwin, "The Slide to Protectionism to the Great Depression: Who Succumbed and Why?" *The Journal of Economic History* 70, no. 4, (December 2010): 871–897.

22. Christina D. Romer, "The Great Crash and the Onset of the Depression," *Quarterly Journal of Economics* 105, no. 3 (August 1990): 597–624; Frederic S. Mishkin, "The Household Balance Sheet and the Great Depression," *The Journal of Economic History* 38, no. 4 (December 1978): 918–937; Martha L. Olney, "The Role of Credit in the Consumption Collapse of 1930," *Quarterly Journal of Economics* 114, no. 1 (February 1999): 319–335; and Christopher Brown, "Consumer Credit and the Propensity to Consume: Evidence from 1930," *Journal of Post-Keynesian Economics* 19, no. 4 (1997): 617–638.

23. US DOC, "Indebtedness in the United States, 1929–1941," Government Printing Office, Washington, DC, 1942), Table 1 and Table 9; for footnote, Federal Reserve Board, "Financial Accounts of the United States, Z.1," Table.D3 and NIPA Table 1.1.5.

24. Charles Calomiris, "Financial Factors in the Great Depression," *Journal of Financial Perspectives* 7, no. 2 (Spring 1993): 61–85; Ali Anari, James Kolari, and Joseph Mason, "Bank Asset Liquidation and the Propagation of the U.S. Great Depression," *Journal of Money, Credit, and Banking* 37, no. 4 (August 2005): 753–773; Alexander J. Field, "A New Interpretation of the Onset of the Great Depression," *The Journal of Economic History* 44, no. 2 (1984): 489–498; Ben Bernanke, "Nonmonetary Effects of the Financial Crisis in the Propagation of the Great Depression," in Bernanke, *Essays on the Great Depression* (Princeton, NJ: Princeton University Press, 2000), 41–69, by permission of the *American Economic Review* 73 (1983).

25. *Historical Statistics*, Table Ba4361; and Emmanuel Saez and Thomas Piketty, "Income Inequality in the United States, 1913–1998," *Quarterly Journal of Economics* 118, no. 1 (2003): 1–39 (tables and figures updated to 2015 in Excel Format), Figure 2.

26. D. E. Moggridge, *British Monetary Policy 1924–1931: The Norman Conquest of $4.86* (Cambridge, England: Cambridge University Press, 1972), Table 10, 121.

27. The German narrative below is drawn entirely from Thomas Ferguson and Peter Termin's splendid, "Made in Germany: The German Currency Crisis of July 1931," *Research in Economic History* (2003), 21, 1–53.

28. Milton Friedman and Anna Jacobson Schwartz, *A Monetary History of the United States, 1867–1960* (Princeton, NJ: Princeton University Press, 1963), 392–393.

29. Charles Calomiris, "Financial Factors in the Great Depression," *Journal of Financial Perspectives* 7, no. 2 (Spring 1993): 61–85, 73, 67.

30. Theo Balderston, *Economics and Politics in the Weimar Republic* (New York: Cambridge University Press, 2002), 101.

31. Alan Greenspan, testimony before the House Committee on Banking and Financial Services, September 16, 1998.

32. Alan Greenspan, remarks to the Chicago Conference on Banking and Financial Services, May 8, 2003.

APPENDIX: MILKING THE INSULL STRUCTURE

1. The example is adapted from a presentation in US Trade Commission, "Utilities Corporations: Summary Report of the Federal Trade Commission to the Senate of the United States, Pursuant to Senate Resolution No. 83, 70th Congress, 1st Session, on Economic, Financial, and Corporate Phases of Holding and Operating Companies of Electric and Gas Utilities," No. 72A, filed December 18, 1934, 154–164. More than eight hundred pages long, the report is impressive in its sweep and detail, although occasionally excessively hostile in its interpretations. The report is part of an eighty-four-volume investigative record undertaken by the US Trade Commission under various Senate resolutions.

2. Forrest McDonald, *Insull* (Chicago IL: University of Chicago Press, 1962), 126–127; US Trade Commission, "Utilities Corporations," 570, 504.

INDEX

AAA. *See* Agricultural Adjustment Act

AB. *See* Aid to the Blind

Abnormal Importation Act (1931), 311

Abramovitz, Moses, 298

AC. *See* alternating current technology

Acheson, Dean, 251, 253–254, 256

Acheson-Warburg group, 253

ACLU. *See* American Civil Liberties Union

Adams, Edward Dean, 26

ADC. *See* Aid to Dependent Children

AFL. *See* American Federation of Labor

African Americans. *See* blacks

Agricultural Adjustment Act (AAA), 264, 276
    Thomas Amendment to, 248–249, 250

Agricultural Marketing Act, 142

agriculture
    cultural loss, 105
    economics of, 105
    farm price index drop, 247
    global crisis, 308–310, 309 (fig.)
    Great Depression and, 103
    Hoover, H., relief policy, 142–144, 306
    industrial, 246–247
    New Deal bill, 262
    parity ratio, 247
    Roosevelt, F., monetary policy for, 246
    US crop and meat prices, 104–105, 104 (fig.)
    See also farms

Aid to Dependent Children (ADC), 270

Aid to the Blind (AB), 270

Alabama Sharecroppers' Union, 69

Alcoa. *See* Aluminum Company of America

Allen, Frederick Lewis, 62

Alternating current (AC) technology,
77, 80–81, 294, 295
manufacturing productivity and, 98
of Westinghouse, 25–26
Aluminum Company of America
(Alcoa) monopoly, 100–101
American Civil Liberties Union
(ACLU), 58
American Federation of Labor (AFL),
289
American Municipal Association,
108–109
American Psychological Association,
63
American Rolling Mill Company
(ARMCO), 102
American Sociological Association,
63
Amos 'n Andy (radio), 40–41
Anari, Ali, 314
ANB. See Austrian National Bank
Anderson, Sherwood, 42
Angell, Norman, 5–6
Anthei, Georges, 20
anti-monopoly, electrical utility
company backlash of, 28–29
Arden, Elizabeth, 53–54
ARMCO. See American Rolling Mill
Company
Armstrong, Louis, 46
Army Corps of Engineers, 269
asset risk, 153
AT&T telephone market, 40
Austria, 7, 8, 303
banking crisis in, 149
customs union, 317, 319
Ferdinand assassination response, 4
Kreditanstalt bank of, 234–235

stand-still agreements, 235
Versailles Peace Conference and,
14, 304
Austrian National Bank (ANB), 234
credit line from Bank of England,
BIS, and Federal Reserve, 235
automobile industries, 34, 77, 84–91,
97
Ford domination of, 38
Great Depression and, 294–295
1923 sales year, 93
1929 increase in, 135
See also specific automobile industries
automobiles, 70–71
market crash of 1920, 90
as mobile houses of prostitution,
56–57
Muncie, Indiana affordable, 55
technology, 31, 35–36

Bagehot, Walter, 183
Baker, Josephine, 47
Balderston, Theo, 228, 320
Baldwin, Stanley, 157, 210
bank crises, of Great Depression, 154
bank holidays, 149, 152–153, 264
currency hoarding, 151–152
fundamental failures, 150
risk management, 153
rural banks, 150–151, 248
sale of banks, 151 (photo)
Bank for International Settlements
(BIS)
ANB credit line from, 235
as Young Plan reparations agent,
228
bank holidays, 149, 152–153, 264
Bank of England, 184–185, 214, 232

ANB credit line from, 235
post WWI progress, 209
Bank of France, 308
pegging franc to dollar, 219
price stability maintained by, 232
Bank of the United States (BUS), 149,
151
bankers' pool, 119–121
banking, cooperation end, 224
conference agenda, 221–222
currency management, 222–223
bankruptcies
of CSC, IUI, and MWU, 161–163
of Ivar Kreuger companies, 167–
177
of farms, 310
banks
deplorable conditions of German,
317
failures in rural areas, 150–151, 248
margin lending reductions, 226
RFC loans to, 152, 244, 273
See also specific banks
Barton, Bruce, 82
Baruch, Bernard, 73, 115
Battle of the Marne, 11–12
The Beautiful and the Damned
(Fitzgerald, S.), 19, 20
BEF. *See* British Expeditionary Force
beggar-my-neighbor policies, 239, 255,
256
Belgium, 1
Germany war declaration against, 4
Ruhr region invasion by, 191, 193, 197
WWI losses, 14
Benchley, Robert, 41
Benny, Jack, 41
Benz, Karl, 31

Bergdorf Goodman, 49
Berlin, Germany, 13, 95, 191, 222, 226,
317
post WWI condition, 304
stock market drop, 235
Berlin, Irving, 107
Bernanke, Ben, 153, 314, 321, 322
Bethlehem Steel, 160
Biblical literalism, 62
bill of exchange, in British World
System, 182–183
binders, in real estate, 106–107
BIS. *See* Bank for International
Settlements
von Bismarck, Otto, 5
Black Monday, 120
Black Thursday, 174
Black Tuesday, 120
blacks
anti-black movement, 46
in Harlem, New York, 46
mass population movement North,
45–46, 76
Bloc National, 218
blue-collar workers, 52, 293, 295
unemployment of, 137
bonds
capital tax exemption for foreign
purchasers, 226
Federal Reserve System issuance of,
73–74
Germany issuance of, in 1927,
226–227
for Germany war reparations, 190
Kreuger forged, 177
war, 73–74, 74 (fig.)
The Book of the Month Club, 42
book publishing, 42

Booms and Depressions (Fisher, I.), 130–131, 134

Bow, Clara, 21, 44

Boyle, Mike, 79

Bresnahan, Timothy, 295

Brewster, Walter, 155

Briand, Aristide, 217, 219, 223, 317, 319

Bridges, Harry, 257

British Expeditionary Force (BEF), 9–10, 11

The British Gazette, 216

British World System, 182–183

broker loans, Federal Reserve system on, 112

Brooks, Louise, 44

Brown, Christopher, 313

Brüning, Heinrich, 236, 308, 317

Bryan, William Jennings, 58, 60–62, 107

Budenz, Louis, 267

Buick, David, 84–91

Buick Motor Company
    Durant, W., financing of, 84–85
    Model B, 84
    racing entry, 86
    sales, 85 (fig.), 86–87

building boom, in Miami, Florida, 106, 107

von Bülow, Karl, 10–11

Bureau of Standards, 128

BUS. *See* Bank of the United States

Byrd, Richard, 42

Cadillac Motor company, 32, 86, 87

Caldwell Corporation, 150

Calloway, Cab, 46

Calomiris, Charles, 150, 153, 314, 319–320

capital account, in Great Britain, 208

capital risk, 153

capital tax exemption, for foreign bond purchasers, 226

Carnegie, Andrew, 101

Cartel des Gauches, 218

Casablanca (movie), 44

Cassel, Gustav, 188, 210

Cather, Willa, 42

Catholics, American, 62

CBS. *See* Columbia Broadcasting System

CCC. *See* Civilian Conservation Corps

Cerf, Bennett, 42

Chamberlain, Austen, 223, 231

Champion, Albert, 86

Chandler, Lester, 133

Chevrolet, Louis, 86, 87

Chevrolet Company
    Model T competition from, 92
    sales, 87–88, 93

Chicago
    franchises and politics in, 79
    Great Depression impact on, 140–141

Chrysler, Walter, 87, 88, 91

Churchill, Winston, 2, 238, 318
    on Great Britain return to gold standard, 210–213
    on Hoover, H., 126
    on Roosevelt Statement, 252

Civil War, American, 2

Civilian Conservation Corps (CCC), 262, 266–267

Civilian Works Administration (CWA), 262, 267–268

Clarke, Stephen V. O., 238–239

Clémenceau, Georges, 14, 15 (photo)
coal companies, 79–80
Cocteau, Jean, 20
Code, in movies, 44, 55–56
Colt, Samuel, 97
Columbia Broadcasting System
    (CBS), 41
Columbia Graphophone, 112
commensurate taxation, of Germany,
    201
Commercial and Financial Chronicle,
    264
Commission for Relief in Belgium
    (CRB), 125–126
commodity prices, 252–253
    elevation of, 246
common people
    rising incomes, 23
    shift post WWI, 22
Commonwealth Edison company, of
    Chicago, 78, 155, 161
communication hub, New York City
    as, 41
complete markets, 321
construction
    employment collapse, 137
    Great Depression influence on, 109
consumer credit, 54–55, 260, 314
consumer society, post WWI, 23
Continental Securities, 171
Continental Shares, 158, 165–166
contraception, 57
Cooley, Charles Horton, 271
Coolidge, Calvin "Silent Cal," 128, 187,
    196–197, 227
Cooper, Lady Diana, 21
corporate capital flotations, 1926–
    1938, 163 (fig.)

Corporation Securities Company
    (CSC), of Chicago, 159–160
    bankruptcy, 161–163
Coughlin, Charles, 257, 259 (photo),
    260
couture industry, 48–49
Couzens, James, 33, 141
    five dollar per day wage, 37–38, 296
Cox, James M., 249
Crane, Hart, 42
Crawford, Joan, 44
CRB. *See* Commission for Relief in
    Belgium
credit
    ANB line of, 235
    consumer, 54–55, 260, 314
    France deflation, 233
    in Germany, 316
CSC. *See* Corporation Securities
    Company
Cullen, Countee, 46
cultural changes, post WWI, 22–23
    agriculture loss, 105
cultural transgression, in couture
    industry, 48–49
currency
    bank crises hoarding of, 151–152
    banking management of, 222–223
    depreciation, 255–256
    Germany Reischsmark plunge, 192,
        193 (photo), 195
    inflation local devaluation of, 184
    Rentenmark, in Germany, 195
    Stresemann-Schacht 1924 reform
        of, 316
    World Monetary and Economic
        Conference stabilization
        agreement, 249–250

current account, in Great Britain, 207 (fig.), 208
Curtius, Julius, 225
customs union, in Austria, 317, 319
CWA. *See* Civilian Works Administration

Daily News, 41
Daimler, Gottlieb, 31
Daimler-Benz Co., 31
Darrow, Clarence, 58–60
Darwin, Charles, 60, 63
Darwin, John, 182
Darwinism, 58, 61
Dawes, Charles G., 195–205
Dawes Plan, 195–205, 223, 225, 315
DC. *See* direct current technology
de Rothschild, Edouard, 220
de Wendel, François, 220
Dearborn Engineering Laboratory, 94
death toll, during WWI, 8, 10, 12, 13
deflation, 104, 105, 109, 133, 134, 233
    Fisher, I., on, 130–131, 234
    Fisherian debt, 310, 318
    French position of, 250, 251
    global, in 1930, 308
    Mellon on, 197
    1937, 282–283
    Roosevelt, F., and, 264
    tariffs impacted by, 144–145
Dempsey, Jack, 40
deposit risk, 153
Depression
    France and, 239
    of Germany, 240
    global agricultural glut, 306
    gold-based currencies, 306
    international catastrophe, 306

world trade collapse, 306
WWI and, 303
See also Great Depression
The Descent of Man (Darwin), 60
Detroit
    Great Depression impact on, 141
    relief program, 138–139
Detroit Edison generating plant, 30–31
devaluation
    of dollar, 246–256, 307
    of franc, 217–220, 231, 239, 308
    of local currency, inflation and, 184
Dewey, John, 63, 271
Dickens, Charles, 107
Dietrich, Marlene, 44
DIJA. *See* Dow Jones Industrial Average
Dillon, Clarence, 112
Dillon, Read and Company, 112, 197
direct current (DC) technology
    of Edison, 25–26
    manufacturing productivity and, 98
disarmament, of Germany, 203, 223
dollar
    bulging, of Fisher, I., 131
    devaluation of, 246–256, 307
    franc pegged to, 231
Dos Passos, John, 20
Double Indemnity (movie), 44
double-decime, 218
Douglas, Lewis, 251
Dow Jones Industrial Average (DIJA), 120, 122
    monthly close, 122 (fig.)
Dow Jones Industrial Index, 110–111, 113, 158

Dreadnought battleship building, Germany, 7

Dreiser, Theodore, 42

Drift and Mastery (Lippmann), 271

DSGE. *See* dynamic stochastic general equilibrium

Du Pont, Pierre, 88–90

Dulles, John Foster, 124

DuPont company, 88, 115–116

Durant, Ariel, 42

Durant, Donald, 170–175

Durant, William Crapo "Billy," 85–86, 90–91, 120, 121
  Buick Model B financing by, 84
  holding company creation, 87–88
  United Motors Company consolidation by, 88

Duryea, Frank, 31

Duryea, Charles, 31

Dust Bowl, 142

dynamic stochastic general equilibrium (DSGE) model, 265

Eaton, Cyrus S., 158–164

Eaton, William, 86

Ebert, Friederich, 13

Eccles, Marriner, 284

econometric analyses, 274–279

The Economic Consequences of Mr. Churchill (Keynes), 213–215, 228, 237

The Economic Consequences of the Peace (Keynes), 15, 197–198, 316

The Economist, 183
  on internal French prices, 232

Edison, Thomas, 27–29

DC technology of, 25–26

electric lighting system of, 24–25

Ford and, 31–32

Edison power companies, 25–27
  Commonwealth Edison, of Chicago, 78, 155, 161

efficiency wage, 37–38

efficient market theorists, 110

Eggertsson, Gauti, 265, 284

Eichengreen, Barry, 255, 256, 312

Eisenhower, Dwight, 147

Electric Bond and Share Company, 156

electric lighting system, of Edison, 24–25

electric power industry, TFP growth and, 300

electrical utility companies, 78
  anti-monopoly and, 28–29

Ellington, Duke, 46

Elmer Gantry (Lewis), 56

embezzlement
  of Insull, S., 164–165
  Whitney, R., conviction for, 121

employment
  construction collapse, 137
  manufacturing decrease, 137
  See also unemployment

Ericsson, L. M., 172, 176–177

Ernst & Ernst accounting, 172

Erzberger, Matthias, 13, 316

Europe
  Germany economic and military power, 8
  gold standard return, 203
  military spending, 7, 7 (fig.)
  proportional representation in, 192

evolution
    Darwinism and, 58, 61
    scientific evidence for, 60
    teaching of, 58

Factor, Max, 53–54
Fair Labor Standards Acts, 289, 296
Farley, Jim, 259–260
Farm Board, Federal, 142–143
Farm Credit Administration, of
    Roosevelt, F., 248
farm price index, 255 (fig.)
farms
    bankruptcies, 310
    in Muncie, Indiana, 50, 53, 103
    parity ratio of, 247
    price collapse, 309, 309 (fig.)
    productivity, 299
Faulkner, William, 42, 44
federal
    liabilities increase during New
        Deal, 263, 263 (fig.)
    New Deal debt, 278
    RFC borrowings, 263, 278, 284
Federal Emergency Relief
    Administration (FERA), 262, 267
Federal Housing Administration
    (FHA), on short blocks, 108
Federal Reserve System, 113, 187, 212,
    308
    ANB credit line from, 235
    bond agency, 73–74
    on broker loans, 112
    Friedman and Schwartz on
        deflation arrest by, 133
    reserve rules, 132–133
    Wicker on, 253
    WWI and, 72

Federal Trade Commission, 144, 272
Federico, Giovanni, 103, 310
Feis, Herbert, 249
FERA. See Federal Emergency Relief
    Administration
Ferdinand, Franz, 3–4
Ferguson, Thomas, 319
FHA. See Federal Housing
    Administration
Field, Alexander, 108, 109, 298, 300,
    314, 319
Field, Marshall, 78
fiscal consequences, of WWI
    borrowing, 73–74
    GNP, 74–75, 75 (fig.), 77, 130
    inflation, 73–75
    productivity shocks, 77
    recession, 76–77
    tight labor market, 76
    war expenditures, 73
Fishback, Price, 272, 275
Fisher, Carl, 106
Fisher, Irving, 134, 188, 210
    on deflation, 130–131, 234
    on dollar bulging, 131
Fisher Body company, 88–89, 106
Fisherian debt, 310
Fitzgerald, Scott, 19–22, 41, 42, 44, 48
Fitzgerald, Zelda, 19–22, 41, 48
Flagler, Henry, 106
Flaming Youth (movie), 55–56, 56 (fig.)
Foch, Ferdinand, 10, 11
food relief programs, of Hoover, H., 126
Ford, Edsel, 92
Ford, Henry, 33–36, 39, 101, 141
    automobile industry domination, 38
    at Detroit Edison generating plant,
        30–31

Edison and, 31–32
five dollar per day wage, 37–38, 296
Malcomson Model A (1903
    original) financing, 32
Quadricycle, 31, 32
Ford Motors, 92, 96
    assembly line, 36 (photo)
    line turnover, 37, 38
    Model A (1903 model), 32, 33
    Model A (1927 model), 71, 93–95
    Model N, 33–34
    Model T, 34–35, 38–39, 55, 69, 77,
        92–94, 247
    productivity, 97
    sales, 33, 34, 39, 87, 93, 96 (fig.)
    worker recruitment and retention,
        36–38
Fordism, 97, 294
Fordney-McCumber tariff, 311
Ford-style plants, in Muncie, Indiana,
    51–52
Fourteen Points, of Wilson, W., 14
franc
    devaluation of, 217–220, 231, 239,
        308
    French Monetary Law and new
        gold, 231–232
    pegged to dollar, 231
France
    credit deflation, 233
    deflation position, 250, 251
    double-decime, 218
    foreign exchange, 232
    franc devaluation, 217–220, 231, 239,
        308
    German war declaration against, 4
    National Union Government, 219
    post WWI condition, 304–305

price movements, 232–233
primitive monetary system, 217
reconstruction debt, 217
Ruhr region invasion by, 191, 193, 197
Ruhr withdrawal by, 202, 218, 292
on war debts and reparations
    moratorium, 236
WWI losses, 13–14
WWI Paris defense, 9–12
WWI war strategy, 9
franchises, 79, 80
Franco-Prussian War (1870–1871), 2,
    9, 204–205, 225
French Monetary Law (1928), new
    gold franc, 231–232
French Radical Party, 249
Friedman, Milton, 132, 149, 283, 285,
    314, 318
fundamental failures, in banks, 150
fundamentalism, 58–59, 62
The Fundamentals, 59

Galbraith, John Kenneth, 110, 116
Garanta company, 171
Garbo, Greta. *See* Gustafsson, Greta
Garfield, John, 45
Gary, Elbert H., 101–102
GDP. *See* gross domestic product
General Electric (GE)
    Marconi's Wireless purchase by, 40
    power management group
        approach, 98
    radio market, 40
General Motors (GM), 32, 38, 77,
    115–116, 121
    Pontiac division, 86
    sales, 86, 89, 91, 93, 96 (fig.), 102
George, David Lloyd, 14, 15 (photo)

George V (king), 243
Germany, 240, 304
  banks deplorable conditions, 317
  bond issuance, of 1927, 226–227
  credit, 316
  disarmament, 203, 223
  Dreadnought battleship building, 7
  foreign money and inflation,
    225–226
  France and Belgium war
    declaration by, 4
  Great Britain war declaration
    against, 4
  international accounts frozen, 237
  Kennedy on economic and military
    power of, 8
  Kreuger match monopoly, 173–174
  military opposition, 7
  politics conditions, 317
  post WWI, 315–318
  prewar industrial output, 206
  unraveling of, 225–230
  weapon technologies, 8
  WWI Belgium attack by, 9
  WWI war reparations, 15–16, 181,
    187, 189–195, 190 (fig.), 224
  See also Berlin
Germany, 1919–1925, 189–190,
    190 (fig.)
  commensurate taxation of, 201
  disarmament mandates ignored by,
    203
  hyperinflation, 194, 194 (fig.), 201
  monetary chaos, 191–192
  national railroad system
    privatization, 201
  November Revolution in, 191
  postwar poverty, 225

rearmament drive, 203–204
Reischsmark currency plunge, 192,
  193 (photo), 195
Rentenmark currency in, 195
Ruhr region invasion by France and
  Belgium, 191, 193, 197
war trials, 203
Weimar Republic in, 191–192, 228,
  307, 316
GI Bill of Rights, 260–261
Gilbert, S. Parker, 203, 226–227
Girdler, Tom, 161
Gish, Lillian, 20
Glassford, Pelham, 146, 147
global agricultural glut, of
  Depression, 306
global agriculture crisis, 308–310,
  309 (fig.)
global deflation, in 1930, 308
global monetary gains, in New York
  City, 40
global trading relations, Great Britain
  and, 182
GM. *See* General Motors
GNP. *See* Gross National Product
gold
  foreign exchange loss and, 235, 237
  price, 253–254, 260
  reserve, Reichsmark creation of, 201
  US holdings of, 232
Gold Bloc, 250–251
gold standard, 75–76, 136, 182–187, 238
  Austrian standstill agreements,
    234, 237
  Europe return to, 203
  gold-exchange standard from, 188
  Great Britain departure from, 149,
    152, 239, 311

Great Britain return to, 208–213,
306, 307
Kreditanstalt, of Austria, standstill
agreement, 234
Strong on, 209–213, 307
US off of, 249
gold-based currencies, at prewar
parities, 306–308
golden age, of Weimar Republic, 228
gold-exchange standard, from gold
standard, 188
Goldman Sachs, 110
Goodman, Edwin, 49–50
The Grammar of Science (Pearson, K.),
63
Great Britain, 7, 202, 238
Germany war declaration by, 4
global trading relations, 182
gold and foreign exchange reserves
loss, 237
gold standard departure, 149, 152,
239, 311
industrial production, 206, 237
Industrial Revolution and, 182, 206
merchandise trade deficit, 184
post WWI, 315
reflation position, 250–251
return to gold standard, 208–213,
306, 307
stock market drop, 120
unemployment doubling, 237
US alliance with, 231
war loans, 189
WWI BEF, 9–10
Great Britain, 1919–1925
Bank of England financials
progress, 209
capital account, 208

current account balances, 207 (fig.),
208
invisibles account, 184, 207–208,
207 (fig.), 237
merchandise account, 208
mining, 215–216, 216 (photo)
Moggridge on, 207–208
prewar steel leadership, 207
recession, 212
return to gold standard, 208–213
sheltered goods, 215
US industrial output compared to,
206
wartime inflation, 209
The Great Crash, 1929 (Galbraith), 110
Great Depression, 139 (photo),
307–312
automobile industry and, 294–295
bank crises of, 149–154, 264, 268
Chicago impacted by, 140–141
construction hit during, 109
deflationary momentum, 306
details, 312–319
Detroit impacted by, 141
Detroit relief program, 138–139
Muncie, Indiana and, 50
national morale and, 138
New York City relief efforts, 140
rural collapse and, 103, 139–142, 144
Smoot-Hawley tariff negative
impact on, 144, 311
unemployment among industries,
296–297
The Great Gatsby (Fitzgerald, S.), 21
The Great Illusion (Angell), 5–6
Great Moderation, 321–322
Great Recession, of 2007, 263, 322
Greenspan, Alan, 111, 321–322

Grigg, P. J., 210–213
gross domestic product (GDP), 72, 77,
 113, 287, 289
 WWI war effort and, 73
gross national product (GNP)
 US real and nominal, 1929–1937,
  131 (fig.)
 WWI fiscal consequences in,
  74–75, 75 (fig.), 77, 130
Gustafsson, Greta (Greta Garbo), 44,
 172

Hadden, Brit, 41
Haig, Douglas, 8
Halsey, Stewart and Company, 82,
 162–163
Hamlin, Charles, 308
Harding, Warren, 76, 127–128, 196
Harlem, black people in, 46
"Harlem Renaissance," 46
Harrison, George, 222, 238
Hart, Liddel, 3
The Harvard Classics, 42
Harvey, Ernest, 239, 318
Hatry, Clarence, 120
Hawtrey, Ralph, 187–188
Haynes, Elwood, 31
Hemingway, Ernest, 20, 42
Henderson, Arthur, 237
Herriot, Édouard, 202, 204, 218, 249
high-end service industries, 49
History of Crises Under the National
 Banking System (Sprague), 133–134
Hitler, Adolf, 203, 240
Hofstadter, Richard, 62
HOLC. See Home Owners' Loan
 Corporation
holding companies

Durant, W., creation of, 87–88
 of Insull, S., 155–157
Holiday, Billie, 46
home mortgage finance industry, 314
Home Owners' Loan Corporation
 (HOLC), 273, 274–275, 278, 314
Hoover, Herbert, 122–124, 127, 187, 197
 agriculture relief policy, 142–144,
  306
 aid to poor opposition, 145
 Bureau of Standards, 128
 Churchill and Leuchtenburg on, 126
 CRB of, 125–126
 farm programs, 306
 humanitarian work, 125
 PECE, 138
 recession and, 135–136
 RFC of, 136, 145, 152, 244, 253–254,
  263, 264, 273, 278, 284
 social spending, 272–273, 273 (fig.)
 tariff increase policy, 144–145, 311
 US food relief programs, 126
 veteran bonus marchers and,
  145–148, 146 (photo)
 voluntary agencies, 137–138
 war debts and reparations
  moratorium, 236
Hoover, J. Edgar, 76
Hoover, Lou Henry, 124
Hope, Bob, 41
Hopkins, Harry, 267–269, 277, 284
hourly pay, of workers
 1919–1941, 261 (fig.). 260
 changes in, 291–292, 291 (fig.)
House, Edward, 14
House of Baring collapse, 184–185
"hucksterism" of stock brokers, 112
Hughes, Charles Evans, 197

Hughes, Langston, 42, 46, 47
Hull, Cordell, 249, 250–251
humanism, Lippman on, 64
Hume, David, 184
Hundred Days legislative program, of
    Roosevelt, F., 267
Hurston, Zora Neale, 46
hyperinflation, in Germany, 194,
    194 (fig.), 201

Icahn, Carl, 161
Ickes, Harold, 169, 284
Import Duties Act (1932), 311
industrial agriculture, 246–247
industrial production
    Great Britain, 206, 237
    NBER on, 115–116
    1920–1929, 113–114, 114 (fig.)
    1933–1940, 280 (fig.)
    See also manufacturing
        productivity; total factor
        productivity
Industrial Revolution, 182, 206
industrial unions, 50–51, 79, 282, 289
industries
    Great Depression-era
        unemployment among, 296–297
    in post WWI recession, 77
    See also specific industries
inflation
    automobile market crash of 1920, 90
    farmers and, 134
    German foreign money and,
        225–226
    Great Britain wartime, 209
    local currency devalued in, 184
    1914 rate of, 72
    of 1970s, 320–321

Rathenau on German, 193
    US, 214
    wartime, 73–75, 209
    Weimar Republic and, 192, 307
Inherit the Wind (movie), 61, 62
Insull, Martin, 144, 156, 159
Insull, Samuel, 24–29, 154, 164–166
    Commonwealth Edison of, 78, 155,
        161
    CSC of, 159–163
    Eaton, C., holdings purchase from,
        158–164
    financing strategy, 82–83
    franchises, 79, 80
    holding companies of, 155–157
    IUI of, 159–163
    MWU of, 155–158, 161–163
    Peoples Gas, Light, and Coke
        Company of, 155
    Public Service of Northern Illinois
        of, 155
    sales strategies, 81
    union dealings, 79
Insull Securities Company (IUI), of
    Chicago, 159–163
interbank payments clearing, 228
international catastrophe, of
    Depression, 306
international finance, 181, 187, 237
International Harvester, 104, 142
International Match, 170, 172, 173
International Telephone and
    Telegraph (IT&T), 176–177
Interstate Commerce Commission,
    262
invisibles account, in Great Britain,
    184, 207–208, 207 (fig.), 237
Irwin, Douglas, 312

IT&T. *See* International Telephone and Telegraph

IUI. *See* Insull Securities Company

James, William, 64, 303
Jazz Age, 19–23
The Jazz Singer (movie), 44
Jeffers, Robinson, 42
Jenkins, Roy, 213
Jensen, Richard, 295–296
Joffre, Joseph, 9–10
Johnson, Hiram, 127, 272
Johnson, James Weldon, 46, 47
Jolson, Al, 44
Jones, Jesse, 254
Josephson, Matthew, 194

Kaiser Aluminum, 101
Keegan, John, 3
Kennedy, Paul, 8
Kerr, Robert, 21
Keynes, John Maynard, 4–5, 15, 132, 188, 197–198, 210, 316
  on deflation, 234
  on Great Britain sheltered goods, 215
  on Hoover, H., 127
  on Roosevelt Statement, 252
  on sticky wages, 288
Kindleberger, Charles, 253, 264, 309, 315
von Kluck, Alexander, 10–11
Knopf, Alfred A., 42
Kreditanstalt bank, of Austria, 234–235
Kreuger, Ivar, 154
  forged Italian bonds, 177
  fraud of, 168

French bond business theft, 173
holdings, 168 (fig.)
IT&T controlling position sale, 176–177
match monopoly, 169–174
Ponzi game, 176
suicide of, 167, 177
Kreuger & Toll, 169–170
Krutch, Joseph Wood, 64
Kuhn, Loeb and Company, 197
Kuznets, Simon, 283, 289

labor market, post WWI, 76
Lamont, Thomas, 13, 119, 187, 197, 199, 202, 236
Land O'Lakes butter cooperative, 142
Lange, Jessica, 45
Lardner, Ring, 41
Laval, Pierre, 317, 319
League of Nations, 16, 196, 203
Lebergott, Stanley, 288
Lee, Higgison investment company, 170, 172, 174–175
Leffingwell, Russell, 188, 307
Legion of Decency, 44
Leland, Henry, 32, 86
Leuchtenburg, William, 126
Lewis, John L., 80
Lewis, Sinclair, 22, 56
Liberty airplane engine, 72
Liberty Bonds, 73
Lincoln Motor Company, 32
Lindbergh, Charles, 42
Lippman, Walter, 41, 64, 244, 271
Liveright, Horace, 42
Lloyd, Harold, 55
Lloyd, Henry Demarest, 271

Locarno Treaties (1925), 223–224, 228, 231

Lodge, Henry Cabot, 126

Lombard Street (Bagehot), 183

Long, Huey, 258–260, 259 (photo)

Long, Lois, 48

Long-Term Capital Management (LTCM), 321

Lorre, Peter, 44

LTCM. *See* Long-Term Capital Management

Luce, Henry, 41

Luther, Hans, 235–236, 317–318

Lynd, Helen M., 50, 99

Lynd, Robert S., 50, 99

MacArthur, Douglas, 147

MacDonald, Ramsay, 204, 237, 238, 243–244, 249

Macfadden, Bernarr, 41

MacLeish, Archibald, 20

Macmillan Report, 237

Madsen, Jakob, 308–309, 310, 311, 312

Maginot Line, 224

majoritarianism, 63

Malcomson, Alexander, 32

Malkiel, Burton, 113

The Maltese Falcon (movie), 44–45

Manufacturing general
  changes in hours, real and nominal wages, 291–292, 291 (fig.)
  employment collapse, 137
  payrolls and gross revenues, 289–290, 290 (fig.)
  US durable/nondurable production and pricing strategies, 293, 293 (fig.)
  US prices and gross revenues, 292 (fig.)

worker hourly pay, 1919–1941, 261 (fig.). 260

Manufacturing productivity, 97–99

Marconi's Wireless
  General Electric purchase of, 40
  Sarnoff as wireless operator at, 40

Marsh & McLennan insurance, 160

Marshall, George, 266

Mason, Joseph, 150, 153

mass manufacturing technologies, 23, 34

mass population movement, of blacks North, 45–46, 76

McCarthy, Joe, 257

McDonald, Forest, 160, 163

McKenna, Reginald, 211

McLennan, Donald, 160, 161

media use, by Roosevelt, F., 257–258

Mellon, Andrew, 101, 121, 122, 197, 223, 227, 236

Meltzer, Allan H., 113

Mencken, H. L., 42, 59, 60

merchandise account, in Great Britain, 208

Miami, Florida
  building boom, 106, 107
  real estate collapse, 108

Middle West Utilities (MWU), 155–158, 161–163

Mildred Pierce (movie), 44

military spending, European, 7, 7 (fig.)

Miller, G. William, 320

Mills, Frederick C., 289, 309

Mills, Ogden, 221

mining, in Great Britain, 215
  strike, 216, 216 (photo)

Minsky, Hyman, 176

Mishkin, Frederic S., 313
Mitchell, Charles E., 120–121
Modern Library, 42
The Modern Temper (Krutch), 64
Moggridge, D. E., 207–208
Moley, Raymond, 248–249, 250–251
von Moltke, Helmuth "the Elder," 1–2
von Moltke, Helmuth "the Younger,"
 1–2, 10–11
Mondrian, Piet, 20
monetary gold, 228
 holdings, 186–187, 186 (fig.)
 maldistribution of, 186
 Roosevelt, F., on, 249
 US control of, 196
Monetary History of the United States
 (Friedman and Schwartz), 132,
 149, 150, 283
monopoly
 of Alcoa, 100–101
 anti-, electrical utility companies
 and, 28–29
 Kreuger match, 169–174
"Moon Shines in Coral Gables"
 (song), 107
Moore, George Gordon, 21
Moreau, Émile, 220, 232, 308
 1927 Long Island conference,
 221–224
 franc pegged to dollar by, 231
Moret, Clément, 238
Morgan, John Pierpont ("J. P."), 24,
 26, 101, 119, 197
 caricature of, 111 (fig.)
Morgan, John Pierpont, Jr. ("Jack"),
 175, 177, 198
 Roosevelt, F., policies support by,
 265

Morgenthau, Henry, 248, 251, 252,
 253, 283
Mott, Charles Stewart, 85
movies, 43–44, 55–56
Mumford, Lewis, 49
Muncie, Indiana
 affordable automobile in, 55
 consumer credit in, 54–55
 contraception, 57
 cosmetics and clothing standards,
 54
 factory workers bleakness, 52–53
 farming, 50, 53, 103
 financial pressures, 53–54
 Fordism, 51–52, 294
 Great Depression and, 50
 industrial accidents, 51
 Lynd, R. and Lynd, H., study of,
 50, 99
 pre-Code movies, 55–56
 prostitution in, 56–57
 as union town, 50–51
Murphy, Frank, 141
Murphy, Gerald, 20–21
Murphy, Sara, 20–21
Murphy, Thomas, 32
MWU. *See* Middle West Utilities
My Years with General Motors (Sloan),
 90–91

The Naked City (movie), 44
The Nation and Athenaeum (Keynes),
 200
National Broadcasting Company
 (NBC), 40
National Bureau of Economic
 Research (NBER), 115–116, 290,
 309

National Industrial Conference
Board (NICB), 289
National Industrial Recovery Act
(NIRA), 44, 262, 271–272, 296
National Labor Relations Act
(Wagner Act), 272, 282, 289, 296
National Union Government, in
France, 219
nationalization, of companies, 73
NBC. *See* National Broadcasting
Company
NBER. *See* National Bureau of
Economic Research
Nevins, Allan, 33, 37, 95
New Deal, 73, 144, 165, 240, 272–274
creation of, 257–261
detail of, 266–271
federal debt, 278
federal liabilities increase, 263,
263 (fig.)
overview, 262–266
New York City
BUS failure, 149
as communication hub, 40
couture industry in, 48–49
global monetary gains in, 40
Great Depression relief efforts,
140
Harlem black people, 46
high-end service industries, 49
mass population movements, 45
movies, 43–44
national print media concentration
in, 41
Prohibition in, 47–48
relief efforts, 140
skyscrapers in, 49
New York Evening Graphic, 41

New York Stock Exchange, 113, 119–123
The New Yorker, 41, 48
Niagara electrical project, 24–29, 27
(fig.), 80
NICB. *See* National Industrial
Conference Board
Nicholas (Tsar), 4
Nicholson, Jack, 45
Niemeyer, Otto, 211–213
1929 stock market crash, 313
Black Monday, 120
Black Thursday, 174
Black Tuesday, 120
eve of, 110–115
Great Britain market drop, 120
"hucksterism" of stock brokers, 112
industrial production, 1920–1929,
113–114, 114 (fig.)
margin regulation, 112
overpricing, 112–113
rapid growth in, 110
NIRA. *See* National Industrial
Recovery Act
Nixon, Richard, 320–321
Norman, Montagu, 197, 235, 238, 307,
318
1927 Long Island conference,
221–224
on Great Britain return to gold
standard, 210–213
North, mass black population
movement into, 45–46, 76
November Revolution, in Germany,
191
Noyes, Alexander Dana, 122, 281

OASI. *See* Old Age and Survivors'
Insurance

Ohanian, Lee, 286
Old Age and Survivors' Insurance (OASI), 270
Olds, Ransom, 31
Olds Motor Vehicle Company, 86
Olney, Martha, 313
On the Waterfront (movie), 44
O'Neill, Eugene, 42
Only Yesterday (Allen), 62
Orlando, Vittorio, 15 (photo)
Otis and Company, 158
Otto, Nikolaus, 31

Painlevé, Paul, 219
Paley, William, 41
Palmer, A. Mitchell, 76
Paris, WWI defense of, 9–12
parity ratio, of farms, 247
Parker, Dorothy, 20, 41
Partnoy, Frank, 176
Payne, John Barton, 140
payrolls and gross revenues, in manufacturing, 289–290, 290 (fig.)
Peabody, Endicott, 254
Peabody, Francis, 79–80
Peace Conference, 3–4
Pearson, Frank A., 252–253, 256
Pearson, Karl, 63
PECE. *See* President's Emergency Committee on Employment
Pegler, Westbrook, 41
Peoples Gas, Light, and Coke Company, 155
Perkins, Maxwell, 42
Pickford, Mary, 21
Pinchot, Gifford, 140

Poincaré, Raymond, 173, 176, 197, 218, 219–220, 231
politics
    in Chicago, 79
    in Germany, 317
Pontiac division, of GM, 86
Ponzi, Charles, 176
Ponzi game, 176
The Postman Always Rings Twice (movie), 44
postwar prosperity, 298–300
poverty, postwar, 225
A Preface to Morals (Krutch), 64
President's Council of Economic Advisors, 322
President's Emergency Committee on Employment (PECE), 138
price-specie flow mechanism, 184
Principles of Mining (Hoover, H.), 125
print media, 41
private nonfarm economy, 299
productivity
    farms, 299
    Ford Motors, 97
    growth, 1920–1941, 298–299, 299 (fig.)
    shocks, 77
    See also industrial production; manufacturing productivity; total factor productivity
Progressive Era, 28
Prohibition, 57
proportional representation, in Europe, 192
Prosser, Seward, 140
protectionism, 311–312
Protestantism, 59
Public Service of Northern Illinois, 155

Public Works Administration (PWA), 267, 268 (photo), 269, 284

Quadricycle, of Ford, 31, 32
Quesnay, Pierre, 220, 308

Race to the Sea, 11
radio, 40–41
Radio Corporation of America (RCA), 40
Raff, Daniel, 295
railroads
    Germany national system privatization, 201
    TFP and, 300
Rappleyea, George, 58
Raskob, John, 88, 89, 115–116
rate of interest, 183
Rathenau, Walter, 193, 316
RCA. See Radio Corporation of America
real estate, 109
    binders, 106–107
    Miami building boom, 106, 107
    Miami collapse, 108
rearmament drive, in Germany, 203–204
recession, of 1937, 279–285, 294–295
    See also Great Recession, of 2007
recession, post WWI, 76
    of 1920–1921, 90, 103, 313
    Hoover, H., and, 135–136
    industries in, 77
reconstruction debt, of France, 217
Reconstruction Finance Corporation (RFC), 136, 145, 264
    bank loans, 152, 244, 273
    federal borrowings, 263, 278, 284

gold price raised through, 253–254
Red Scare, by Hoover, J., and Palmer, 76
reflation, 134, 252–256
    commodity price elevation, 246
    farm bloc and, 246
    Roosevelt, F., support of, 264
    US and Great Britain position of, 250–251
Reichsbank, Germany, 225, 235, 236, 317–318
Reichsmark currency plunge, in Germany, 192, 193 (photo), 201
Reinhold, Peter, 226
Rentenmark currency, in Germany, 195
reparations, Germany, 15–16, 181, 187, 189–195, 190 (fig.), 315, 316
    bonds for, 190
    Lamont on moratorium for, 236
    from new foreign loans, 225
    possible loan defaults, 225
    revised schedule for, 227–228
Reparations Commission, 189–190
    commensurate taxation of Germany, 201
    Dawes Plan, 195–205, 223, 225, 315
    France withdrawal from Ruhr, 292
    on Germany hyperinflation, 201
    on Germany national railroad system privatization, 201
    Germany phase in of payments, 201
    Germany temporary transport tax, 201
    Gilbert as agent of, 203
    Great Britain support of, 202
    Young Plan, 195–205, 227–228, 236, 317

The Report of the First Committee of Experts to the Reparation Commission, 200
Republic Steel, 121, 160, 161
residual, in TFP growth factors, 298
return to normalcy campaign, of Harding, 76
Reuther, Walter, 289
Review of Economics and Statistics, for 1937, 279
Reynolds Aluminum, 101
RFC. *See* Reconstruction Finance Corporation
Rhineland, withdrawal from, 204, 224
risk management, in bank crises, 153
Rist, Charles, 220, 233, 308
 1927 Long Island conference, 221
Rizzo, Fiore, 266
Robeson, Paul, 47
Rockefeller, John D., 106, 115, 121, 158, 169–170
Rockefeller, Percy, 115, 172–173
Romer, Christina D., 265, 313
Roose, Kenneth, 294–295
Roosevelt, Eleanor, 127, 129
Roosevelt, Franklin, 48, 127, 148, 240, 278 (fig.)
 1937 recession and, 279–284
 background of, 244
 on deflation and reflation, 264
 dollar devaluation, 247
 Farm Credit Administration of, 248
 Hundred Days legislative program of, 267
 mass media use, 257–258
 on monetary gold, 249

monetary policy, 246, 248–249
Morgan, J. P., Jr., policies support, 265
recovery factor, 263–264
social spending, 272–273, 273 (fig.)
Stimson on, 244–245
tax on net undistributed earnings, 285
World Monetary and Economic Conference delegation of, 249–251
WWII declaration of war, 300
Roosevelt Statement, to World Monetary and Economic Conference, 251–252, 264
Rope of Sand (movie), 44
Ross, Harold, 41
Rubenstein, Helena, 53–54
Ruhr, Germany invasion by France and Belgium, 191, 193, 197
 France withdrawal from, 202, 218, 292
Runyon, Damon, 41
rural
 bank failures, 150–151, 248
 collapse, in Great Depression, 103, 139–142, 144
 poverty, 141–142
 unemployment, 296
Russell, Bertrand, 64
Russia, 1–2, 4, 7–8

Sachs, Jeffrey, 255, 256
SAE. *See* Society of Automobile Engineers
Sarnoff, David, 40
Save Me the Waltz (Fitzgerald, Z.), 21–22

Schacht, Hjalmar, 194–195, 197, 204, 225, 232
bank margin lending reductions, 226
1927 Long Island conference, 221–224
capital tax exemption for foreign bond purchasers, 226
discount rates dropped by, 226
stock market and, 226
Schecter Poultry v. United States, 272
Schlesinger, Arthur, Jr., 250
von Schlieffen, Alfred, 1–2
Schlieffen Plan, 1–3
Schuker, Stephen, 218
Schwartz, Anna Jacobson, 132, 149, 283, 285, 314, 318
scientific progressivism, 63–65
Scopes, John, 58, 59–60
Scopes Monkey Trial, 58–62
Securities Exchange Commission (SEC), 157, 262
Von Seeckt, Hans, 203–204
Seldes, Gilbert, 20
Sellers, Coleman, Jr., 26
service industries, high-end, 49
Share Our Wealth program, of Long, H., 259–260
sharecropping, 69
Shaw, Hannah, 69
Shaw, Nate, 69–71
sheltered goods, of Great Britain, 215
short blocks, of FHA, 108
Sion, John, 238
Skidelsky, Robert, 214
skyscrapers, 49, 101, 109, 110, 115, 169
Slater, Samuel, 293

Sloan, Alfred, 84–91, 90, 95–96
Smith, Al, 128
Smoot-Hawley tariff, 144, 311
Snowden, Philip, 228, 237, 238
revised reparation schedule, 227
Social Security, 262
social spending, of Hoover, H., 272–273, 273 (fig.)
Society of Automobile Engineers (SAE), 102
Solow, Robert, 298
Spanish flu pandemic, 303–304
Sprague, Oliver M. W., 133–134, 244, 250, 308
St. Vincent Millay, Edna, 41
Stamp, Josiah, 198–199
Standard Oil, 100, 106, 121, 258
stand-still agreements, Austria and, 235
steam power, 80
steel industry, 91, 101, 102, 115, 119, 160, 207
Stein, Gertrude, 20
Stevens, Wallace, 42
sticky prices, 292
sticky wages, 288
Stimson, Henry, 236, 244–245
Stinnes, Hugo, 199
stock market, 226
Great Britain drop in, 120
See also 1929 stock market crash
Stravinsky, Igor, 20
Stresemann, Gustav, 194, 195, 204, 223, 225
death of, 228
on revised reparation schedule, 227
Stresemann-Schacht 1924 currency reform, 316

Strong, Benjamin, 133, 187, 197, 200, 231
  1927 Long Island conference, 221–224
  death of, 222
  on Great Britain return to gold standard, 209–213, 307
Stuart, Harold, 83, 155, 157
Sunday, Billy, 59
Survey of Current Business, 135
  on agriculture, of 1929, 104
  Hoover, H., creation of, 128
  on industrial production, in 1929, 114–115
Swedish Bank Inspection Board, 171
Swedish Match, 169–170

tariffs
  deflation impact on, 144–145
  Fordney-McCumber, 311
  Hoover increase policy, 144–145, 311
  Smoot-Hawley, 144, 311
telephone, AT&T market of, 40
television industry, 40–41
Temin, Peter, 150, 152–153, 264, 319
Tender Is the Night (Fitzgerald, S.), 20–21
Tesla, Nikola, 24–29
Texaco, 100
TFP. *See* total factor productivity
This Side of Paradise (Fitzgerald, S.), 19
Thomas, Elmer, 248
Thomas Amendment, to AAA, 248–249, 250
Thomson-Houston, 25
Time, 41
Tin Pan Alley, 49

Titanic, 40
Toll, Paul, 169
Toscanini, Arturo, 40, 41
total factor productivity (TFP)
  electric power industry, 300
  private nonfarm economy and, 299–300
  railroads and, 300
  residual in growth factors, 298
  wholesale and retail distribution, 300
Townsend, Francis, 259 (photo), 260
Trades Union Congress (TUC), 215–216
Treatise on Money (Keynes), 134
Treaty of Brest-Litovsk (1918), 12
Treaty of Versailles, 187, 189
  Germany disarmament mandates ignored, 203
  Hitler repudiation of, 240
  US Senate failure to ratify, 196
trickle-down economics, 69–71
TUC. *See* Trades Union Congress
Turner, Lana, 45

UAW. *See* United Auto Workers
UI. *See* Unemployment Insurance
unemployment, 287–295, 306
  of blue-collar workers, 137
  Great Britain doubling of, 237
  Great Depression-era among industries, 296–297
  1926–1941 rates of, 138 (fig.)
  rural, 296
  US, 1929–1940, 287 (fig.), 288
Unemployment Insurance (UI), 270
Union Oil, 100

Union Party, 260
United Auto Workers (UAW), 289
United Motors Company, 88, 90
United States (US), 2, 313
    crop and meat prices, 104–105, 104
        (fig.)
    farming price collapse, 309
    gold holdings, 232
    Great Britain alliance with, 231
    Great Britain industrial output
        compared to, 206
    Great Recession, of 2007, 263, 322
    inflation, 214
    monetary gold control by, 196
    prewar steel production, 207
    productivity growth, 1920–1941,
        298–299, 299 (fig.)
    real and nominal GNP, 1929–1937,
        131 (fig.)
    reflation position, 250–251
    Treaty of Versailles ratification
        failure, 196
    unemployment, 1929–1940, 287
        (fig.), 288
US Steel, 91, 101, 102, 119

Van Vechten, Carl, 46–47
Versailles Peace Conference
    Austria and, 14, 304
    Germany exclusion from, 14–15
    war settlements, 15–16
    See also Treaty of Versailles
veteran bonus marchers, 145–148, 146
    (photo)
Victor phonograph company, 40
Victory Bonds, 73, 76
Volcker, Paul, 321
Volstead Act, 47

von Hindenburg, Paul, 317

wage cuts, 290–292, 291 (fig.)
Wagner, Robert, 145
Wagner Act. See National Labor
    Relations Act
Wallis, John, 272
war
    Angell on mainstream acceptance
        of, 5–6
    bonds, 73–74, 74 (fig.)
    debt settlements, 15–16, 223, 236
    expenditures, 73
    loans, of Great Britain, 189
    production, 72–73
    costs, 13
    trials, of Germany, 203
    virtues of, 303
War Industries Board, 73
war reparations, of Germany. See
    reparations, Germany
Warburg, James, 249–250
Warburg, Max, 6
Warburg, Paul, 133
The Warmth of Other Suns
    (Wilkerson), 45
Warren, George F., 252–253, 256
    gold price target, 260
Warren-Pearson Indices, 252
wartime inflation, 73–75, 209
Waters, Ethel, 47
weapon technologies, of Germany, 8
Weimar Republic, 191, 316
    golden age of, 228
    inflationary mechanism, 192, 307
West, Mae, 44
Westinghouse, George, 24, 27–29
    AC technology, 25–26

Westinghouse Electric, 25
Whiteman, Paul, 41
Whitney, Richard, 119–120, 174
    embezzlement conviction, 121
Wicker, Elmus, 150, 152–153, 253
Wiggin, Albert, 121
Wigmore, Barrie, 110–111, 150, 152–153,
    264
Wilhelm II, 1, 6
Wilkerson, Isabel, 45
Wilson, Berry, 150, 153
Wilson, Woodrow, 13, 14, 15 (photo),
    72, 73, 181, 196
Winchell, Walter, 41
Winthrop, John, 119
Wolfe, Thomas, 42
Wooley, Monty, 20
workers
    blue-collar, 52, 137, 293, 295
    Ford Motors recruitment and
        retention, 36–38
    hourly pay of, 261 (fig.). 260,
        291–292, 291 (fig.)
    Muncie, Indiana bleakness of
        factory, 52–53
Works Progress Administration
    (WPA), 270, 276–277, 284, 297
World in Depression (Kindleberger),
    309
World Monetary and Economic
    Conference, 245
    Acheson-Warburg group, 253
    currency stabilization agreement,
        249–250
    French deflation position, 250, 251
    MacDonald organization of,
        243–244
    on nationalism in economics, 243

Roosevelt, F., delegation to,
    249–251
    Roosevelt Statement to, 251–252,
        264
    US and Great Britain reflation
        position, 250–251
world trade collapse, 306, 311–312
World War I (WWI), 6–7, 11 (photo)
    Battle of the Marne, 11–12
    BEF, 9–10
    Belgium losses in, 14
    common people shift, 22
    death toll during, 8, 10, 12, 13
    Depression and, 303
    Federal Reserve system and, 72
    fiscal consequences of, 73–77,
        75 (fig.), 130
    France losses in, 13–14
    France war strategy, 9
    GDP and war effort, 73
    Germany war reparations, 15–16,
        181, 189–195, 190 (fig.), 224
    international debt from, 187
    Keynes on, 4–5
    legacy of, 303–305
    military increase, 72
    Paris defense, by France, 9–12
    peace cost, 13–16
    Race to the Sea, 11
    reasons for, 1–4
    Russia mobilization during, 1–2
    Schlieffen Plan during, 1–3
    war spending costs, 13
World War I (WWI), post
    Bank of England progress, 209
    Berlin conditions, 304
    common people shift, 22
    consumer society, 23

cultural changes, 22–23, 105
France condition, 304–305
Germany and, 315–318
Great Britain, 315
industries in recession, 77
labor market, 76
recession, 76–77, 90, 103, 135–136, 313
World War II (WWII), 300
WPA. *See* Works Progress Administration
Wright, Gavin, 277

WWI. *See* World War I
WWII. *See* World War II

Young, Arthur, 165
Young, Owen D., 195–205, 227–228, 236, 317
Young Plan, 317
    BIS reparations agent, 228
    Brüning complaint about, 236
    revised reparation plan, 227–228
Youngstown Sheet and Tube Company, 160

photo © Andrew Popper

A Rabble of Dead Money is **Charles R. Morris's** fifteenth book. Other books include *The Cost of Good Intentions,* a *New York Times* selection as an "Editor's Choice for 1980"; *The Tycoons,* a Barron's Best Book of 2005; *The Trillion Dollar Meltdown,* winner of the 2008 Gerald Loeb Award and a *New York Times* bestseller; and *The Dawn of Innovation,* a *Wall Street Journal* Best Business Book of 2012. A lawyer and former banker, Mr. Morris's articles and reviews have appeared in many publications, including the *Atlantic Monthly,* the *New York Times,* and the *Wall Street Journal,* and his books have been translated into eighteen languages. He is a fellow of the Century Foundation and a member of the Council on Foreign Relations.

PublicAffairs is a publishing house founded in 1997. It is a tribute to the standards, values, and flair of three persons who have served as mentors to countless reporters, writers, editors, and book people of all kinds, including me.

I. F. STONE, proprietor of *I. F. Stone's Weekly*, combined a commitment to the First Amendment with entrepreneurial zeal and reporting skill and became one of the great independent journalists in American history. At the age of eighty, Izzy published *The Trial of Socrates*, which was a national bestseller. He wrote the book after he taught himself ancient Greek.

BENJAMIN C. BRADLEE was for nearly thirty years the charismatic editorial leader of *The Washington Post*. It was Ben who gave the *Post* the range and courage to pursue such historic issues as Watergate. He supported his reporters with a tenacity that made them fearless and it is no accident that so many became authors of influential, best-selling books.

ROBERT L. BERNSTEIN, the chief executive of Random House for more than a quarter century, guided one of the nation's premier publishing houses. Bob was personally responsible for many books of political dissent and argument that challenged tyranny around the globe. He is also the founder and longtime chair of Human Rights Watch, one of the most respected human rights organizations in the world.

·   ·   ·

For fifty years, the banner of Public Affairs Press was carried by its owner Morris B. Schnapper, who published Gandhi, Nasser, Toynbee, Truman, and about 1,500 other authors. In 1983, Schnapper was described by *The Washington Post* as "a redoubtable gadfly." His legacy will endure in the books to come.

Peter Osnos, *Founder and Editor-at-Large*